CW01021244

INSURANCE AND WEATHER DERIVATIVES

From Exotic Options to Exotic Underlyings

INSURANCE AND WEATHER DERIVATIVES

From Exotic Options to Exotic Underlyings

Edited by Hélyette Geman

Published by Risk Books, a division of Risk Publications.

Haymarket House
28–29 Haymarket
London SW1Y 4RX
Tel: +44 (0)171 484 9700
Fax: +44 (0)171 930 2238
E-mail: books@risk.co.uk
Home Page: http://www.riskpublications.com

Every effort has been made to secure the permission of individual copyright holders for
inclusion.

© Financial Engineering Ltd, 1999

ISBN 1 899332 57 X

British Library Cataloguing in Publication Data
A catalogue record for this book is available from the British Library

Risk Books Commissioning Editor: Laurie Donaldson
Project Editor: Avril Eglinton
Desk Editor: Lindsey Hofmeister
Copy Editor: Miles Smith-Morris
Typesetter: Marie Doherty

Printed and bound in Great Britain by Bookcraft (Bath) Ltd, Somerset.

Conditions of sale
All rights reserved. No part of this publication may be reproduced in any material form whether by
photocopying or storing in any medium by electronic means whether or not transiently or incidentally to
some other use for this publication without the prior written consent of the copyright owner except in
accordance with the provisions of the Copyright, Designs and Patents Act 1988 or under the terms of a
licence issued by the Copyright Licensing Agency Limited of 90 Tottenham Court Road, London W1P 0LP.

Warning: the doing of any unauthorised act in relation to this work may result in both civil and criminal
liability.

Every effort has been made to ensure the accuracy of the text at the time of publication. However, no
responsibility for loss occasioned to any person acting or refraining from acting as a result of the material
contained in this publication will be accepted by Financial Engineering Ltd.

Many of the product names contained in this publication are registered trade marks, and Risk Books has
made every effort to print them with the capitalisation and punctuation used by the trademark owner. For
reasons of textual clarity, it is not our house style to use symbols such as TM, ®, etc. However, the absence
of such symbols should not be taken to indicate absence of trademark protection; anyone wishing to use
product names in the public domain should first clear such use with the product owner.

CONTENTS

WEATHER DERIVATIVES

CONTRIBUTORS

Marie Odile Albizzati is professor of management science at the Pantheon Assas University in Paris. Her research is on risk management in insurance, using stochastic financial models. She is also a consultant at Groupama Asset Management. Marie holds the "agrégation" in mathematics and diplomas from the Ecole Polytechnique in Palaiseau and Ecole Nationale de la Statiotique et de l'administration Economique in Paris.

David Beaglehole is a director and head of OTC Derivatives Research for North America at Deutsche Bank. Prior to working for Deutsche Bank he worked for five years for Goldman Sachs in their derivatives modelling group. Before this David was an assistant professor of finance at the University of Iowa where he taught options pricing theory and investments and was also a consultant to the exotic FX options trading group at Barclays Bank. David has published articles in the *Journal of Financial Economics*, the *Journal of Fixed Income* and the *Journal of Portfolio Management*. He has also served as a reviewer of articles for a number of major finance journals. He earned his PhD degree in finance and economics at the University of Chicago and is an associate of the Society of Actuaries.

Gail Belonsky is head of the securitisation group at Swiss Re.

This group originates and structures securitisations as well as related products transferring risk from the insurance industry to the capital markets. Gail joined Swiss Re in 1995 and has also been an economic consultant at the New York Stock Exchange and a vice president in the mortgage-backed securities department at Drexel Burnham Lambert. As part of the mortgage trading and research groups at Drexel, she was responsible for structuring collateralised mortgage obligations, trading CMO equity residuals, product development, and marketing. Gail holds a PhD in finance from the University of California at Berkeley, a MSc from the Univeristy of Guelph and a BS from Cornell University.

Eric Briys is a director in the strategic solutions group at Merrill Lynch in London. He heads the firm's European insurance and reinsurance coverage. Eric specialises in asset-liability management and alternative risk transfer techniques. He was previously heading the European insurance and reinsurance coverage at Lehman Brothers in London. Prior to this Eric was a senior consultant at Tillinghast-Towers Perrin and a financial officer at the World Bank. He has also spent 10 years in the academic world as a professor of finance. He held positions at HEC School of Management, CERAM and University of Montreal. Eric

has published over 35 papers in refereed journals, six books and is an associate editor of several scientific journals. He holds a PhD in economics from the University of Geneva and the ITP from Stockholm School of Economics. Eric is a graduate from the HEC School of Management.

Michael Canter joined AIG Risk Finance as a senior vice president, head of the insurance securitisation group, in May 1998. At AIG he is working on originating, structuring, and marketing insurance securitisation transactions. Prior to joining AIG, Michael was a vice president of trading at Hedge Financial Products, Inc., a wholly-owned subsidiary of CNA Financial Corporation. Here Michael's responsibilities involved securitisation as well as the structuring of insurance products that integrate financial risks and insurance risks into one policy. Michael has published scholarly articles on derivatives and securitisation in "Derivatives Handbook", *Journal of Futures Markets*, *Journal of Applied Corporate Finance*, *Journal of Derivatives* and other publications. He received a BA in economics and mathematics from Northwestern University and a PhD in finance from the Columbia University School of Business.

Lynda Clemmons is a vice president at Enron North America, with primary responsibility for Enron's global weather risk management business. She is also a co-founder and vice president of an industry trade group, the Weather Risk Management Association. In addition to weather derivative experience, Lynda built and managed the SO2 and NOx emission allowance trading desk for four years. Prior to joining ENA, she worked in the investment banking group at NationsBank (now Bank of America).

Joseph B. Cole is chief operating officer of Hedge Financial Products, Inc., where he is involved in new product development in the emerging markets for insurance derivatives, securitised indemnities and other tradable event-risks. Previously he was a managing director of Centre Financial Products Limited where he worked on product and account development and the marketing of structured financial instruments for insurance and environmental trading. Joseph has also served as senior vice president and special projects manager in the derivative products group of Kidder, Peabody & Co. Incorporated. He has spoken at numerous seminars and conferences on financial futures and options trading, commodity and oil-related hedging, asset-liability management, SO2 allowance trading and insurance derivatives. Joseph has a BSc in mathematics from Briar Cliff College and a MBA from the University of South Dakota. He also holds a PhD in business administration from the University of Iowa.

J. David Cummins is the Henry J. Loman professor of insurance and risk management and executive director of the S.S. Huebner Foundation for insurance

education at the Wharton School of the University of Pennsylvania. His primary research interests are financial management of insurance companies, the economics of insurance markets, and insurance rate of return and solvency regulation. Dr. Cummins has served as editor of the *Journal of Risk and Insurance* and is past president of the American Risk and Insurance Association and the Risk Theory Society. He has written or edited a number of books and published more than forty journal articles in numerous publications. His current research interests include the pricing and basis risk of catastrophic loss securities and frontier efficiency analysis of insurance firms. Dr. Cummins has consulted and testified on the cost of capital in insurance for organisations such as the National Council on Compensation Insurance and Liberty Mutual Insurance Group. Dr. Cummins received his BA in economics and actuarial science from the University of Nebraska and MA and PhD degrees from the Wharton School of the University of Pennsylvania.

Robert S. Dischel is a consultant to the weather market and a seminar leader. He is a meteorologist, oceanographer and capital markets analyst who has developed models of options, mortgage-backed securities, interest rate sensitive portfolios, ocean currents, the weather and now weather derivatives. Bob was a managing director in the Portfolio Department of Aetna Insurance Company, a Director of Quantitative Research at MetLife Insurance Company, and a quantitative analyst at PaineWebber Inc. In these positions he focused on measuring the risk to portfolios that held equity, real estate, fixed

income assets and insurance liabilities. He also developed new methods of portfolio management based on optimised stochastic total return. Before his work in the capital markets, Bob was a university professor. He worked as a consultant to environmental impact studies for a broad spread of clients from energy companies to scientific institutes. He has published ten articles on the weather risk market that can be found at www.WxPx.com, in *Risk*, *Energy and Power Risk Management* and at the Applied Derivatives Trading website, www.adtrading.com. He holds a Ph.D. from New York University, Department of Meteorology and Oceanography, and is certified by the American Meteorological Society as a Consulting Meteorologist (CCM). He is registered in New York State as a professional engineer

Weimin Dong is chief technical officer and senior vice president of research and development for Risk Management Solutions, Inc. (RMS), a firm dedicated to the transfer of natural disaster related technology from research to the consumer, as well as furthering technology development. Dr. Dong has over 30 years of industrial, teaching and research experience and has specialised in seismic hazard evaluation and risk assessment. Recently, his research focus has been on catastrophe risk securitisation, modern portfolio theory of combining Cat risk with Market risk to optimise the return. He is the chair of the Steering Committee for the EERI project on risk-based financing. He has participated in many joint venture projects (US–China, US–Japan) to share knowledge in hazard mitigation with other countries with similar concerns. Currently he is co-principal investigator for two projects with

Wharton School on insurance risk management. During his career Dr. Dong has published a number of books and over 100 papers and technical reports. He received his PhD from Stanford University.

David Durbin is the head of economic research and consulting in North America for Swiss Re. He is responsible for directing a wide-ranging research program for understanding the relationships and interactions between the general economy, capital markets, and the insurance and reinsurance markets as well as strategic consulting in North America. David has been involved in insurance related research for 18 years. He has published extensively on economic factors affecting insurance markets and on optimal design of insurance programs. His work has appeared in *American Economic Review*, *Journal of Risk and Insurance* and *Journal of Risk and Uncertainty*. David has also testified on insurance issues including profitability and the cost of capital in regulatory proceedings. David has a PhD in economics from the City University of New York

Hélyette Geman is professor of finance at the University Paris IX Dauphine and at ESSEC Graduate Business School. She is a member of honor of the French Society of Actuaries. Hélyette was previously a director at Caisse des Dépôts in charge of research and development and is currently a scientific adviser for major financial institutions and industrial companies. Hélyette has extensively published in international journals and in 1993 received the first prize of the Merrill Lynch awards for her work on exotic options. In 1995 she was awarded the first Actuarial Approach for Financial Risk

(AFIR) international prize for her pioneering research on catastrophe and extreme events derivatives. Hélyette is the co-founder and editor of European Finance Review, associate editor of the journal of Mathematical Finance, Geneva Papers on Insurance and other international journals. She is co-chair of the French branch of the International Association of Financial Engineers. Hélyette is a graduate from Ecole Normale Supérieure, holds a master's degree in theoretical physics and a PhD in mathematics from the University Paris VI Pierre et Marie Curie and a PhD in finance from the University Paris I Panthéon Sorbonne. She is president of the Bachelier Finance Society.

Joseph H. Hrgovcic is a manager in Enron's research department, where he developed the models used to price and structure the deals in Enron's weather book. Other specialties include the application of neural networks and other AI techniques to pricing and forecasting in the energy markets. Prior to joining Enron, Joseph worked at the Laboratory for Computer Science at MIT in applying massively parallel computers to quantum and statistical physics. He received a BA magna cum laude from Rice University and a PhD in physics from MIT.

Vincent Kaminski is a vice president and head of research in the risk analysis and control (RAC) group of Enron Corp. Vince joined Enron in June of 1992. Previously, he was a vice president in the research department of Salomon Brothers in New York (Bond Portfolio Analysis Group) and a manager in AT&T Communications (Long Lines) in Bedminster, New Jersey. In his current position, Vince is

responsible for the development of analytical tools for the pricing of commodity options and other commodity transactions, hedging strategies, optimisation of financial and physical transactions, as well as development of Value-at-Risk systems. Enron Capital & Trade Resources manages the largest portfolio of fixed-price and derivative natural gas contracts in the world and has invested a lot of time and effort in the development of state-of-art risk management systems. Vince is a recipient of the 1999 James H. McGraw Award for Energy Risk Management (Energy Risk Manager of the Year). He holds a MS degree in international economics and a PhD degree in mathematical economics from the Main School of Planning and Statistics in Warsaw, Poland. He also has a MBA from Fordham University in New York.

R. McFall Lamm, Jr. is chief investment strategist at Bankers Trust Private Banking in New York. He manages asset allocation, quantitative analysis and portfolio strategy. In addition Dr. Lamm has written extensively no investment analysis over the years and has published numerous articles in professional journals and books. He has made many public appearances and is a noted authority on asset allocation and trading strategies. His current research focus is on the role of non-traditional assets in investor portfolios. Dr. Lamm has 20 years of experience in market analysis, trading, investment management and research.

Morton Lane is senior managing director of the Capital Markets Division at Gerling Global Financial Products. This Division structures and underwrites risks within the capital markets.

Morton pioneered the area of insurance securitisation having placed the first private placement of an insurance-linked note into the capital markets in March 1997. Morton was awarded with Reinsurance Broking Initiative of the Year in 1999 by *The Review*. Before founding Lane Financial, Morton was president of Discount Corp. of New York Futures ("Futures House of the Year 1989"); senior managing director and head of commodities of Bear Stearns & Co.; president of Lind–Waldock & Co.; investment officer for The World Bank; and lecturer at the London Graduate School of Business Studies. Morton is the author of numerous articles on insurance and securitisation and is the co-author of two books, "The Treasury Bond Basis" and "Eurodollar Futures". Morton earned his BSc. from Birmingham University, England, and his PhD in mathematics, business administration and computer science from the University of Texas at Austin.

David Laster is a senior economist in Swiss Re's North American economic research and consulting unit. Specialising in capital market topics, he is engaged in a variety of strategic consulting projects for Swiss Re and their clients. His current areas of research include asset-liability management, the demutualisation of insurers, integrated risk management, and the securitisation of insurance risk. Prior to joining Swiss Re, David was a financial economist at the Federal Reserve Bank of New York. His work has appeared in the *Financial Analysts Journal, Journal of Investing* and *Quarterly Journal of Economics*. David earned a BA in mathematics from Yale University and a PhD in economics from Columbia University.

Robert H. Litzenberger is a managing director at Goldman, Sachs and Co. where he serves as the Firmwide risk manager. Prior to joining Goldman, Sachs he taught finance at the Wharton School of the University of Pennsylvania where he was the Edward Hopkinson professor of investment banking. Before this he was the C. O. G. Miller Distinguished professor of finance at the Stanford Graduate School of Business. He is co-author of "Foundations of Financial Economics" (1988) and has published more than 50 articles in the leading academic finance journals, with a focus on the theory of valuation and the empirical testing of asset pricing models.

Oleg Y. Movchan currently works at UBS Brinson, as a member of the risk analysis group at the asset allocation/currency division. As a quantitative risk analyst, he is responsible for implementation, refinement and development of risk measurement and forecasting tools and techniques. He contributes to such areas as multi-factor models, volatility measurement and estimation and analysis of large data sets. Oleg had worked as a structuring analyst at Sedgwick Lane Financial L.L.C. since the firm's inception. He was responsible for quantitative risk analysis and structuring of insurance-linked and fixed income securities. He also built statistical and mathematical models and conducted extensive research on industry related topics. Oleg earned his MS degree in applied mathematics and physics from Kharkov State University, Ukraine, and his MS degree in financial mathematics from The University of Chicago. He is currently pursuing his MBA degree at The University of Chicago, majoring in

analytic finance, econometrics and statistics and international business.

Sailesh Ramaurtie is risk control officer at Southern Company Energy Marketing. Previously he was a member of the faculty of finance at Georgia State University and has acted as a visiting scholar to the Federal Reserve Bank of Atlanta, where he participated in financial market studies and interest rate forecasting. Sailesh is a member of the American Finance Association, American Mathematical Society and the Econometric Society. He has published papers in *Journal of Finance* and *Economic Letters* and has presented papers on investments and asset valuation at various conferences in the US.

Craig Reynolds is the head trader of European OTC derivatives at Goldman Sachs. He previously spent two years in the derivatives research group at Goldman Sachs. Craig has a BA in econometrics from the Wharton School and the University of Pennsylvania.

Richard L. Sandor is chairman and chief executive officer of Environmental Financial Products LLC which specialises in developing and trading in new environmental, financial, and commodity markets. He is also chairman of the board of Hedge Financial. For two years Dr Sandor served as second vice chairman of the Chicago Board of Trade. He is a senior advisor to PricewaterhouseCoopers on greenhouse gas emissions trading. Dr. Sandor is a director of Central and South West Corp., providing electric power, telecommunication, energy efficiency and financial services. He is also a director of the Zurich-based Sustainable Performance

Group. For more than three years, he was vice president and chief economist at the Chicago Board of Trade, in recognition of his work Dr. Sandor was named the "father of financial futures" by the Chicago Board of Trade and the City of Chicago. He is also a visiting scholar at Northwestern University and received his BA degree from the City University of New York, Brooklyn College. He earned his PhD in economics from the University of Minnesota.

Haresh Shah is The Obayashi Professor of Engineering, Emeritus at Stanford University and currently serves as director of RMS. He was the original principal investigator for the development of IRAS. Dr. Shah specialises in applying probability and reliability theory to structural and earthquake engineering. His achievements include founding the Blume Earthquake Engineering Center at Stanford University, where he served as director; the founding of Stanford's Center for Integrated Facilities Engineering (CIFE); service on almost every earthquake policy and conference committee in the US; membership on the Board of Directors of the Earthquake Engineering Research Institute (EERI); steering the Department of Civil Engineering at Stanford University, as its chairman, to its prominent position within the US; extensive consulting experience with domestic and international government agencies and engineering firms, and author of over 150 publications. Dr Shah is the chairman of the board of Liquid Software and also for the World Seismic Safety Initiative (WSSI).

David C. Shimko is currently a senior lecturer in the finance department of the Harvard Business School. Before this position he was principal and subsequently head of the risk management advisory group at Bankers Trust (Deutsche Bank). Prior to this he was vice present and head of risk management research at J.P. Morgan Securities, responsible for ongoing research into strategic and analytical risk management questions for the company and their clients. Dr. Shimko has also been responsible for commodity derivatives research on J.P. Morgan's trading desk. Before joining J.P. Morgan in 1993, Dr. Shimko was assistant professor of finance at the University of Southern California and a private consultant to financial institutions. He writes a monthly end-user column in *Risk* magazine. Dr. Shimko received his PhD in managerial economics/finance and his BA in economics from Northwestern University.

Michael J. Tomas is group manager for the financial products group at the Chicago Board of Trade. Here his responsibilities include managing: new product development and research; applied research projects for CBOT strategic decision making; contract maintenance programs for existing financial products; and evaluation of education research foundation grant applications. The financial products traded at the CBOT include: the PCS Catastophe options, Treasury Bond and Note futures and options, Dow Jones Industrial Average futures and options, Municipal Bond futures and options, and Federal Funds futures. Michael is also an instructor at Loyola University in Chicago, in the Finance Department. He has a PhD in finance from Syracuse University, a MBA in international business and a BS in applied mathematics from the University of Akron.

Felix Wong is a principal of Weidlinger Associates, Inc., a consulting engineering firm that specialises in the study of the dynamic response of structures. He is a distinguished researcher, planner and manager, with over 25 years of consulting experience in structural dynamics, control and guidance systems, blast and shock effects, earthquake and lifeline engineering, software development, and knowledge engineering. An expert in the vulnerability and survivability of structures subjected to blast or seismic loads, he pioneers the use of the response surface as a bridge joining detailed finite-element models to probabilistic risk assessment (PRA) applications. He advocates the use of fuzzy sets and approximate reasoning techniques in modelling and analysing expert knowledge, to create a unified framework for quantifying all the important uncertainties in engineering decisions. Felix holds a doctoral degree from the California Institute of Technology and has published over 50 professional papers on the aforementioned topics.

Marc Yor is a professor of mathematics at the University Pierre et Marie Curie. He is one of the most famous probabilists worldwide and an expert on stochastic processes in general and Brownian motion in particular. He has published a considerable number of articles in the best mathematical journals and is associate editor of leading mathematical journals. Marc holds a PhD in mathematics from the University Pierre et Marie Curie and is the author of a number of books in probability, the most famous one being "Continuous Martingales and Brownian Motion". He is a correspondent of the French Academy of Sciences.

PREFACE

ince the beginning of the 1970s, deregulation and disintermediation have redefined the profile of the finance and insurance worlds, with bankers facing the competition from new financial structures and insurers discovering the impact on their balance-sheet of volatile interest rates. In the context of its discussion of insurance and weather derivatives, their valuation and hedging, this book aims to shed light on other important developments in the financial markets.

These trends include the transformation in the structure of financial markets from providers of capital transfer to providers of risk transfer through the process of securitisation. Against this background there has been a convergence of the fields of finance and insurance in the design of alternative forms of risk transfer such as structured securities, catastrophe bonds or synthetic collateralised bond obligations. There has also been the introduction, after exotic options on financial assets (stocks, interest rates, currencies), of derivative contracts written on exotic underlyings (such as insurance, weather or electricity) as necessary hedging instruments for various sectors of the economy.

The simplicity of the Nobel prize-winning Black–Scholes–Merton formula (1973) for pricing equity options created an explosion in the growth of derivatives markets, first for stocks, then for currencies and lastly, in the mid-1980s, for interest rates and commodities. These options started as "plain vanilla", in the sense that the cashflow received at maturity by the option holder depends solely on the terminal value of the underlying asset. Rapidly, new types of options, called exotic (or path-dependent) emerged as better solutions to a number of problems. For instance, Asian (or average rate) options, whose payout is related to the average value of the underlying over the lifetime of the option, allow treasurers of multinational corporations to hedge with a single instrument the exchange rate risk associated with a series of cashflows denominated in a foreign currency. In the case of oil, Asian options are the natural contracts since oil indexes are defined as averages.

The first and third sections of this book are dedicated to a new class of complex options – sometimes called "third generation" – whose exotic nature resides also in the underlying source of risk. These instruments raise a variety of delicate issues, among them:

❑ the introduction of an index, neither opaque nor capable of manipulation, to which the derivative contract is tied;
❑ the appropriate stochastic modelling of the index dynamics; and
❑ the design of the hedging portfolio under the severe constraints generated by the non-tradable and non-storable nature of the underlying.

The second section of the book does not analyse derivatives as such, but rather structured products such as catastrophe or nature-related bonds, which represent a key example of insurance risk transfer through securitisation. These bonds, whose coupon (and possibly principal) payment is contingent upon the non-occurrence of a well-defined catastrophic event, offer higher returns than Treasury bonds while having virtually no correlation with stocks and interest rates. Hence they provide all the benefits of diversification to investors' portfolios. One may argue further that these instruments improve the general welfare since they distribute part of nature or ecology risk among a larger number of counterparties than solely (re)insurance companies.

The third section of the book also analyses the specific features of weather derivatives, which started trading on the electronic platform of the Chicago Mercantile Exchange on September 29, 1999. Given the Asian form of the option payout and the nature of the underlying, these are exotic instruments "par excellence". Reconciling their valuation and hedging with the fundamental references, the actuarial sciences and the Black–Scholes–Merton model represents a challenge as significant as the economic relevance of these ethereal securities.

Hélyette Geman, September 1999

Introduction

Richard L. Sandor[1]

Hedge Financial Products

During the decade of the 1970s, three strangers had careers that appeared to be worlds apart: a business professor, a wheat trader and a graduate student in English. In the course of a 20-year period Bob Goshay, Les Rosenthal and Michael Palm would all play critical roles in the convergence of the insurance and capital markets, as well as the development of alternative risk transfer tools.

The last seven years of the millennium have seen the development of an unprecedented number of financial innovations in the insurance industry. These include exchange-traded catastrophe options, over-the-counter (OTC) swaps and options, CAT bonds, CatEPuts, and capital surplus notes. Related organised and OTC markets in weather derivatives have also emerged.

This exciting new publication offers a diverse kit to the reader interested in insurance derivatives, securitisation and weather derivatives. Important insights into pricing these exotic options and descriptions of this new asset class are covered in great detail. Further insights into weather derivatives are then presented. The book concludes with a chapter that helps us to understand both weather and insurance derivatives.

This brief Introduction includes some personal remembrances that may offer some insight into the process of developing new markets. The foundation and success of these new markets is due to a variety of complex factors and space limits any complete analysis.

Robert Goshay was a professor in the Graduate School of Business at the University of California, Berkeley. He was trained at Wharton in insurance in the traditional and time-honoured way. Radicalism at Berkeley in the 1960s extended to the new field of finance, and Bob was quick to understand this change. He inspired the author of this Introduction to collaborate on a paper published in the *Journal of Business Finance* in 1973,[2] that crudely outlined the possibility of insurance derivatives. It was this paper that ultimately provided the basis for the Chicago Board of Trade's commitment to the development of insurance futures and options two decades later. Bob took a sabbatical in 1973 and spent the year at Lloyds attempting to convince the leadership that new tools were necessary. His academic efforts were slow to be embraced, but represented the first educational efforts in this field. The success of new markets often depends on an intellectual underpinning by academics as well as their efforts to transfer their knowledge to industry practitioners.

Les Rosenthal was a very successful broker and trader in the Chicago Board of Trade wheat pit. He went on to build one of the most successful brokerage and proprietary trading firms at the exchange. Les is a natural leader and became a member of the board of directors of the exchange and ultimately chairman of the board. His political skills and championing of new products were responsible for the entire Treasury debt complex at the exchange. Les enjoyed the process and not the laurels. Well after his terms as chairman were finished he continued to take risks and he championed the idea of insurance derivatives for nearly five years. The new product research effort began with automotive risk and eventually moved on to medical insurance. Events of the late 1980s and early 1990s such as hurricane Hugo and the Loma Pietra earthquake ultimately generated industry support for the concept.

An overt expression of interest by the financial sector provided the last step in finalising the details and bringing the catastrophe contracts to the Board. In spite of the sound intellectual basis for the concept and support of the industry there was still opposition. One director of the exchange, who sincerely thought the concept was both irrational and that it could take down the clearing house, mounted a campaign to kill the concept. It ultimately took the support of Bill O'Connor, who was chairman of the Board of Trade, and another exchange pioneer. After a significant debate the board of directors voted to launch the new contracts. New markets require champions. Leaders who are willing to take personal risks are indispensable in organised markets where a political process determines the outcome of research and development.

Michael Palm was probably one of the most unlikely individuals to become an executive in the insurance industry. One could easily envision him as an English professor or as a great classical pianist. In a fortuitous meeting with Steven Gluckstern, while they were both teaching in Iran, they become personal friends and ultimately business partners. After a series of independent careers they both ended up working for Warren Buffet in the 1980s. It was at that time that they came up with the concept of finite insurance. A search for capital led them to Rolf Huppi, an individual with the vision to understand the convergence of the capital and insurance markets and the talent to implement his ideas. Zurich Insurance began its transformation from a traditional insurance company with the establishment of the Bermuda-based Centre Re.

A mutual friend introduced me to Michael Palm in 1992, after learning of the Chicago Board of Trade's initiatives. Michael's immediate grasp of the subject, and the innovative spirit of Rolf resulted in one of the major insurance companies of the world establishing a joint venture to explore commercial opportunities in insurance derivatives. This new company would play an integral part in the use of these tools and would motivate interest by other members of their community. Once again the lessons seem clear. The sound intellectual base for these new tools was established. A major exchange had committed itself to develop the markets. It was part of a self-fulfilling prophecy. Champions emerged within the insurance industry with Michael Palm and Steven Gluckstern. Rolf Huppi's support really made it all happen.

In the last five years consolidation has occurred in all segments of the industry. Zurich acquired Farmers, St Paul bought USF&G, Excel purchased MidOcean Reinsurance Co, Berkshire Hathaway acquired General Re, Excel purchased Tempest Re

and Cigna's Property and Casualty business. A similar trend is occurring with intermediaries. Benfield's purchase of Greg Fester is worth noting. In spite of enormous capacity, better capitalised companies and lower rates making traditional risk transfer cost effective, the trend toward securitisation continues.

Lending even more reason for optimism about the future of insurance derivatives is the financial and human capital committed by the firms participating in the process. These developments form the basis of a self-fulfilling prophecy. The investment and commercial banks involved in securitised transactions include Merrill Lynch, Goldman Sachs, Chase Securities and Donaldson Lufkin & Jenrette. Lehman Brothers has also formed a Bermudan entity. US and European insurers and reinsurers such as AIG, CNA, Zurich and Swiss Re have set up specialty units. Leading intermediaries such as Marsh, McLennan, Aon and Benfield Grieg have also devoted substantial resources to these emerging markets.

The trend is clear – securitisation is growing and evolving. Hurricane and earthquake risks are readily being transferred to the capital markets. Corporations are directly transferring risk to the capital markets. The recent issuance of a CAT bond related to an earthquake in Disneyland Japan is an example of such an effort. Hedge funds, pension funds, insurance companies and high net-worth individuals who are buying the new types of assets have extended their interest from single-year to multi-year risk.

The CBOT's invention of markets in interest rate futures and options in the 1970s helped spur the OTC swaps and options market, which soared from less than US$1 trillion in 1987 to almost US$30 trillion in 1998. A similar pattern is emerging in catastrophe securitisation, with OTC catastrophe issues increasing from less than US$200 million in June 1996 to over US$2 billion by July 1998. At the time of writing, autumn 1999, over the last two and a half years approximately 20 separate insurers, including US, European, Japanese and Bermudan companies have securitised more than US$3 billion in risk.

Hélyette Geman was part of the process of building the intellectual foundation for this industry, and her tireless efforts in both writing and lecturing have played an integral role in establishing this new market. This collection provides an excellent overview, from both an academic and a practitioner perspective, of these new and exciting markets.

1 *Richard L. Sandor is Chairman of Hedge Financial Products Inc, Chairman and CEO of Environmental Financial Products LLC, Senior Advisor to PricewaterhouseCoopers LLP, and Visiting Scholar at Northwestern University.*

2 *Goshay, Robert C. and Richard L. Sandor, 1973, "An Inquiry into the Feasibility of a Reinsurance Futures Market", Journal of Business Finance V(2).*

INSURANCE DERIVATIVES

1

From Options on Stocks and Currencies to Options on Insurance, Credit and Weather

Hélyette Geman

University Paris IX Dauphine and ESSEC

More than 25 years ago, the celebrated work by Black and Scholes (1973) and Merton (1973) on the valuation of equity options paved the way for the explosion of derivatives markets around the world. In the following decade, these results were extended to options on futures contracts (Black, 1976), options on currencies (Garman and Kohlhagen, 1983) and so forth. All these new formulas are in the same vein as the Black–Scholes–Merton formula. This chapter will try to explain why options on insurance, credit or weather present new challenges in several respects.

To start with a straightforward but crucial observation, we need to note that in the so-called "first-generation" of options, the quantity that defines the option payout at maturity T is the price of a traded stock or asset, S. This has a number of key consequences. First, the number $S(T)$, and hence the terminal value, $max(0, S(T) - k)$ of the call option, is fully observable. So is the stock price $S(l)$ at any date l during the lifetime of the option. This property obviously does not hold in the case of options on insurance, credit or weather, for which a clear *definition* of the underlying instrument or an *index* is necessary to avoid litigation on a contract that was improperly underwritten.

Second, the seller of an equity or currency option is able to hedge his/her position continuously by holding the underlying instrument in a quantity equal to the delta of the option. Hence, except for rare occurrences of "liquidity holes", hedging plain-vanilla options on stocks does not

pose any real difficulties. Delta-hedging a weather derivative through a long (or short) position in a temperature index is obviously not feasible, however. Other answers need to be found. These answers will have neither the accuracy nor the elegant simplicity of the Black–Scholes hedging portfolio.

Third, the mathematical modelling of the underlying state variable dynamics, namely the claim index for insurance derivatives or the firm's rating for credit options, involves stochastic processes whose proper identification and calibration require a database. Obviously, such data are readily and widely available in the case of financial options. This is not necessarily the case for other types of underlying sources of risk.

To clarify these points, in particular the crucial discussion of derivatives hedging, we will review the Black–Scholes–Merton formula and identify the steps in the proof that may not extend easily to insurance and weather derivatives.

The Black–Scholes–Merton formula (1973)

Let us first review the classical graphs corresponding to the payouts and gains at maturity T of simple put and call options, or combinations thereof, written on a stock S. Keeping in mind that the respective payouts of call and put options are $C(T) = max(0, S(T) - k)$ and $P(T) = max(0, k - S(T))$, where k is the strike price of the option, we obtain the familiar graphs shown in Figures 1a and 1b.

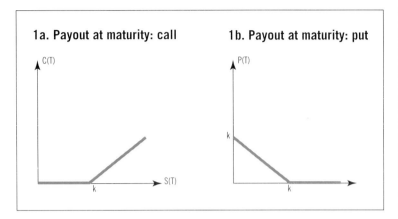

1a. Payout at maturity: call

1b. Payout at maturity: put

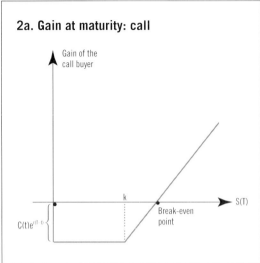

2a. Gain at maturity: call

If an investor has paid C(t) (respectively P(t)) to buy the call (put) at date t, his algebraic gain profile at maturity, expressed in US dollars of date T, is shown in Figures 2a and 2b.

Among the simple combinations of puts and calls that one can easily construct, let us mention one which will be particularly relevant for insurance derivatives, the *call spread*. A call spread is the combination of a long position in a call with strike price k_1 and a short position in a call with strike price $k_2 > k_1$, both being written on the same underlying instrument S and having the same maturity T. As will be made precise below, but is straightforward, the call price is higher for a lower strike price; hence the value CS(t) at time t of a call spread is positive and the gain profile at maturity is as shown in Figure 3.

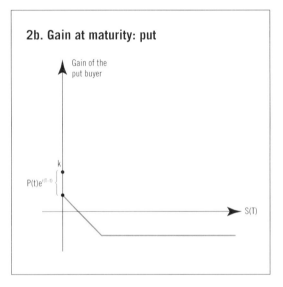

2b. Gain at maturity: put

PUT–CALL PARITY

Before turning to the problem of valuing a call option, we establish the relation prevailing, at any time t, between a call and a put written on the same underlying stock S, with the same strike price k and maturity T. It is worth noting that the result holds under fairly general assumptions, namely

A_1 The market is supposed to be frictionless (no taxes, no transaction costs).

A_2 The stock does not pay any dividend over the lifetime [0, T] of the option. (This assumption can easily be relaxed.)

A_3 The risk-free rate of borrowing or lending r is supposed to be constant over the period [0, T].

A_4 There are no arbitrage opportunities in the market, ie any riskless portfolio must have a return equal to the risk-free rate, r.

Then the following relationship holds at any date t

$$S(t) + P(t) = C(t) + ke^{-r(T-t)}$$

where C(t) is the call price, P(t) the put price, S(t) the stock price and k the strike price.

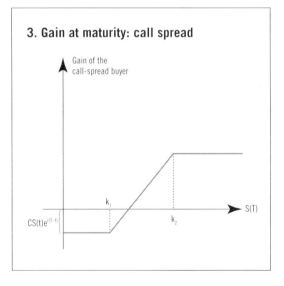

3. Gain at maturity: call spread

The proof is straightforward and consists, as usual in finance, in considering an appropriate portfolio. Here, we build a position at date t that comprises a stock, a put and a short position in the call. The position is held and liquidated at date T.

5

FROM
OPTIONS ON
STOCKS AND
CURRENCIES
TO OPTIONS
ON
INSURANCE,
CREDIT AND
WEATHER

	t	T	
		S(T) < k	S(T) ≥ k
Buy a stock	−S(t)	S(T)	S(T)
Buy a put	−P(t)	k − S(T)	0
Sell a call	C(t)	0	k − S(T)
		k	k

We see that in *all states of the world*, the terminal value of the portfolio is equal to k, a fixed quantity *known* at date t. Hence the portfolio is *riskless*, since risk in finance (and in insurance) is equivalent to randomness. The no-arbitrage assumption then implies that the initial dollar value at date t of this portfolio is +ke$^{-r(T-t)}$, which needs to be invested to build the position. This proves the put–call parity relation. It is extremely important to observe that:

❑ This result does not depend on a particular choice for the spot price evolution between t and T. In particular, the stock price process S(t) may have continuous or discontinuous trajectories.
❑ A key point, however, is the possibility of buying the stock at date t and holding it to time T.

When we turn to credit, insurance or weather derivatives, it will become difficult to buy a temperature or insurance index or a credit rating and keep it in a portfolio or in a position until maturity. The proofs of the Black–Scholes–Merton results must be kept in mind to identify the situations where their extension becomes hazardous.

To conclude on the put–call parity, let us make a final observation on a simple but fundamental use of the put option. Suppose one buys at date t a stock S(t) and a put written on the stock, with maturity T and strike price k. At date T, the value of this portfolio P is

$$V(T) = S(T) + \max(0, k - S(T))$$
$$= \max(k, S(T))$$

This expression shows that the investor will benefit from a rise in the stock market, since the portfolio value V(T) at date T will be equal to S(T). However, in the case of a collapse of the stock market, V(T) will not vanish to zero but will be equal to k. The portfolio P is called an *insured portfolio* and k is called the floor of the portfolio insurance strategy. This use of put options plays a central role in the management of portfolios, for both small and institutional investors. It also illuminates the function of *insurance* that is built in the structure of all financial options.

THE BLACK-SCHOLES-MERTON FORMULA (1973)
We can observe first that if we kept only the assumptions used to establish the put-call parity, we would not be able to find the price at date t (equally fair to the buyer and the seller) of the call option. One key assumption is missing - the one that describes the evolution of the stock price between t and T.

The Black-Scholes-Merton model We make again the assumptions A$_1$ to A$_4$ and add the assumption

$$A_5 \qquad \frac{dS_t}{S_t} = \mu dt + \sigma dW_t \qquad (1)$$

where $(W_t)_{t\geq 0}$ denotes the Brownian motion and the positive constant σ denotes the so-called volatility of the stock price.

We can observe that, since the stock does not pay any dividend, the return over the interval (t, t + dt) comes from the algebraic gain in capital represented by S(t + dt) − S(t); hence it is the left-hand side of equation (1). Since the right-hand side (an affine function of dW$_t$) follows a normal distribution, it appears that the normality of returns is a key condition of applicability of the Black-Scholes formula and of its possible extension to other underlying instruments.

Moreover, if S$_t$ is replaced by an index I$_t$ of aggregate catastrophe claims when pricing an insurance derivative, the continuity of the trajectories implied by equation (1) may not be desirable, since it will poorly reflect the jumps in losses on the amount insured following the occurrence of an earthquake or a hurricane. In the case of weather derivatives, S$_t$ is replaced by a temperature index (or an arithmetic average of temperatures) and it is not clear that the relative change dI$_t$/I$_t$ over the time interval (t, t + dt) is best represented by a normal distribution. Hence, in both cases, the mathematical modelling of the underlying source of uncertainly needs to be rethought and an adequate option pricing formula established.

Besides the nature of the stochastic process itself, another key ingredient in the proof of the Black-Scholes-Merton formula is the *risk-neutrality* argument applied to a portfolio consisting of financial instruments, the underlying stock and the option. When the option is written on insurance, credit or weather, the portfolio to which one may apply this argument is more difficult to identify - if it exists at all.

Coming to the mathematics of the Black-Scholes-Merton formula, the well-known proof given by the authors is the following: the call price

6

FROM
OPTIONS ON
STOCKS AND
CURRENCIES
TO OPTIONS
ON
INSURANCE,
CREDIT AND
WEATHER

$C(t)$ at date t may be viewed as a function of the two state variables t and S_t, namely $C(t) = f(t, St)$.

By application of Itô's lemma

$$dC_t = \frac{\partial C_t}{\partial t} + \frac{\partial C_t}{\partial S_t} \partial S_t + \frac{1}{2} \frac{\partial^2 C}{\partial S_t^2} (\partial S_t)^2$$

where, from equation (1),

$$dS_t = \mu S_t\, dt + \sigma S_t\, dW_t \qquad (1')$$

Hence

$$dC_t = \left[\frac{\partial C_t}{\partial t} + \mu S_t \frac{\partial C_t}{\partial S_t} \right. $$
$$\left. + \frac{1}{2} \sigma^2 S_t^2 \frac{\partial^2 C}{\partial S_t^2} \right] dt + \sigma S_t \frac{\partial C_t}{\partial S_t} dW_t \qquad (2)$$

To eliminate the risk expressed only by the presence of the Brownian motion (W_t), it suffices to consider the portfolio P built at time t with one call option and n stocks, where n is a real number held constant over the time interval $(t, t + dt)$.

The portfolio value at date t is

$$V_p(t) = C_t + nS_t$$

Hence

$$dV_P(t) = dC_t + ndS_t$$
$$= dt\left[\frac{\partial C_t}{\partial t} + \mu S_t \frac{\partial C_t}{\partial S_t} + \frac{1}{2} \sigma^2 S^2 \frac{\partial^2 C}{\partial S^2} \right.$$
$$\left. + nS_t\mu \right] + dW_t\left[\sigma S_t \frac{\partial C_t}{\partial S_t} + n\mu S_t \right] \qquad (3)$$

By choosing $n = -(\partial C_t/\partial S_t)$, the coefficient of dW_t is nullified and the portfolio P becomes *riskless* over the interval $(t, t + dt)$.

Hence $V_p(t + dt)$, is non-random at date t. By the *no-arbitrage* assumption A_4, the return on this riskless portfolio has to be equal to the risk-free rate r and we obtain a second expression for $dV_p(t)$

$$dV_P(t) = rV_P(t)dt = r\left[C_t - \frac{\partial C_t}{\partial S_t} S_t \right]dt \qquad (4)$$

The comparison of equations (3) and (4) leads to the fundamental *partial differential equation*:

$$\frac{\partial C_t}{\partial t} + rSt \frac{\partial C_t}{\partial S_t} + \frac{1}{2} \sigma^2 S_t^2 \frac{\partial^2 C_t}{\partial S_t^2} - rC_t = 0 \qquad (5)$$

with the boundary condition $C(T) = \max(0, S(T) - k)$.

Up to a change of variables, equation (5) may be reduced to the *heat equation* solved by Einstein. This leads to the call price at date t

$$C_t = S(t)N(d_1) - ke^{-r(T-t)}N(d_2) \qquad (6)$$

where:

N denotes the cumulative function of a normal variable with mean 0 and variance 1

$$d_1 = \frac{\ln\left(\frac{S_t}{ke^{-r(T-t)}}\right) + \frac{1}{2} \sigma^2(T - t)}{\sigma\sqrt{T - t}}$$

$$d_2 = d_1 - \sigma\sqrt{T - t}$$

Before turning to the computation of the call price sensitivities to the different variables (the Greeks), some important observations are in order. Equation (4) establishes that the portfolio consisting of a long call and a number of stocks, equal to $-\partial C_t/\partial S_t$ ($\partial C_t/\partial S_t$ will be defined below as the delta of the option), behaves over the interval $(t, t + dt)$ like a money market account; equivalently, the call is replicated on the interval $(t, t + dt)$ by Δ shares and some cash amount (in fact negative), the two quantities being functions of time (for instance, $\partial C_t/\partial S_t$ obviously varies with time), hence needing to be adjusted over time. This is *the dynamic replication* of the call the seller must perform over the interval $[0, T]$ to come up with the payout of the option, $\max(0, S(T) - k)$, in all states of the world at time T.

This continuous replication of the option with the underlying instrument (and the cash, which is held by any institution) is obviously problematic for electricity, insurance and weather derivatives. In each case, an appropriate solution in terms of a hedging portfolio – if it exists – needs to be exhibited.

SENSITIVITIES OF THE CALL PRICE TO THE DIFFERENT VARIABLES

Delta of the call The first quantity whose impact on the option price needs to be monitored is obviously the underlying source of risk S_t; hence the importance of the so-called delta of the call

$$\Delta = \frac{\partial C_t}{\partial S_t} = N(d_1)$$

as computed from equation (6).

7

FROM
OPTIONS ON
STOCKS AND
CURRENCIES
TO OPTIONS
ON
INSURANCE,
CREDIT AND
WEATHER

Hence, this sensitivity is positive, which is not surprising: the higher the stock price, the higher the option price. Moreover, Δ is smaller than 1, which shows that one uses less than one stock at any date t to replicate the call. Lastly, observing that over a time interval δt, one can write

$$\delta C_t \approx \Delta . \delta S_t$$

$$\frac{\delta C_t}{C_t} \approx \frac{\delta S_t}{S_t} \frac{S_t}{C_t} . \Delta$$

From equation (6),

$$S_t . \Delta > C_t$$

which leads to

$$\left| \frac{\delta C_t}{C_t} \right| > \left| \frac{\delta S_t}{S_t} \right|$$

The return generated over (t, t + dt) by investing in the call has the same sign as an investment in the stock but is always greater in absolute value, hence the *leverage effect* obtained by investing the same amount of money in the call rather than in the underlying stock when one has a view (upward or downward) on the stock moves. Lastly, we can observe that the delta of the put can be easily derived from the delta of the call, which has the same strike price and maturity. Returning to the put–call parity relationship $S(t) + P(t) = C(t) + ke^{-r(T-t)}$, it suffices to take the partial derivative with respect to S_t on both sides to obtain $\Delta_{put} = \Delta_{call} - 1$.

This shows that the put is, at any date t, a decreasing function of the stock price (this is obvious at time T from the expression max $(0, k - S(T))$ of the put price) and that the dynamic replication of the put will involve a short position in the underlying stock.

Gamma of the call   Given the importance of the delta of the call, a quantity of interest is the sensitivity of the delta itself to the stock price, namely

$$\Gamma = \frac{\partial \Delta_t}{\partial S_t} = \frac{\partial^2 C}{\partial S_t^2} = N'(d_1) \frac{\partial d_1}{\partial S_t} = \frac{1}{S_t} \frac{N'(d_1)}{\sigma \sqrt{T-t}}$$

which is obviously positive.

Hence at any date t, the call price is a convex function of the underlying stock price.

Sensitivity to time

$$\Theta = \frac{-\partial S_t}{\partial t}$$

$$= -\left[e^{-r(T-t)} kN(d_2) + \frac{\sigma e^{-r(T-t)}}{2\sqrt{T-t}} kN'(d_1) \right] < 0$$

As time goes by, the period during which the stock price may move to very high values before maturity shrinks (the downward moves below k remaining constantly translated into a zero pay-out of the call at date T) and the *time value* of the call price diminishes.

Sensitivity to the volatility: vega of the option

$$\frac{\partial C}{\partial \sigma} = S\sqrt{T-t} \, N'(d_1) > 0$$

A number of comments are in order at this point. These are particularly important from a practical standpoint. Firstly, let us mention that, even though the volatility parameter σ is supposed to be constant in the Black–Scholes model, practitioners have for more than 20 years computed the *implied volatility* $\sigma_{imp}(t)$ embedded in the option market price C(t) at date t (in a unique manner since $\partial C/\partial \sigma = >0$). In contrast with the model assumption, $\sigma_{imp}(t)$, as reconstructed daily from prices of options written on a given stock, varies with time. Among the number of questions on this issue, the first one – widely documented in the finance literature without any decisive conclusion – is the following: if one writes an option at time t for the maturity T, what is the best quantity to incorporate for σ in the Black–Scholes formula to obtain a quasi-perfect replication of the option by delta hedging? The main quantities that have been and are tested are the historical volatility, computed on a time series of past prices of the underlying stock, and the implied volatility, derived from current option prices. As far as the latter is concerned, another difficulty arises from the fact that it also only varies with the strike price k of the option, generating the famous volatility smile $\sigma_{impl}(k)$ prevailing at date t.

Extensions of the Black–Scholes–Merton formula

A number of deviations from the original Black–Scholes–Merton model have been documented both by academics and practitioners over the past 25 years. We noted in the previous paragraph

FROM
OPTIONS ON
STOCKS AND
CURRENCIES
TO OPTIONS
ON
INSURANCE,
CREDIT AND
WEATHER

that the implied volatility rapidly became a time-varying parameter $\sigma_{imp}(t)$, depending also not only on the strike price of the option under analysis but also on its maturity T (for instance, options with a short time to maturity have a much higher volatility than the one predicted by the Black–Scholes formula). This dependence in t and T defines the so-called term structure of volatilities at date t, $\sigma_{impl}(t, T)$, whose dependence in k as well translates into the volatility surface $\sigma_{impl}(k, T)$ at date t.

The celebrated formula has been extended in several ways. These can be roughly classified in three categories:

❑ replacement of the classical geometric Brownian motion to represent the underlying price process by a more complicated stochastic process;
❑ replacement of the classical call option payoff, max(0, S(T) – k) by an "exotic" payoff involving not only S(T) but the trajectory of the process S(t) over the lifetime [0, T] of the option; and
❑ replacement of the stock price as the underlying source of risk in the option by interest rates, currencies and, very recently, by credit, insurance, weather and electricity. As this book will try to show, all these extensions apply to the case of derivatives on insurance, electricity or weather.

ALTERNATIVE REPRESENTATIONS OF THE UNDERLYING SOURCE OF RISK DYNAMICS
We observed in the previous section that equation (1), representing the return of the stock price over the interval (t, t + dt) as the quantity $\mu dt + \sigma dW_t$, hence a normal distribution, was a key assumption in the Black–Scholes model. On the other hand, a huge literature in finance has been dedicated to the analysis of the normality of asset returns, since this property plays a central role in the construction of the Markowitz frontier of efficient portfolios and the Capital Asset Pricing Model. The property of normality also has an impact on the nature of the *tails* of the distribution, which represent extreme events and are conveyed by the $(1 - \alpha)$ quantile ($\alpha = 0.95$ for instance), called value-at-risk, at the level of confidence α and playing a major role as a risk indicator. Deviations of returns from normality have been consistently exhibited in the finance literature. This is all the more true as the time period becomes shorter – such as a day or a week, a time length which has become for practical purposes the horizon in portfolio management (see Geman and Ané, 1996). Besides the fat

tails or kurtosis, the distribution of observed returns is more skewed than the normal distribution. One way of addressing the issue of skewness and kurtosis is to introduce jumps in the representation of the stock price dynamics.

Jump diffusion processes for the underlying asset price In 1976, Merton proposed to extend the model proposed in Black and Scholes (1973) and Merton (1973) for the stock price dynamics by adding a jump component, namely

$$\frac{dS_t}{S_t} = \mu dt + \sigma dW_t + U dN_t \qquad (7)$$

where:
(N_t) is a Poisson process with intensity λ;
U is a real-valued random variable; and
the other quantities have the same meaning as before.

This assumption has a number of consequences:

❑ From a mathematical viewpoint, the solution of (7) is obviously more complicated than the solution of (1) (in particular, it is no longer explicit, but involves the so-called Doléans–Dade exponential).
❑ From an economic viewpoint, the number of sources of randomness driving the stock price has been drastically increased, not only because of the presence of the Poisson process (N_t) but also because the magnitude of the jumps U is a random quantity. Hence, it is no longer possible to duplicate the call option with the underlying stock and the money-market account. In fact, an *infinite number* of hedging instruments are necessary and do not exist in practice.

To eliminate this market incompleteness, Merton (1976) made the simplifying assumption that the jump risk could be diversified away. This eliminated the most important difficulty. And some mathematical considerations allowed the option price to be exhibited in this new setting. This assumption of a null *market price of jump risk* is clearly unacceptable for catastrophic insurance risk. Nor is it valid in the case of electricity derivatives. After the spike of June 1998 in the Illinois region, when the spot price of electricity went from US$25 to US$7,500, options with a strike price of US$1,000 had their market prices multiplied by 100, clearly indicating the existence of risk aversion and a risk premium associated with the jump.

FROM
OPTIONS ON
STOCKS AND
CURRENCIES
TO OPTIONS
ON
INSURANCE,
CREDIT AND
WEATHER

Time-varying volatility for the underlying asset price Another way of explaining the volatility smile mentioned above, as well as the fact that the implied volatility $\sigma_{impl}(t)$ derived from a call option written on a given stock varies with time, is to introduce explicitly in equation (1) a volatility that varies with time.

As a first approach, $\sigma(t)$ may be expressed as a deterministic function of time

$$\frac{dS_t}{S_t} = \mu dt + \sigma(t)dW_t$$

It is then easy to show that all Black–Scholes results hold, including the hedging strategy. It is sufficient to replace σ with Σ everywhere, including in the valuation equation (6), where Σ is defined by

$$\Sigma^2(T - t) = \int_t^T \sigma^2(u)du$$

Going one step further, $\sigma(t)$ becomes stochastic but has the property of being a function of $S(t)$. In this case, we still have only one source of randomness, namely the Brownian motion involved in the dynamics of $(S(t))$. Hence, the option price (as well as the hedging portfolio) is unique. It can be obtained as a closed-form expression if $\sigma(S_t)$ is a simple function; otherwise, $C(t)$ may be computed using Monte-Carlo simulations.

In the most general *stochastic volatility model*, $\sigma(t)$ is a stochastic process; hence, assuming diffusion processes for the stock and the volatility, the dynamics of $(S(t))$ are defined by the two stochastic differential equations

$$dS_t = \mu_1(t,S_t)dt + \sigma(t,S_t)dW_t^1$$

$$dy(t) = \mu_2(t,y_t)dt + \eta(t,y(t))dW_t^2$$

where

$$y(t) = [\sigma(t)]^2; \quad dW_t^1 . dW_t^2 = \rho(t)dt$$

The coefficient $\rho(t)$ allows for dependence of the Brownian motions $W_1(t)$ and $W_2(t)$; the functions μ_1 and μ_2 may eventually translate a property of mean reversion for the stock price or volatility. In this case, not only do the closed-form solutions for option prices become problematic but the uniqueness of the call value and of the hedging portfolio is lost, since we still have only two hedging instruments and an extra

source of risk represented by the Brownian motion (W_t^2). A possible answer to this market incompleteness is to consider that the at-the-money call C^m (ie with a strike price equal to the value of the stock today) is a *basic security* whose price is agreed upon by all market players.

It then becomes possible to hedge all other calls and puts using the stock, the money-market account and the call C^m. The existence of this very liquid option completing the market is quite legitimate for options on stocks, on stock indexes or on currencies; it is certainly problematic for insurance or weather derivatives, where the generality of a stochastic volatility model is paid for by the loss of a unique price for the options.

EXOTIC PAY-OFFS
Since the beginning of the 1980s, "exotic" options have been introduced to answer the hedging needs of financial and industrial firms as well as the search for new opportunities on the part of investors. We will describe the most popular exotic options – Asian and barrier options.

Asian or average-rate options Instead of the Black–Scholes payoff, $\max(0, S_T - k)$, the buyer of an Asian call option receives at maturity, T, $\max(0, A_T - k)$, where A_T represents the arithmetic average of the stock price computed over the lifetime $[0, T]$ or over a subinterval of $[0, T]$.

Asian options are much used for thinly traded assets, such as gold, since they obviously prevent a possible manipulation of prices on the maturity date of standard options by institutions holding large positions in the underlying asset. They represent a large percentage of the options traded on oil or oil spreads, since oil indexes are themselves defined as averages of spot prices over a period. In the foreign exchange markets, they allow corporate treasurers to hedge a series of cashflows by buying a single average-rate option, as an alternative to a portfolio of standard options associated with each payment date, hence reducing the cost of currency risk management.

Other examples of Asian options will be presented in this book, with explanations of why their valuation is such an important issue. Unfortunately, it is not a straightforward problem. The difficulties stem from the fact that an average of prices, S_t, satisfying equation (1) does not satisfy an equation of the same type or, in other words, is not a geometric Brownian motion. The main methods used today to value

10

FROM
OPTIONS ON
STOCKS AND
CURRENCIES
TO OPTIONS
ON
INSURANCE,
CREDIT AND
WEATHER

Asian options are the following:

❏ The approximation of the true distribution of the average A_T by the lognormal distribution of S_T, with adjustment of the first two moments (see Lévy, 1992).

❏ The use of Monte Carlo simulations: different paths of the stock price are generated, providing for each the values $S(t_1) \dots S(t_n)$, which are averaged to exhibit one outcome O_i of $\max(0, A_T - k)$, where k is the strike price of the Asian call.

From the law of large numbers, we know that the quantity $\sum_{i=1}^{N} O_i/N$ will converge to the expectation of the payoff which, discounted, gives the price of the Asian call at time zero.

❏ An exact approach to Asian option valuation and hedging. Geman and Yor (1993) used sophisticated mathematical tools to compute the Laplace transform of the call price with respect to maturity. Geman and Eydeland (1995), on one hand, and Fu, Madan and Wang (1996), on the other, apply different algorithms to invert the Geman–Yor formula, but come up with remarkably similar results. The former authors demonstrate the superiority of their results over those obtained through Monte Carlo simulations, in particular in terms of the accuracy of delta hedging.

Barrier and double-barrier options These have become increasingly popular in equity markets, and even more so in foreign exchange and commodity markets. A barrier call option provides at maturity the classical Black–Scholes payoff, $\max(0, S_T - k)$ only if (unless) the underlying asset S has touched a prespecified barrier L over the lifetime [0, T] of the option. For instance, if a non-zero payoff is contingent on the fact that the value L is reached at some date t, the call is said to be "up-and-in" or "down-and-in".

It appears immediately that the price of a barrier call at time 0 is smaller than the standard call with the same strike and maturity (since it pays zero more often). Hence a barrier option is an inexpensive hedge against extreme events. An "up-and-in" option will be activated only if an insurance index, a foreign currency or the spot price of electricity reaches a very high level (defined as the barrier in the option contract).

A vast body of recent literature has been dedicated to barrier options. The pricing of "single-barrier" options is not particularly difficult in the classical Black–Scholes–Merton framework and explicit formulas have existed for some time (see Merton, 1973; Goldman, Sosin and Gatto, 1979).

For instance, if the barrier L is less than or equal to the strike price, the value at date 0 of a down-and-in call written on a non-dividend-paying stock is

$$C(0) = S(0) \left[\frac{L}{S(0)} \right]^{2\alpha} N(d_1) - ke^{-rT} \left[\frac{L}{S(0)} \right]^{2\alpha} N(d_2)$$

$$\text{where} \quad \alpha = \frac{r + \dfrac{\sigma^2}{2}}{\sigma^2}$$

and d_1 and d_2 have the same expressions as in formula (6).

Double-barrier options yield the Black–Scholes payout, $\max(0, S_T - k)$, at maturity under the condition that S_t has not touched either of two barriers, denoted L (lower barrier) and U (upper barrier), during the lifetime of the option [0, T]. They are then called *corridor* options and allow traders or investors to take a view on the range of a stock, a commodity or an index price. Another type of double-barrier option is activated by the fact that one (at least) of the two barriers has been crossed by the trajectory of S_t between 0 and T. All types of double-barrier options are more difficult to price than simple barrier options. In both cases, Monte Carlo methods may be dangerous: the discrete trajectories simulated may misrepresent the continuous possibility of (de-)activation of the barrier option over the interval [0, T]. Geman and Yor (1996) provide the Laplace transforms of the exact prices of double-barrier options and of their deltas, gammas and other sensitivities as well.

Options on exotic underlyings Over the past six years, a variety of non-financial assets have become the source of risk on which standard and path-dependent options are written. Insurance derivatives were launched in December 1993 by the Chicago Board of Trade and are traded today both on exchanges and in over-the-counter (OTC) markets. An index, precluding manipulations and opacity, needed to be constructed for its value at maturity T to determine the option payout. This index is now the PCS (Property Claim Services) index. Since it is defined as an aggregate amount of losses – that is an average (up to constant) – insurance derivative give rise to Asian-type problems. At the same time, the nature of the underlying instrument – an index that spikes in the case of an earthquake or a hurricane – requires the presence of a jump process in its modelling.

11

FROM
OPTIONS ON
STOCKS AND
CURRENCIES
TO OPTIONS
ON
INSURANCE,
CREDIT AND
WEATHER

More recently, as a result of the credit events that shook financial markets, from the Asian crisis to the Russian turmoil, credit derivatives developed as hedging instruments. These cover not only bonds on which default is possible, but also swaps and transactions with counterparties that bear the risk of default – all OTC transactions, in other words. Again, credit not being a traded instrument, a precise definition of the option contract and of the *insured risk* is necessary to avoid possible litigation later on.

Lastly, with deregulation of electricity taking place around the world, and in the US in particular, weather derivatives have been introduced to allow utilities to hedge their electricity risk since, in the US, spikes in electricity prices tend to coincide with extreme weather conditions. Weather derivatives have quickly become a very useful instrument for farmers, construction companies or even clothing manufacturers.

As will be discussed in the third section of this book, weather derivatives raise two types of difficulties. The first is technical, since the payoff of the option is related to an average of temperature spreads (65°F representing the "ideal" temperature), hence it is again an Asian-type problem. A much bigger difficulty, however, is of an economic nature and resides in the fact that the seller of a weather derivative cannot delta hedge, since this procedure would involve *owning* the underlying source of risk – the temperature index.

The pricing and hedging of weather derivatives therefore require new answers, much closer to actuarial and insurance techniques than to the *dynamic hedging* of options written on traded assets.

BIBLIOGRAPHY

Black, F. and M. Scholes, 1973, "The Pricing of Options and Corporate Liabilities", *Journal of Political Economy*, 81, pp. 637-54.

Clark, P., 1973, "A Subordinated Stochastic Process with Finite Variance for Speculative Price", *Econometrica*, 41(1), pp. 135-56.

Fu, M., D. Madan and T. Wang, 1996, "Pricing Continuous Time Asian Options: A Comparison of Analytical and Monte Carlo Methods", preprint, University of Maryland.

Geman, H. and T. Ané, 1996, "Stochastic Subordination", *Risk*, September, pp. 146-49.

Geman, H. and A. Eydeland, 1995, "Domino Effect: Inverting the Laplace Transform", *Risk*, April, pp. 64-7.

Geman, H. and M. Yor, 1993, "Bessel Processes, Asian Options and Perpetuities", *Mathematical Finance*, 3(4), pp. 349-75.

Geman, H. and M. Yor, 1996, "Pricing and Hedging Path-Dependent Options: A Probabilistic Approach", *Mathematical Finance*, 6(4), pp. 365-78.

Goldman, M., H. Sosin and M. Gatto, 1979, "Path Dependent Options: Buy at the Low, Sell at the High", *Journal of Finance*, 34, pp. 111-27.

Harrison, J.M. and D. Kreps, 1979, "Martingales and Arbitrage in Multiperiod Securities Markets", *Journal of Economic Theory*, 20, pp. 381-408.

Harrison, J.M. and S.R. Pliska, 1981, "Martingales and Stochastic Integrals in the Theory of Continuous Trading", *Stochastic Processes and their Applications*, 11, pp. 215-60.

Ingersoll, J., 1987, *Theory of Rational Decision Making*, Rowman and Littlefield.

Kemna, A. and T. Vorst, 1990, "A Pricing Method for Options Based on Average Asset Values", *Journal of Banking and Finance* 14, pp. 113-29.

Kunitomo, N. and M. Ikeda, 1992, "Pricing Options with Curved Boundaries", *Mathematical Finance*, 2(4), pp. 275-91.

Merton, R.C., 1973, "Theory of Rational Option Pricing", *Bell Journal of Economics and Management Science*, 4, pp. 141-83.

2

The Valuation of Multiple Claim Insurance Contracts

David C. Shimko
Harvard Business School

This chapter provides a closed-form solution for the value of a multiple claim insurance contract that is subject to a deductible amount and/or an upper limit on claims. The solution is a time integral of European option prices. The model provides three important insights. First, systematic risk in insurance policies is altered in the presence of deductibles and maximum indemnity levels. Second, idiosyncratic risk affects policy valuation and the required rates of return on underwriting portfolios. Finally, contrary to traditional actuarial intuition, changes in the risk-free interest rate may either increase or reduce policy values.

The contingent claims approach to insurance valuation can be traced to Merton (1977) and Smith (1979), who use this methodology to value specific types of insurance policies. While qualitative comparisons to stock options valuation are straightforward, the calculation of insurance premia presents a difficult problem for at least three reasons:

❏ For many lines of insurance, a policyholder may submit multiple claims.
❏ Policies are typically written with prescribed deductibles and maximum coverage limits. The non-linear nature of these loss-sharing rules creates aggregation problems similar to those encountered in the valuation of portfolios of options.
❏ The size and frequency of losses may vary systematically, which requires the calculation of a risk premium that is also affected by the option-like characteristics of the insurance policies.

This chapter explicitly resolves these valuation problems, and applies the results to rate-making

practices for insurance lines. The model abstracts from problems of market imperfections, non-competitiveness, non-observability, adverse selection and moral hazard, and examines the pricing of insurance policies in an environment where claims are generated according to exogenously specified stochastic processes. For the lognormal loss case, closed form solutions are derived for policy value and required rate of return. The solutions are shown to be equivalent to linear combinations of time integrals of European option pricing formulas. Based on these solutions, the following results are established:

❏ The systematic risk and required rate of return of an insurance policy depend on the size of the deductible and maximum indemnity level.
❏ In the presence of a deductible or maximum indemnity level, idiosyncratic underwriting risks affect policy valuation and the required rate of return on insurance policies.
❏ Higher interest rates may lead to higher or lower policy values.

Kraus and Ross (1982) studied the impact of systematic risk in underwriting portfolios; the

This chapter was first published in Journal of Financial and Qualitative Analysis, *Vol 27, no 2, 1992. This copyrighted material is reprinted with permission from The University of Washington, USA. The author thanks Stephen Buser, Tim Campbell, Dennis Draper, Bruno Gerard, Francis Longstaff, Robert McDonald, Daniel Siegel, Randolph Westerfield and an anonymous JFQA referee for their suggestions and guidance. Residual errors remain the author's responsibility. Research support from the State Farm Companies Foundation is gratefully acknowledged.*

14

THE
VALUATION
OF MULTIPLE
CLAIM
INSURANCE
CONTRACTS

first observation admits loss truncation and examines the differential effect on systematic risk. Doherty and Garven (1986) and Cummins (1988) analysed insurer insolvency risk and showed that idiosyncratic risk may affect policy valuation and returns; the second observation provides another reason why volatility may be priced. The third observation contradicts traditional actuarial practice in policy valuation.

The chapter is organised in the following manner. The next section formulates and solves the insurance model in closed form. The third section examines special cases of the general solution that highlight the properties of proportional coinsurance (when deductibles are expressed as percentages of loses), the effects of maximum indemnity levels (which are shown to produce effects symmetric to those for deductibles), and policy termination provisions. The fourth section studies limiting cases and presents comparative static results, and the final section presents conclusions.

The model

CONSTRUCTION

We consider the problem of pricing an individual insurance indemnity contract. An indemnity contract binds the insurer to pay the insured whatever amount of loss is incurred, minus a previously agreed-upon deductible payment D, if the difference is positive. Whenever a claim is made with indemnity (loss) level C_t at time t, the insurance company pays its policyholder

$$S_t = \min[\max(C_t - D, 0), M] \qquad (1)$$

For convenience, assume that the policy begins coverage at time zero, and expires at time T, τ periods from now. The interest rate is assumed constant, and equal to r. The constant (M) specifies the maximum recovery per claim.[1]

Let the claim (conditional on the claim being made) for the individual follow the geometric Brownian motion process generated by the stochastic differential equation given below.

$$dC_t = \alpha_c C_t dt + \sigma_c C_t dZ_{ct}; \quad C(0) = C \qquad (2)$$

When the policyholder experiences a loss, the loss is of value C_t. The insurance company then pays the insured S_t, which is given by equation (1).

The constant α_c reflects the non-stochastic element in the expected growth or decline in the level of claims. The constant σ_c determines the

instantaneous volatility of the process. The term dZ_{ct} represents a standard Wiener process, with mean zero and variance dt. The conditional claim process is correlated with the market portfolio of Merton (1973); the correlation coefficient is ρ_{cm}.

We characterise the arrival of claims as a non-stationary Poisson process. At any given moment, the expected intensity (claims per period) of the arrival process (λ_t) is modelled as a geometric diffusion process.

$$d\lambda_t = \alpha_\lambda \lambda_t dt + \sigma_\lambda \lambda_t dZ_{\lambda t}; \quad \lambda(0) = \lambda \qquad (3)$$

The constant α_λ measures the expected growth in claim frequency, while the constant σ_λ is the instantaneous volatility. The term dZ_λ represents a standard Wiener process, which may be correlated with dC. Let $dZ_c dZ_\lambda = \rho_{c\lambda} dt$ represent the instantaneous correlation between C and λ.

At any point in time, the probability an individual will make a claim is given by $\lambda_t dt$.[2] This probability changes stochastically through time, in relation to systematic factors.[3] The correlation between the claim frequency process and the market portfolio is given by $\rho_{\lambda m}$. In this model, conditional on a jump (a cash loss to the insurance company), the size of the jump is independent of market factors; it is given contemporaneously by the level of S_{it}. Recall that the loss to the insurance company, S, is derived from C through equation (1). Although the increments of the jump size S_{it} are correlated with aggregate wealth, the jump size itself is conditionally uncorrelated with aggregate wealth; its value is known at time t. Therefore, for pricing purposes, the jump size may be considered diversifiable, although changes in the jump size are not.

To the structure presented above, we add the following assumptions for the insurance company and the economy:

A1. Intermediary role. The insurance company holds an arbitrarily large number in identically parameterised policies. Claim realisations differ across policies.

A2. Atomistic equity financing. There exist an arbitrarily large number of shareholders who own the intermediary and disburse proportional cash payments to policyholders who experience losses. There are no debtholders.

A3. Symmetric information. The insurance company enjoys full observability of the underlying claim processes. Claims arise exogenously, absent of any influence on the part of the policyholder. There are no moral hazard and no adverse selection problems.

15

THE
VALUATION
OF MULTIPLE
CLAIM
INSURANCE
CONTRACTS

A4. Equilibrium. The assumptions of the Cox, Ingersoll and Ross (1985) model of intertemporal capital asset pricing hold. These assumptions include: (i) existence of a single consumption/investment good; (ii) existence of a set of linear production activities where changes in productivity follow exogenously specified Wiener processes; (iii) existence of a finite dimensional state variable vector whose components follow Wiener processes; (iv) free entry and exit with competitive price-taking individuals and firms; (v) common riskless borrowing and lending rates; (vi) markets for contingent claims where the claims follow Wiener processes with endogenously determined parameters; (vii) a fixed number of identical individuals with homogenous expectations and von Neumann-Morganstern utility functions, and (viii) continuous and frictionless trading.

A5. Preferences and investment opportunities. Investors have intertemporal utility functions that exhibit constant relative risk aversion. The investment opportunity set (including the riskless rate of interest) is constant. See Merton (1973) for further description.

DISCUSSION

Assumptions A1, A2, and A4 allow the discrete cash disbursements to be treated as a continuous cashflow stream. For a proof, see Shimko (1989). Assumption A5 admits a unique market portfolio and a constant risk premium for each of the state variables. Assumption A3 restricts the current study to issues of asset valuations in the absence of strategic behaviour on the part of policyholders and the insurance company.

The general formulation does not limit the number of claims that might be made within the claim period. The actual claim dates are assumed random, where the distribution of these claim dates depends on the number of claims that occur within the period of coverage.[4]

The structure of the claim (C) may be compared to previous financial models. Primarily, note that C does not represent the value of an asset, but the conditional value of a cashflow. This implies that there will be no necessary equilibrium relationship between α, σ, and the riskless interest rate, as might exist for a traded asset. At random times, the process is observed, and the policyholder suffers a discrete loss of (C_t).[5]

The insurance company eliminates diversifiable risk by pooling a large group of policies, and divides the claim payments among a large group of shareholders. The resulting cash payouts (on a per-share basis) are continuous, stochastic and bear priced risk. The shareholders find the present value of these liabilities and set the value equal to the (actuarially fair) premium value. The discount rate is found according to Merton's (1973) intertemporal capital asset pricing model.[6]

For pricing purposes, the insurance company need not perform the diversification function if the insurance company is held by well-diversified shareholders. However, to invoke a continuous asset pricing model to value the cashflows, the cashflows must be continuous as well. The diversification assumption therefore facilitates the solution of the problem without loss of generality.

SOLUTION

For the moment, we assume no maximum indemnity level. Under Assumptions A1–A5, the dollar value of the policy must evolve according to the following partial differential equation, where subscripts of V denote partial derivatives,

$$\tfrac{1}{2}V_{cc}\sigma_c^2C^2 + \tfrac{1}{2}V_{\lambda\lambda}\sigma_\lambda^2\lambda^2 + V_{C\lambda}\rho_{C\lambda}\sigma_c\sigma_\lambda C\lambda + V_c\alpha_c^*C$$
$$+ V_\lambda\alpha_\lambda^*\lambda - V_\tau + \lambda g - rV = 0 \qquad (4)$$

In equation (4), the variable τ represents time to expiration, and the riskless constant discount rate is given by r. Time subscripts are omitted. In addition, the following parameter restrictions apply:

$$\alpha_c^* = \alpha_c - \phi_c\sigma_c \qquad \phi_c = (\alpha_m - r)\rho_{cm}/\sigma_m$$
$$\alpha_\lambda^* = \alpha_\lambda - \phi_\lambda\sigma_\lambda \qquad \phi_\lambda = (\alpha_m - r)\rho_{\lambda m}/\sigma_\lambda$$
$$g = \max(C - D,0)$$

This is a special case of the fundamental equilibrium valuation equation given in Cox–Ingersoll–Ross (1985). The market portfolio (M) follows geometric Brownian motion with constant drift (α_m) and volatility (σ_m) parameters. Correlations (ρ) between C, λ and M are implied by their subscripts. The terms ϕ_c and ϕ_λ represent the market price of risk of claim level and frequency risk, respectively. The terms α_c^* and α_λ^* can be thought of as certainty-equivalent growth rates for claim levels and frequencies, as discussed by Constantinides (1978).

The expected cashflow term is given by λg. We have assumed that the policy is of the renewing type, ie, the policy does not terminate upon payment of the first (or any) claim.[7] The equation states that the expected cashflow term equals λmax(C − D,0), reflecting the fact that (a) the policy is not cancelled after a claim is made and

(b) the policy value is unaffected by an instantaneous loss realisation. For a discussion of the partial differential equation in a similar environment, see the appendix in Brennan and Schwartz (1982). Shimko (1989) details the specifics of various cashflow treatments.

The policy value must satisfy several boundary conditions. In τ periods, the policy expires worthless, therefore, $V(C,\lambda,0) = 0$. To this we add four additional boundary conditions, $V(0,\lambda,\tau) = V(C,0,\tau) = 0$, $|V_c(\infty,\lambda,\tau)| < \infty$, and $|V_\lambda(C,\infty,\tau)| < \infty$. The first two reflect that when either C or λ reaches zero (a zero probability event), they remain at zero, and the policy is worthless. The second two conditions require that the hedge ratios be bounded. This completes the specification.

The solution method has been relegated to the Appendix. The solution for V can be given by

$$V(C,\lambda,\tau; D) = \lambda W(C,\tau; D) \qquad (5)$$

$$W = AD(C/D)^{\gamma + \nu}N(b_1) + BD(C/D)^{\gamma - \nu}N(b_2)$$

$$-\left[\frac{Ce^{-\delta\tau}}{\delta}N(d_1) - \frac{De^{-r_2\tau}}{r_2}N(d_2)\right]$$

$$-\left[AD(C/D)^{\gamma + \nu} + BD(C/D)^{\gamma - \nu} - \frac{C}{\delta} + \frac{D}{r_2}\right]1_{\{C > D\}}$$

$$\nu = \frac{m}{a}$$

$$b_1 = \frac{Ln(C/D)}{\sigma\sqrt{\tau}} + \sigma\nu\sqrt{\tau}, \quad b_2 = \frac{Ln(C/D)}{\sigma\sqrt{\tau}} - \sigma\nu\sqrt{\tau}$$

$$d_1 = \frac{Ln(C/D) + (r_1 + \frac{1}{2}\sigma^2)\tau}{\sigma\sqrt{\tau}}$$

$$d_2 = \frac{Ln(C/D) + (r_1 - \frac{1}{2}\sigma^2)\tau}{\sigma\sqrt{\tau}}$$

$$A = [r_2 - r_1(\gamma - \nu)] \div [2\delta r_2\nu]$$

$$B = [r_1(\gamma + \nu) - r_2] \div [2\delta r_2\nu]$$

$$m^2 = r_2 + a^2\gamma^2, \quad a^2 = \frac{1}{2}\sigma^2, \quad \gamma = [a^2 - r_1]/[2a^2]$$

$$\delta = r_2 - r_1, \quad u = a(1 - \gamma), \quad p = a\gamma$$

where $1_{\{A\}}$ is the indicator function of set A.[8] Note that $\sigma \equiv \sigma_c$. $N(\cdot)$ represents the standard cumulative normal distribution function. The uniqueness of the solution follows from Friedman (1964). The function (V) is continuous and continuously differentiable at the point of equality ($C = D$), as shown in the Appendix.

The value of an insurance contract of any term can be expressed as a time integral of the appropriately modified Black–Scholes formulas.

Consider the expected payout at any moment in the future. The current level of C is known, and the parameters of its lognormal distribution at time t. The actual claim payout at time t (if a claim is paid) is $\max(C - D,0)$, similar to the terminal payout of a call option. The expected payout at t is given by the future value of the dividend-adjusted Black–Scholes equation. The present value of the Black–Scholes equation requires an adjustment for the rate of return shortfall in the underlying stock (McDonald and Siegel, 1984).[9] To verify this claim, one can calculate $\partial W/\partial \tau$; the result is the Black–Scholes option pricing model with $C \exp(-\delta\tau)$ for the stock price, and $D \exp(-r_2\tau)$ for the present value of the exercise price. The constant $\delta = r_2 - r_1$.

MAXIMUM RECOVERY LEVELS
Many insurance contracts include provisions limiting the maximum indemnity of the insurance company. If this maximum indemnity level is expressed on a per-claim basis, then the valuation of equation (5) can be easily adapted to value the insurance contract. Let $Y(C,\lambda,\tau; D,M)$ represent the value of this insurance policy, and M represent the maximum indemnity level. Then $Y(C,\lambda,\tau; D,M) = \lambda W(C,\tau;D) - \lambda W(C,\tau;M)$. The payout to the insured party resembles the payout of a call option that is truncated from above. In effect, the insured party reinsures the insurance company against the possibility of very high losses. The deductible on the reinsurance policy is the same as the maximum indemnity level for the insurance policy.

INTERPRETATIONS
The intuitive interpretation of the individual components of V is difficult.[10] The valuation reflects the present values of the cashflows required to replicate the expected payouts of the insurance contract. The strategy is as follows:
(a) At time 0, if C > D, purchase a perpetuity that pays λCdt continuously (value = $\lambda C/\delta$). Sell a risk-free perpetuity that pays λDdt continuously (value = $\lambda D/r_2$). If C < D, do nothing.
(b) Continuously revise the position. Whenever C > D, hold the long and short perpetuity; whenever C < D, hold nothing.
(c) At the termination date, liquidate the perpetuities.

The first, second, fifth and sixth terms in (5) correspond to the present value of the interim cashflows described in (b). The calculation depends on the financing costs $[\lambda D(1/\delta - 1/r_2)]$ and the local time financing effects generated by

17

THE
VALUATION
OF MULTIPLE
CLAIM
INSURANCE
CONTRACTS

the infinite crossing property of the Brownian motion process of C at D.[11] The third and fourth terms are the present value of the expected liquidation costs, as described in (c). The last two terms reflect the initial cost of the strategy.

In the solution process, we require that $\delta > 0$, or that $r_2 > r_1$. Therefore, in order to obtain a solution, the interest rate must exceed the risk-adjusted expected loss rate: $r > \alpha_c^* + \alpha_\lambda^* + \rho_{c\lambda}\sigma_c\sigma_\lambda$. If this condition is not met in the perpetual case, the "no insurance" solution applies; value is infinite. In the finite case, this restriction may limit the ability to calculate premium values.

IMPLICATIONS FOR RATE OF RETURN
LEGISLATION
The required rate of return on the insurance policy can be calculated using Itô's lemma and Merton's intertemporal capital asset pricing model relationship,

$$r_v = r + (\eta_c\beta_c + \beta_\lambda)(\alpha_m - r) \qquad (6)$$

where $\beta_i = \rho_{im}\sigma_i/\sigma_m$, and $\eta_c = V_cC/V > 1$ is the price elasticity of the insurance policy with respect to the underlying loss process. Note that $\eta_\lambda = 1$. The partial derivatives of V are calculated in closed form in the next section. The risk premium on the insurance contract with a deductible is greater (less) than for the zero-deductible case. Since $\partial\eta_c/\partial D > 0$, the risk premium is increasing (decreasing) with the level of the deductible if the loss beta is positive (negative).

If the value of the equity of the insurance company (E) can be written as the difference between asset value (A) and premium values (V),[12] then we have E = A - V, and $\beta_e = \beta_a + (\beta_a - \beta_v)/V/E$, where $\beta_v = \eta_c\beta_c + \beta_\lambda$. For fixed asset characteristics, the equity value increases with the level of the deductible. The required rate of return on equity decreases (increases) with the level of the deductible if the loss beta is positive (negative).

Applications
In this section, we use the general valuation equation (5) to investigate the implications of three common features of insurance contracts: a proportional deductible that is typical for coinsurance contracts (eg, health insurance); a maximum indemnity level (eg, policy face value); and a claim-terminating policy (eg, life insurance, which only admits one claim).

We can model the first two cases with appropriate specifications of the reimbursement to

policyholders. If the loss level is C, the reimbursement level is

$$S = \min[(1 - \pi) \max(C - D, 0), M] \qquad (7)$$

We define π to be the proportion of the loss paid by the policyholder. For proportional coinsurance, D = 0, M = ∞, and $0 \le \pi \le 1$. For a standard deductible contract up to a maximum indemnity level M, we have $\pi = 0$.

Because of the linearity of the policy value in the expected cashflows, we can write the solution for the policy value V, in this more general case;

$$V = (1 - \pi)\lambda W(C, \tau; D) - \lambda W(C, \tau; M) \qquad (8)$$

where $W(C, \tau; X)$ is taken from equation (5).

PROPORTIONAL COINSURANCE
Letting D = 0 and M = ∞, we derive for the high case only (the low case is irrelevant),

$$V = \frac{(1 - \pi)\lambda C}{\delta}\left[1 - e^{-\delta\tau}\right] \qquad (9)$$

This simple expression represents the present value of a continuously paid annuity of $\lambda C(1 - \pi)$ when the discount rate is δ. The most striking feature of the valuation formula in this context is the fact that policy value does not depend on idiosyncratic risk.

This result highlights an important contrast between insurance and financial methods of risk adjustment. Insurers typically adjust the expected claim $[\lambda C(1 - \pi)]$ upward to account for its risk and discount at the riskless rate; financial theorists might call this term a certainty equivalent. This adjustment is valid if the policy bears market risk; it is equivalent to discounting cashflows at a risky discount rate (δ). However, many insurance pricing models add a multiple of standard deviation or variance to the expected payout before discounting. For several examples, see Goovaerts *et al* (1984). In the intertemporal capital asset pricing model, one adds a multiple of a covariance term to the expected value before discounting at the riskless rate. In the absence of market risk, the addition of a risk factor to expected payout cannot be justified; non-market risk is important only if a deductible is present.

Consider an analogy between an insurance contract and a stock option. Idiosyncratic risk impacts options prices only if the exercise price is strictly positive; similarly, idiosyncratic risk affects

18

THE
VALUATION
OF MULTIPLE
CLAIM
INSURANCE
CONTRACTS

insurance premium values only in the presence of a deductible.

MAXIMUM INDEMNITY LEVELS

For some lines of insurance, the truncation of the coverage from above creates a greater effect than the truncation from below. This would be the case in many lines of liability insurance, for example.

The effect of maximum indemnity levels can be measured by taking the difference between two policy values (see note 1). The maximum indemnity level adds an integral of short call option-like positions to the underwriting portfolio. If the deductible is zero, the presence of a maximum indemnity level creates exactly the opposite pricing effect as one would expect in the presence of deductibles. If one compares two policies, the first with no maximum level, several conclusions will be drawn: the value of the first policy is greater than the second, and its required rate of return is lower (higher) if the loss beta is positive (negative). The effect on equity pricing and risk is exactly the opposite. Therefore, in the presence of both deductibles and maximum indemnity levels, either effect may dominate; comparative statics are ambiguous.

CLAIM-TERMINATING POLICIES

Some policies may allow only one claim to be made within a contract period. This is the case for cancellable insurance and life insurance, for example. So far we have considered only insurance policies of the renewing type; claims for this type of contract do not cause a policy to terminate. To value a policy of the terminating type, one makes a few minor adjustments. In the original partial differential equation (4), we replace $g(C,V) = \max(C - D,0)$ with $g(C,V) = \max(C - D,0) - V$. Originally, the value of the insurance policy jumped by the amount of the cashflow; now we must surrender the policy (give up V) as well. The change has no effect on the boundary conditions. Rearrangement of the equation verifies that the same solution obtains, if we replace r_2 with $r_2 + \lambda$. See Merton (1976) for a similar conclusion. If interest rates themselves are stochastic, a parallel but non-equivalent substitution can be made.

If the insured behaves strategically, the result does not hold. In particular, when the insured observes a loss less than the deductible, he will not report the loss; the insurance company will not be able to cancel the contract. The insured will not report the loss unless the value of the policy falls short of the value of the loss minus the deductible. Therefore, the cashflow term becomes $\max(\max(C - D,0) - V,0)$, and one would value a continuous expected cashflow stream associated with the terminal payoff of an option on an option.

Limiting cases and comparative statics

The premium value is increasing and convex in the conditional claim level. The hedge ratio, $V_c = \partial V / \partial C$, is given below.

$$V_c(C,\lambda,\tau; D) = \lambda W_c(C,\tau; D) \qquad (10)$$

$$\begin{aligned}
W_c = {} & A(\gamma + \nu)(C/D)^{\gamma+\nu-1}N(b_1) \\
& + B(\gamma - \nu)(C/D)^{\gamma-\nu-1}N(b_2) \quad \frac{e^{-\delta\tau}}{\delta} N(d_1) \\
& - \left[A(\gamma + \nu)(C/D)^{\gamma+\nu-1} \right. \\
& \left. + B(\gamma - \nu)(C/D)^{\gamma-\nu-1} - \frac{1}{\delta} \right] 1_{\{C > D\}}
\end{aligned}$$

The hedge ratio for C can be used to calculate the risk of variable claim levels on policies with deductibles. In the absence of a tradable security, these results may also be used to calculate the optimal hedge ratios of an imperfect cross hedge. For example, if one knew the correlation between the Standard & Poor's 500 index and the conditional loss process, one could easily determine the instantaneous correlation between the return on the index and the return on this policy. The hedge ratio with respect to λ can be found easily; $V_\lambda = V/\lambda$. Using Itô's lemma, one can calculate the instantaneous correlation between changes in the policy value and changes in the market portfolio; $dVdZ_m = (V_c\sigma_c C\rho_{cm} + V_\lambda\sigma_\lambda\lambda\rho_{\lambda m})dt$. This information may be used to formulate an investment position to hedge dynamically some underwriting risk with equity futures contracts. Note that, in this situation, while market risk may be hedged, arbitrage arguments alone will not suffice to value the insurance policy.

Taking the partial derivative of the hedge ratio with respect to time, we find that, independent of the value of C, the value is given by $\exp(-\delta\tau)N(d_1)$. This is the hedge ratio of the modified Black–Scholes formula. It also describes the evolution in time of the insurance hedge ratio.

As the term of the contract, τ, approaches infinity, the value of the insurance premium approaches the following expressions:

$$V_{Low} = \lambda AD(C/D)^{\gamma+\nu} \qquad (\text{if } C \le D),$$

$$V_{High} = \frac{\lambda C}{\delta} - \frac{\lambda D}{r_2} - \lambda BD(C/D)^{\gamma+\nu} \qquad (\text{if } C \ge D)$$

$$(11)$$

THE
VALUATION
OF MULTIPLE
CLAIM
INSURANCE
CONTRACTS

The perpetual expressions suggest immediate similarities to other perpetual option pricing formulas. In particular, the functional form of V (Low) in (11) is proportional to Samuelson's (1965) expression for the value of a perpetual warrant. As the term to maturity nears zero, the value of the insurance premium tends to zero as well. The time derivative, V_τ, is the Black–Scholes option price for a stock that pays a proportional dividend of δ.

EXTENSIONS OF KNOWN OPTION COMPARATIVE STATICS

Many comparative statics results can be easily derived from our current understanding of option pricing theory. Since the premium value is a time integral of dividend-adjusted Black–Scholes option prices, any comparative static result that is true for each option price must be true for the integral of those prices. If the maximum indemnity level is finite, then the solution is the difference between two Black–Scholes time integrals.

The deductible of an insurance policy has the same effect as the exercise price of a call option. A policy with a lower deductible costs more. A policy with a higher maximum indemnity level costs more.

The volatility of an insurance policy derives from the volatility of claim levels and claim frequencies. It can be compared to the volatility of a stock in valuing a call option. For the moment, assume the maximum indemnity level is infinite. Then, higher claim volatility increases premium values as long as the deductible is strictly positive. When the deductible is zero, the premium value does not depend upon idiosyncratic volatility. This is analogous to the argument that idiosyncratic risk has no effect on security prices, but affects options written against those securities. If there is no deductible, and there is a finite maximum indemnity level, volatility reduces premium value. If both a deductible and maximum indemnity level are present, then the effect of volatility on premium value is ambiguous.

Once again, assume no maximum indemnity level. Policies with higher deductibles vary less in dollar terms and more in percentage terms with changes in the market portfolio. This result is consistent with the observation that call options deltas (ΔOption/ΔStock) are less than unity, but option betas (= β(Stock) $\times$ Delta $\times$ Stock/Option) exceed stock betas in absolute value. In the presence of a maximum indemnity level, these results may be modified or reversed.

Recall that $r_2 = r - \alpha_\lambda^*$ and $r_1 = \alpha_c^* + \rho_{c\lambda}\sigma_c\sigma_\lambda$. In the absence of a maximum indemnity level, the premium value can either increase or decrease with increases in r_2 (the interest rate factor) and increases with r_1 (the conditional claim risk-adjusted growth factor). The ambiguity with respect to r_2 results from our assumption of what may change. If the difference between r_2 and r_1 stays constant, the premium may fall when r rises. Normally, call option prices rise when interest rates rise.

In the presence of a maximum indemnity level, these results are again ambiguous. In most actuarial models of insurance pricing, the premium decreases strictly with increases in the risk-free discount rate. In the current model, changes in the interest rate also affect the certainty-equivalent growth rate of the conditional claim process. Since the reimbursement is truncated from below, the increase in the certainty equivalent growth rate may increase the policy value, in contrast with actuarial intuition.

Summary and conclusions

This chapter develops an equilibrium premium valuation model for multiple claim insurance policies subject to non-linear loss-sharing rules, ie, deductibles and maximum indemnity levels. Changes in the sharing rules change the systematic risk of a policy and the required rate of return on insurance equity; regulators concerned with appropriate rates of return on equity should consider these effects in rate determination. Idiosyncratic underwriting risk is priced (in this model) only when losses are divided in a non-linear manner. Finally, for some parameter values, these rules create the surprising property that policy values may increase with increases in the interest rate.

For a continuous lognormal specification of the structure of claim levels and frequencies, this chapter offers a closed form solution for the value of the insurance premium in mostly observable variables. The unobserved variables in the model can be estimated using standard insurance practices. For example, cohorts of policies may be studied to estimate the expected claim level and frequency, the volatility of the claim level and frequency, and the correlations between these variables.

There are numerous applications for the generic pricing result exposited in this chapter. Any asset with continuous expected payouts that resemble option payouts can be valued using this model. An American option that is exercised autonomously according to a Poisson arrival

20

**THE
VALUATION
OF MULTIPLE
CLAIM
INSURANCE
CONTRACTS**

process can be valued readily. Together with numerical techniques, an extension can be made to price junk bonds, which are subject to both optimal and autonomous call policies. A firm that makes project decisions at points in time governed by a Poisson arrival process can be valued directly if the contemporaneous value of the project benefits follows a geometric process, and projects are adopted if benefits exceed a fixed cost level.

Appendix

To solve the differential equation in (4) for the premium value V, we guess the solution $V(C,\lambda,\tau) = \lambda W(C,\tau)$, and verify that this assumption satisfies the basic partial differential equation. After simplifying, the following differential equation obtains for W,

$$\tfrac{1}{2}W_{cc}\sigma_c^2 C^2 + r_1 W_c C - r_2 W - W_\tau = -\max(C - D,0) \tag{A1}$$

where $r_1 = \alpha_c^* + \rho_{c\lambda}\sigma_c\sigma_\lambda$, $r_2 = r - \alpha_\lambda^*$.

In this form, we have recomputed the Black–Scholes (1973) option pricing formula, with the exceptions that (a) the option pays a continuous expected dividend of $\max(C - D,0)$ and (b) the option expires worthless at $\tau = 0$. The function W inherits boundary conditions from the original function V; $W(C,0) = W(0,\tau) = 0$, and $|W_c(\infty,\tau)| < \infty$. In the special case where $T \to \infty$, W_τ must approach zero; valuation is independent of calendar time. When $T \to \infty$, the resulting differential equation represents the Laplace transform (infinite discounted time integral) of the Black–Scholes (1973) option pricing differential equation, where the parameter of the Laplace transform (discount rate) equals $r_2 - r_1$. This observation provides an extension to the Buser (1986) study of financial applications of Laplace transforms. A similar result has been independently established by Carr, Jarrow and Myneni (1990).

The term a^2 is defined to be equal to $\tfrac{1}{2}\sigma_c^2$. For the moment, let $D \equiv 1$. Subscripts denote partial derivatives. The equation may be solved using various techniques. This appendix demonstrates the Laplace transform method, following an example by Ingersoll (1982). A substitution facilitates the solution process,

$$W = \exp(-m^2\tau)H(X,\tau) \tag{A2}$$

where $X = C^\gamma$ and $m^2 = r_2 + a^2\gamma^2$. This substitution assumes $r_2 > -a^2\gamma^2$. We allow $\gamma = (a^2 - r_1)/(2a^2)$, $p = a\gamma$, and $\delta = r_2 - r_1$. Calculating the necessary partial derivatives and combining terms, we find

$$p^2 X^2 H_{xx} - p^2 X H_x + p^2 H - H_\tau$$
$$= -\exp(m^2\tau)\max(X^{1/\gamma} - 1,0) \tag{A3}$$

Let $G = \mathcal{L}_q\{H\}$, where $\mathcal{L}_q$ indicates the Laplace transform of H with parameter q. General properties of Laplace transforms are tabulated in Abramowitz and Stegun (1972). The function G satisfies

$$p^2 X^2 G_{xx} - p^2 X\, G_x + (p^2 - q)G$$
$$= \begin{bmatrix} (1 - X^{1/\gamma})/(q - m^2) & (X > 1) \\ 0 & (X < 1) \end{bmatrix} \tag{A4}$$

When $X > 1$, the solution is called the "high" case, and when $X < 1$, the solution is termed the "low" case. We allow $u = a(1 - \gamma)$. A specific solution for the high case can be given by

$$G = \frac{X^{1/\gamma}}{|q - m^2||q - u^2|} + \frac{-1}{|q - m^2||q - p^2|} \tag{A5}$$

Homogeneous solutions take the form $G = KX^\epsilon$. The characteristic equation permits two values of ϵ to satisfy the homogeneous equation: $\epsilon_1 = 1 + \sqrt{q/p}$ and $\epsilon_2 = 1 - \sqrt{q/p}$. Note that $\epsilon_1 > 1$ and $\epsilon_2 < 0$ for sufficiently large values of q. The boundary conditions require that when $X > 1$, the coefficient of X^{ϵ_1} be zero (boundedness of the derivative), and that when $X < 1$, the coefficient of X^{ϵ_2} be zero $[W(0,\tau) = 0]$. Therefore,

$$G = \begin{bmatrix} K_2 X^{\epsilon_2} + \text{specific solution} & (X > 1) \\ K_1 X^{\epsilon_1} & (X > 1) \end{bmatrix} \tag{A6}$$

Since we assumed W twice continuously differentiable with respect to S, we must impose three continuity conditions at $X = 1$,

$$\begin{array}{ccc} \text{HIGH CASE} & G = G & \text{LOW CASE} \\ & G_x = G_x & \\ & G_{xx} = G_{xx} & \end{array} \tag{A7}$$

The three conditions are simultaneously satisfied only if

$$K_1 = \frac{a + au/\sqrt{q}}{2|q - m^2||q - u^2||\sqrt{q} + p|}$$

$$K_2 = \frac{a - au/\sqrt{q}}{2|q - m^2||q - u^2||\sqrt{q} - p|} \tag{A8}$$

21

THE
VALUATION
OF MULTIPLE
CLAIM
INSURANCE
CONTRACTS

We proceed to solve the low case. To facilitate inversion of the Laplace transform, we can rewrite

$$K_1 = \left[\frac{F}{\sqrt{q}} + G\right]\left[\frac{A}{\sqrt{q} + p} + \frac{B}{\sqrt{q} - m}\right.$$

$$\left. + \frac{C}{\sqrt{q} + m} + \frac{D}{\sqrt{q} - u} + \frac{E}{\sqrt{q} + u}\right]$$

$$A = \frac{1}{r_1 r_2}, \quad B = \frac{1}{2\delta m(p + m)}, \quad C = \frac{-1}{2\delta m(p - m)}$$

$$D = \frac{1}{2\delta u(p + u)}, \quad E = \frac{1}{2\delta u(p - u)},$$

$$F = \frac{au}{2}, \quad G = \frac{a}{2} \qquad \text{(A9)}$$

Note that X^{ϵ_1} can be expressed as $(X \exp(-k\sqrt{q}))$ with $k = -(\text{Ln } X)/p$. Also, for later reference, $A + B + C + D + E = 0$. From a table of Laplace transforms, we have (erfc($\bullet$) as the complementary error function),

$$\mathcal{L}_q \{[XC_1C_3 - XC_2C_3C_4] \exp (C_4k + C_4^2\tau) \text{ erfc}[C_4\sqrt{\tau}$$

$$+ k/(2\sqrt{\tau})] + XC_2C_3 \exp[-k^2/(4\tau)]/\sqrt{(\pi\tau)}\}$$

$$= X \exp(-k\sqrt{q})[C_1/\sqrt{q} + C_2][C_3/(\sqrt{q} + C_4)]$$

$$\text{(A10)}$$

for arbitrary constants, $C_1 \ldots C_4$. We invert G to find H, and make the substitutions required to obtain the solution for W in the low case. We define $W = Y$ if $C < D$ and $W = Y + Q$ if $C > D$.

$$Y = AC^{\gamma+\nu}N(b_1) + BC^{\gamma-\nu}N(b_2)$$

$$- \frac{C \exp(-\delta\tau)}{\delta}N(d_1) + \frac{\exp(-r_2\tau)}{r_2}N(d_2), \ (X < 1)$$

$$\nu = \frac{m}{a}$$

$$b_1 = \frac{\text{Ln}(C)}{\sigma\sqrt{\tau}} + \sigma\nu\sqrt{\tau}, \quad b_2 = \frac{\text{Ln}(C)}{\sigma\sqrt{\tau}} - \sigma\nu\sqrt{\tau}$$

$$d_1 = \frac{\text{Ln}(C) + (r_1 + \frac{1}{2}\sigma^2)\tau}{\sigma\sqrt{\tau}}$$

$$d_2 = \frac{\text{Ln}(C) + (r_1 - \frac{1}{2}\sigma^2)\tau}{\sigma\sqrt{\tau}}$$

$$A = [r_2 - r_1(\gamma - \nu)] \div [2\delta r_2\nu]$$

$$B = [r_1(\gamma + \nu) - r_2] \div [2\delta r_2\nu]$$

$$m^2 = r_2 + a^2\gamma^2, \quad a^2 = \frac{1}{2}\sigma^2, \quad \gamma = [a^2 - r_1]/[2a^2]$$

$$\delta = r_2 - r_1, \quad u = a(1 - \gamma), \quad p = a\gamma$$

$$\text{(A11)}$$

$N(\bullet)$ is the cumulative normal (Gaussian) distribution function. The constants A and B exhibit the following properties,

$$A + B = r_1/(\delta r_2) = 1/\delta - 1/r_2$$

$$A - B = [r_2 - \gamma r_1]/[\delta r_2\nu]$$

$$A(\gamma + \nu) + B(\gamma - \nu) = 1/\delta$$

$$Am(\gamma + \nu) - Bm(\gamma - \nu) = u/\delta$$

$$A(\gamma + \nu)(\gamma + \nu - 1) + B(\gamma - \nu)(\gamma - \nu - 1) = 0$$

$$\text{(A12)}$$

Two additional relationships between the constants are useful in verifying (A1),

$$a^2(\gamma + \nu)(\gamma + \nu - 1) + r_1(\gamma + \nu) - r_2 = 0$$

$$a^2(\gamma - \nu)(\gamma - \nu - 1) + r_1(\gamma - \nu) - r_2 = 0$$

$$\text{(A13)}$$

Finally, the following identities simplify the calculation of the partial derivatives,

$$C^{\gamma+\nu}N'(b_1) = C^{\gamma-\nu}N'(b_2) = C \exp(-\delta\tau)N'(d_1)$$

$$= \exp(-r_2\tau)N'(d_2) \qquad \text{(A14)}$$

The partial derivatives of Y are given by the following expressions,

$$Y_\tau = C \exp(-\delta\tau)N(d_1) - \exp(-r_2\tau)N(d_2) \qquad \text{(A15)}$$

$$Y_c = A(\gamma + \nu)C^{\gamma+\nu-1}N(b_1)$$

$$+ B(\gamma - \nu)C^{\gamma-\nu-1}N(b_2) - \frac{\exp(-\delta\tau)}{\delta}N(d_1)$$

$$\text{(A16)}$$

$$Y_{cc} = A(\gamma + \nu)(\gamma + \nu - 1)C^{\gamma+\nu-2}N(b_1)$$

$$+ B(\gamma - \nu)(\gamma - \nu - 1)C^{\gamma-\nu-2}N(b_2) \qquad \text{(A17)}$$

$$Y_{c\tau} = \exp(-\delta\tau)N(d_1) \qquad \text{(A18)}$$

The identities in (A12) serve to verify that the homogeneous part of the partial differential equation (A1) is satisfied. The solution for $X > 1$ can be given by a function of C and not τ. In particular, if $Q = W(\text{High}) - W(\text{Low})$, then

$$Q = \frac{C}{\delta} - \frac{1}{r_2} - AC^{\gamma+\nu} - BC^{\gamma-\nu} \qquad \text{(A19)}$$

$$Q_c = \frac{1}{\delta} - A(\gamma + \nu)C^{\gamma+\nu-1} - B(\gamma - \nu)C^{\gamma-\nu-1} \qquad \text{(A20)}$$

$$Q_{cc} = -A(\gamma + \nu)(\gamma + \nu - 1)C^{\gamma+\nu-2}$$

$$- B(\gamma - \nu)(\gamma - \nu - 1)C^{\gamma-\nu-2} \qquad \text{(A21)}$$

Inspection of Q and its derivatives, together with the identities in (A12), reveals that $Q = Q_c = Q_{cc} = 0$ at the point $X = 1$; these are the continuity

22

THE
VALUATION
OF MULTIPLE
CLAIM
INSURANCE
CONTRACTS

criteria. The solution in the high case can also be written as

$$Y + Q$$

$$= \frac{C}{\delta} - \frac{1}{r_2} - AC^{\gamma+\nu}N(-b_1) - BC^{\gamma-\nu}N(-b_2)$$

$$- \frac{C\exp(-\delta\tau)}{\delta}N(d_1) + \frac{\exp(-r_2\tau)}{r_2}N(d_2), \ (X > 1)$$

$$(A22)$$

The general solution for W is simply $W = Y + Q1_{(C>D)}$, where $1_{(A)}$ is the indicator function on set A. Note that when Q is substituted for W in (A1), the partial differential equation reduces to value $(1 - C)$. The solutions for the low and high case differ because the function cannot be thrice continuously differentiable; this can be seen from (A1).

In the derivation, we assumed the deductible was identically equal to 1. For the more general case, we note that W is homogeneous in the deductible,

$$W(C,\tau; D) = D \times W(C',\tau; 1)$$
$$\text{where } C' = C/D \qquad (A23)$$

Since W is the integral of Black–Scholes functions, which are homogeneous in the deductible, W is also homogeneous in the deductible.

Two interesting results from this derivation include the calculation of the intermediate Black–Scholes integrals,

$$\int_0^\tau Ce^{-\delta t}N\big|d_1(t)\big|dt = W_1(C,\tau;D) \qquad (A24)$$

$$\int_0^\tau De^{-r_2 t}N\big|d_2(t)\big|dt = W_2(C,\tau;D) \qquad (A25)$$

where $d_1(t) = [Ln(C/D) + (r_1 + \frac{1}{2}\sigma^2)t]$ and $d_2(t) = d_1(t) - \sigma\sqrt{t}$. The solutions are given below.

$$W_1 = A_1 D(C/D)^{\gamma+\nu}N(b_1) + B_1 D(C/D)^{\gamma-\nu}N(b_2)$$
$$- Ce^{-\delta\tau}N(d_1)/\delta$$
$$- \left[A_1 D(C/D)^{\gamma+\nu} + B_1 D(C/D)^{\gamma-\nu} - \frac{C}{\delta} \right] I_{(C>D)}$$

$$(A26)$$

$$W_2 = A_2 D(C/D)^{\gamma+\nu}N(b_1) + B_2 D(C/D)^{\gamma-\nu}N(b_2)$$
$$- De^{-r_2\tau}N(d_2)/r_2$$
$$- \left[A_2 D(C/D)^{\gamma+\nu} + B_2 D(C/D)^{\gamma-\nu} - \frac{D}{r_2} \right] I_{(C>D)}$$

$$(A27)$$

where $A_1 = (\nu + 1 - \gamma)/(2\delta\nu)$, $B_1 = (\nu - 1 + \gamma)/(2\delta\nu)$, $A_2 = (\nu - \gamma)/(2\nu r_2)$, and $B_2 = (\nu + \gamma)/(2\nu r_2)$. The functions b_1 and b_2 are defined as: $b_1(C,\tau; D) = [Ln(C/D)/(\sigma\sqrt{\tau})] + \sigma\nu\sqrt{\tau}$ and $b_2(C,\tau; D) = [Ln(C/D)/(\sigma\sqrt{\tau})] - \sigma\nu\sqrt{\tau}$. The constants were defined in (A11). The indicator function is $I = 1$ if the condition in brackets is met $(C > D)$; otherwise $I = 0$.

Note that the expressions in (A26) and (A27) are twice continuously differentiable everywhere except at the point $C = D$, where they are once continuously differentiable. The difference, $W = W_1 - W_2$, is twice continuously differentiable for all values of $C > 0$. The value of the insurance policy then is $V = \lambda W$.

---

1 *For the claim structure represented here, the value of a policy in the presence of a maximum indemnity clause may be calculated by taking the difference in value between two policies, the first with a deductible equal to the policy deductible, and the second with a deductible equal to the maximum level of indemnity. The result does not apply when the insured party has some influence on the outcome of the claim.*

2 *Technically, λdt represents the expected number of claims in the next interval dt. Since the probability of two claims in the next moment is of order dt^2, this is a close approximation.*

3 *The probability changes through time because the individual policyholder's behaviour is not independent of aggregate behaviour; some events affect the probability that all individuals will make a claim. The probability may also change as a result of individual-specific events. The former may be a source of systematic risk. While the probability of claim occurrence varies systematically, however, conditional on the levels of the joint processes, the timing of the jump is independent of the level and changes of the state variables.*

4 *While the claim dates are random, it is important to emphasise that the timing of the claims is driven by an exogenous process.*

5 *This approach both parallels and contrasts Constantinides' (1978) treatment of continuous cashflows. At random points in time, a discrete loss of C_t is incurred. In Constantinides' treatment, an infinitesimal loss of C_t dt might be incurred.*

6 *A more general equilibrium specification can be made within the Cox, Ingersoll and Ross (1985) framework with little difficulty. Under the CIR model, one specifies the relevant state variables and the market price of risk for each of these variables. In the likely absence of a closed form solution technology, the value of the premium could then be determined with numerical approximation methods.*

7 *The terminology is taken from Shimko (1989). When renewing cashflows occur, the policy continues to stay in force; the value of the policy is unaffected by the loss. When terminating cashflows occur, the policy dies with the claim.*

23

THE
VALUATION
OF MULTIPLE
CLAIM
INSURANCE
CONTRACTS

Both renewing and terminating cashflows can occur in finite or infinite time horizon contracts.

8 *The solution is twice continuously differentiable. To see why it cannot be thrice continuously differentiable, examine equation (4), whose right-hand side is not continuously differentiable. Therefore, the differential of the left-hand side (and W_{ccc} in particular) cannot be continuous. This leads to different expressions for V when $C > D$ and $C < D$. If we had formulated the problem so that the expected cashflow term were continuously differentiable indefinitely, the solution for V would be as well.*

9 *The adjustment is similar to the adjustment made in calculating the value of an option on a futures contract. Since the futures contract (like the conditional cashflow) is not an asset, no equilibrium relationship need prevail between the parameters of the driving process and the interest rate.*

10 *Intuitively, W represents the area between the sample path of C and the constant D when $C > D$. The present value of the associated cashflows is expressed in (A26) and (A27).*

11 *The local time concept and its impact on option pricing is exposited in Carr and Jarrow (1990). Infinite crossings in replication strategies have an effect on option pricing that is proportional to the quadratic variation of the underlying process at the refinancing boundary.*

12 *In order to write the balance sheet identity, one must assume that equityholders have unlimited liability, that markets are perfect, and that investment policy is fixed. Without loss of generality, we assume the stock of policies is adequately represented by a single policy.*

BIBLIOGRAPHY

Abramowitz, M. and I.A. Stegun, 1972, *Handbook of Mathematical Functions,* New York, NY: Dover Publications.

Black, F. and M. Scholes, 1973, "The Pricing of Options and Corporate Liabilities", *Journal of Political Economy*, 81, pp. 637-59.

Brennan, M. and E. Schwartz, 1982, "Consistent Regulatory Policy under Uncertainty", *Bell Journal of Economics*, 13, pp. 506-21.

Buser, S., 1986, "LaPlace Transforms as Present Value Rules: A Note", *Journal of Finance* 41, pp. 243-47.

Carr, P.P. and R.A. Jarrow, 1990, "The Stop-Loss Start-Gain Paradox and Option Valuation: A New Decomposition into Intrinsic and Time Value", *Review of Financial Studies*, 3(3), pp. 469-92.

Carr, P.P., R.A. Jarrow and R. Myneni, 1990, "Alternative Characterizations of American Put Options", Working Paper, Cornell University, Johnson Graduate School of Management, Ithaca, NY.

Constantinides, G.M., 1978, "Market Risk Adjustment in Project Valuation", *Journal of Finance*, 33, pp. 603-16.

Cox, J.C., J.E. Ingersoll and S.A. Ross, 1985, "An Intertemporal General Equilibrium Model of Asset Prices", *Econometrica*, 53, pp. 363-84.

Cummins, J.D., 1988, "Risk-Based Premiums for Insurance Guaranty Funds", *Journal of Finance*, 43, pp. 823-40.

Doherty, N.A. and J.R. Garven, 1986, "Price Regulation in Property-Liability Insurance: A Contingent Claims Approach", *Journal of Finance*, 41, pp. 1031-50.

Friedman, A., 1964, *A Partial Differential Equation of Parabolic Type,* Englewood Cliffs, NJ: Prentice-Hall, Chapter 6, Section 7.

Goovaerts, M.J., F. deVylder and J. Haezendonck, 1984, *Insurance Premiums.* Amsterdam: North Holland-Elsevier Science Publishing, pp. 16-94.

Ingersoll, J.E., 1982, *Notes of the Theory of Financial Decisions: Class Lecture Notes* (#16). Unpublished manuscript.

Kraus, A. and S. Ross, 1982, "The Determination of Fair Profits for the Property-Liability Insurance Firm", *Journal of Finance*, 37, pp. 1015-28.

McDonald, R. and D. Siegel, March 1984, "Option Pricing when the Underlying Asset Earns a Below-Equilibrium Rate of Return: A Note", *Journal of Finance*, 39, pp. 261-65.

Merton, R.C., September 1973, "An Intertemporal Capital Asset Pricing Model", *Econometrica*, 41, pp. 867-87.

Merton, R.C., 1976, "Option Pricing when Underlying Stock Returns are Discontinuous", *Journal of Financial Economics*, 3, pp. 125-44.

Merton, R.C., 1977, "An Analytic Derivation of the Cost of Deposit Insurance and Loan Guarantees: An Application of Modern Option Pricing Theory", *Journal of Banking and Finance*, 1, pp. 3-11.

Samuelson, P.A. and H.P. McKean, Jr, 1972, "Rational Theory of Warrant Pricing", *Industrial management Review.* Reprinted in *The Collected Scientific Papers of Paul A. Samuelson.* R.C. Merton, ed. Boston: MIT Press, pp. 791-871.

Shimko, D., 1989, "The Equilibrium, Valuation of Risky Discrete Cash Flows in Continuous Time", *Journal of Finance*, 44, pp. 1373-83.

Smith, C., 1979, "Applications of Option Pricing Analysis", in *Handbook of Financial Economics*, J.I. Bicksler, ed. Amsterdam: North Holland, Chapter 4.

3

CAT Calls

Hélyette Geman*

University Paris IX Dauphine and ESSEC

Until 1993, the only way insurers could hedge their underwriting risk was through reinsurance. Although they were able to use financial derivatives to hedge their asset portfolios and interest-rate sensitive liabilities, there were no traded instruments available to cover the increasing claims arising from losses in property and casualty lines of insurance. Demand for such instruments was heightened by the growing costs of catastrophes and the consequent effect on reinsurance available.

From 1990–92 the Chicago Board of Trade studied the feasibility of introducing health, automobile or home-owners' futures contracts but concluded these were not the main priority. The first solution was catastrophe insurance (CAT) futures contracts, which started trading at the beginning of 1993. Options on the futures followed that summer and call spreads proved particularly successful.

CAT futures contracts are not easy to define given the absence of an underlying traded security and the specific nature of insurance. They can best be described through an example. There are four contracts over the year: March, June, September, December. Let us consider the March 1994 contract. It trades from the beginning of January until the end of June; the period between January 1 and March 31 is called the event quarter, the period between January and the end of June the reporting period. (The contract keeps trading after the end of the reporting period but as the volume is very low, this feature is unlikely to continue and is ignored in this chapter.)

Four types of CAT futures contracts are traded today: Eastern, Midwestern, Western and National. Before trading began, the Insurance Services Office (ISO), an independent statistical firm to which more than 100 US insurance companies

report, selected a sample of 26 insurance companies, diversified in size, lines of business and states, to create these representative national and regional pools. The September 1994 Eastern contract, for instance, is very popular in July, at the beginning of the hurricane season.

The causes of losses denominated as catastrophes – wind, hail, earthquake, riot and flood – and the applicable lines of insurance are clearly defined. Consequently, the amount of property premium (Π) associated with the policies in the pool (estimated on the basis of the most recent statutory annual statements filed by the reporting companies) is known before the contract starts trading.

At maturity T (end of June 1994), the settlement price of the March futures contract is:

$$F(T) = \text{US\$25,000 } \min\left(\frac{L(T)}{\Pi}, 2\right) \qquad (1)$$

where $L(T)$ is the aggregate amount of losses associated with the ISO pool of policies, incurred during the first quarter of 1994 and reported during the first or second quarter of 1994; Π is the

The author wishes to acknowledge the help of Antoine Poidatz for running Monte Carlo simulations and of CERESSEC for financial support.

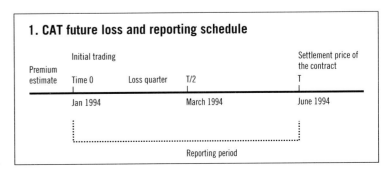

1. CAT future loss and reporting schedule

first quarter property premium; L(T)/Π represents the loss ratio; the settlement value of the contract is capped at 200% or US$50,000 (for comparison, in the case of hurricane Andrew, the loss ratio did not reach one in the National contract and was around 1.6 in the Eastern contract). The small face value of the contract is intended to help insurers accurately design their hedge.

Futures prices are quoted in points (US$250) and tenths of a point (US$25). Obviously, an intermediary price F(t), where t is some time between 0 and contract expiry T, will reflect the market's expectation of the terminal price.

An insurer who wants to hedge against a possible excess of losses over a given quarter will *buy* a futures contract. Let us suppose, for simplicity, that the contract is bought at time 0 and held to maturity. If severe catastrophes occur, the gain F(T) – F(0) generated by each long position in a futures contract will offset the high amount of claims to be paid; the hedge will be all the better as the correlation between the insurer's losses and the ISO pool losses is close to one (see Geman, 1994).

A more popular hedge than a long futures position is a call spread. A CAT call spread, like any other, involves buying a call at a strike price (k_1) and selling a call at a higher strike (k_2), both calls having the same maturity. Where it differs is that both calls are written on the futures contract: k_1 and k_2 are called loss ratio attachment points. A long position in a call spread gives coverage, once the premium is paid, between two loss ratio attachment points. In principle, all layers are available for trading; in practice, most traded spreads have a range of 20, between the values 20 and 120 (eg, [20, 40] ... [100,120]). If we take the example of the September 1994 Eastern 40-60 call spread bought at a premium of eight, we see in Figure 2 the pay-off profile at maturity.

Call spreads are more heavily traded than the futures contracts for obvious reasons. The amount of risk at stake, whether taking a short or long position, is much more limited, a desirable feature for a new instrument and for insurers who are not familiar with derivatives. Also, the pay-off profile generated by a CAT spread (Figure 2) bears a striking similarity to that for a layer of reinsurance, so that insurers and reinsurers have an idea of what the "fair price" of a call spread should be. Remember that the pay-off of a call spread maturing at time T is:

$$\Phi(T) = \min\{\max(F(T) - k_1, 0), k_2 - k_1\}$$

Turning to the sellers of CAT futures and call spreads, these tend to be construction companies which benefit from catastrophes, some reinsurance companies and speculators willing to take risk in order to make profits. In all cases, a pricing methodology is desirable to allow hedgers to know how much they should pay for a CAT call spread and for reinsurers to uncover possible arbitrage opportunities.

In insurance, the classical modelling of claims involves Poisson processes or compound Poisson processes, and the methodology used to price a liability or any random cashflow consists in taking its expectation under the objective (ie, historical) probability and adding a risk premium. To reflect the financial nature of the CAT futures contract, Cummins and Geman (1993) proposed a new approach, founded on an arbitrage pricing methodology and a representation of the instantaneous claim process by a diffusion process with a jump component.

Extending the results obtained by Geman and Yor (1992, 1993) on the exact pricing of Asian options to the case of a diffusion process plus a Poisson process, they were able to derive a closed-form solution for the futures price. This approach is described below and extended to CAT futures call spreads but Monte Carlo simulations are needed for these as closed-form solutions do not yet exist.

Since claims are reported every day to insurance companies, the representation of the instantaneous claim process S(t) by a diffusion process seems pretty accurate; the aggregate losses L(T) involved in the settlement price of the futures contract can be written as:

$$L(T) = \int_0^T S(s)ds$$

However, the two quarters of the trading period don't play the same role. To reflect this

2. September 1994 Eastern 40–60 call spread at maturity

where:
- maximum loss = premium (compounded over the period);
- maximum profit = spread ($k_2 - k_1$) – compounded premium;
- BE = break even point = lower strike price + compounded premium

feature, Cummins–Geman propose juxtaposing two stochastic processes. Representing the uncertainty of the economy by a probability space (Ω, F, P), where P is the objective probability, the instantaneous claim process $S(t)$ is described on the interval $[0,T/2]$, which is the event quarter, by a diffusion process plus a jump, that is, its dynamics under P are driven by the stochastic differential equation:

$$dS(t) = S(t^-)[\mu dt + \sigma dW_t] + \kappa dN(t) \quad (2)$$

where $\mu \in R$ and $\sigma \in R^{+*}$ are the coefficients of the geometric Brownian motion; W_t is a standard Brownian motion under P, $\kappa \in RR^{+*}$ represents the severity of a jump; and $N(t)$ is a Poisson process with intensity λ, where λ represents the frequency of the catastrophes.

We can observe immediately that the parameters μ, σ, κ, λ must be adjusted for the different traded contracts. The constants κ and λ, for instance, should be higher for the September maturity in the case of the Eastern contract.

During the second quarter $[T/2,T]$ of the reporting period, the instantaneous claim process $S(t)$ verifies the following stochastic differential equation:

$$dS(t) = S(t)[\mu' dt + \sigma dW_t] \quad (3)$$

where $\mu' \in R$, $S(T/2)$ is derived from equation (2) and the volatility σ in the reporting process is supposed to be the same for the whole period $[0,T]$ – but this assumption can be relaxed without any difficulty.

Returning to equation (1), it can be written as:

$$F(T) = US\$25{,}000\left[\frac{L(T)}{\Pi} - \max\left(\frac{L(T)}{\Pi} - 2,0\right)\right]$$
$$(4)$$

where we recognise in the second term the payoff of a call option written on the loss ratio.

Introducing the risk-neutral probability measure Q, the arbitrage price of the futures contract is:

$$F(t) = E_Q[F(T)/F_t]$$

where F_t is the information available at time t and the dynamics of $S(t)$ are expressed under the probability measure Q.

One can observe that the CAT futures contracts and call spreads are attainable assets in the sense of Harrison and Kreps (1979) since we have two non-redundant derivatives traded and layers of reinsurance as a cash market; consequently, we have enough traded assets in

comparison with the number of sources of risk for the CAT futures and call spreads to have an arbitrage price. If t is in the interval $[T/2, T]$,

$$L(T) = \int_0^t S(s)ds + \int_t^T S(s)ds$$

and

$$E_Q[L(T)/F_t] = \int_0^t S(s)ds + E_Q\left[\int_t^T S(s)ds/F_t\right] \quad (5)$$

The first term on the right hand side is totally known as long as ISO provides a regular information release on the claims already reported. The second term in (5) involves the first moment of the integral of a geometric Brownian motion which was calculated by Geman and Yor (1992).

To obtain the expectation of $F(T)$ defined in equation (4), it suffices to compute

$$E_Q\left[\max\left(\frac{L(T)}{\Pi} - 2,0\right)/F_t\right]$$
$$= \frac{T}{\Pi} E_Q\left[\max\left(A(T) - \frac{2\Pi}{T},0\right)/F_t\right] \quad (6)$$

where:

$$A(T) = \frac{1}{T}\int_0^T S(s)ds$$

can be interpreted as the average price of a stock S over the period $[0,T]$, when the time interval between two fixings is small. Consequently, (6) can be obtained from the exact pricing formula of Asian options proposed by Geman and Yor (1993) and so is the arbitrage price of the futures contract on the interval $[T/2,T]$.

When t is in the interval $[0,T/2]$, the problem is more complicated since:

$$L(T) = \int_0^t S(s)ds + \int_t^{T/2} S(s)ds + \int_{T/2}^T S(s)ds$$

where $S(s)$ is a geometric Brownian motion plus a jump on the interval $[t,T/2]$

$$E_Q[L(T)/F_t] = \int_0^t S(s)ds + E_Q\left[\int_t^T S(s)ds/F_t\right]$$
$$+ E_Q\left[\int_{T/2}^T S(s)ds/F_t\right]$$

The third term on the right is calculated according to the methodology described earlier; in the second term, $S(s)$ is given by the Doléans–Dade exponential and, again, the explicit expression of the expectation of the integral can be obtained at

Table 1. Monte Carlo simulations of the Doléans–Dade exponential

Time to maturity	Call spread strikes		
	CAT 20/40	CAT 40/60	CAT 60/80
0.05	0.48	0.28	0.03
0.10	0.96	0.45	0.05
0.15	1.38	0.48	0.07
0.20	1.70	0.51	0.09
0.25	1.96	0.52	0.10
0.30	1.97	0.52	0.10
0.35	1.98	0.52	0.10
0.40	1.98	0.53	0.10
0.45	1.99	0.55	0.10

the cost of more complicated computations (see Cummins and Geman 1993). One can observe that the parameters σ, κ, λ and the risk-neutral drifts α and α' may be derived from actual market prices and our pricing methodology. These implied values are all the more relevant as the derivative contracts are heavily traded. Independently, one can use historical data provided by ISO or PCS to estimate μ and μ'.

We saw earlier that the pay-off at time T of a call spread with k_1 and k_2 as the loss ratio attachment points is equal to

$$\Phi(T) = \min\{\max(F(T) - k_1, 0), k_2 - k_1\} \qquad (7)$$

Consequently, the value C(t) at time t of this call spread is equal to the expectation under the risk-neutral probability measure Q of the discounted terminal pay-off (in fact, CAT call spreads are American options but we will ignore this feature in the present study).

Since an exact pricing formula seems hopeless at this point in the context of our complicated (but probably accurate) modelling of the instantaneous claim process, we are running Monte Carlo simulations of the Doléans–Dade exponential.

The most important results are the following:

❑ the introduction of a jump process on top of the diffusion process, rather than a change of the parameters in the diffusion process, definitely gives a representation of the claim process much closer to the one observed in historical insurance data; the Poisson process takes care of the "major" catastrophes, the diffusion process of the randomness in reporting and of the "small" catastrophes;

❑ the pricing model is sensitive to a change in the set of parameters, but with a robustness somewhat similar to the one which exists in the celebrated Black and Scholes formula. This property implies that when the market in CAT call spreads is very liquid and the bid–ask interval quite narrow, it will be possible to derive the parameters from market prices; and

❑ to obtain a spread premium with an error smaller than 1%, it is necessary at this point to run 100,000 simulations of the Doléans–Dade exponential for each value C(t), at time t, between 0 and T, which is costly in computer time.

The results with only 10,000 simulations are shown in the table above. The integral was calculated with a discretisation step of one day; the premium $\Pi = 5,718,769,130$ dollars was the premium of the Eastern contract for the third quarter of 1993. The parameters α, r and α' were set respectively at 0.1, 0.1 and 0.15, σ at 0.5 (higher volatility than in the stock markets), λ at 0.5 and κ at the level of 0.8 Π; S(0) was derived from the loss ratio estimated on the period and the value Π defined earlier.

As expected, the CAT spread premium is higher as the layer of reinsurance is set at a lower claims level. We are conducting a range of new simulations on the most liquid traded call spreads with different sets of parameters.

In conclusion, the increasing popularity of CAT call spreads can be explained by the additional capacity of reinsurance they give the marketplace, the low transaction costs, the possibility of unwinding a position and the financial integrity of the Chicago Board of Trade as a counterparty. OTC hybrid insurance derivatives, such as foreign exchange CATs, are now being offered by a number of financial institutions.

BIBLIOGRAPHY

Cummins D. and H. Geman, 1993, "An Asian Option Approach to the Valuation of Insurance Futures Contracts", AFFI Conference, La Baule.

Geman H., 1994, "Pricing CAT Futures and Call Spreads", Chicago Board of Trade Catastrophe Insurance Seminar, London.

Geman H., 1994, "Changes of Numéraire and Correlation Risk Management", Risk Conference on Correlation, London.

Geman H. and M. Yor, 1992, "Fonctions Confluentes Hypergéométriques et Options Asiatiques, *Comptes Rendus de l'Academie des Sciences*.

Geman H. and M. Yor, 1993, "Bessel Processes, Asian Options and Perpetuities", *Mathematical Finance*.

Harrison J. and D. Kreps, 1979, "Martingale and Arbitrage in Multipersonal Securities Markets", *Journal of Economic Theory*.

4

Pricing Catastrophe Insurance Futures and Call Spreads
An Arbitrage Approach

J. David Cummins and Hélyette Geman
The Wharton School; University Paris IX Dauphine and ESSEC

While insurers have a variety of instruments readily available to hedge the risk of assets and interest rate-sensitive liabilities, until recently reinsurance has been the only mechanism for hedging underwriting risk. Despite its desirable characteristics, reinsurance has its limitations. Reinsurance markets are subject to periodic price and availability cycles, and reinsurance market inefficiencies played a major role in exacerbating the general liability insurance crisis of 1984–86 (see Berger, Cummins, and Tennyson, 1992). The catastrophe insurance futures contracts introduced by the Chicago Board of Trade (CBOT) in 1992 and the catastrophe call spreads introduced by the CBOT in 1993 have a potentially important role to play in stabilising insurance markets by providing an alternative hedging mechanism for underwriting risk.

Unlike reinsurance, hedging through futures and options has the advantage of reversibility; any position may be closed before the maturity of the futures or option contract if the overall exposure of the insurer has diminished. Although reinsurance, in principle, is also reversible, in practice reversing a reinsurance transaction exposes the insurer to relatively high transaction costs as well as additional charges to protect the reinsurer against adverse selection. Because futures and option contracts are anonymous rather than negotiated between two specific parties, both the potential for adverse selection and the accompanying administrative costs are greatly diminished. An insurance futures market should offer the advantages of liquidity and low transaction costs that are common to futures and options.

Unlike most derivatives traded on the CBOT, insurance futures and options are based on an accumulation of insured losses over a period of time rather than on the price of a commodity or asset at the end of a period of time. Consequently, the classic relationships between the spot price and the futures price do not hold. On the other hand, the fact that the price of the catastrophe insurance contract at maturity will reflect a sum of claim payments makes these contracts similar to an Asian option, for which the underlying asset is an average, ie a sum of spot prices (up to a multiplicative constant).

Insurance futures and call spreads

First we provide a brief overview of property catastrophes, the type of loss that the CBOT insurance futures contracts are designed to hedge. We then discuss the CBOT insurance futures and call spreads, and provide examples of hedging using these derivative instruments.

PROPERTY CATASTROPHES
Property catastrophes represent a significant risk for property owners and insurers. The insurance industry defines a catastrophe as "an event which causes in excess of US$5 million in insured property damage and affects a significant number of insureds and insurers" (Property Claims Services, 1993). As the definition implies, catastrophes involve large losses and, what is

This chapter was first published in Journal of Fixed Income, *4, 1995. This copyrighted material is reprinted with permission from Institutional Investor.*

PRICING

CATASTROPHE

INSURANCE

FUTURES AND

CALL

SPREADS

even more fundamental, constitute a violation of the most basic tenet of insurance – the independence and diversifiability of risk.

In principle – so far, at least – very few events have worldwide consequences, so catastrophe losses should be diversifiable internationally through the reinsurance market. In practice, reinsurance markets often experience price and availability problems because of information asymmetries, parameter estimation uncertainty, and large concentrations of property values in disaster-prone areas such as the Eastern seaboard and Gulf Coast in the US. Futures markets thus have a potentially important role to play in hedging through these derivative instruments.

During the period 1970 through mid-1993, an average of thirty-four catastrophes occurred each year, causing an annual average of US$2.5 billion in losses. Figure 1 shows catastrophe losses by quarter since 1949. As the figure suggests, most catastrophes are relatively small (less than US$250 million), but the potential for much larger catastrophes clearly exists. For example, hurricane Andrew caused twice as much damage (US$10.7 billion) as the next largest catastrophe (period since 1949) hurricane Hugo (US$4.2 billion). Hurricane Iniki, the fourth largest catastrophe since 1949, also occurred during the second quarter of 1992, accounting for the extremely high losses during this period.

Property catastrophes thus represent a significant threat to insurers. The lines of insurance subject to property catastrophes account for about 40% of total US property and liability

insurance premium volume, and for many insurers the exposure is much higher.

Hurricane Andrew alone, for example, caused insured losses totalling about 20% of 1992 premium volume in the affected lines of insurance and resulted in several insurance company insolvencies. The likelihood that losses of this magnitude will occur in the future provides insurers with a powerful incentive to hedge catastrophic risk.

THE CBOT INSURANCE FUTURES

The CBOT introduced insurance futures in December 1992 to provide a hedge against catastrophic property insurance losses. Separate contracts are available for National, Eastern, Midwestern and Western catastrophes.[1] One reason for the CBOT's focus on property losses is that such losses settle relatively quickly, and thus are not subject to the lengthy payout period and accompanying loss estimation errors that characterise other risky coverages such as commercial liability insurance. Property losses are relatively insulated from insurer mis-statements and manipulations of loss reserves.

Because there is no traded underlying instrument, the CBOT created an index to which the futures contract is linked; this index consists of losses reported each quarter to the Insurance Services Office (ISO), an independent statistical firm to which approximately 100 companies regularly report loss data.[2] The settlement values for insurance futures are based on losses incurred by a pool of companies selected by ISO on the basis of size, diversity of business, and quality of reported data. (The contracts covering 1994 losses are based on a pool of 25 insurers.)

The companies included in the pool for any given futures are announced by the CBOT prior to the beginning of the trading period for that contract. The CBOT also announces the premium volume for the pool prior to the start of the trading period for each catastrophe contract. Thus, the premiums in the pool are a known constant throughout the trading period, and price changes are attributable solely to changes in the market's expectations of loss liabilities.

Catastrophe insurance futures trade on a quarterly cycle, with contract months March, June, September and December. A contract for any given calendar quarter (the "event quarter") is based on losses occurring in the listed quarter that are reported to the participating companies by the end of the following quarter (the "run-off quarter"). The six-month period following the

1. Property catastrophes – US insured losses, quarterly 1949–93

start of the event quarter is known as the "reporting period". The three additional reporting months following the close of the event quarter are to allow for loss settlement lags.

Trading is conducted from the date the contract is listed until the settlement date. Contracts are listed as early as four quarters prior to the beginning of the event quarter.

The relevant quarters for the March 1995 contract are shown in Figure 2. This contract covers losses from events occurring during the first quarter of 1995 (January–March) as reported to the participating companies by the end of June 1995. At any given time, contracts are available for trading covering the current event quarter and the following four quarters. This forward-starting property permits insurers to implement hedging strategies in advance, much as they would do with reinsurance.

Although not all losses are reported by the end of the reporting period, reported pool losses should represent a high proportion of eventual paid losses. Losses included in the pool consist of all property losses incurred by reporting companies arising from the perils of windstorm, hail, earthquake, riot and flood.

The nominal value of the contract is US$25,000, and the loss ratio (losses divided by premiums) is capped at 2, which means that the settlement value at maturity T of the contract is defined by

$$F(T) = US\$25,000 \min\left(\frac{L(T)}{\Pi}, 2\right) \quad (1)$$

where $F(T)$ = futures price at maturity, $L(T)$ = reported losses incurred, and Π = premiums earned for the event quarter. The CBOT places a maximum on the settlement value both to reduce credit risk in the event of unusually large losses and to make the contract look more like reinsurance policies, which usually have upper limits.

The price of the futures contract at any given time reflects the market's expectation of the event quarter's catastrophic loss in relation to the earned premiums for that quarter. Obviously, the insurer's net gain from a long position in a futures contract is the settlement price minus the price at the inception date of the contract.

To illustrate the features of insurance futures, we use a simple hedging example. Assume that an insurer anticipates US$5 million in earned premiums on policies subject to catastrophes during the first quarter of the year. The insurer forecasts catastrophic losses of US$600,000 for this

quarter, ie a catastrophic loss ratio of 0.12. The firm wants to hedge against catastrophic losses greater than US$600,000 by purchasing March futures contracts.

The company's actuaries predict that 80% of the losses will be reported by the end of June. The insurance futures contract is traded at the beginning of the period at a given price F(0). To hedge its underwriting risk, the insurer buys a number of futures contracts equal to:

$$N = \frac{P}{25,000} \frac{h}{R} = \frac{5,000,000}{25,000} \frac{1.0}{0.8} = 250 \quad (2)$$

where

N = number of contracts purchased by the insurer;

P = premium volume of the insurer in the line of business being hedged;

h = proportion of its anticipated catastrophe losses the firm desires to hedge; and

R = expected proportion of pool losses reported to ISO by the end of reporting period.

Assume also that the pool's and the insurer's loss ratio are five percentage points higher than expected at the time the futures contracts were purchased. The gain from the futures position [F(T) – F(0)] will be US$1,000 per contract (25,000 × 0.05 × 0.8), and the insurer's total gain from holding 250 contracts equals US$250,000. The gain on the futures contracts obviously equals 5% of the insurer's earned premiums and makes up for the extra losses encountered.

Of course, there will be times when the hedge is less than perfect. If the insurer's and pool's loss ratio movements are not perfectly correlated, the gain from the hedge will not exactly cover the insurer's unexpected losses.

CALL SPREADS
So far, the volume of transactions observed in insurance futures markets has not been high.

2. Catastrophe future loss and reporting schedule for the March 1995 contracts

PRICING
CATASTROPHE
INSURANCE
FUTURES AND
CALL
SPREADS

There are several possible explanations:

❑ Information release by ISO is not as frequent as it should be.

❑ If insurers are natural buyers of these contracts, "natural sellers" are less easy to identify; examples would be construction companies, which benefit from catastrophes, and, as usual, speculators willing to take risk to make profits.

❑ Insurers may be reluctant to buy the futures contracts because they are not necessarily familiar with this type of instrument. On the other hand, their counterparties may feel that insurers have access to more information and that the usual caveats in the presence of asymmetric information apply.

❑ Taking a long position in a futures contract amounts to hedging the risk that the loss ratio is greater than its expected value at the time the contract is purchased. Insurers usually do not want to hedge the risk of relatively small fluctuations around the expected loss, but rather are interested in hedging extremely large or unusual loss shocks.

As we shall see, most of these problems disappear with the catastrophe (CAT) call spreads, which explains why they have been successful since their introduction in 1993 by the CBOT.

Like any other call spread, a catastrophe call spread involves buying a call at a strike price of k_1 and selling a call at a higher strike, k_2, both calls having the same maturity. In the case of the CBOT's catastrophe spreads, the underlying instrument is the catastrophe insurance futures contract, and the maturities of the call spreads are the same as the futures contract maturities. With CAT spreads, the values k_1 and k_2 are called *loss ratio attachment points*, where the loss ratio (the ratio of losses to premiums) is expressed as a percentage and one point = US$250.

A long position in a call spread gives coverage, net of the premium paid, for loss ratios between the two loss ratio attachment points. In principle, all layers between 0 and 200 are available for trading, but in practice most traded spreads have a range of 20 points, such as [20, 40], [50, 70], [70, 90]. Buying catastrophe call spreads thus gives insurers the ability to choose the layer or layers of losses that they prefer to hedge, while retaining the risk of smaller deviations from the expected value of losses.

As an example of a call spread, suppose there is a September 1995 [50, 70] Eastern call spread bought at a premium of 5.0. If the settlement value of the loss ratio index is ≤0.5, or 50% of premiums, the call spread expires worthless, and the hedger's loss equals the premium payment of US$1,250. If the loss ratio index settlement value is ≥0.7, or 70% of premiums, the hedger receives at maturity the maximum payoff from the call spread (20 points). In between the spread's attachment points, the hedger receives the difference between the loss ratio settlement value and a loss ratio of 50 points.

The gain on the call spread at maturity is diagrammed in Figure 3. In the figure, the maximum loss is the premium (compounded over the period); the maximum points ($k_2 - k_1$); and the break-even point is the lower strike price plus the compounded premium. Graphs such as this are standard in finance to express the profit generated by a long position in a call spread. In insurance, the graph is remarkable because of the striking similarity it offers with the gain profile after buying a layer of reinsurance.

Reinsurance is the practice by which one insurer transfers to another insurer some of the potential losses on insurance contracts the first insurer has issued or will issue in the future. Typically, reinsurers spread out the transferred risk by writing layers of reinsurance – ie each reinsurer provides coverage between two predetermined amounts of loss.

Figure 3 illustrates the main reasons for the success of the CAT call spreads:

❑ the amount of money at risk is bounded, whether one takes a short or long position;
❑ call spreads look familiar to insurers, as reinsurance has been traded for centuries;
❑ competition in reinsurance markets entails the existence of some kind of market price for a given layer; and
❑ by choosing among layers, each insurer is able to hedge only those loss layers of most relevance in terms of its desired risk profile.

3. Gain at maturity – 40/60 call spread

where:
- maximum loss = premium (compounded over the period);
- maximum profit = spread ($k_2 - k_1$) – compounded premium;
- BE = break even point = lower strike price + compounded premium

33

PRICING
CATASTROPHE
INSURANCE
FUTURES AND
CALL
SPREADS

Valuation of insurance futures and call spreads

Actuaries have traditionally valued insurance claim accumulations such as those underlying catastrophe insurance futures as random sums. The number of claims is a random variable modelled by a discrete probability distribution such as the Poisson or negative binomial, while the claim amounts (also random) usually are modelled by a continuous distribution such as the gamma, lognormal or pareto distribution.

The price of insurance according to this model is typically equal to the expected value plus an additive function of the second moment of the distribution (eg, a constant times the variance or standard deviation). This pricing approach is particularly inconsistent with the value additivity principle that prevails in financial markets, as has been observed by some leading actuaries (eg Buhlmann, 1980).

In contrast, even though catastrophe futures and call spreads are related to insurance, we view them as financial instruments. This is reflected both in the continuous-time modelling of the claim process and in the use of arbitrage arguments in our valuation methodology.

THE INSTANTANEOUS CLAIM PROCESS

We define $[S(t)]_{t \geq 0}$ as the *instantaneous* claim process, meaning that for any date t in the trading period and for a small length of time dt (representing, for instance, a day), the amount of claims reported to the insurance companies in the pool during the interval $[t, t + dt]$ is equal to $S(t)dt$. The value of aggregate claims $L(T)$ that is the numerator of loss-to-premium ratio at maturity T and hence determines the settlement value of the futures contract is equal to

$$L(T) = \int_0^T S(s)ds \qquad (3)$$

We represent the uncertainty in the economy by a probability space $(\Omega, \widetilde{\mathfrak{F}}, \widetilde{\mathfrak{F}}_t, P)$, where $\widetilde{\mathfrak{F}}_t$ is the information available at time t, and P is the objective probability. An important matter is specification of the dynamics under P of the process $[S(t)]$. Since the reporting of claims by policyholders is continuous, we represent $[S(t)]_{t \geq 0}$ to be a diffusion process, obviously taking only positive values, making geometric Brownian motion a natural candidate. Moreover, to represent the difference between the event quarter and the non-event quarter, we add a jump process to the diffusion process during the event quarter. Consequently,

$[S(t)]$ is the juxtaposition of two processes driven by the following dynamics.

$$\text{For } t \in [0, T/2]:$$
$$dS(t) = S(t^-)[\mu dt + \sigma dW(t)] + kdN(t) \qquad (4)$$

where
$[W(t)]_{t \geq 0}$ = a standard Brownian motion;
μ and σ = constants representing the continuous part of the instantaneous claims, which reflects the randomness in reporting as well as "small" catastrophes;
k = a positive constant representing the severity of the loss jump component due to catastrophes; and
$N(t)$ = a Poisson process with intensity λ, where λ represents the frequency of the jumps.

We assume that the processes $[W(t)]$ and $[N(t)]$ are independent, the latter representing only the "major" catastrophes.

$$\text{For } t \in [T/2, T],$$
$$dS(t) = S(t)[\mu'dt + \sigma dW(t)] \qquad (5)$$

where the drift μ' is not necessarily equal to μ. The assumption of equal volatility in the diffusion part during both quarters can be relaxed without adding any complexity to our pricing methodology.

From the seminal articles by Harrison and Kreps (1979) and Harrison and Pliska (1981), the no-arbitrage assumption implies the existence of a risk-adjusted probability measure Q under which the discounted price process of securities traded in financial markets is a martingale. Under this new probability measure, the dynamics of $S(t)$ described in equation (5) become:

$$dS(t) = S(t)[\alpha'dt + \sigma d\hat{W}(t)] \qquad (6)$$

where $[\hat{W}(t)]_{t \geq 0}$ = a Q-Brownian motion, $\mu' = \alpha' + \rho\sigma$, and ρ represents, as in Shimko (1992), the equilibrium market price of claim level risk that we assume to be constant over the period $[0, T]$.

The independence of the processes $[W(t)]$ and $[N(t)]$ implies that the change of probability measure gives the following dynamics of $S(t)$ under Q during the event quarter $[0, T/2]$:

$$dS(t) = S(t^-)[\alpha dt + \sigma d\hat{W}(t)] + kd\hat{N}(t) \qquad (7)$$

where $\mu = \alpha + \rho\sigma$.

34

PRICING
CATASTROPHE
INSURANCE
FUTURES AND
CALL
SPREADS

Having specified the modelling of the reported claims, we now turn to the pricing problem. We know from recent work in finance that the no-arbitrage assumption does not imply completeness of the financial markets. In our situation, however, insurance futures contracts and options are attainable contingent claims and do have a unique price; we have a sufficient number of non-redundant traded securities relative to our two sources of randomness to legitimise the existence of a well-defined arbitrage price for the futures contracts and call spreads.

PRICING THE CAT FUTURES CONTRACTS
It is well-known (see Geman, 1989, and Jamshidian, 1989) that the future price (with no discount factor) is a martingale under the risk-adjusted probability measure. Consequently, at any time $t \in [0, T]$, its market value $F(t)$ is defined as:

$$F(t) = E_Q[F(T) \mid \widetilde{\aleph}_t]$$
$$= \frac{\$25,000}{\Pi}$$
$$\times \{E_Q[L(T) \mid \widetilde{\aleph}_t] - E_Q[Max(L(T) - 2\Pi, 0) \mid \widetilde{\aleph}_t]\}$$
$$(8)$$

where $L(T)$ is given by equation (3).

We observe at this point that the randomness in $L(T)$ resides only in the part $\int_t^T S(s)ds$ of the claims not yet reported, because the quantity $\int_0^t S(s)ds$ should be known from information released on the value of the claims accumulation. Additionally, we observe that the value of the two terms on the right-hand side of equation (8) depends upon the expression for $S(t)$, and hence on t belonging on the first or second quarter.

To price the futures contracts, we start with the simplest case, where $t \in [T/2, T]$:

$$L(T) = \int_0^t S(s)ds + \int_t^T S(s)ds \qquad (9)$$

where the first term is non-random, and the second term involves $S(s)$ as described in equation (5). The expectation under Q of the second term on the right-hand side of equation (9) is exactly the first moment of the integral of geometric Brownian motion, which is fairly easy to compute (see Geman and Yor, 1993), because it is legitimate to commute the expectation and integral operators. The result is:

$$E_Q[L(T) \mid \widetilde{\aleph}_t] = \int_0^t S(s)ds + \frac{S(t)}{\alpha'}\left[e^{\alpha'(T-t)} - 1\right]$$
$$(10)$$

The second term in equation (8), which represents the capping at 2.0 of the loss ratio used as the settlement value, can be neglected for practical purposes, as even hurricane Andrew, the worst catastrophe since records began to be kept in 1948, resulted in a loss ratio less than 1.5. Envisioning the possibility of larger catastrophes, we note that this term can be written as:

$$F(t) = E_Q[Max(L(T) - 2\Pi, 0) \mid \widetilde{\aleph}_t]$$
$$= TE_Q\left[max\left(\frac{1}{T}\int_0^T S(s)ds - \frac{2\Pi}{T}, 0\right)\Big|\widetilde{\aleph}_t\right] \qquad (11)$$

Equation (11) can be seen, up to the factor T, as the value of an Asian option where the integral between two fixings incorporated in the average is very small relative to the lifetime of the option and the strike price equal to $2\Pi/T$. Geman and Yor (1993) provide either an explicit formula for the average rate option price, or an expression of the Laplace transform of this price (which can be inverted by a numerical procedure).

For the case where $t \in [0, T/2]$, we write

$$L(T) = \int_0^t S(s)ds + \int_t^{T/2} S(s)ds + \int_{T/2}^T S(s)ds$$
$$(12)$$

which gives:

$$F(t) = E_Q[L(T) \mid \widetilde{\aleph}_t]$$
$$= \int_0^t S(s)ds + Y_1(t) + Y_2(t) \qquad (13)$$

where

$$Y_1(t) = E_Q\left[\int_t^{T/2} S(s)ds\Big|\widetilde{\aleph}_t\right]$$

and

$$Y_2(t) = E_Q\left[\int_{T/2}^T S(s)ds\Big|\widetilde{\aleph}_t\right]$$

The claim process $S(s)$ involved in $Y_1(t)$ is the Doléans–Dade exponential solution of the stochastic differential equation (7), which involves a diffusion process plus a jump. This makes the computation of $Y_1(t)$ more complex, although a closed-form expression can still be obtained, namely:

$$Y_1(t) = S(t)\left[\frac{e^{(T/2-t)\alpha} - 1}{\alpha}\right]$$
$$+ k\lambda\frac{e^{(T/2-t)\alpha} - (T/2 - t)\alpha - 1}{\alpha^2} \qquad (14)$$

35

PRICING

CATASTROPHE

INSURANCE

FUTURES AND

CALL

SPREADS

(See Appendix A for the computations involved in integrating equation (7) and calculating the expectation of the integral of the claim process.)

The values of S(s) for S ∈ [T/2, T] involved in $Y_2(t)$ are driven by the dynamics of a geometric Brownian motion, but with S(T/2) as the initial value; hence, for s ∈ [T/2, T]

$$S(s) = S\left(\frac{T}{2}\right)e^{\alpha'(s-T/2)+\sigma\hat{W}(s-T/2)-\sigma^2/2(s-T/2)} \quad (15)$$

where S(T/2) is the Doléans–Dade exponential derived from equation (7). Appendix B gives the explicit calculation of $Y_2(t)$, leading to the price of the futures contract on the interval [0, T/2]:

$$V(t) = \int_0^t S(s)ds + S(t)\left[\frac{e^{\alpha(T/2-t)}-1}{\alpha}\right]$$

$$+ k\lambda\left[\frac{e^{(T/2-t)\alpha}-\left(\frac{T}{2}-t\right)\alpha-1}{\alpha^2}\right]$$

$$+ S(0)e^{\alpha'(T/2-t)}\left[\frac{e^{\alpha'T/2}-1}{\alpha'}\right]$$

$$+ k\lambda\left(\frac{e^{\alpha(T/2-t)}-1}{\alpha}\right)\left(\frac{e^{\alpha'T/2}-1}{\alpha'}\right) \quad (16)$$

The exact value of V(t) would reflect the capping at 2.0 of the loss ratio – ie would require the incorporation of a term similar to the value of an average rate option written on an underlying asset following a diffusion process plus a jump. To our knowledge, no closed-form solution has yet been obtained, so pricing requires the use of Monte Carlo simulations described below.

Obviously, all the parameters involved in modelling of the dynamics of the instantaneous claim process under Q could be derived from market prices and the closed-form solutions we have obtained. Taking as many values for the futures price in the intervals [0, T/2] and [T/2, T] as the number of parameters would provide the values of these parameters. A better solution, given that there are days when the trading volume is low, is to use data from all dates where reasonable liquidity is present and estimate the parameters using a least squares approach. Independently, one can use historical data and time series provided by statistical firms such as ISO and the Property Claims Service to estimate μ and μ′.

PRICING CAT CALL SPREADS

At maturity T, the payoff of a call spread has the classic expression obtained as a difference of payoffs of two standard options, which can be written compactly as follows (with the payoff expressed in points):[3]

$$C(T) = \min\left\{\max\left[100\frac{L(T)}{\Pi} - k_1, 0\right], k_2 - k_1\right\} \quad (17)$$

At time t, the price of the call spread is equal to the expectation under the risk-neutral probability measure of the discounted terminal payoff. Even when looking separately at the two calls instead of equation (17), an exact pricing expression does not exist for the reasons mentioned earlier. Consequently, in order to estimate C(t), it is necessary to run Monte Carlo simulations of the possible trajectories of S(t), including the portion that corresponds to the Doléans–Dade exponential.

The Monte Carlo simulations during the event quarter are based on the discrete-time version of equation (7). The Brownian motion term $d\hat{W}(t)$ in (7) is simulated as $z\sqrt{\Delta t}$, where z is a simulated standard normal variate, and Δt is a small time interval (in most of our simulations Δt = 0.0025 years). The Poisson component of (7) is simulated using the fact that the time between arrivals of Poisson events follows the exponential probability distribution.

An arrival time is simulated for each arrival Δt. If the arrival time is ≤Δt, a jump of magnitude k is added in (7); no jump is added if the simulated arrival time is >Δt. During the run-off quarter, the procedure is the same except that the drift term in the Brownian motion process becomes α′ (which may differ from α), and, of course, the jump component of (7) is not included.

The result of any given simulation is a path S(t) from the contract start date (t = 0) to the end of the run-off period (T = 0.5 years). The settlement value is obtained by numerically integrating under S(t) to obtain a realisation of L(T), which is allocated among the call spread layers on the basis of its magnitude. The procedure is then replicated many times, and allocations to each layer are averaged to give the contract prices for the call spreads.

As an example, we simulate a contract with an expected loss ratio of 0.2, which corresponds roughly to the average loss ratios of the September Eastern futures contracts (the contracts covering the hurricane season). We fix the parameters α, α′, and μ at the values 0.1, 0.1, and

36

PRICING
CATASTROPHE
INSURANCE
FUTURES AND
CALL
SPREADS

Table 1. Simulated prices – 20/40 call spreads

Time to maturity (years)	Sigma		
	0.2	0.4	0.6
0	3.234	3.842	4.421
0.05	3.192	3.798	4.376
0.10	3.155	3.760	4.336
0.15	3.122	3.727	4.301
0.20	3.095	3.698	4.270
0.25	3.071	3.674	4.244
0.30	3.052	3.653	4.221
0.35	3.035	3.635	4.202
0.40	3.022	3.620	4.185
0.45	3.010	3.608	4.171
0.50	3.002	3.598	4.160

Note: Prices are quoted in terms of loss ratio percentage points where 1 point = US$250. Strike prices for spreads are also in points. The CAT 20/40 spread provides coverage for loss ratios between 20% and 40%.

Table 2. Simulated prices – 60/80 call spreads

Time to maturity (years)	Sigma		
	0.2	0.4	0.6
0	0.170	0.226	0.362
0.05	0.165	0.220	0.356
0.10	0.159	0.217	0.351
0.15	0.156	0.212	0.347
0.20	0.152	0.210	0.344
0.25	0.150	0.207	0.341
0.30	0.148	0.206	0.339
0.35	0.146	0.204	0.337
0.40	0.146	0.203	0.336
0.45	0.145	0.202	0.334
0.50	0.144	0.202	0.334

Note: Prices are quoted in terms of loss ratio percentage points where 1 point = US$250. Strike prices for spreads are also in points. The CAT 60/80 spread provides coverage for loss ratios between 60% and 80%.

0.15. The risk-free rate is set at 5%. We conduct the simulations for three values of σ, 0.2, 0.4, and 0.6. In accordance with the actuarial literature, we choose $\lambda = 0.5$ and $k = 0.8$.

The results of the simulations are presented in Tables 1 and 2. Table 1 shows prices for the 20/40 call spreads, while Table 2 shows prices for the 60/80 spreads.

As expected, the CAT spread premium is higher when the layer of reinsurance is defined by low attachment points. We observe through our numerical procedure that the pricing model is sensitive to changes in the assumed parameter values, but with a robustness similar to that characterising the famous Black–Scholes formula. The robustness of the results to parameter changes implies that when the market for CAT call spreads is very liquid and the bid–ask spread is very narrow, it will be possible to derive the parameters from market prices.

Conclusions

It is important to emphasise the fact that the CBOT insurance futures and call spreads offer an important new example of risk securitisation. The maintenance of viable insurance markets for high-exposure losses such as property catastrophes and commercial liability is likely to become increasingly dependent on insurance derivatives. In addition to providing needed liquidity, derivatives have the advantage of reducing the impact of information asymmetries that often prevent insurance markets from functioning efficiently. Similar instruments are being studied for other types of insurance such as health, agricultural, and environmental coverage.

Paralleling the exchange-traded futures and options, over-the-counter trading in insurance derivative is also expanding rapidly. A particularly important development is the growth in multiple asset options, such as foreign exchange CAT spreads, which provide a hedge against currency risk. The fact that the business of insurance companies is worldwide is likely to spur the development of "quanto CAT" instruments.

Appendix A: Derivation of $Y_1(t)$

Equation (7) in the text is:

$$dS(t) = S(t^-)[\alpha dt + \sigma d\hat{W}(t)] + kd\hat{N}(t) \quad (A1)$$

We want to integrate (A1) and calculate the expectation of the integral of the claim process.

The first part, $dS(t) = S(t^-)[\alpha dt + \sigma d\hat{W}(t)]$ is the usual lognormal equation with solution: $S(t) = S(0) e^{[X(t)]}$, where $X(t) = (\alpha - \sigma^2/2)t + \sigma W(t)$. Equation (A1) can be solved by the well-known method of "variation of constants," to obtain:

$$S(t) = e^{X(t)}\left[S(0) + k\int_0^t e^{-X(u)}d\hat{N}(u)\right] \quad (A2)$$

We now consider the aggregate claim amount at time T:

$$T(AT) = \int_0^T S(s)ds$$

$$= \int_0^T S(0)e^{X(s)}ds$$

$$+ \int_0^T e^{X(s)}ds \int_0^s e^{-X(u)}kd\hat{N}(u) \qquad (A3)$$

where $u < s < T$. The last integral can also be written as:

$$k\int_0^T d\hat{N}(u) \int_u^T e^{|X(s) - X(u)|}ds \qquad (A4)$$

Clearly,

$$T\,E[A(T) \mid \tilde{\mathfrak{F}}_t]$$
$$= \int_0^t S(s)ds + E\left[\int_t^T S(s)\,ds \mid \tilde{\mathfrak{F}}_t\right]$$

and

$$E\left[\int_t^T S(s)\,ds \mid \tilde{\mathfrak{F}}_t\right]$$

$$= E\left[\int_t^T e^{X(s)}ds\left\{S(0) + k\int_0^s e^{-X(v)}d\hat{N}(v)\right\} \mid \tilde{\mathfrak{F}}_t\right] \qquad (A5)$$

where $t < s < T$, and $0 < v < s$. This last expectation is in turn the sum of three terms that we denote U_1', U_2' and U_3', where

$$U_1' = S(0)e^{X(t)}\int_t^T e^{(s-t)\alpha}\,ds \qquad (A6)$$

(since $X(s)$ is a Brownian motion with drift).

From Fubini's theorem and the conditioning on $\tilde{\mathfrak{F}}_t$, we obtain

$$U_2' = k\int_0^t d\hat{N}(v)e^{-X(v)}\left[e^{X(t)}\int_t^T e^{(s-t)\alpha}ds\right] \qquad (A7)$$

and

$$U_3' = k\lambda\int_t^T dv\int_v^t E[e^{X(s)} - e^{X(v)}]ds \qquad (A8)$$

We first observe that

$$U_1' + U_2' = \frac{e^{(T-t)\alpha} - 1}{\alpha}$$

$$\times \left\{e^{X(t)}\left[1 + k\int_0^t e^{-X(v)}d\hat{N}(v)\right]\right\} \qquad (A9)$$

where we exactly recognise $S(t)$ as the second factor. We compute U_3' with the same arguments as before:

$$U_3' = k\lambda\int_t^T dv\int_v^t E[e^{|X(s) - X(v)|}]ds$$

$$= k\lambda\frac{e^{(T-t)\alpha} - (T-t)\alpha - 1}{\alpha^2} \qquad (A10)$$

Finally, we obtain:

$$T\,E[A(T) \mid \tilde{\mathfrak{F}}_t] = \int_0^t S(s)ds + S(t)\left[\frac{e^{(T-t)\alpha} - 1}{\alpha}\right]$$

$$+ k\lambda\frac{e^{(T-t)\alpha} - (T-t)\alpha - 1}{\alpha^2}$$

$$(A11)$$

Appendix B: Derivation of $Y_2(t)$

Recall that the claims process in the second sub-period $[T/2, T]$ is a pure diffusion process that has the same random term as the continuous part of the claims process over $[0, T/2]$ but a possibly different drift α':

$$dS(t) = \alpha'S(t)dt + \sigma S(t)dW(t) \qquad (B1)$$

We want to calculate $Y_2(t) = E_Q[\int_{T/2}^T S(s)ds \mid \tilde{\mathfrak{F}}_t]$. We know that for $s \geq T/2$:

$$S(s) = S\left(\frac{T}{2}\right)e^{\alpha'(s-T/2)+\sigma W(s-T/2)-\sigma^2/2(s-T/2)} \qquad (B2)$$

where $S(T/2)$ itself is derived from equation (A10) in Appendix A, which gives

$$S(s) = e^{(\alpha-\alpha')T/2}\left[S(0) + k\int_0^{T/2}e^{-X(u)}d\hat{N}(u)\right]e^{X(s)}$$

$$(B3)$$

where $X(s) = (\alpha - \sigma^2/2)s + \sigma W(s)$. Consequently, $Y_2(t)$ itself will be the sum of two terms. The first one, by the arguments developed in the first part of the section "Valuation of insurance futures and call futures" above, is

$$S(t)e^{\alpha(T/2-t)}\left[\frac{e^{\alpha'T/2} - 1}{\alpha'}\right] \qquad (B4)$$

The second component of $Y_2(t)$, by the arguments developed in Appendix A, is equal to

$$k\lambda\left(\frac{e^{\alpha(T/2-t)} - 1}{\alpha}\right)\left(\frac{e^{\alpha'T/2} - 1}{\alpha'}\right) \qquad (B5)$$

and

$$Y_2(t) = S(t)e^{\alpha(T/2-t)}\left[\frac{e^{\alpha'T/2} - 1}{\alpha'}\right]$$

$$+ k\lambda\left(\frac{e^{\alpha(T/2-t)} - 1}{\alpha}\right)\left(\frac{e^{\alpha'T/2} - 1}{\alpha'}\right) \qquad (B6)$$

PRICING
CATASTROPHE
INSURANCE
FUTURES AND
CALL
SPREADS

38

PRICING
CATASTROPHE
INSURANCE
FUTURES AND
CALL
SPREADS

1 *The regional futures are important because of the differing catastrophe exposure in the three regions. Hurricanes are the most significant exposure in the East, while tornadoes are most important in the Midwest, and fires and earthquakes are prominent in the West.*

2 *This discussion is based on the CBOT contracts as they existed prior to September 1995, when the futures contracts were withdrawn. At that time the ISO index was replaced by* an index compiled by Property Claims Services (PCS). The contracts traded today are PCS call spreads. Some additional changes also have been made eg, trading is now conducted in a national contract, five regional contracts, and three state contracts (for California, Florida and Texas).

3 *Recall that for insurance futures, settlement values are expressed as loss ratio percentage points (eg 10.2 points), where one point = US$250.*

BIBLIOGRAPHY

Berger, L., J.D. Cummins and S. Tennyson, 1992, "Reinsurance and the Liability Insurance Crisis", *Journal of Risk and Uncertainty*, 5, No. 3, pp. 253–72.

Buhlmann, H., 1980, "An Economic Premium Principle", *Astin Bulletin*, 11, pp. 52–60.

Geman, H., 1989, "The Importance of the Forward Neutral Probability Measure in a Stochastic Approach of Interest Rates", Working Paper, ESSEC, Cergy-Pontoise, France.

Geman, H. and M. Yor, 1993, "Bessel Processes, Asian Options, and Perpetuities", *Mathematical Finance*, 3, No. 4, pp. 349–75.

Geman, H., 1992, "Quelques Relations Entre processes de Bessel, Options Asiatiques, et Fonctions Confluentes Hypergéometriques", *Comptes Rendus de l'Académie des Sciences de Paris*, Série I, pp. 471–4.

Harrison, J.M. and D. Kreps, 1979, "Martingale and Arbitrage in Multiperiod Securities Markets", *Journal of Economic Theory*, 20, pp. 381–408.

Harrison, J.M. and S.R. Pliska, 1981, "Martingales and Stochastic Integrals in the Theory of Continuous Trading", *Stoch. Proc. Appl*, 11, pp. 215–60.

"Homeowners Futures and Options: Innovative Concepts for Protecting Underwriting Exposure". Chicago Board of Trade, 1992.

Jamshidian, F., 1989, "Bond and Option Valuation in the Gaussian Interest Rate Model", unpublished manuscript, Merrill Lynch Capital Markets, New York.

Property Claims Services, *The Catastrophe Record: 1949-1993*, Rahway, New Jersey, 1993.

Shimko, D., 1992, "The Valuation of Multiple Claim Insurance Contracts", *Journal of Financial and Quantitative Analysis*, 27, No. 2, pp. 229–46.

5

A Rational Approach to Pricing of Catastrophe Insurance

Weimin Dong, Haresh Shah and Felix Wong

Risk Management Solutions Inc; Stanford University; Weidlinger Associates Inc

A methodology for rational pricing of cata-strophe insurance is described. The methodology has two components: a sol-vency- and stability-based pricing framework, and an engine to quantify the loss variability that dri-ves solvency and stability. Generalisation to account for contagious effects of catastrophes and multiple occurrence of peril is presented in detail.

Catastrophes due to natural or man-made causes have three characteristics that distinguish them from other events of property and casualty losses. They occur infrequently and unpre-dictably, but can exact high costs due to their large footprint. For insurers, the large loss and footprint represent a good market opportunity on the one hand but great risk on the other. However, infrequent occurrence drives volatility, which is exacerbated by the absence of norms or precedence. Catastrophes do not happen often enough to establish a track record in the actuarial sense.

Pricing of catastrophe insurance must take these unique characteristics into account. In this paper, we describe how capacity-based pricing models are used as the starting point for a ratio-nal approach to pricing. A key element of the sol-vency and stability model is the loss exceedance probability. The loss exceedance probability of a portfolio determines the capacity inherent in the portfolio, and capacity is a commodity that drives the pricing structure, along with other economic considerations such as profit, investment return and market condition. Quantification of the exceedance probability involves knowing the correlation between any two losses, or the covariance loss matrix. This matrix is difficult to quantify for most insurance applications, but modern computerised techniques such as IRAS[1] have become available for that purpose. IRAS can also be used to compute the loss exceedance probability of a portfolio for complex scenarios, including multi-occurrence of various perils such as earthquakes, hurricanes and floods, which then becomes the foundation for premium deter-mination and risk management.

Details of the methodology are presented in the following sections along with illustration.

Solvency, stability and pricing

One can go into great details in discussing the financial operation of an insurance business (for example, see Pentikainen *et al.*, 1989), such as losses on policies, unallocated loss adjustment expenses, inflation, taxes, operating expenses, commission, reinsurance costs, etc. on the debit side, premium income and investment income from the credit side, the competitive environ-ment, capital markets, overall books of business, and regulatory and geographic constraints. However, we shall focus on the fundamentals, because a basic model of the insurance business suffices for the present purpose.

Succinctly stated, the goal of the insurance busi-ness is to maximise its return on capital while

This chapter was first published in Journal of Risk and Uncertainty, *vol 12, 1996. This copyrighted material is reprinted with permission from Kluwer Academic Publishers. The assistance of Rick Anderson of RMS Inc., who proofread the manuscript and provided many helpful comments, is acknowledged.*

maintaining survival and stability (see also the excellent exposition by Stone, 1973). The *survival (or solvency)* is usually expressed in terms of probability. If probability of ruin per year is defined as 1 – probability of survival per year = P_1, then probability of survival equals $1 - P_1$. For example, P_1 could be one in 100,000. Thus, probability of ruin per year is one in 100,000 and the probability of survival per year is 0.99999. For *stability*, the probability that the combined loss and expense ratio in any year will exceed its target by X percentage points (eg 4%) must be less than P_2, eg one in 100. If L denotes loss, E the expenses, P the premium income and C the capital, these constraints can be expressed as,

$$\Pr[(L + E) \geq (P + C)] < P_1 \qquad (1)$$

and

$$\Pr[(L + E)/P - \text{target} \geq X] < P_2 \qquad (2)$$

The insolvency probability, P_1, and the stability parameters P_2 and X are set formally or implicitly by management. For large insurance companies stability rather than survival is likely to be at issue when a new commitment is being considered.

The profit objective can be expressed as $\max[P - (L + E)]$ if other economic and political considerations such as investment income from capital are ignored for simplicity. However, a more common practice is to set a target rate of return in the form of a combined loss and expense ratio (eg, a ratio of 0.96 means a 4% target rate of return; if the expense ratio is 0.36, then the maximum target loss ratio is 0.60).

Any solvency-stability constraint set (P_1, P_2, X) corresponds to a maximum portfolio *loss exceedance probability (LEP)*. A LEP is depicted in Figure 1, and a point on the curve defines the probability corresponding to a loss threshold, ie, the probability that the dollar loss to the portfolio due to some combination of events is equal to or greater than the threshold. Assuming that the capital structure of the company is such that the maximum loss it can sustain is d_0, then the probability of ruin is p_0 as indicated in the figure. Alternately, if the acceptable probability of ruin is p_0, then the maximum loss sustainable is d_0.

However, if the company reserve can cover a loss higher than d_0, say d_1, as indicated in the figure, the leeway between the maximum LEP and the actual defines the *capacity*. An insurance company with a given capital structure can enhance its stability or lower its insolvency probability by swapping out less attractive policies in the portfolio. Alternately, excess capacity can be traded for income just like a commodity; less attractive policies can be swapped in, in return for higher premiums such as depicted in Figure 2.

Capacity can also be discussed in terms of stability, and for that purpose, the loss probability density function given in Figure 3 is more illustrative than the exceedance probability even though they contain the same information.[2] With reference to the figure, variability in the loss estimate corresponds to the girth of the bell curve, which depends on probability moments such as the standard deviation, σ, etc; the wider the girth, the higher the probability that the loss will exceed income. Hence, girth portends variability and destability. Of the two cases denoted by curves A and B in the figure, portfolio B is less

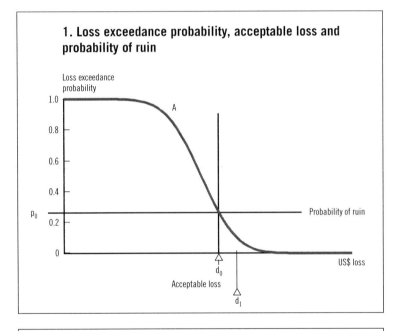

1. Loss exceedance probability, acceptable loss and probability of ruin

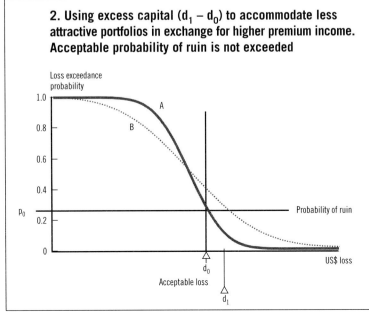

2. Using excess capital ($d_1 - d_0$) to accommodate less attractive portfolios in exchange for higher premium income. Acceptable probability of ruin is not exceeded

attractive because for a given income level, denoted by point I, the probability of negative income (ie the area under the density curve beyond I) is higher for B than for A. Alternately, B can be made acceptable if the premium income is increased sufficiently so that the probability of negative income is now the same as for A.

Although the girth of the bell curve depends on σ and higher (probability) moments, σ is often used as the measure of the girth for simplicity. In fact, the ratio of σ/μ, where μ is the mean loss, is called the *exposure ratio* and has been identified as the major measure of stability (see Stone, 1973).

Finally, for a given portfolio, the capital structure can be adjusted either in parts or in whole, as depicted in Figure 4, to realise risk pass-through while income is maintained at the same level. We shall show how the IRAS computation engine makes these and other management decisions possible by providing a rational, integrated framework in which the exposure ratio, probability density function or loss exceedance probability for treaties, policies and portfolios are computed and studied.

Event loss uncertainty matrix

Several sources of uncertainties are involved in loss estimation, and they include event occurrence uncertainty, uncertainty in the hazard given an event has occurred, building performance (asset damage) uncertainty given a hazard, and incomplete knowledge of the portfolio in general. All contribute to the variability in the loss distribution and all are considered in IRAS. We shall use event uncertainty to illustrate how IRAS is used to support rational pricing. Hence, although only event uncertainty is referenced explicitly, it is understood that losses computed in IRAS include the effects of the other uncertainties by default.

The end result of an IRAS application is an "event loss uncertainty matrix" such as that depicted in Table 1. The matrix gives the mean annual loss due to any event of interest, and, more importantly, the standard deviation of the loss. The latter is a measure of the variability in the loss estimate, but both are important in pricing.

The events include basic events and compound events, and the distinction is made solely for clarity of presentation. First, a list of all reasonable events (earthquakes, hurricanes, tornadoes, floods, etc) that may affect the book of business is made in column (1). Each peril is assumed to have an annual probability of

occurrence, column (2); each such occurrence is considered a basic event. Note that no reference is made to occurrences of other perils (or reoccurrence of the same peril within the year), and damage due to the event is computed independently of other damages. Compound events are combinations of the basic events, ie, more than one event occurs within the year and their losses are compounded. We shall see that compound events or multi-occurrences of peril are important to the variability in loss estimates.

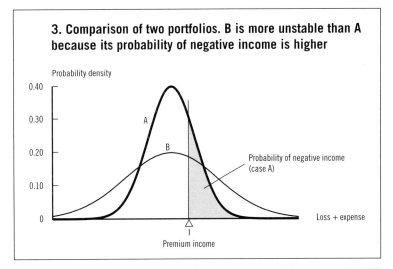

3. Comparison of two portfolios. B is more unstable than A because its probability of negative income is higher

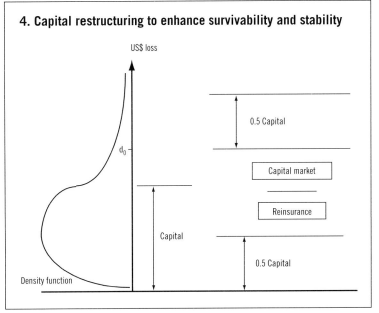

4. Capital restructuring to enhance survivability and stability

Table 1. Sample event loss uncertainty matrix

Event (1)	Annual probability (2)	Mean annual loss (3)	Standard deviation σ (4)
Total		Mean annual loss =	Standard deviation =

Column (3) is symbolic only. Entries in column (3) denote loss from any insurance contract, be it primary, quota share, surplus share, etc or facultatives at the policy or portfolio level. In fact, any loss computed in IRAS can be entered; the methodology remains the same. The loss can also be ground-up loss, gross loss (before reinsurance) or net loss. Column (4) contains the standard deviations associated with the mean losses in column (3); they constitute the product of the extended IRAS methodology.

The event loss uncertainty matrix then contains all the information on loss that is required to compute the LEP. We show how the matrix is developed for basic (singly occurring) events and compound (multiply occurring) events. Multi-occurrences of the same or different kinds of peril within a given time span are less probable than single occurrences of the perils. Nevertheless, multi-occurrences are of interest because the losses can be much higher; in the worst case, they may be the cause of ruin.

When the number of basic events is small, combination logic can be used to exhaust all permutations of multi-occurrences, and the corresponding exceedance probabilities computed exactly. As the number of events increases, combination explosion rules out analytic calculation and numerical methods must be used. We show how stochastic simulation techniques can give a more accurate estimate of the exceedance probability (and, hence, expected loss) at the expense of computation time, when such accuracy is required. We also show that a simple assumption on the correlation of events significantly reduces the simulation time so that the simulation approach offers an attractive compromise between accuracy and expediency.

Loss exceedance probability (LEP)

Consider three probable events such as A, B and C defined below:

$$P(A) = 0.05; \quad P(\bar{A}) = (1.0 - 0.05) = 0.95;$$
$$L(A) = 30$$

$$P(B) = 0.10; \quad P(\bar{B}) = (1.0 - 0.10) = 0.90; \quad (3)$$
$$L(B) = 20$$

$$P(C) = 0.15; \quad P(\bar{C}) = (1.0 - 0.15) = 0.85;$$
$$L(C) = 10$$

Each event has an *annual probability of occurrence* associated with it, denoted by, P(A), P(B), etc. Following common convention, P(Ē) denotes

Table 2. Sample data for three events

Event	Loss (in US$)	Probability
(1)	(2)	(3)
A	30	0.05
B	20	0.10
C	10	0.15

Table 3. The expected loss based on combination of events

Event	Loss (in US$)	Probability	Expected loss
(1)	(2)	(3)	(4) = (2) × (3)
ABC	60	$0.05 \times 0.10 \times 0.15 = 0.00075$	0.0450
ABC	50	$0.05 \times 0.10 \times 0.85 = 0.00425$	0.2125
ABC	40	$0.05 \times 0.90 \times 0.15 = 0.00675$	0.2700
ABC	30	$0.05 \times 0.90 \times 0.85 = 0.03825$	1.1475
ABC	30	$0.95 \times 0.10 \times 0.15 = 0.01425$	0.4275
ABC	20	$0.95 \times 0.10 \times 0.85 = 0.08075$	1.6150
ABC	10	$0.95 \times 0.90 \times 0.15 = 0.12825$	1.2825
ABC	0	$0.95 \times 0.90 \times 0.85 = 0.72675$	0.0000
Total		1.00000	5.0000

the probability that the event E does not occur. Hence, $P(\bar{E}) = 1 - P(E)$. The amount of loss that an event will incur, or *the single-event loss*[3], will be denoted by L(.). Note that the same assets may be affected by more than one event, or the different events may involve distinct groups of assets. That is not an important point as the assumption is made here that all assets will have been repaired before the next event, if any, occurs. Cumulative damage, ie amplification of damage due to pre-existing damaged conditions of the asset, is not considered in this discussion. In other words, the effect of multi-occurrence on loss is caused exclusively by the addition of the single-event losses based on pristine asset condition in each case.

The sample data are collected in Table 2 above. From these basic data, it is easy to compute the probabilities and losses associated with multiple events. For three events A, B and C, there are a total of eight combinations of multiple events as shown in Table 3, where, following convention, ABC stands for the occurrences of event A and B, but not C, and so on. For example, consider the first row. If as denoted by ABC all three events occur, the total loss is 30 + 20 + 10 = US$60, and the probability of this *compound event*[4] is, assuming the events are independent, P(A)*P(B)*P(C) = 0.05*0.10*0.15 = 0.00075. Entries in the other rows are obtained in similar fashion. The process can be visualised most clearly in the form of a Venn diagram such as shown in Figure 5. The loss and probability associated with the eight compound events are as noted in the figure.

5. Venn diagram for example

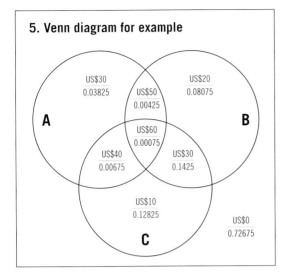

The expected loss for each compound event is computed according to the formula (event loss)*(event probability), and shown as column (4) in Table 3. The *total expected loss* is then the sum of the column, or US$5 in this case.

It is interesting to note that the same total expected loss can be obtained directly from Table 2. As is done for Table 3, for each of the events A, B and C shown in Table 2, we multiply the loss column by the probability column to obtain the expected loss, which is then appended to the table. The complete new table is shown as Table 4, and the total expected loss is US$5, the same as obtained previously by considering all possible combinations of the three events A, B and C in Table 3. Hence, the total expected loss computed based on seemingly only individual events in Table 4 includes the contribution of all multi-events! That this must be so also becomes clear when reference is made to the Venn diagram introduced previously in Figure 5. For example, consider the circle that denotes all events involving A. Each of the two double-overlap portions of the circle is the sum of two parts:

$$\frac{US\$50}{0.00425} = \frac{US\$30}{0.00425} + \frac{US\$20}{0.00425}$$

$$\frac{US\$40}{0.00675} = \frac{US\$30}{0.00675} + \frac{US\$10}{0.00675}$$

Table 4. Expected loss based on annual rates of events

Event (1)	Loss (in US$) (2)	Probability (3)	Expected loss (in US$) (4) = (2) × (3)
A	30	0.05	1.5
B	20	0.10	2.0
C	10	0.15	1.5
Total			5.0

where the first part can be allocated to A, and the second part going to B and C for the first and second line, respectively. Similarly, the triple-overlap portion can be broken into:

$$\frac{US\$60}{0.00075} = \frac{US\$30}{0.00075} + \frac{US\$20}{0.00075} + \frac{US\$10}{0.00075}$$

and the three parts go to A, B and C, respectively. Summing all parts that revert to A, we have:

$$\frac{US\$30}{0.03825} + \frac{US\$30}{0.00425} + \frac{US\$30}{0.00675} + \frac{US\$30}{0.00075}$$

or US$30/0.05, which is also the loss due to event A multiplied by the probability of event A. Other pieces in the diagram can be decomposed and allocated in similar fashion, and the operation of Table 3 is shown to be equivalent to that of Table 4.

Hence, if one is interested only in the total expected loss from all combinations of multi-events and if constituent data such as probabilities and losses from the basic events are available, the simple operations illustrated in Table 4 suffice. In other words, the effect of multi-occurrences is already included in Table 2 (or 4), and there is no need to go to the expanded Table 3. However, Table 3 contains detailed information that is not available in Table 2 *per se*, but is important in loss estimates. In particular, if one is interested in the LEP which gives the probability of the loss exceeding a certain level, such information can be readily extracted from Table 3 but not from Table 2 *per se*. With reference to Table 3, column (2) shows there are seven loss levels (US$0, 10, 20, 30, 40, 50 and 60). Their corresponding exceedance probabilities can be constructed from column (3) as follows. Only one compound event ABC can attain the highest loss level of US$60, with a probability of 0.00075. Next, we see that two compound events can exceed a loss level of US$50, viz, ABC and ABC; hence, the composite probability for that loss level is 0.00075 + 0.00425. This process is continued for other levels of loss, and the result is plotted in Figure 6. The exceedance probability curve is monotonically decreasing, starting with 1 for a loss of zero and approaching zero as the loss level increases.

To reiterate, we see that as opposed to the total expected loss, the exceedance probability curve cannot be obtained directly from Table 2. It must be done through its expanded counterpart, Table 3, because all possible loss levels from various combinations of events are directly available from the expanded table.

6. Exceedance probability for various loss levels

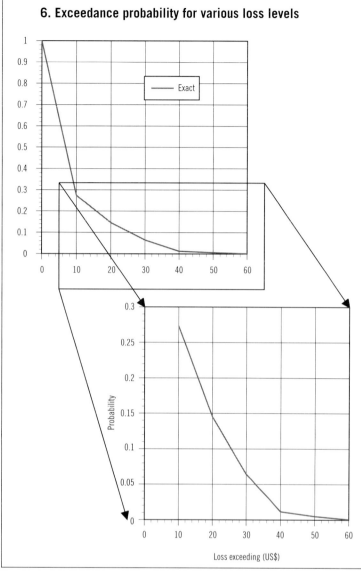

Exact

Probability

Loss exceeding (US$)

7. Probability of exceedance for example

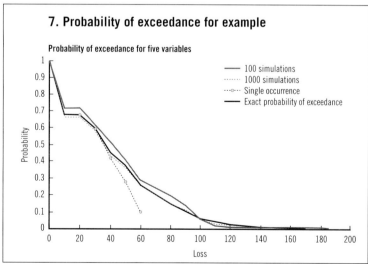

Probability of exceedance for five variables

- 100 simulations
- 1000 simulations
- Single occurrence
- Exact probability of exceedance

Probability

Loss

To generalise, when the number of events is N, the basic table will have N entries, but the expanded table will have 2^N entries. Hence, the size of the tables can become large very quickly as N increases. For this and other reasons, numerical

Event no.	Loss (US$)	Probability
1	60	0.1
2	50	0.2
3	40	0.2
4	30	0.3
5	20	0.2

Table 5. Data for example

methods are favoured. In subsequent sections, we describe current IRAS methodology in relation to multi-occurrences of perils, and how stochastic simulation is used to compute the expected losses under those circumstances.

Loss exceedance probability from stochastic simulation

LEPs that consider the effects of multi-occurrences of perils are difficult to obtain analytically except for the simplest cases involving a few events. Even then, the portfolio structure presents complications which are likely to rule out analytic procedures. This suggests that numerical methods be used. We describe in the following some results obtained with stochastic simulation techniques.

The probability of exceedance for any loss X can be computed by integrating the probability density function for loss from X to ∞. The probability density function for loss can be estimated by simulation as follows:

❏ for each event generate a random number between 0–1. If the generated random number is larger than the probability of the event, the event will occur. Repeat for all events of interest to identify the events that are "occurring" from those that are not;
❏ find the total loss of all occurring events;
❏ increment the counter of the total loss by 1, representing another round of event on-off selection, and repeat the first two steps;
❏ repeat above steps a large number of times (>1,000); and
❏ divide the loss counters from all simulations by the total number of simulations to get an estimate of the probability density function.

We illustrate the procedure with an example. Consider the five events in Table 5. Figure 7 compares the exact probability of exceedance (solid line) with that obtained using simulations (dotted lines). It is seen also that the accuracy of the probability of exceedance obtained by simulation increases as the number of simulations increases. At 1,000 simulations the simulated probability of exceedance is close to the exact value. The curve marked with single-occurrence denotes the probability of exceedance that would have been obtained if the effects of multi-occurrence are ignored[5]. Note that neglecting the effects of multi-occurrence can lead to significant error in the LEP.

Capacity-based pricing

Assume for the moment that pricing is based solely on the rate of return on capital, ie without regard to survival and stability constraints. The corresponding premium, called the *economic premium*, is simply the loss ratio:

$$P = \frac{\bar{L} + \bar{E}}{(1 - r)} \qquad (4)$$

or

$$P = \frac{\bar{L}}{(1 - r - e)} \qquad (5)$$

where $\bar{L}$ is the long-term annual loss expectation and $\bar{E}$ is the expected expense incurred by underwriting the risk, r the underwriting profit ratio, and e the expense ratio. For instance, for a risk with average US$100 per year in loss, an expense ratio of 35% and a required profit ratio of 5%, the economic premium based on equation (5) is $100/(1 - 0.35 - 0.05) = \$167$.

However, in an uncertain insurance environment, a portfolio of a given size and expected return within the stability and survival constraints is worth more than a portfolio of identical size with the same expected return outside of the constraints, everything else being the same. A portfolio with substantial excess capacity is even more valuable. *Survivability and stability are positively priced commodities and risks that generate capacity are more valuable to an insurer than capacity consumers* (see Stone, 1973).

Hence, if the two classes of risk are available only at their economic premiums, insurers would show a distinct preference for the capacity generators, which will then be bid below the economic premium. Conversely, capacity risks will be underwritten above their economic premiums. Hence, pricing must be based on capacity effect as well as the expected loss, and a first effort may be as follows:

$$P = \frac{\bar{L}}{1 - r - e - d} \qquad (6)$$

where d is the differential based on capacity (stability) considerations.

Equation (6) is the basis for capacity/stability-based pricing. The magnitude of d in any specific case will depend on the exposure ratio of the risk, the size of the risk, the size and composition of the portfolio, the constraints observed by the insuring company, and competitive factors relating to the capacity and exposure of the insurance industry as a whole. Generally speaking, d could be negative for those risks which add substantial capacity to the portfolio, while d is likely to be highly positive for most of the capacity risks. The greater the uncertainty of the risk characteristics, the greater would be the additional differential.

Capacity-based pricing formulas currently in use include:[6]

❑ standard deviation principle: $P = E(L) + \alpha\sigma(L)$
❑ variance principle: $P = E(L) + \beta\sigma^2(L)$

where α and β are parameters, $E(L)$ is the expected loss, $\sigma(L)$ the standard deviation of the loss. The inclusion of the parameters α (or β) in the capacity-based formulas denotes the insurer's reluctance to take on the risk measured by $\sigma(L)$ (or $\sigma^2(L)$). For this reason, the product $\alpha\sigma(L)$ (or $\beta\sigma^2(L)$) is also called the *risk load*, in the sense that it is the extra cost associated with the assumed risk.

For instance, Kreps (1990) has shown that

$$\alpha = \frac{yz(2SC + \sigma)}{1 + y(S' + S)} \qquad (7)$$

where S and S′ are the standard deviations of the expected loss for the existing and new book, respectively, C the correlation of the new contract with the existing book, z the level of stability required, and y the yield rate in the capital markets. When $C = 1$, and $S \gg \sigma$, Equation (7) reduces to $\alpha = yz/(1 + y)$ and the risk load is independent of σ. Meyers (1994) has derived a formula for risk load that is of the form:

$$R = \tilde{\lambda}\left\{\sigma^2(L) + 2\sum_{i=1}^{n} Cov(\bar{x}_i, L)\right\} \qquad (8)$$

where $\bar{x}_i$ are the expected losses of existing policies in the portfolio, and $Cov(.,.)$ denotes the covariance. $\tilde{\lambda}$ is called the risk load multiplier, and is a function of the marginal rate of return and marginal cost of capital.

We use an illustration to show how IRAS can be used to support capacity-based pricing. Consider the following table as an example of an existing book of business. Event A1 is associated with fault A, B1 with fault B and so on.[7] The events are assumed independent for now.

Event A1 is assumed to have an annual probability p_i of 0.1 or 10%. If it occurs, it will incur a net loss x_i of 3.0. Hence, the mean annual loss $E[x_i]$ where $E[.]$ is the expectation operation, is then $p_i*x_i = 3.0*0.1 = 0.3$. The variance of the loss for this case is 0.81.[8] Entries in the other rows of Table 6 have similar meanings and no further elaboration is needed.

Table 6. Sample book of business

Event, i (1)	Annual probability, p_i (2)	Net loss, x_i (3)	Mean annual loss, $E[x_i]$ (4)	$E[x_i^2]$ (5)	Variance $=\sigma^2[x_i]$ (6)	$\sigma[x_i]$ (7)
A1	0.10	3.0	0.30	0.900	0.81	0.90
B1	0.20	1.5	0.30	0.450	0.36	0.60
C1	0.30	0.5	0.15	0.075	0.0525	0.23
D1	0.05	5.0	0.25	1.250	1.1875	1.09
E1	0.10	2.5	0.25	0.625	0.5625	0.75
F1	0.30	0.5	0.15	0.075	0.0525	0.23
Total			1.40	3.375	3.025	1.74

Table 7. Data for sample new contracts

Event (1)	Annual probability (2)	Net loss (3)	Mean annual loss (4)	Variance (6)	Standard deviation, σ (5)
X1	0.05	6.0	0.30	1.71	1.31
Y1	0.05	3.0	0.15	0.4275	0.65
Total			0.45	2.1375	1.46

Table 8. New Book 1

Event, i (1)	Annual probability, p_i (2)	Net loss, x_i (3)	Mean annual loss, $E[x_i]$ (4)	$E[x_i^2]$ (5)	Variance $=\sigma^2[x_i]$ (6)	$\sigma[x_i]$ (7)
A1	0.10	3.0	0.30	0.900	0.81	0.90
B1	0.20	1.5	0.30	0.450	0.36	0.60
C1	0.30	0.5	0.15	0.075	0.0525	0.23
D1	0.05	5.0	0.25	1.250	1.1875	1.09
E1	0.10	2.5	0.25	0.625	0.5625	0.75
F1	0.30	0.5	0.15	0.075	0.0525	0.23
X1	0.05	6.0	0.30	1.8	1.71	1.31
Y1	0.05	3.0	0.15	0.45	0.4275	0.65
Total			1.85	5.625	5.1625	2.27

Table 9. New Book 2

Event, i (1)	Annual probability, p_i (2)	Net loss, x_i (3)	Mean annual loss, $E[x_i]$ (4)	$E[x_i^2]$ (5)	Variance $=\sigma^2[x_i]$ (6)	$\sigma[x_i]$ (7)
A1	0.10	3.0	0.30	0.900	0.81	0.90
B1	0.20	1.5	0.30	0.450	0.36	0.60
C1	0.30	0.5	0.15	0.075	0.0525	0.23
D1	0.05	5.0	0.25	1.250	1.1875	1.09
E1	0.10	2.5	0.25	0.625	0.5625	0.75
F1	0.30	0.5	0.15	0.075	0.0525	0.23
D2	0.05	6.0	0.30	1.8	1.71	1.31
D3	0.05	3.0	0.15	0.45	0.4275	0.65
Total			1.85		11.14	3.34

Hence, the sum of the mean annual loss from the six events is 1.40 and the sum of the variance is 3.025.[9] For uncorrelated events, the variance of the book is the sum of the variances of the contracts in the book. Hence, the standard deviation for the book is $\sqrt{3.025} = 1.74$, and the coefficient of variation for the book, cv, is $1.74/1.4 = 1.24$.

Suppose two new contracts, X1 and Y1, are added to the book, and that they are affected by faults X and Y which are uncorrelated with faults A–F, ie, their losses are not correlated with the A, B, .., F events. Data for the new contracts are given in Table 7.

The sum of the mean losses for the new contracts is 0.45, the sum of their variances is 2.1375, the standard deviation is 1.46, and the cv is $1.46/0.45 = 3.24$. Hence, a book consisting of only these two contracts has low stability.

We examine how adding the new contracts will affect the book of business. The new book, denoted by New Book 1, is as shown in Table 8.

New Book 1 has a total mean loss of 1.85 and a sum of variance of 5.1625. The cv is then $\sqrt{5.1625}/1.85 = 1.23$, which is much smaller than that of the two contracts X1 and Y1 by themselves (viz., 3.24), and even smaller than that of the original book (viz, 1.24). *Hence, adding contracts which are independent of existing contracts in a book can decrease the volatility of the book even if the new contracts are themselves more volatile.*

Suppose the contracts added are not independent, and indeed the losses are affected by an event on fault D. To denote this dependency, we denote X1 by D2 and Y1 by D3, and the new book by New Book 2. Hence, data for New Book 2 are as shown in Table 9.

Hence, an event on fault D will lead to losses in rows D1, D2 and D3. The impact of this correlation is that the variance of the book is increased by $2*1.09*1.31 = 2.86$ (for correlation between D1 and D2), by $2*1.09*0.65 = 1.42$ (for D1 and D3) and by $2*1.31*0.65 = 1.70$ (for D2 and D3)[10]. The variance of the New Book 2 is $5.1625 + 2.86 + 1.42 + 1.70 = 11.14$, and the cv is $\sqrt{11.14}/1.85 = 1.80$. While still lower compared with that of the new contracts (3.24), the volatility of New Book 2 is higher than the original book (1.24) and New Book 1 (1.23). *Hence, adding contracts which are correlated with existing contracts in a book increases the volatility of the book.*

The quantitative impact of correlation depends on the degree of correlation and the standard deviations of the events involved. For instance, a cursory look at column (7) of New Book 2 above indicates that the destabilising impact will be smaller if the new contracts are correlated with F1 instead of D1 as the standard deviation of F1 is only 0.23/1.09 or 21% of D1. A smaller degree of correlation, represented by the value of the correlation coefficient, has a similar effect. In the present context, the coefficient has a maximum value of one and a minimum value of zero. The latter case corresponds to the independent events examined in New Book 1.

Summary

Catastrophe risk is very different from other more common and less devastating risks such as auto and fire: losses from catastrophes are large, highly unpredictable and contagious. Furthermore, the uncertainty associated with the occurrence of catastrophes is large because they do not happen very often; the actuarial database from which cause/effect information may be gathered is small. For earthquakes, the time scale is of the order of hundreds of years, and even when loss data could be recorded as in recent events, the data are fragmentary and uncertain. More important, such loss experiences are unlikely to be representative of modern society due to constant changes in the built environment, technology, business infrastructure, asset valuation and demographic distribution.

Because the effects of catastrophes are felt by a much larger region than, say, isolated auto accidents or fires, geographic diversification takes on new scale and meaning[11]. Domino effects in catastrophes are also prominent. A damaged asset will in turn enhance the damage to another asset, either directly such as debris from a collapsed building may create havoc on its neighbors (called collocation or collateral damage), or indirectly such as loss of power exacerbates communication functions and recovery efforts (called functional or dependency damage). Losses from catastrophe are said to be spatially and functionally correlated.

A rational approach for pricing that takes these unique characteristics into account has been described. Capacity-based pricing models are used as a starting point; the models account for the

important interaction between catastrophe loss, survival and stability. A key pricing parameter in these models is the exposure ratio, viz., the ratio of the standard deviation of the loss to the mean loss. The exposure ratio of the risk (policy) being contemplated denotes its destabilising potential, and the aggregate ratio indicates whether the risk is a capacity generator (stabilising) or a capacity consumer (destabilising). Hence, capacity is a commodity and should be recognised in the pricing structure along with economic considerations such as profit, investment return and market condition and regulatory/political constraints. It is shown how computerised loss estimation systems such as IRAS can be used to quantify the exposure ratio of each policy, the aggregate exposure ratio of a portfolio, and the loss exceedance probability for credible scenarios.

Paramount in any rational pricing paradigm is the accounting of the contagious effects of catastrophes and the effects due to multiple occurrence of peril. Quantification of contagious effects requires knowing the correlation relation between any two losses, or the covariance matrix. This matrix is difficult to quantify for most applications except by simulation techniques such as IRAS. Losses due to multi-occurrences of the same or different kinds of peril can be much larger than that due to a single peril, and these "excess" losses are important to solvency even though they have very small probability of occurring. We have shown how they can be quantified using the IRAS framework. In short, all quantitative information on potential losses needed for rational pricing is provided.

In summary, IRAS can be viewed as the engine that powers the pricing vehicle. Quantitative estimates of losses and their variability constitute the "drive train". The IRAS finance module, details of which will be deferred to another article, is the "transmission" that converts loss information at the treaty, policy or portfolio level and management preferences into a pricing structure.

The same IRAS framework can be used for many elements of insurance planning other than pricing. For example, treaty screening and reinsurance strategy can be addressed as is obvious from the previous discussion.

1 *Investment and Insurance Risk Assessment System, an application software by Risk Management Solutions Inc.*

2 *Recall that the relation between LEP and density function is* $LEP(L) = \int_L^\infty p(x)dx$ *where* $p(x)$ *denotes the loss probability density function and* L *the loss level of interest.*

3 *In IRAS terminology, this loss can be the maximum loss, the mean loss, etc, given that the event occurs. The uncertainty in loss is caused by uncertainties in hazards such as attenuated ground shock and building performance. We denote it simply as loss; the uncertainty hereinafter is caused by uncertainty of the event and the probability of exceedance caused by the probability of occurrence of the event.*

4 *To eliminate confusion, we shall henceforth refer to events that occur singly as the basic events, and events that occur together as compound events.*

5 *When the effects of multi-occurrence are ignored, the LEP can be derived readily by using the range probability, ie, the probability that the loss is within certain ranges. Details are not included herein as they are not germane to the discussion.*

6 *The formulas have been greatly simplified as they do not include the many other factors that enter into pricing. This is done to highlight the role of IRAS.*

7 *Faults stand for some source of hazards, which can be hurricanes, floods, etc.*

8 *The variance of* x, *denoted by* $\mathrm{Var}[x]$ *is* $\mathrm{Var}[x] = E[x^2] - E[x]*E[x]$, *and the standard deviation* σ *is related to the variance by* $\sigma[x]*\sigma[x] = \mathrm{Var}[x]$.

9 *In general, not equal to* $\sum E[x_i^2] - (\sum E[x_i])^2$ *or 1.415.*

10 *When two losses are correlated, the increment in variance is given by* $2p_{ij}\sigma_i\sigma_j$, *where* p_{ij} *is the correlation coefficient,* σ_i *the standard deviation of event* i, *and* σ_j *that of event* j. *The correlation coefficient has been assumed to be 1, the maximum value possible, for simplicity.*

11 *For example, consider the impact of the Northridge earthquake on small, local insurance companies whose portfolios are mainly in the Southern California area.*

BIBLIOGRAPHY

Kreps, R., 1990, "Reinsurer Risk Loads From Marginal Surplus Requirements", *Proceedings of the Casualty Actuarial Society*, 76, pp.196–203.

Meyers, G., 1994, "Managing the Catastrophe Risk", 4th International Conference on Insurer Solvency, Philadelphia, Pennsylvania, April.

Pentikainen, et al, 1989, *Insurance Solvency and Financial Strength,* Finnish Insurance Training and Publishing Company Ltd, Helsinki.

Stone, J.M., 1973, "A Theory of Capacity and the Insurance of Catastrophe Risks", *Journal of Risk and Insurance*, 40(2), pp. 231–44 and pp. 339–56.

6

Stochastic Time Changes in Catastrophe Option Pricing

Hélyette Geman and Marc Yor

University Paris IX Dauphine and ESSEC; University Paris VI

Catastrophe insurance derivatives (futures and options) were introduced in December 1992 by the Chicago Board of Trade to offer insurers new ways of hedging their underwriting risk. Only CAT options and combinations of options such as call spreads are traded today, and the ISO index has been replaced by the PCS index. Otherwise, the economic goal of these instruments continues to be for insurers an alternative to reinsurance and for portfolio managers a new class of assets to invest in.

The pricing methodology of these derivatives relies on some crucial elements: the choice of the stochastic modelling of the aggregate reported claim index dynamics (since the terminal value of this index defines the payoff of the CAT options); the decision on a financial versus actuarial approach to the valuation, and the number of sources of randomness in the model and the determination of a "martingale measure" for insurance and reinsurance instruments.

We represent in this paper the dynamics of the *aggregate* claim index by the sum of a geometric Brownian motion which accounts for the randomness in the reporting of the claims and a Poisson process which accounts for the occurrence of catastrophes (only catastrophic claims are incorporated in the index). Geman (1994) and Cummins and Geman (1995) took this modelling for the *instantaneous* claim process. Our choice here is closer to the classical actuarial representation, while preserving the quasi-completeness of insurance derivative markets obtained by applying the Delbaen and Haezendonck (1989) methodology to the class of layers of reinsurance replicating the call spreads. Moreover, we obtain semi-analytical solutions for the CAT options and

call spreads by extending to the jump-diffusion case the method of the Laplace transform and stochastic time changes introduced in Geman and Yor (1993, 1996) in order to price financial path-dependent options through the properties of excursion theory.

The catastrophe insurance derivatives introduced in December 1992 by the Chicago Board of Trade continue to experience a steady development; over-the-counter (OTC) markets are growing even faster. Regarding the exchange-traded instruments, the original Insurance Statistical Office (ISO)-denominated contracts, futures and options, were changed in September 1995 into Property Claim Services (PCS) contracts; in this second generation of products, the futures contracts on which the options were written are no longer traded. Hence, the payoff at maturity of the options is directly related to the aggregate claims index, which becomes the key quantity in the option valuation. So far, and despite the huge interest these derivatives have received among not only insurers and reinsurers but also portfolio managers, who find a new class of assets to invest in with full diversification, the literature offering a pricing methodology for these instruments has been rather scarce. But prices are necessary to generate liquidity for the instruments, while reliable valuation formulas are likely to create a bigger volume.

This chapter was first published in Insurance: Mathematics and Economics, *21, 1997. This copyrighted material is reprinted with permission from Elsevier Science BV. Hélyette Geman is grateful to Hans Föllmer for a fruitful discussion on the model in May 1996.*

STOCHASTIC
TIME
CHANGES IN
CATASTROPHE
OPTION
PRICING

The articles on the subject (at least the ones we are aware of) fall roughly into three categories:

❏ Geman (1994) and Cummins and Geman (1995) propose an arbitrage approach to the valuation of these derivatives, somewhat similar to the celebrated Black–Scholes model for stock options, except for three major differences: (a) in the case of insurance derivatives, there is no underlying asset traded on the markets; we will come back to this crucial point; (b) it is the *increment* (for instance, daily) of the claim index L, defining the option pay-off, whose dynamics are modelled by a stochastic differential equation over the lifetime [0,T] of the option; (c) this increment is represented by a geometric Brownian motion (to account for the randomness in the reporting of the claim) plus a jump process (since only catastrophic claims are incorporate in the index).

❏ Aase (1995) offers interesting observations on the likelihood of reduction of adverse selection in insurance markets, since more traded instruments imply more available information, and proposes to obtain derivative prices through the principle of utility maximisation. To obtain unique prices, however, this methodology would need the assumption of the same utility function for all participants in these markets, whether they be insurers, reinsurer, insurance brokers, portfolio managers or investment bankers.

❏ Wang *et al* (1996) propose a "randomised operational time" approach to pricing CAT options. Their stochastic time change is uniquely and totally determined by the transactions on futures contracts and they "price the options directly with respect to the traded CAT futures contracts". This approach, which has the merit of illuminating the information conveyed by transactions (see Clark, 1973; Geman and Ané, 1996) is unfortunately totally inappropriate in the current situation (and already was in December 1996 when the paper was published) since the futures contracts stopped trading in 1995 and no "transaction time" can be derived from them in order to price options.

We propose in this chapter to directly model the aggregate claim process $(L(t))_{t \geq 0}$ as a jump-diffusion process.

This specification is closer to the actuarial representation than the one adopted in Geman (1994) and Cummins and Geman (1995). Moreover, it seems to be a more accurate (obviously not perfect) model since, leaving aside the randomness in

the reporting represented by the geometric Brownian motion, the effect of a catastrophic event pushes (through the jump term) the index L(t) very high but not necessarily the daily increment S(t) until the end of the lifetime of the option.

Lastly, besides the possibility of using Monte Carlo simulations (with their easy implementation and their possible pitfalls), we are able to recover "quasi-analytical" solutions for CAT option price through the use of stochastic time changes and Laplace transforms, both being deeply related to excursion theory as explained in Geman and Yor (1996).

The model

The uncertainty of the universe is represented by a probability space $(\Omega, \mathcal{F}, (\mathcal{F}_t)_{t \geq 0}, P)$ where Ω denotes the set of states of nature, $\mathcal{F}_t$ the information available at time t and P the historical probability measure.

The call option payoff is defined at maturity T by the quantity $(L(T) - k)^+$, where k is the strike price of the option and L(T) is the amount of aggregate claims incurred during the event quarter and reported during the development period. (In the PCS contracts, the event or loss period covers a quarter $[0,T_1]$, and the development period $[T_1,T]$ covers the following six months or 12 months to allow for a lag between the occurrence of a catastrophe and the time necessary to accurately report the claim.)

We assume no arbitrage in the insurance markets which, following the seminal work by Harrison and Kreps (1979) and Harrison and Pliska (1981) - extended by a number of other fundamental papers - implies the existence of a risk-adjusted probability measure Q equivalent to P under which the discounted prices of basic securities are martingales. However, even if this assumption was totally legitimate, another fundamental property we need to derive a unique arbitrage price for insurance derivatives is the insurance market completeness. To our knowledge, the literature on this crucial issue is rather scarce, except for the major paper by Delbaen and Haezendonck (1989). The two authors, among other points, observe that insurance markets are incomplete. This is still probably true, even though one can argue that, in the meantime, these markets have undergone a huge transformation (in particular, an "invasion" by financial institutions, investment bankers and portfolio managers). New instruments, such as the recently issued catastrophe bonds, have certainly added some completeness to these markets. Leaving the debate on the subject open, we use the

51

STOCHASTIC
TIME
CHANGES IN
CATASTROPHE
OPTION
PRICING

key property provided by the identity of the payoff profile between CAT call spreads and layers of reinsurance (see Geman, 1994) and choosing the Poisson-diffusion representation of the index process described below, we know from Jeanblanc and Pontier (1991) that the class of equivalent martingale measure preserving the structure of the process is not void. Following Delbaen and Haezendonck (1989), we select in this class the measure Q which best fits prices of reinsurance layers as they can be observed, in particular through the prices quoted by the financial subsidiaries of major reinsurance companies. Stating that insurance derivative prices are Q-martingales seems to us a reasonable approximation and this approximation should gain accuracy with the increasing number of market participants.

We represent the dynamics of the aggregate reported claim index $(L(t))$ during the loss quarter $[0, T_1]$ by a Poisson-diffusion process, ie, we suppose that the dynamics of the process $(L(t))$ are driven under Q by the stochastic differential equation:

$$dL(t) = S(t)dt + \theta dN_t$$

where:
$S(t)$ denotes a geometric Brownian motion with drift which represents the randomness in the reporting of the claims;
(N_t) is a Poisson process with intensity which represents the major catastrophes and is assumed to be independent of $(S(t))$; and
θ is a positive constant representing the magnitude of the jumps.

For simplicity, we take $S(t) = \exp 2(W_t + vt)$, where (W_t) is a Q-Brownian motion, but using the scaling property of Brownian motion, the following methodology can easily be extended to a volatility σ different from two.

During the development period, the major news about catastrophes is already known and the randomness results only from the adjustment of the claim amounts. Hence, we choose to represent $L(t)$ on the interval $[T_1, T]$ as

$$dL(t) = S(t)dt$$

where $(S(t))$ could be replaced by a geometric Brownian motion with different parameters.

The identity of gain profiles generated by the purchase of a CAT call spread (ie, the combination of a long position in a call with strike price k_1 and a short position in a call with strike price $k_2 > k_1$, k_1 and k_2 being called the attachment

points of the call spread) and a layer of reinsurance and the availability of a vast class of layers with different attachment points provides (see Geman, 1994) enough "basic" securities with respect to the number of sources of randomness in our model to imply completeness of the insurance derivative markets. Hence, assuming a constant interest rate r over the lifetime $[0,T]$ of the option, the CAT call price at time t is equal to

$$C(t) = e^{-r(T-t)} E_Q[(L(T) - k)^+ / \mathcal{F}_t]$$

where k denotes the strike price of the call.

The conditioning by the information $\mathcal{F}_t$ available at time t naturally leads us to write

$$L(T) - k = (L(t) - k) + \int_t^T dL_u$$

❏ We see that in the particular case where $L(t) - k > 0$, we already know at time t that the call option will end in-the-money and its price at time t reduces to

$$C(t) = e^{-r(T-t)} \left\{ (L(t) - k) + E_Q \left(\int_t^T dL_u \right) \right\}$$

(in what follows, E_Q is denoted as E).

If this date t belongs to $[T_1, T]$ (the most likely case if $L(t) > k$), then $dL_u = S(u)du$, where $(S(u))$ is a geometric Brownian motion. The quantity $E[\int_t^T S(u)du]$ is then easy to compute (see Geman and Yor, 1993) and the call price is obtained under a closed form expression.

If this date t belongs to the interval $[0, T_1]$, we need to write

$$\int_t^T dL_u = \int_t^{T_1} dL_u + \int_{T_1}^T dL_u$$

$$= \int_t^{T_1} S(u)du + \int_t^{T_1} \theta dN_u + \int_{T_1}^T S(u)du$$

Since $E[\int_t^{T_1} \theta dN_u] = \theta\lambda(T_1 - t)$, the computation of the call price reduces again to writing explicitly $E[\int_t^T S(u)du]$.

Consequently, at any date t such that the amount of reported claims is bigger than the strike price k of the call option, we obtain a simple closed-form solution for the call price.

❏ Obviously, we observe most often $L(t) < k$.

(1) In the case where $t \in [T_1, T]$,

$$L(T) = L(t) + \int_t^T S(u)du$$

52

STOCHASTIC
TIME
CHANGES IN
CATASTROPHE
OPTION
PRICING

hence

$$E[(L(T) - k)^+/\mathcal{F}_t]$$

$$= E\left[\left(\int_t^T S(u)du - (k - L(t))\right)^+/\mathcal{F}_t\right]$$

and we need to compute the price of an Asian option when the underlying asset price is a geometric Brownian motion. The problem was addressed through different types of approximations by several authors. Geman and Yor (1993) obtained the Laplace transform of the exact price, and Geman and Eydeland (1995) proposed an inversion of this Laplace transform.

(2) In the case where $t \in [0,T_1]$

$$L(T) = L(t) + \int_t^T S(u)du + \int_t^{T_1} \theta dN_u$$

Since this is, mathematically, the most difficult situation, we are going in a first stage to conduct the computations under the assumption $T_1 = T$ (Poisson-diffusion process over the whole trading period) and then extend the methodology to $T_1 < T$.

Using the property of independence of the increments of the Brownian motion (W_t) and of the Poisson process (N_t) and the independence of the two processes, we reduce the problem to the situation $t = 0$.

To circumvent the difficulty created by the fixed time T in the combination of $E[(L(t) - k)^+]$, we replace this fixed time by an exponential time τ independent of (W_t) and (N_t). This boils down (see Geman and Yor, 1993, 1996) to computing the Laplace transform of this quantity with respect to the maturity T, ie the function

$$\psi(\lambda) = E\left[\int_0^\infty dT e^{-\lambda T}\left(\int_0^T dv S(v) + \theta N_T - k\right)^+\right]$$

and then making the stochastic time change $T = \int_0^u ds/R_s^2 \equiv A_u$ where (R_s) is the Bessel process with index ν originating at 1 such that

$$\exp(B_s + \nu s) \equiv (S(s))^{1/2}$$

$$= R\left(\int_0^s du \exp 2(B_u + \nu u)\right)$$

Since $(A_u, u \geq 0)$ is the inverse of $(\int_0^s dv\, S(v), s \geq 0)$, we obtain

$$\psi(\lambda) = E^{(\nu)}\left[\int_0^\infty \frac{du}{R_u^2} e^{-\lambda A_u}(u + \theta N_{A_u} - k)^+\right]$$

where $E^{(\nu)}$ denotes the expectation with respect to the Bessel process (R_u).

We write

$$\psi(\lambda) = E^{(\nu)}\left[\int_k^{+\infty} \frac{du}{R_u^2} e^{-\lambda A_u}((u - k) + \theta N_{A_u})\right]$$

$$+ E^{(\nu)}\left[\int_0^k \frac{du}{R_u^2} e^{-\lambda A_u}(\theta N_{A_u} - (k - u))^+\right]$$

$$\equiv \psi_1(\lambda) + \psi_2(\lambda)$$

Observing that $(N_t - \alpha t, t \geq 0)$ is a martingale, we can write, thanks to the independence of the processes (N_t) and (R_t)

$$\psi_1(\lambda) = \int_k^\infty du(u - k)E^{(\nu)}\left[e^{-\lambda A_u}\frac{1}{R_u^2}\right]$$

$$+ \theta\alpha\int_k^\infty du\, E^{(\nu)}\left[A_u\, e^{-\lambda A_u}\frac{1}{R_u^2}\right]$$

If we denote by $\varphi_\nu(\lambda)$ the first expectation in $\psi_1(\lambda)$, the second one is precisely $-\varphi_\nu'(\lambda)$.

In order to compute $\varphi_\nu(\lambda)$ and related quantities, we shall use several times the following.

PROPOSITION
(Yor, 1980). Let $\nu > -1$, and let $\Phi_u \geq 0$ be a $\mathcal{F}_u$ measurable variable defined on the canonical space $(C(\mathbb{R}_+,\mathbb{R}_+); \mathcal{F}_\infty)$, where $\mathcal{F}_u = \sigma\{R_s(\omega) \equiv \omega(s), s \leq u\}$.

Then, for $r > 0$, and $\lambda > 0$, one has

$$E_r^{(\nu)}\left[\Phi_u \exp\left(-\lambda\int_0^u \frac{ds}{R_s^2}\right)\right] = E_r^{(\gamma)}\left[\Phi_u\left(\frac{r}{R_u}\right)^{\gamma - \nu}\right]$$

where $\gamma = \sqrt{\nu^2 + 2\lambda}$.

COROLLARY
(We keep the above notation). The function

$$\varphi_\nu(\lambda) \equiv E_1^{(\nu)}\left[\exp(-\lambda A_u)\frac{1}{R_u^2}\right]$$

is equal to

$$E_1^{(\gamma)}\left[\frac{1}{R_u^{2+\gamma-\nu}}\right] = \frac{1}{\Gamma(1 + (\gamma - \nu)/2)}$$

$$\times \int_0^{1/2u} dv\, e^{-v}v^{(1 + (\gamma - \nu)/2)}(1 - 2uv)^{(\gamma + \nu)/2 - 1}$$

The derivative with respect to λ of this last quantity involves the three terms where γ

53

STOCHASTIC
TIME
CHANGES IN
CATASTROPHE
OPTION
PRICING

appears and $\psi_1(\lambda)$ can be written as a double integral which may be computed numerically.

Coming to $\psi_2(\lambda)$, we use again the independence of (N_t) and (R_t) and the fact that, for any $\mathbb{R}_+$ valued function

$$E[\varphi(N_t)] = \sum_{n=0}^{\infty} \varphi(n) e^{-\alpha t} \frac{(\alpha t)^n}{n!}$$

to obtain

$$\psi_2(\lambda) = \sum_{n=0}^{\infty} \int_0^k du(\theta n - (k - u))^+$$

$$\times E^{(v)}\left[\frac{1}{R_u^2} e^{-(\lambda + \alpha)A_u}\left(\frac{\alpha^n}{n!}\right)A_u^n\right]$$

Hence, denoting $\sigma = \lambda + \alpha$, we remark that

$$\varphi_v^{(n)}(\sigma) \stackrel{def}{=} E^{(v)}\left[\frac{1}{R_u^2} e^{-\sigma A_u} A_u^n\right] = (-1)^n \frac{d^n}{d\sigma^n} \varphi_v(\sigma)$$

The quantity $\varphi_v(\sigma)$ which needs to be derived n times was computed earlier and depends on σ in a complicated manner.

However, from the proposition, we also deduce another expression for $\varphi_v^{(n)}(\sigma)$

$$\varphi_v^{(n)}(\sigma) = E^{(\gamma)}\left[A_u^n \frac{1}{R_u^{2+\gamma-v}}\right]$$

Hence, $\psi_1(\lambda)$ and $\psi_2(\lambda)$ are in principle fully known.

For practical purposes, one can truncate the Poisson process to the value $n = 5$ if 5 is an upper bound of the worst possible situation in terms of catastrophe estimation. In this case, the summation in $\psi_2(\lambda)$ would be limited to six terms.

Having obtained $\psi(\lambda)$ as the sum of $\psi_1(\lambda)$ and $\psi_2(\lambda)$, an inversion of the Laplace transform, for instance according to the methodology developed in Geman and Eydeland (1995) remains to be performed.

We now develop an extension of the above methodology to the more complicated (but more appropriate) model:

$$\begin{aligned}
&\text{on } [0,T_1], &&dL(t) = S(t)dt + \theta dN_t \\
&\text{on } [T_1,T], &&dL(t) = S(t)dt
\end{aligned}$$

Probabilistically, our method consists in randomising both T_1 and T; precisely: we take T_1 to be an exponential variable with parameter λ, and $T = T_1 + T_2$, where T_2 is a second independent exponential variable with parameter μ.

Thus, our method boils down to the computation of the double Laplace transform:

$$I \stackrel{def}{=} E\left[\int_0^{\infty} \lambda e^{-\lambda T_1} dT_1 \int_0^{\infty} \mu \epsilon^{-\mu T_2} dT_2 Z(T_1, T_2)\right] \quad (1)$$

where

$$Z(T_1, T_2) = \left\{\int_0^{T_1} du\, S(u) + \theta_1 N_{T_1}\right.$$

$$\left. + \theta_2 \int_{T_1}^{T_1 + T_2} du\, S(u) - k\right\}^+$$

T_1 and T_2 being given, we can write

$$\int_{T_1}^{T_1+T_2} du\, S(u) = S(T_1) \int_0^{T_2} dt\, \widetilde{S}(t)$$

with $(\widetilde{S}(t), t \geq 0)$ independent of $(S(u), u \leq T_1)$, and $\widetilde{S} \stackrel{(law)}{=} S$.

Next, we use Fubini's theorem to express I in terms of the two independent processes S and $\widetilde{S}$, and we perform the time changes as above. Thus, we obtain

$$I = \lambda\mu \mathbb{E}^{(v)}$$

$$\times \left[\int_0^{\infty} \frac{du}{R_u^2} \exp(-\lambda A_u) \int_0^{\infty} \frac{dt}{\widetilde{R}_t^2} \exp(-\mu \widetilde{A}_t) \hat{Z}(u,t)\right]$$

$$(2)$$

where $\mathbb{P}^{(v)} \equiv P^{(v)} \otimes \widetilde{P}^{(v)}$ denotes the product law of the two independent Bessel processes R and $\widetilde{R}$, issued from (1), and with common index v,

$$A_u \equiv \int_0^u \frac{ds}{R_s^2} \qquad \widetilde{A}_t \equiv \int_0^t \frac{dv}{\widetilde{R}_v^2}$$

$$\hat{Z}(u,v) = (u + \theta_1 N_{A_u} + \theta_2 (R_u^2)v - k)^+$$

(note in particular that the expression of $\hat{Z}$ does not contain the process $\widetilde{R}$ any more).

We now use the proposition which allows us to "get rid" of the exponentials $\exp(-\lambda A_u)$ and $\exp(-u\widetilde{A}_t)$, at the cost of changing the indexes of R and $\widetilde{R}$. Thus, we obtain

$$I = \lambda u \mathbb{E}^{(\gamma_1, \gamma_2)}\left[\int_0^{\infty} \frac{du}{R_v^{2+\gamma_1-v}} \int_0^{\infty} \frac{dv}{\widetilde{R}_v^{2+\gamma_2-v}} \hat{Z}(u,v)\right] \quad (3)$$

where $\gamma_1 = \sqrt{2\lambda + v^2}$, $\gamma_2 = \sqrt{2\mu + v^2}$ and $\mathbb{P}^{(\gamma_1, \gamma_2)}$

STOCHASTIC
TIME
CHANGES IN
CATASTROPHE
OPTION
PRICING

is the product law of the processes R and $\widetilde{R}$, which are now respectively Bessel processes, starting from 1, with indices γ_1 and γ_2.

Since $\widetilde{R}$ does not appear in the expression of $\hat{Z}$, we obtain

$$I = \lambda\mu \int_0^\infty d\upsilon\, h_2(\upsilon) E^{\gamma_1}\left[\int_0^\infty \frac{du}{R_u^{2+\gamma_1-\nu}}\, \hat{Z}(u,\upsilon)\right] \quad (4)$$

where $h_2(\upsilon) \overset{\text{def}}{=} E^{\gamma_2}\left[1/R_\upsilon^{2+\gamma_2-\nu}\right]$ is given by the formula in the above corollary.

Hence, from equation (4), it now remains to compute

$$H_1(\upsilon) \overset{\text{def}}{=} E^{\gamma_1}\left[\int_0^\infty \frac{du}{R_u^{2+\gamma_1-\nu}}\, \hat{Z}(u,\upsilon)\right] \quad (5)$$

and this expression is of the same order of complexity as the expression we denoted by $\psi(\lambda)$ earlier.

Although at this point, we do not find it useful to develop further our methodology, let us sketch a few more steps: from the formula,

$$E\left[\varphi(N_t)\right] = \sum_n \varphi(n)\exp(-\alpha t)\, \frac{(\alpha t)^n}{n!} \quad (\varphi : \mathbb{N} \to \mathbb{R}_+)$$

we obtain

$$H_1(\upsilon) = \sum_{n=0}^\infty \times E^{\gamma_1}\left[\int_0^\infty \frac{du}{R_u^{2+\gamma_1-\nu}}\exp(-\alpha A_u)\,\frac{(\alpha A_u)^n}{n!}\right.$$
$$\left. \times (u + \theta_1 n + \theta_2 R_u^2\upsilon - k)^+\right] \quad (6)$$

hence, the computation now hinges on that of

$$E^\gamma\left[f(R_u\exp(-\alpha A_u)A_u^n\right]$$
$$= (-1)^n\,\frac{d^n}{d\alpha^n}\left(E^\gamma\left[f(R_u)\exp(-\alpha A_u)\right]\right)$$

and the latter expression may be deduced again from the proposition.

As a conclusion, one can observe that the introduction of jumps in the aggregate claims process during the loss period is necessary from a modelling viewpoint to represent the occurrence of catastrophes (the diffusion term accounting for the randomness in claim reporting) and, at the same time, gives rise to interesting mathematical problems. Besides the computations mentioned above, key quantities necessary to obtain numbers for the option and call spread prices are the parameters involved in the risk-adjusted dynamics of the aggregate claim index. When insurance derivatives markets become liquid, it will be possible to obtain them as implied parameters from market prices.

BIBLIOGRAPHY

Aase, K.K., 1995, "An Equilibrium Model of Catastrophe Insurance Futures and Spreads", Reprint.

Clark, P.K., 1973, "A Subordinated Stochastic Process with Finite Variance for Speculative Price", *Econometrica*, 41, pp. 135–56.

Cummins, D. and H. Geman, 1995, "Pricing Catastrophe Insurance Futures and Call Spreads: An Arbitrage Approach", *Journal of Fixed Income*, March, pp. 46–57; reprinted as Chapter 4 of the present volume.

Delbaen, F. and J. Haezendonck, 1989, "A Martingale Approach to Premium Calculation", *Insurance: Mathematics and Economics*, 8, pp. 269–77.

Geman, H., 1994, "CAT Calls", *Risk*, September, pp. 86–9; reprinted as Chapter 3 of the present volume.

Geman, H. and T. Ané, 1996, "Stochastic Subordination", *Risk*, September, pp. 145–9.

Geman, H. and A. Eydeland, 1995, "Domino Effect: Inverting the Laplace Transform", *Risk*, April, pp. 65–7.

Geman, H. and M. Yor, 1993, "Bessel Processes, Asian Options and Perpetuities", *Mathematical Finance*, 3(4), pp. 349–75.

Geman, H. and M. Yor, 1996, "Pricing and Hedging Double-Barrier Options: A Probabilistic Approach", *Mathematical Finance*, 6(4), pp. 365–78.

Harrison, J.-M. and D. Kreps, 1979, "Martingale and arbitrage in multiperiod securities markets", *Journal of Economic Theory*, 20, pp. 381–408.

Harrison, J.-M. and S.-R. Pliska, 1981, "Martingales and Stochastic Integrals in the Theory of Continuous Trading", *Stochastic Processes and their Applications*, 11, pp. 215–60.

Jeanblanc, M. and M. Pontier, 1991, "Optimal Portfolio for a Small Investor in a Market Model with Discontinuous Prices", *Applied Mathematics Option*, 22, pp. 287–310.

Shimko, D., 1992, "The Valuation of Multiple Claim Insurance Contracts", *Journal of Financial and Quantitative Analysis*, 27(2), pp. 229–46; reprinted as Chapter 2 of the present volume.

Wang, C., J. Wang and M. Yu, 1996, "Pricing Catastrophe Insurance. Future Call Spreads: A Randomized Operational Time Approach", *Journal of Risk and Insurance*, 63(4), pp. 599–617.

Yor, M., 1980, "Loi de l'indice du lacet brownien et distribution de Hartman-Watson", *Zeit. für Wahr*, 53, pp. 71–95.

Interest Rate Risk Management and Valuation of the Surrender Option in Life Insurance Policies

Marie Odile Albizzati and Hélyette Geman

Pantheon Assas University, Paris; University Paris IX Dauphine and ESSEC

The valuation of the prepayment option embedded in mortgages has been for some time a subject of attention for practitioners and academics (see Schwartz and Torous,1989), both because of its direct negative effect on the financial value of a bank balance sheet in case of a drop of interest rates and also because of its impact on the design and pricing of mortgage-backed securities. In the same manner, the right for the holder of a life insurance policy to surrender his contract and take advantage of higher yields available in the financial markets is a source of concern for life insurance companies, particularly in the light of the high volatility of interest rates that has prevailed for more than 20 years. To take into account the possibility of early termination of life insurance policies, Asay, Bouyoucos and Marciano, (1989), have offered an option-adjusted spread approach to estimate the financial value for the insurer of outstanding policies. This interesting approach does not however provide the methodology developed by the authors to estimate this spread, since it is the one used by Goldman Sachs in its own pricing models of callable bonds or mortgage-backed securities using its proprietary interest rate lattice. Moreover, as pointed out by Babbel and Zenios (1992), this spread is not easy to estimate in practice and strongly depends on the volatility assumption introduced in the model. We wish in this chapter to address the surrender option pricing problem directly as the valuation of a contingent claim on the insurance company, where the contingency is closely related to the level of interest rates and propose to price by arbitrage arguments the surrender option embedded in life insurance policies. A closed-form solution is derived in the case of a single-premium policy when the investment portfolio consists of a fixed-term zero-coupon bond and the dynamics of stochastic interest rates are driven by the Heath–Jarrow–Morton model. The price of the option is computed in the case of French contracts both using the closed-form expression and through Monte Carlo simulations.

Economic and financial developments over the past 15 years have brought both new opportunities and new challenges for life insurers. On one hand, the uncertainty about pay-as-you-go retirement schemes generated by longer life expectancy and lower birth rates has entailed a shift of savings towards life insurance policies. Non-mortality-related contracts account today for more than 80% of life insurance contracts in France and they amounted to Ffr250 billion in 1993, climbing from Ffr49 billion in 1983.

On the other hand, volatile interest rates, disintermediation and competition from banks and financial institutions offering similar types of products have forced life insurers to promise and guarantee higher rates and hence, to assume the investment risks associated with higher book yields. Moreover, if the guaranteed return is not

Reprinted with permission from the American Risk and Insurance Association. The article first appeared in the Journal of Risk and Insurance, *December 1994.*

INTEREST
RATE RISK
MANAGEMENT
AND
VALUATION OF
THE
SURRENDER
OPTION IN
LIFE
INSURANCE
POLICIES

high enough in comparison with other forms of investment, mainly in the event of a rise in interest rates, policyholders may opt for an early termination of their existing policies and choose a higher-yield alternative offered in the capital markets, such as money market funds. It is the valuation of this surrender option in the context of stochastic interest rates that this chapter addresses, after a quick overview of interest rate risk management for life insurers.

As mentioned earlier, the option-adjusted approach requires the explicit identification of the relevant option in order not to be opaque. Moreover, whether one looks at a single contract or at a pool of contracts, the property of path-dependency has to be taken into account, since several lapses cannot be observed on the same policy. This chapter proposes to look at the problem the other way around and to directly calculate the value of the surrender option embedded in life insurance policies.

This option, which is indeed an exchange option, cannot be priced by the formula provided by Margrabe (1978). Margrabe had the same simplifying assumption of deterministic interest rates as Black–Scholes. Our problem, by definition, is set in the framework of stochastic interest rates. Moreover, Margrabe's exchange option was a European option (with a fixed maturity); in contrast the surrender option has a random exercise date, which is an optimal stopping time. We partly solve the latter difficulty by considering a pool of homogeneous life insurance policies and using the fundamental averaging effect of the insurance mechanism. This leads to evaluating the option by arbitrage under the risk-neutral probability as the expectation of random cashflows occurring at well-defined dates and discounted with stochastic interest rates. We use in a generalised form the forward neutral probability measure introduced by Geman (1989) and Jamshidian (1989), which has already proved very powerful in pricing interest rate derivative instruments, such as floating-rate notes and interest rate swaps (El Karoui–Geman, 1991, 1994).

This chapter is organised as follows: the next section presents some elements on asset liability management in life insurance companies. The following section provides a closed-form expression of the surrender option value in the case of a single-premium policy, when its dollar amount is invested in a fixed-term zero-coupon bond and the dynamics of the term structure of interest rates are assumed to be driven by a one-factor model with

a deterministic term structure of volatilities. Then the option price is computed under different settings of interest rate volatilities, both using the closed-form expression obtained below and through Monte Carlo simulations. The chapter ends with concluding comments.

Managing interest rate risk in European life insurance companies

For decades, the management of insurance companies in Europe was very different from bank management. Real estate located in expensive urban districts consistently appreciated over time, enhancing the firms' assets. The technical management of such companies was essentially the responsibility of insurers having a solid statistical and actuarial culture but not necessarily a full knowledge of modern finance.

It is only in the past 10–15 years that a more financial component has been introduced – by choice or by necessity – for a number of converging reasons. First, the developing reality of the European Economic Community has resulted in tougher competition between banks, insurance companies and financial institutions, within and across countries. Second, the process of mergers and acquisitions has widely developed among insurance companies, inside Europe and worldwide. In the case of an acquisition, the market value of the target firm has to be estimated as precisely as possible; the same applies to mutual companies becoming stock companies. Third, real estate has gone down in value in Europe, even though the decline has been less dramatic than in the US. Last but not least, the gloomy prospects for pay-as-you-go retirement schemes in Europe have generated big opportunities for private pension funds.

The Netherlands today has the highest amount of capital per inhabitant invested in pension funds. In France, there has been over the past few years an explosion of demand for life insurance contracts with no mortality-related component.[1] Intense competition from banks and other financial institutions has led insurers to be concerned about the yields they are able to offer their clients on this type of instrument. One answer has been the marketing of *contrats à taux garanti*, very similar to the American guaranteed insurance contracts (GICs), and requiring the same financial skills in their management. These instruments are accumulation savings vehicles, essentially with no life insurance content (upon death, the policyholder's estate gets the invested money plus accrued interest) and with a

57

INTEREST
RATE RISK
MANAGEMENT
AND
VALUATION OF
THE
SURRENDER
OPTION IN
LIFE
INSURANCE
POLICIES

major tax advantage if there is no early surrender of the policy. In the US, the difficulties and the subsequent necessary adaptation occurred earlier. Very high volatilities of interest rates were already observed in the 1970s; disintermediation had entailed strong competition from other sectors of the financial services industry and insurance companies replied by offering guaranteed yields (eg GICs), sometimes incompatible with a desirable equilibrium of the balance sheet.

For insurance companies, interest rate volatility generates a surplus volatility that needs to be estimated. When interest rates go up, the portfolio of the insurance company, which consists mainly of bonds, decreases in value. At the same time, customers may surrender their existing policies to buy new contracts offering higher yields. Both assets and liabilities are negatively affected. Bankers experience an analogous and equally difficult situation when interest rates go down and rational customers exercise the prepayment option of their mortgages (this has massively been the case in the US in 1992 and 1993). This prepayment has received the attention it deserved from both the academic and professional communities (see, for instance, Schwartz and Torous, 1989). When interest rates go down, life insurance policies may become hardly more attractive than savings passbooks. If this decline occurs after a return has been guaranteed to the policyholders and a proper hedge has not been built, the asset portfolio may not be able to meet the future stream of liabilities.

Consequently, to prevent failures, governmental and federal authorities in the US have imposed more severe regulation on equity requirements (eg risk-based capital). As for the insurers, they have become more aware of asset liability management techniques – both in life insurance and in other sectors of the insurance industry.

Macaulay-type risk indicators measure price responses to shape-preserving (parallel) shocks to the term structure of interest rates. Beyond duration (Macaulay or modified duration), which measures the first order sensitivity to interest rates moves, convexity and even higher order derivatives are used to take into account the fact that interest rate moves are no longer infinitesimal in both developing and developed countries (for example, during the summer of 1992, the overnight interest rate in Sweden climbed to 200%). Moreover, to represent the fact that moves of the yield curve are not parallel, two complementary types of methods are being implemented in most insurance companies.[2]

These methods are, on the one hand, simulations of interest rate variations and of their impact on asset and liability values, on the other hand, a stochastic modelling of the term structure dynamics incorporating the current yield curve and *allowing only for arbitrage free interest rate moves*. Obviously, this stochastic modelling of the yield curve is necessary to price any optional feature embedded in the balance sheet, such as the surrender option that will be studied later in this chapter.

In Europe, a similar evolution is being observed. The same or more severe regulatory rules are being established both within each country and at the EEC level. The most famous is the Cooke ratio (defined by the July 1988 Basle Agreement on Banking Regulations and Supervisory Practices), which defines an equity requirement for all European banks. It imposes a minimum value of 8% for the ratio of capital divided by a weighted sum of the assets, the weights being an increasing function of default risk. The analogous constraints would not be too binding for insurance companies since European insurers (German, Swiss and French) hold a high amount of equity and reserves. In France, though, profits have decreased and insurers need to enhance their competitiveness and the quality of their management. In particular, life insurers are concerned by the possibility of experiencing a wave of early termination of policies in the event of a rise of interest rates. They are as much concerned by the surrender option as their banker colleagues are by the prepayment options embedded in mortgages. This surrender option is studied at length in the next section.

Valuation of the surrender option
The first part of this section describes the characteristics of the insurance policy under analysis as well as the tax rules applying to it. We then introduce a stochastic modelling of the term structure dynamics allowing only for arbitrage-free movements and price in this setting the surrender option when exercised at a well-defined date. Using the insurance pooling of risks principle, we are able to take into account the random nature of the time of occurrence of policies lapses and provide a closed-form expression for the surrender option.

DESCRIPTION OF THE CONTRACT
❏ The insurance policy may be bought in a lump sum or a series of payments. As in Asay *et al* (1991), who deal with single-premium deferred

INTEREST
RATE RISK
MANAGEMENT
AND
VALUATION OF
THE
SURRENDER
OPTION IN
LIFE
INSURANCE
POLICIES

annuities, we suppose in our model that a single premium is paid at inception of the contract and denote by K_0 the proceeds for the insurer at time 0 after the up-front fees have been paid. (The up-front fees can be categorised as investment and administrative expenses and are significant since they represent 5% of the policyholder's investment.)

❏ The lifetime of the policy is $T = 8$ years if there is neither early termination nor rollover.

❏ Corresponding to this liability, French insurance companies build a portfolio consisting mainly of bonds. For simplicity, we will assume that the assets associated with these policies are zero-coupon bonds having the same maturity as the contract.

❏ For a contract that is held for eight years, a guaranteed minimum return is paid to the policyholder. We represent the return effectively paid to the policyholder as $\lambda R(0,T)$ where λ is a positive constant not greater than one and $R(0,T)$ denotes the yield on a zero-coupon bond maturing at time T. $\lambda = 0.9$ is an accurate description of French insurers' practice. Consequently, at maturity, the value of the policy is $K(T) = K_0 e^{\lambda TR(0,T)}$; for simplicity, we will take $K_0 = 1$.

❏ The contract under analysis, "*contrat à taux garanti*", is a tax-advantaged savings product offered by life insurers. Interest income on the policy is tax-free in France if it is held for eight years. In the case of early surrender, the tax rate is different depending on whether surrender occurs before or after four years. A proper representation of this tax rate at time t is:

$$x(t) = 0.381 \; I_{(t<4)} + 0.181 \; I_{(4 \leq t < 8)}$$

where I denotes the indicator function.

❏ Because of competition, the penalty on early surrender, limited by the regulator, is in practice very small. For simplicity, we will assume there is none. Consequently, the capital received by a policyholder terminating his contract at time t, also called the cash surrender value, amounts to $V_s(t) = e^{\lambda t R(0,T)}$.

After tax, the payoff for the policyholder reduces to:

$$K(t) = 1 + (e^{\lambda t R(0,T)} - 1)(1 - x(t))$$

❏ The interest rate that would prevail on a new contract of the same nature bought at time t is $R(t,T)$, yield on a zero-coupon bond maturing at time $t + T$, whose market value is:

$$B(t,T + t) = e^{-TR(t,T)}$$

VALUATION OF A EUROPEAN SURRENDER OPTION

For the insurer the market value of the zero-coupon bonds (in number $1/B(0,T)$ when the up-front proceeds amount to US$1) associated with this contract in the assets portfolio is:

$$V_m(t) = \frac{B(t,T)}{B(0,T)}$$

We can write:

$$V_s(t) = e^{\lambda R(0,T)t} = V_m(t) + h(t) \qquad (1)$$

where the cashflow $h(t)$ (positive or negative) is guaranteed by the insurer. The rational policyholder compares, at any time t, the terminal value of his contract held to maturity, $K(T)$, with the terminal value of a new contract initiated at time t under the same financial conditions, ie:

$$K(t)(1 - \beta)e^{\lambda(T-t)R(t,T)}$$

where β represents the up-front management fees if starting a new contract.

Remembering that $K(T) = e^{\lambda TR(0,T)}$, we see that a necessary condition for surrender at time t is $D(t) > 1$ where

$$D(t) = \frac{(1 - \beta)K(t)e^{\lambda(T-t)R(t,T)}}{e^{\lambda TR(0,T)}} \qquad (2)$$

will be called the decision criterion and also be denoted D_t.

The option will be exercised at time t by the rational policyholder only if $D_t > 1$. We can observe that $D(t) > 1 \Leftrightarrow R(t,T) > \gamma(t)$ where:

$$\gamma(t) = \frac{T}{T - t} R(0,T) - \frac{1}{\lambda(T - t)} \ln\left|(1 - \beta)K(t)\right| \qquad (3)$$

These different quantities are represented in Figures 1 and 2. Figure 1, which plots over time the cash surrender value $V_s(t)$ and the after tax pay-off to the policyholder $K(t)$, illustrates the case where $D_t > 1$ for $t = 3$. Figure 2 plots over time the values of $R(t,T)$ for which $D(t) = 1$ when the guaranteed return at time 0 is equal to 6%, the up-front management fees β when starting a new contract equal to 5% and assuming there are no surrender charges. Remembering that the surrender option is in fact an American option since it does not have a maturity known at inception of the contract, we represent in

Figure 3 the random cashflow provided by the exercise of the American option, namely the quantity:

$$h(t)I_{(D(t)>1)} \quad \text{where} \quad t \in [0,T]$$

In a first stage, we are going to assume that this option can only be exercised at a well-defined time t. We will justify later how this assumption fits into the real situation of an insurance company managing a pool of contracts. The uncertainty in the economy is represented by a probability space (Ω, F, P). The accruing information available to all agents is represented by the filtration $(F_r)_{t\geq0}$ satisfying the usual conditions. Assuming the surrender option could only be exercised at time t (t deterministic and belonging to the interval $[0,T]$), its value at date 0 that we denote by $C^t(0)$, even though it is in fact a put option, is

$$C^t(0) = E_Q\left[h(t) I_{(D(t)>1)} e^{-\int_0^t r(s)ds}\right] \quad (4)$$

where:

❏ $(r(s))_{s\geq0}$ denotes the short-term interest rate process; $r(t)$ is supposed to be F_t-measurable.
❏ Q denotes the risk-adjusted probability measure equivalent to P under which basic securities discounted prices are martingales (see Harrison–Kreps, 1979; Harrison–Pliska, 1981); moreover, we assume market completeness, which ensures the existence of a price for any contingent claim (in our model described below, this is not even an assumption since we have one source of randomness and certainly at least two non-redundant securities are traded in the market).
❏ $h(t)$ has been defined as

$$h(t) = V_s(t) - V_m(t) = e^{\lambda t R(0,T)} - \frac{B(t,T)}{B(0,T)}$$

STOCHASTIC MODELLING OF THE TERM STRUCTURE DYNAMICS

We describe the interest rate movements through the zero-coupon bond dynamics under Q and assume the latter are driven by a particular case of the Heath–Jarrow–Morton model:

$$\frac{dB(t,T)}{B(t,T)} = r(t)dt + \sigma(t,T)dW_t \quad (5)$$

where $(W(t))_{t\geq0}$ is a Q-Brownian motion and where we assume deterministic volatilities of the

form $\sigma(t,T) = \sigma[1 - e^{-a(T-t)}/a]$ with a and σ positive constants. This specification of the volatility term structure leads to Gaussian interest rates and closed-form expressions for most interest rate derivative instruments prices (see Cohen and Heath, 1992). We want to underline the fact that, as of today, the superiority of two (or more) factors over one-factor models of interest rates is still a matter of debate in the financial literature (see Cohen and Heath, 1992). Consequently, it appears that overcoming the difficulties involved

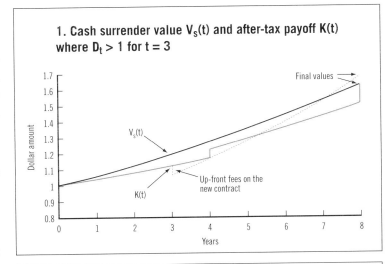

1. Cash surrender value $V_s(t)$ and after-tax payoff $K(t)$ where $D_t > 1$ for $t = 3$

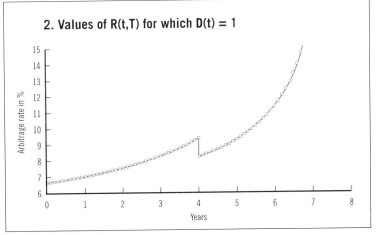

2. Values of $R(t,T)$ for which $D(t) = 1$

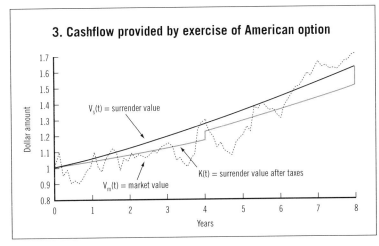

3. Cashflow provided by exercise of American option

INTEREST
RATE RISK
MANAGEMENT
AND
VALUATION OF
THE
SURRENDER
OPTION IN
LIFE
INSURANCE
POLICIES

in the surrender option pricing and providing a closed-form solution easy to compute with the specific parameters of each insurance company may be quite useful, even in the context of a one-factor model.

The first difficulty in the calculation of C in equation (4) is to pull the discount factor out of the expectation operator; for that, we introduce the forward neutral probability measure Q_t relative to time t, defined by its Radon–Nikodym derivative with respect to Q:

$$\frac{dQ_t}{dQ} = \frac{e^{-\int_0^t r(s)ds}}{B(0,t)}$$

$$= \exp\left\{\int_0^t \sigma(s,t)dW_s - \frac{1}{2}\int_0^t |\sigma(s,t)|^2 ds\right\}$$

(see Geman, 1989), and, from Girsanov's theorem, the relationship:

$$dW_s^t = dW_s - \sigma(s,t)ds \qquad (6)$$

defines $(W_s^t)_{s\geq 0}$ as a Q_t-Brownian motion.

We can observe that this change of probability measure, meant to absorb the stochastic nature of interest rates up to time t, consists in fact in taking as a new numéraire the zero-coupon bond maturing at time t.

From equation (5) and the relationship $B(t,T+t) = e^{-TR(t,T)}$ we derive:

$$R(t,T) = f(0,t,T) - \int_0^t \frac{\sigma(s,T+t) - \sigma(s,t)}{T} dW_s$$

$$+ \frac{1}{2}\int_0^t \frac{\sigma^2(s,T+t) - \sigma^2(s,t)}{T} ds$$

where $f(0,t,T)$ represents the forward rate observed at time 0 relative to the period $[t,t+T]$.

Using (6), we can also write:

$$R(t,T) = f(0,t,T) - \int_0^t \frac{\sigma(s,T+t) - \sigma(s,t)}{T} dW_s^t$$

$$+ \frac{T}{2} \text{Var } R(t,T)$$

$$(7)$$

where:

$$\text{Var } R(t,T) = \int_0^t \frac{|\sigma(s,T+t) - \sigma(s,t)|^2}{T^2} ds$$

$$= \frac{\sigma^2}{2T^2}\left(\frac{1-e^{-aT}}{a}\right)^2\left(\frac{1-e^{-2at}}{a}\right)$$

Coming back to equation (4) and using the expression of h(t) derived from equation (3), we obtain:

$$C^t(0) = E_Q\left[e^{\lambda t R(0,T)}e^{-\int_0^t r(s)ds}\,I_{(D(t)>1)}\right]$$

$$- E_Q\left[\frac{B(t,T)}{B(0,T)}\,e^{-\int_0^t r(s)ds}\,I_{(D(t)>1)}\right]$$

Introducing the new probability measure Q_t, the first expectation can easily be written as:

$$B(0,t)e^{\lambda t R(0,T)}E_{Q_t}\left(I_{(D(t)>1)}\right)$$

The second one, in the same manner, is equal to:

$$\frac{B(0,t)}{B(0,T)}\,E_{Q_t}\left(B(t,T)I_{(D(t)>1)}\right)$$

Using the general change of numéraires formula established in Geman–El Karoui–Rochet (1992):

$$X(0)E_{Q_X}[Y(T)\phi] = Y(0)E_{Q_y}[X(T)\phi]$$

where X and Y are two arbitrary securities and ϕ an F_T-measurable random cashflow, the second expectation simply reduces to

$$E_{Q_T}\left(I_{(D(t)>1)}\right)$$

and the put option price $C^t(0)$ appears as:

$$C^t(0) = e^{\lambda t R(0,T)}B(0,t)E_{Q_t}\left(I_{(D(t)>1)}\right) - E_{Q_T}\left(I_{(D(t)>1)}\right)$$

$$(8)$$

We observed that $D(t) > 1 \Leftrightarrow R(t,T) > \gamma(t)$. Using the dynamics of $R(t,T)$ described in equation (7) and the fact that $(R(s,T))_{s\geq 0}$ is a Gaussian process under Q_t, it is easy to show with standard probability arguments that:

$$E_{Q_T}\left(I_{(D(T)>1)}\right) = N(d_1^t)$$

where N denotes the cumulative function of the normal distribution and:

$$d_1^t = \frac{-\gamma(t) + f(0,t,T) + \frac{T}{2}\text{Var } R(t,T)}{\sqrt{\text{Var } R(t,T)}}$$

61

INTEREST
RATE RISK
MANAGEMENT
AND
VALUATION OF
THE
SURRENDER
OPTION IN
LIFE
INSURANCE
POLICIES

Let us emphasise here that the hypothesis of deterministic volatilities in (5) induces Gaussian interest rates and a significant tractability in the calculations.

We now introduce for $u > t$ a similar Brownian motion change as in (6):

$$dW_s^u = dW_s - \sigma(s,u)ds$$

and can write

$$R(t,T) = f(0,t,T) + \frac{T}{2} \text{Var } R(t,T)$$
$$- (u - t)\text{Cov}(R(t,T),R(t,(u - t)))$$
$$- \int_0^t \frac{\sigma(s,T + t) - \sigma(s,t)}{T} dW_s^u$$

Consequently, for $u > t$,

$$E_{Q_u}[R(t,T)] = E_{Qt}[R(t,T)]$$
$$- (u - t)\text{Cov}(R(t,T),R(t,u - t))$$

where:

$$\text{Cov}(R(t,T),R(t,u - t))$$
$$= \frac{T}{u - t} \text{Var } R(t,T) \frac{1 - e^{-a(u - t)}}{1 - e^{-aT}}$$

Coming back to equation (8), we can write:

$$E_{Q_T}\left(I_{(D(t) > 1)}\right) = N(d_2^t)$$

where:

$$d_2^t = d_1^t - \frac{(T - t)\text{cov}(R(t,T - t),R(t,T))}{\sqrt{\text{Var } R(t,T)}}$$

which finally gives:

$$C^t(0) = e^{\lambda t R(0,T)}B(0,t)N(d_1^t) - N(d_2^t) \quad (8')$$

Equation (8') now looks like the Black–Scholes formula, or more precisely like Margrabe's formula generalised to stochastic interest rates. This is not surprising, since the surrender option is nothing but an exchange option, in a context of interest rates necessarily non-deterministic (otherwise, the option would not exist).

Numerical values are calculated for the European options with maturities $t = 1,2,...,7$ for different parameter values. The initial term structure of interest rates is taken on June 25, 1993, which is date 0. The parameter a, proved

in earlier studies (El Karoui–Geman, 1991, 1993) to be stable over large periods of time, is set at the value 0.1; from the study of liquid interest rate derivative securities at different dates the second parameter σ, crucial in the term structure of volatilities, is shown by the same authors to be comprised between 2% and 3%. The value $\beta = 5\%$ represents the standard up-front management fees in France. We run the calculations for $\lambda = 0.9$ which is a fair representation of the real situation and also, for the sake of comparison in two other cases $\lambda = 0.75$ and $\lambda = 1$. Figures 4a and 4b plot the value at time 0 of the surrender option as a function of the date of exercise for the volatility parameter σ set equal to 2% and 3%.

At this point, we want to make two important observations, one practical, the other theoretical:

❏ At variance with a belief shared by a number of insurers preoccupied by this problem, the

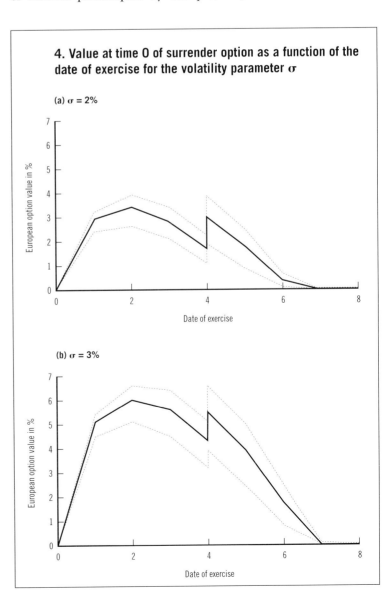

4. Value at time 0 of surrender option as a function of the date of exercise for the volatility parameter σ

(a) $\sigma = 2\%$

(b) $\sigma = 3\%$

62

INTEREST
RATE RISK
MANAGEMENT
AND
VALUATION OF
THE
SURRENDER
OPTION IN
LIFE
INSURANCE
POLICIES

maximum value of the "European" option is observed for maturities falling between two and four years after inception of the contract and not for maturities greater than four years. This shows that the tax effect is dominated by the time value of the option.

❏ One must keep in mind that, as is always the case for American options, the surrender option on a policy has a greater value than the supremum of the values of the corresponding European option for different possible exercise dates.

THE CASE OF A POOL OF LIFE INSURANCE POLICIES

The fundamental feature of insurance is the pooling of risks. From the viewpoint of the insurer, the surrender option on a pool of life insurance policies can be represented by the frequency $p(t)$ of the policies which are early terminated at time t, where $t = 1, 2, ..., (T-1)$, since policy covenants permit only lapses at the end of the calendar year.

This property, typical of the insurance mechanism, will allow us to address the difficulty raised by the American nature of the surrender option and is consequently crucial to exhibit a closed form expression for the surrender option.

Lapse behaviour We denote by $p(t)$ or p_t the proportion of lapses at date t among the contracts still alive in the pool and express $p(t)$ as a deterministic function f of the decision criterion D_t. Moreover, as it is often assumed in models of mortgage prepayments (see d'Andria, Elie, Boulier, 1990, for instance), we represent f as a non-decreasing piecewise linear function of the variable D_t. The existence of lapses reflecting policyholders' personal circumstances (including death) and independent of financial considerations accounts for a non-zero value for p_t even when D_t is below the value D_1 corresponding to the minimum threshold worth undertaking the paperwork of early surrender. These "irrational" lapses are analogous to non-economic prepayments on low-rate mortgages. In the same manner, some rational lapses never occur and a reasonable specification of p_t is described in Figure 5.

As observed earlier, we are led to the valuation of a set of European options with different dates of exercise. The cashflows associated with the pool of insurance policies (taking into account the possible surrenders at times

$1, 2, ..., T-1$) are the following:

Dates	0	1...	t	T
Liabilities	0	$p_1 V_s(1)$	$a_t p_t V_s(t)$	$a_T V_s(T)$
Assets	0			$\dfrac{1}{B(0,T)}$

where a_t denotes the proportion of policies in the pool still alive at time t. If there was no surrender, the cashflows on the pool would be:

Dates	0	1...	t	T
Liabilities	0	0	0	$a_T V_s(T)$
Assets	0		$a_T \dfrac{1}{B(0,T)}$	

and we obtain by difference the flows corresponding to the surrender option:

Dates	0	1...	t	T
Liabilities	0	$p_1 V_s(1)$	$a_t p_t V_s(t)$	0
Assets	0		$(1 - a_T) \dfrac{1}{B(0,T)}$	

where $V_s(t) = e^{\lambda t R(0,T)}$.

We can observe that the cashflows in the last table – which correspond to the cost for the insurer of the surrender option – depend on the management policy decided by the insurance company, both through the choice of the assets portfolio associated with the contracts under analysis (in our model, zero-coupon bonds) and through the coefficient λ which defines how much of the portfolio yield goes to the policyholder.

The value C at time 0 of the surrender option is obtained by arbitrage arguments from the series of cashflows described above:

$$C = E_Q \left[\sum_{t=1}^{T-1} e^{-\int_0^t r(s)ds} p_t a_t V_s(t) \right.$$

$$\left. - e^{-\int_0^T r(s)ds}(1 - a_T) \frac{1}{B(0,T)} \right]$$

$$= \sum_{t=1}^{T-1} B(0,t) E_{Q_t}[p_t a_t V_s(t)] - E_{Q_t}(1 - a_T)$$

This formula features the fact that the surrender option on a pool of policies is a portfolio of Black and Scholes-type options and is very similar to the expression of a coupon-bond option under Gaussian interest rates.

Observing that

$$a_T + \sum_{j=1}^{T-1} p_j a_j = 1$$

63

INTEREST
RATE RISK
MANAGEMENT
AND
VALUATION OF
THE
SURRENDER
OPTION IN
LIFE
INSURANCE
POLICIES

we can also write:

$$C = \sum_{t=1}^{T-1} E_{Q_t}\left[e^{-\int_0^t r(s)ds} p_t a_t\left(V_s(t) - \frac{B(t,T)}{B(0,T)}\right)\right]$$

This latter expression exhibits the loss at each time t due to the early termination of the policies, namely:

$$p_t a_t (V_s(t) - V_m(t))$$

where, as was defined before, $V_s(t)$ is the value of the policy when terminated at date t and $V_m(t)$ is the market value of the assets portfolio.

At this point, we will address the numerical problem both by going further into the analytical solution and also by using Monte Carlo simulations. We will compare the values obtained by the two methods.

Numerical valuation of the surrender option

We will first compute the option value using the closed-form expression exhibited in the previous section of this chapter.

Returning to equation (9):

$$C = \sum_{t=1}^{T-1} B(0,t) E_{Q_t}[p_t a_t V_s(t)] - E_{Q_T}(1 - a_T)$$

We must observe that, for $2 \leq t \leq T$,

$$a_t = \prod_{k=1}^{t-1}(1 - p_k)$$

As $V_s(t) = e^{\lambda t R(0,T)}$ is deterministic, the difficulty remaining after the introduction of the new set of probability measures Q_t is the computation of:

$$E_{Q_t}\left[p_t \prod_{k=1}^{t-1}(1 - p_k)\right]$$

Since p_t depends on the interest rates prevailing at time t and the p_k, for $k < t$, depend on the interest rates at time k prior to t, these quantities are not independent. Assuming this independence – and again, this approximation can be justified by the insurance mechanism – we can write, for $u \geq t$:

$$E_{Q_u}(p_u a_u) = E_{Q_u}(p_u) \prod_{t=1}^{u-1} E_{Q_u}(1 - p_t)$$

where:

$$p_t = f(D_t) = p_{min} I_{(D(t)<D_1)}$$

$$+ \left(\frac{p_{max} - p_{min}}{D_2 - D_1} D_t + \frac{p_{max}D_1 - p_{min}D_2}{D_1 - D_2}\right) I_{(D_1 \leq D_t < D_2)}$$

$$+ p_{max} I_{(D(t) \geq D_2)}$$

Using the same calculations as the ones following equation (8), we can determine real numbers e_u^t and ε_u^t such that:

$$E_{Q_u}\left(I_{(D(t) \geq D_1)}\right) = N(e_u^t)$$

and:

$$E_{Q_u}\left(I_{(D(t) \geq D_2)}\right) = N(\varepsilon_u^t)$$

The only remaining difficulty now comes from the computation of

$$E_{Q_u}\left(D_t \, I_{D(t) \geq D_1}\right)$$

and the analogous expression with D_2.

Remembering that $D(t) = (1 - \beta)e^{-\lambda TR(0,T)}K(t) e^{\lambda(T-t)R(t,T)}$, we can factor the deterministic part $g(t) = (1 - \beta)e^{-\lambda TR(0,T)}K(t)$ and write:

$$D(t) = g(t)e^{\lambda(T-t)R(t,T)}$$

Moreover, we can observe that $D(t) \geq D_1 \Leftrightarrow R(t,T) \geq h(t)$ where:

$$h(t) = \frac{1}{\lambda(T-t)} \ln\left(\frac{D_1}{g(t)}\right)$$

and:

$$E_{Q_u}\left(D(t) \, I_{(D(t) \geq D_1)}\right) = g(t)E_{Q_u}\left[e^{\lambda(T-t)R(t,T)} \, I_{(R(t,T) \geq h(t))}\right]$$

Introducing a final change of probability measure Q_{u^*} and the Q_{u^*}-Brownian motion $(W_s^{u^*})$ defined through Girsanov's theorem by:

$$dW_s^{u^*} = dW_s^u + \lambda\left(\frac{T-t}{T}\right)(\sigma(s,T+t) - \sigma(s,t))ds$$

we obtain:

$$E_{Q_u}\left(D(t) \, I_{(D(t) \geq D_1)}\right)$$

$$= g(t)\exp\left[\lambda(T-t)E_{Q_u}(R(t,T))\right]$$

$$\times E_{Q_u}\left[\exp\left(\frac{\lambda^2(T-t)^2}{2} \text{ Var } R(t,T) \, I_{(R(t,T) \geq h(t))}\right)\right]$$

64

INTEREST
RATE RISK
MANAGEMENT
AND
VALUATION OF
THE
SURRENDER
OPTION IN
LIFE
INSURANCE
POLICIES

Table 1. Sensitivity to the slope of the initial yield curve

Slope	$\sigma = 2\%$	$\sigma = 3\%$
Negative	C = 0	C = 1.69
Null	C = 0.29	C = 2.16
Positive	C = 0.73	C = 2.85

Table 2. Sensitivity to the level of the initial yield curve

Level	$\sigma = 2\%$	$\sigma = 3\%$
Yield curve of June 25, 1993	C = 0.73	C = 2.85
Downward parallel move of 1%	C = 0.91	C = 3.11
Upward parallel move of 1%	C = 0.57	C = 2.61

$$= g(t)\exp\left[\frac{\lambda^2(T-t)^2}{2} Var\,R(t,T)\right.$$

$$\left. + \lambda(T-t)E_{Q_u}R(t,T)\right]E_{Q_u}\left[I_{(R(t,T)\geq h(t))}\right]$$

We can observe again that the assumption of deterministic interest rates allowed us to provide such an explicit formula.

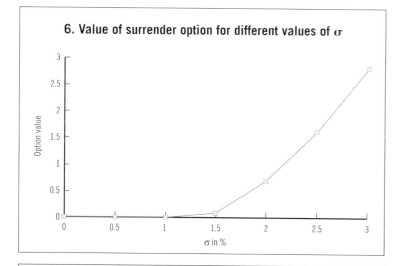

6. Value of surrender option for different values of σ

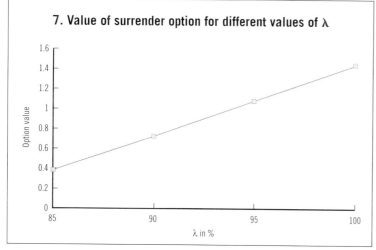

7. Value of surrender option for different values of λ

At this point, we can compute the different quantities obtained in this expression. We use again the term structure observed on June 25, 1993 (date 0) and the parameters a and σ described earlier. As mentioned before, $D_1 = 1$; $D_2 = 1.5$: $P_{min} = 0.03$; $P_{max} = 0.6$.

We obtain for the surrender option values the following results:

$$\sigma = 2\% \qquad \sigma = 3\%$$
$$C = 0.7 \qquad C = 2.9$$

Another method, which avoids the approximation in the expectation of the product of the probabilities p_k, is to use directly in equation (9) Monte Carlo simulations which allow us to fully take into account the fact that the cashflows associated with the pool of insurance policies under analysis are path-dependent. The cashflow in any given period depends not only upon the current levels of interest rates through p_t, but also upon the entire history of interest rates relevant to the pool through the numbers

$$a_t = \prod_{(k<t)}(1 - p_k)$$

As observed earlier, for $k = 1,2, \dots T - 1$, p_k is a function of $R(k,T)$. Starting from the yield curve observed at time 0 (which provides in particular the forward rates), we simulate the quantities:

$$R(k,T) = f(0,k,T) - \int_0^k \frac{\sigma(s,T+k) - \sigma(s,k)}{T}dW_s$$

$$+ \frac{1}{2}\int_0^k \frac{\sigma^2(s,T+k) - \sigma^2(s,k)}{T}ds$$

We calculate an approximate value for the stochastic integral involved in the second term and, using 500 draws, the simulations provide the following intervals of values:

$$\sigma = 2\% \qquad \sigma = 3\%$$
$$[0.65; 0.76] \qquad [2.2; 2.6]$$

The width of these intervals may be explained by the long time to maturity (eight years) of the surrender option.

SENSITIVITY OF THE OPTION PRICE TO DIFFERENT FACTORS

Influence of the initial yield curve The initial yield curve is a significant parameter in the evaluation of the option. The price of the surrender

65

INTEREST
RATE RISK
MANAGEMENT
AND
VALUATION OF
THE
SURRENDER
OPTION IN
LIFE
INSURANCE
POLICIES

option increases with the slope of the initial yield curve and decreases with the level of the initial yield curve (see Tables 1 and 2 on the previous page).

Sensitivity to the volatility of interest rates
The two parameters involved in the term structure of volatilities are a and σ. We observed earlier that the parameter a is very stable over time and we set it equal to 0.1. Figure 6 plots the values of the surrender option on the pool of contracts for different values of σ between 0 and 3%.

Sensitivity to the choice of λ Figure 7 represents the values of the option empirically obtained for different values of λ. Interestingly, the value of the surrender option on the pool of contracts appears as an affine function of the coefficient λ, at least for realistic values of this parameter.

Sensitivity to the specification of the function f
The choice of the surrender rate function f plays an essential role. The price of the option increases with the slope of this function which reflects the "intensity" of rational behaviour in the pool. The price of the option also naturally increases with the width of the interval $[p_{min}, p_{max}]$, which expresses again a more rational behaviour of the policyholders on both ends.

Conclusion
The possibility of early surrender of life insurance policies is a systemic risk for insurers since the option value is a significant percentage of the policy value, which amounts in France to several billion francs. Insurers face two difficult choices: either experiencing early terminations of life insurance contracts or guaranteeing a high yield to avoid these surrenders – in which case the management of the corresponding assets portfolio becomes difficult.

Consequently, it is necessary for insurers to estimate the value of the existing surrender options in the portfolio of insurance policies and to hedge the risk they represent. This hedge can be achieved by incorporating floating-rate notes in the assets portfolio and other financial instruments, in particular interest rate caps, which are commonly available for seven to 10-year maturities and would suit the insurer's needs. These caps should be tied to the interest rate index most closely related to the policy lapses which need to be hedged – in our example the TMO (the taux moyen obligataire), an average T-bond yield. At variance with reinsurance, early termination of the coverage is easy to achieve when it is no longer necessary. The insurer can recoup part of the initial premium either by selling back to the issuer the remaining portion of the cap or by taking an opposite position in a new cap with characteristics identical to the remaining part of the first one. Obviously, these caps would only be an efficient hedge against interest rate-related policy surrenders. As far as other lapses are concerned (whether they are due to mortality or other factors), the appropriate funding is determined through actuarial expertise. In either case, the coverage cost must be incorporated in the coefficient λ and in the up-front fees when defining the marketing policy of the company.

Appendix

Numerical valuation of the option
The lifetime of the option (and of the policy, if no surrender occurs) is $T = 8$ years. Lapses can only occur at times $t = 1, 2 ..., 7$.

The set of parameters is the following

❑ To describe the function $p_t = f(D_t)$
  $P_{min} = 3\%$; $P_{max} = 60\%$
  $d_1 = 1$; $d_2 = 1.5$

❑ To describe the term structure dynamics

  • The yield curve at time 0 has the following increasing shape:

θ	0	1	2	3	4	5	6	7	8	9	10	11	12	13	14	15
$R(0,\theta)$ in %	6	6.1	6.2	6.3	6.4	6.5	6.6	6.7	6.8	6.9	7	7.1	7.2	7.3	7.4	7.5

  • The parameter a is set equal to 0.1

  • The parameter σ observed at time 0 is equal to 2% but we also run the calculations for a higher volatility $\sigma = 3\%$

❑ To describe the management fees

  $\lambda = 0.9$; $\beta = 5\%$

66

INTEREST
RATE RISK
MANAGEMENT
AND
VALUATION OF
THE
SURRENDER
OPTION IN
LIFE
INSURANCE
POLICIES

Computation of $E_{Q_u}(pt)$ for $u \geq t$

(a) $\sigma = 2\%$

	t=1	t=2	t=3	t=4	t=5	t=6	t=7
u=1	0.047						
u=2	0.047	0.050					
u=3	0.047	0.049	0.045				
u=4	0.046	0.048	0.044	0.046			
u=5	0.046	0.048	0.043	0.047	0.038		
u=6	0.046	0.047	0.043	0.046	0.038	0.031	
u=7	0.045	0.047	0.042	0.046	0.037	0.031	0.030
u=8	0.045	0.047	0.042	0.045	0.037	0.031	0.030

(b) $\sigma = 3\%$

	t=1	t=2	t=3	t=4	t=5	t=6	t=7
u=1	0.070						
u=2	0.068	0.076					
u=3	0.067	0.074	0.069				
u=4	0.066	0.072	0.067	0.072			
u=5	0.065	0.070	0.065	0.070	0.055		
u=6	0.064	0.069	0.063	0.070	0.053	0.038	
u=7	0.063	0.067	0.061	0.065	0.051	0.037	0.030
u=8	0.062	0.066	0.060	0.064	0.050	0.036	0.030

$P_{Q_u}(D_t < 1) = N(D(t,u,1))$

(a) $\sigma = 2\%$

	t=1	t=2	t=3	t=4	t=5	t=6	t=7
u=1	0.736						
u=2	0.742	0.744					
u=3	0.747	0.752	0.796				
u=4	0.752	0.758	0.804	0.726			
u=5	0.756	0.765	0.811	0.737	0.832		
u=6	0.760	0.770	0.818	0.746	0.830	0.950	
u=7	0.763	0.775	0.823	0.754	0.838	0.953	
u=8	0.766	0.780	0.828	0.762	0.845	0.956	

(b) $\sigma = 3\%$

	t=1	t=2	t=3	t=4	t=5	t=6	t=7
u=1	0.647						
u=2	0.657	0.647					
u=3	0.666	0.661	0.686				
u=4	0.674	0.673	0.701	0.627			
u=5	0.681	0.684	0.714	0.645	0.703		
u=6	0.688	0.693	0.726	0.661	0.720	0.844	
u=7	0.693	0.702	0.736	0.675	0.736	0.856	0.994
u=8	0.699	0.709	0.746	0.688	0.749	0.867	0.995

$E_{Q_u}(D_t 1_{D_t<1})$

(a) $\sigma = 2\%$

	t=1	t=2	t=3	t=4	t=5	t=6	t=7
u=1	0.668						
u=2	0.673	0.665					
u=3	0.677	0.671	0.707				
u=4	0.681	0.676	0.713	0.815			
u=5	0.684	0.681	0.718	0.819	0.751		
u=6	0.687	0.685	0.722	0.823	0.758	0.869	
u=7	0.690	0.689	0.726	0.825	0.764	0.871	0.900
u=8	0.693	0.692	0.730	0.829	0.769	0.872	0.899

(b) $\sigma = 3\%$

	t=1	t=2	t=3	t=4	t=5	t=6	t=7
u=1	0.570						
u=2	0.578	0.559					
u=3	0.585	0.570	0.590				
u=4	0.591	0.579	0.601	0.688			
u=5	0.597	0.587	0.611	0.699	0.630		
u=6	0.602	0.594	0.620	0.708	0.644	0.765	
u=7	0.606	0.600	0.627	0.716	0.655	0.774	0.898
u=8	0.610	0.605	0.633	0.723	0.666	0.782	0.897

Var(R(t,T)) in %

(a) $\sigma = 2\%$

	t=1	t=2	t=3	t=4	t=5	t=6	t=7
T=8	0.017	0.031	0.043	0.052	0.060	0.066	0.071

(b) $\sigma = 3\%$

	t=1	t=2	t=3	t=4	t=5	t=6	t=7
T=8	0.039	0.070	0.096	0.117	0.135	0.149	0.161

$E_{Q_u}(R(t,T))$ in %, T = 8 years

(a) $\sigma = 2\%$

	t=1	t=2	t=3	t=4	t=5	t=6	t=7
u=1	7.1						
u=2	7	7.3					
u=3	7	7.3	7.6				
u=4	7	7.2	7.5	7.8			
u=5	7	7.2	7.5	7.7	8		
u=6	7	7.2	7.4	7.7	8	8.3	
u=7	7	7.1	7.4	7.6	7.9	8.2	8.5
u=8	6.9	7.1	7.3	7.6	7.8	8.1	8.4

(b) $\sigma = 3\%$

	t=1	t=2	t=3	t=4	t=5	t=6	t=7
u=1	7.2						
u=2	7.1	7.5					
u=3	7.1	7.4	7.8				
u=4	7	7.3	7.7	8.1			
u=5	7	7.2	7.5	7.9	8.3		
u=6	6.9	7.1	7.4	7.8	8.2	8.6	
u=7	6.9	7.1	7.3	7.6	8	8.4	8.8
u=8	6.9	7	7.2	7.5	7.8	8.2	8.6

Numerical value of the option: $\sigma = 2\%$ C = 0.76%; $\sigma = 3\%$ C = 2.9%

1 Pension Funds and their Advisers, *1993, AP Information Services.*

2 *Idem.*

BIBLIOGRAPHY

d'Andria, P., J.F. Boulier and L. Elie, 1991, "Modele Analytique d'Evaluation des Options de Remboursement Anticipe", *Finance*, 12 (2).

Asay, M., P. Bouyaoucos and A. Marciano, 1989, "An Economic Approach to Valuation of Single Premium Deferred Annuities", Goldman Sachs research paper.

Babbel, D.F. and S.A. Zenios, 1992, "Pitfalls in the Analysis of Option-Adjusted Spreads", *Financial Analysts Journal*, July–August.

Black, F. and M. Scholes, 1973, "The Pricing of Options and Corporate Liabilities", *Journal of Political Economy*, 81.

Cohen, H. and D. Heath, 1992, "Testing Models for Valuation of Interest Rate Dependent Securities", Conference on Mathematical Finance, Paris.

El Karoui, N. and H. Geman, 1991, "A Stochastic Approach to Pricing FRNs", *Risk*, March.

El Karoui, N. and H. Geman, 1994, "A Probabilistic Approach to the Valuation of Floating Rate Notes with an Aplication to Interest Rate Swaps", *Advances in Options and Futures Research*, 7 (forthcoming).

Geman, H., 1989, "The Importance of the Forward Neutral Probability Measure in a Stochastic Approach to Interest Rates", ESSEC Working Paper.

Geman, H., N. El Karoui and J.C. Rochet, 1995, "Changes of Numeraire, Changes of Probability Measure and Option Pricing", *Journal of Applied Probability*, June.

Harrison, J.M. and D. Kreps, 1979, "Martingales and Arbitrage in Multiperiod Securities Markets", *Journal of Economic Theory*, 20.

Harrison, J.M. and S. Pliska, 1981, "Martingales and Stochastic Integrals in the Theory of Continuous Trading", *Stochastic Processes and their Applications*, 11.

Heath, D., R. Jarrow and A. Morton, 1992, "Bond Pricing and the Term Structure of Interest Rates ; a New Methodology for Contingent Claims Valuation", *Econometrica*, 60.

Jamshidian, F., 1989, "An Exact Bond Pricing Formula", *Journal of Finance*.

Margrabe, W., 1978, "The Value of an Option to Exchange One Asset for Another". *Journal of Finance*, 33.

Merton, R.C., 1973, "Theory of Rational Option Pricing", *Bell Journal of Economics and Management Science*, 4.

Schwartz, E. and W. Torous, 1989, "Prepayment and the Valuation of Mortgage-Backed Securities", *Journal of Finance*.

Spahr, R.W. and M.R. Sunderman, 1990, "The Effect of Freepaiement Modeling in Pricing Mortgage-Backed Securities", *Journal of Housing Research*, 3.

Tilley, J.A., 1990, "A Stochastic Yield Curve Model for Asset-Liability Simulations", Proceedings of the first AFIR Colloquium, Paris.

INTEREST
RATE RISK
MANAGEMENT
AND
VALUATION OF
THE
SURRENDER
OPTION IN
LIFE
INSURANCE
POLICIES

SECURITISATION

8

The Catastrophe Reinsurance Market
Economic Gyrations and Innovations Amid Major Structural Transformation

R. McFall Lamm Jr
Bankers Trust

The US property and casualty reinsurance industry has been rocked by several major cataclysms in recent years. First, hurricane Hugo in 1989 set a new record for insured losses. Three years later, hurricane Andrew devastated Florida and caused damage three times that of Hugo. Then came a devastating earthquake in Northridge, California, creating losses nearly as high as those of Andrew. These events stimulated a genuine scramble for new sources of risk capital to support a business shaken by a major revaluation of perceived risk (see Figures 1 and 2).

The ensuing industry restructuring witnessed the establishment of new reinsurance companies in Bermuda, as well as the creation of new risk-management tools and structures to manage catastrophe risks. These included an insurance exchange (Catex): options trading on the Chicago Board of Trade; contingent financing, and securitisation of insurance risks. It is premature to speculate whether Catex or exchange-traded options will ultimately be successful. In contrast, both contingency financing and securitisation improve efficiency and their use has become commonplace. This parallels the evolution of more sophisticated risk-management tools in other businesses.

Insurance securities have now emerged as a new asset class for some portfolio managers. A major factor influencing how fast they are adopted by a wider audience is the reinsurance business cycle. Catastrophe reinsurance is unique in that the prime determinant of rates (prices) is the

occurrence of natural events that are uncorrelated with volatility in other financial markets. When new and larger disasters occur, they increase risk and reinsurance demand. In response, rates

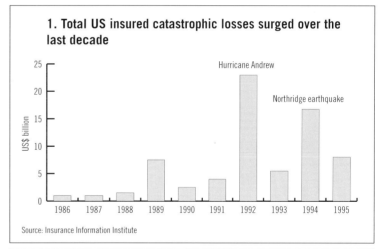

1. Total US insured catastrophic losses surged over the last decade

Source: Insurance Information Institute

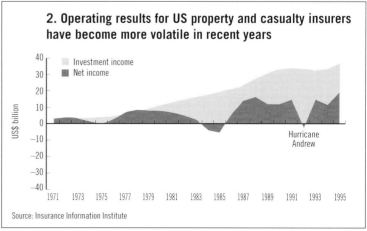

2. Operating results for US property and casualty insurers have become more volatile in recent years

Source: Insurance Information Institute

sometimes rise dramatically. Reinsurance supply ultimately expands, but with a lag.

The reinsurance industry is now well into its current cycle: rates are declining but remain relatively high. For this reason, reinsurance securities now represent a good opportunity for investors before yields decline further.

The reinsurance market experienced a major upheaval over the last decade. In the aftermath of hurricane Andrew, reinsurance demand surged as perceived catastrophe risk shot up. This precipitated a large inflow of capital (estimated at as much as US$5 billion) when several companies established operations in Bermuda in 1993.[1]

Even so, the injection of capital was not enough to moderate a reinsurance capacity crisis for major property and casualty insurers. In fact, reinsurance rates doubled and certain large insurers' total requirements for catastrophe reinsurance went unmet. A search for new sources of capital to reduce the risks of major insurers followed, leading to the development of new risk management vehicles and solutions.

Total reinsurance market capital is now estimated at about US$25 billion, of which approximately US$9 billion is catastrophe insurance. This relatively small market size, and the limited number of reinsurance suppliers, means that there are response lags and inefficiencies when risk and reinsurance demand increase simultaneously – it takes time for reinsurance capacity to react and for the market to adjust.

The new risk management instruments now available are primarily a supply response to eliminate market inefficiencies. Importantly, they augment traditional reinsurance and provide increased funding capacity for the industry. In addition, they represent a method of channelling capital flows from other sectors in search of higher returns.

Reinsurance market overview

THE BERMUDA TRIANGLE
Following hurricane Andrew in 1992, the reinsurance business went through a tremendous structural overhaul as it became obvious that additional reinsurance capacity was needed to cover a much larger exposure than was previously recognised. Industry capacity shifted to Bermuda and the firms that established operations there from 1993 onward were largely responsible for meeting the new surge in demand. Their business continues to expand. For example, another new reinsurer – New Cap Reinsurance Corp – established operations in Bermuda at

the end of 1996 with capital of US$150 million. Another US$60 million injection is expected.

THE FUNDING GAP
Despite industry adjustments, a widely acknowledged "funding gap" remains. As already noted, this gap surfaced as large losses became a more frequent occurrence and the market marked up the probability of catastrophe. Not only did reinsurance become expensive, but insurers could not purchase sufficient size to meet their needs. The resulting discontinuity stimulated the search for new solutions.

THE INDUSTRY RESPONSE
To mitigate higher business risks, insurers followed several strategies. First, they made a conscious effort to rebalance their exposures geographically and by business line. Thus, firms with heavy exposure to Florida sought to reduce it, or at least to offset it by expanding exposure to other states.

Second, some firms sought out merger and acquisition opportunities to reduce risk. This lessened exposure because the insurance portfolio of the combined entity typically was more balanced geographically and by business line.[2] Third, insurers began to seek and encourage new sources of funding, realising that even with greater capital inflow to the industry, they were still captive to a small number of reinsurance suppliers.

At the same time insurers were seeking new methods of managing risk, third parties recognised the industry disequilibrium and introduced new products that expanded reinsurance capacity and improved efficiency (see Table 1).[3] These included:

❏ the creation of an insurance exchange (Catex);
❏ the introduction of insurance futures and options of the CBOT;
❏ the development of bank contingency financing as a partial substitute for reinsurance; and
❏ the securitisation of reinsurance which allowed access to investor capital from outside the industry for the first time.

The reinsurance business cycle
Before we discuss these new innovations and their relative success, it is important to explain the economics of the reinsurance business cycle and its relationship with new product development.

DEMAND
In an economic context, increased catastrophic losses imply a greater probability of future

Table 1. Risk management tools in the catastrophe reinsurance industry

Instrument	Market participants	Characteristics	Status
Traditional reinsurance	Insurance companies; reinsurers	One-on-one negotiation; an opaque or translucent market	In place for decades
Catex	Insurance companies; reinsurers	An electronic exchange to improve market transparency by allowing participants to communicate more effectively	Attempting to start up
CBOT option spreads	Insurance companies; third parties; reinsurers	A mechanism to increase transparency and bring in outside capital through exchange trading of standardised contracts	A market in its infancy
Contingency financing	Insurance companies; banks	Non-traditional financing that brings bank capital into the market as a substitute for reinsurance	Accepted as an alternative to reinsurance
Securitisation	Insurance companies; noninsurance investors	Security creation that allows outside investors to enter the reinsurance market	Expanding

damage. This stimulates demand for reinsurance as a way to hedge this exposure. As a result, insurers are willing to pay more and rates rise when losses increase.

For example, following hurricane Andrew and the Northridge earthquake, reinsurance demand exploded as the market revalued up the potential of huge losses from catastrophic events of such magnitudes. The cost of reinsurance (price) more than doubled (see Figure 3) and exacerbated the industry's funding gap.

In contrast, the last two years were fairly benign in terms of catastrophic losses. This tempered perceived risk, softened reinsurance demand, and brought about some downward pressure on prices (see Figure 4 for a conceptual representation).[4]

SUPPLY

On the supply side, there is a lag before the capital markets respond to higher reinsurance prices. Consequently, the wave of reinsurance risk-management innovations seen over the past year and more is in part a supply reaction to the extraordinary surge in reinsurance rates of 1993 and 1994. Though the response may be a little late from the perspective of insurers, it is real and significant.[5]

Importantly, the recent supply response took the form of both product innovation and a flow of funds into reinsurance from other sectors. Product innovation was already on the drawing board, but the funds flow from other sectors is due to declining returns on alternative investments. Not only are bond yields down, but rates on high-yield securities have plummeted. For this reason, there is a lot of capital seeking a better home – even if it is an earthquake zone.

REINSURANCE CYCLE DYNAMICS

In summary, there is a dynamic pattern in the reinsurance industry that progresses sequentially. First, an extraordinary shock triggers increased

demand, driving up prices. Second, this brings increased supply after a lag. Third, demand moderates, as long as no event occurs. Fourth, softening demand and increased supply drive rates back down. The cycle then repeats itself when another major catastrophe strikes.

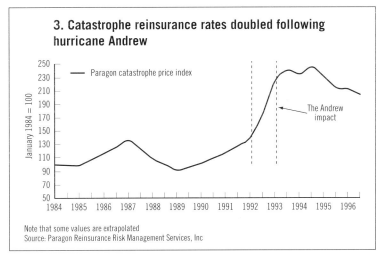

3. Catastrophe reinsurance rates doubled following hurricane Andrew

Note that some values are extrapolated
Source: Paragon Reinsurance Risk Management Services, Inc

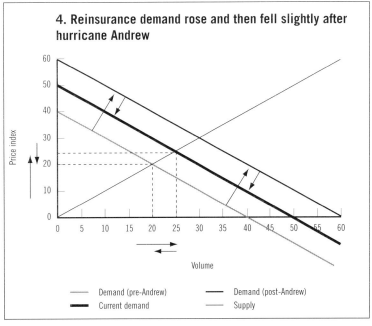

4. Reinsurance demand rose and then fell slightly after hurricane Andrew

CURRENT SITUATION

Where are we in the reinsurance cycle now? With some reduction in demand and escalating supply, it would appear that we are well into the current cycle. However, prices have fallen only slightly, indicating there may be a distance to travel before a floor is reached. For this reason, it can be argued that reinsurance securities now represent a good investment.

The major uncertainty is that another catastrophe could drive up demand and prices at any time, if one believes the frequency of large-loss earthquakes and hurricanes has risen. Otherwise, reinsurance rates should soften further as it becomes more clear that Andrew and Northridge so close together do not represent an increased frequency of catastrophic events.

The new instruments: risk management innovations

As already indicated, there are four major supply innovations that expanded reinsurance capacity and risk-management capability:

❑ *Catex* (the Catastrophic Risk Exchange), which allows the trading of reinsurance contracts electronically. It is designed to increase market liquidity, efficiency, and transparency by bringing reinsurance buyers and sellers together through a centralised facility.[6]
❑ *Catastrophic insurance options*, which trade on the Chicago Board of Trade. These instruments increase reinsurance capital liquidity, efficiency, and transparency through a standardised contract.
❑ *Contingent financing*, which gives the insurer access to a loan facility that can be used in the event of a catastrophe. This vehicle exposes the lender to credit risk.
❑ *Securitisation*, which is a form of contingency financing that involves the issue of securities such as catastrophe bonds, earthquake bonds, and similar instruments.

Each of these reinsurance methods has advantages and disadvantages. For the insurer, the vehicle or solution selected typically depends on the amount of capital needed, the cost, the urgency of need, the duration of coverage and the structural composition of existing coverage.

As of this writing, risks are posted on Catex but no transactions have been completed. Catastrophe options are trading on the CBOT, but volume remains low although it is increasing. In contrast, contingent financing and securitisation

are accepted alternatives to traditional reinsurance and are playing a major role in the market – they are more customised and address the specific needs of the insurer. We now review each in more detail.

CATEX

Purpose of the exchange Catex allows insurance companies, reinsurers and insurance brokers to trade bundles of specific catastrophic risks segmented by type and region of loss. Transactions are processed electronically, with Catex providing a benchmark rate based on historical losses and the most recent realised trades. The market then establishes new prices off these benchmarks in response to current demand and supply conditions.

Market acceptance Catex was to begin trading in October 1996 with 13 member firms. Unfortunately, trading was delayed by systems installation problems. For this reason, it is clearly too early to make any judgement about whether Catex will work. While Catex is essentially a good idea, the apparent lack of enthusiastic market acceptance may be due to the fact that the reinsurance industry is unaccustomed to open trading and sees little value in it – opaqueness is useful for firms that possess information not readily available to others.

The new Catex – into the Bermuda Triangle? On November 20, 1996 Catex announced the creation of a Bermuda subsidiary that would not only allow reinsurers to swap risks, but would also open the market to outside participants such as hedge funds. In addition, the Bermuda subsidiary will allow non-US domiciled firms to trade. And importantly, Bermuda offers a somewhat less regulated environment that should facilitate market activity.

As originally designed, Catex did not really increase the capital base available for use in the industry since only current insurance market participants were to be involved in trading. The Bermuda Catex will allow outside capital and other participants to find their way into the market, however. Maybe Catex will ultimately be successful in warmer water.

EXCHANGE-TRADED OPTIONS

Origins of the contracts The CBOT originally launched futures and options trading in catastrophe risk in late 1992. The initial purpose of trading was to improve market efficiency by bringing additional capital to the reinsurance market, while increasing transparency among existing market participants.

Initial trading began with great fanfare and a large thud. Few transactions occurred. Rather than abandon ship, the contracts were extensively revised, and trading is now concentrated in options on nine catastrophic-loss indexes. The contracts are cash-settled and based on indexes of insured property and casualty losses maintained by Property Claims Services (PCS).

The indexes, which cover the entire US, the East, Northeast, Southeast, West, Midwest, Florida, Texas, and California, represent reported quarterly losses. Each index point measures US$100 million in losses and is the basis for contract settlement. The contracts themselves are either six or 12 months in duration and are traded primarily as call spreads that provide a buyer with a partial hedge against a catastrophe while sellers obtain partial exposure.

Spread trading and layered protection To illustrate the way trading works, consider an insurer that wants to hedge national catastrophe risk. The insurer might buy 100 call options at an index value of 200 while simultaneously selling 100 calls at 250. This would lock in coverage between US$20 and US$25 billion in potential losses at a price equal to the cost of the 200 call, offset by the income from selling the 250 call.[7] This "call spread" trading evolved because it is analogous to the way insurers establish layers of protection against catastrophic risk.

Recently, open interest has surged in PCS options (see Figure 5). In addition, Travellers/ Aetna Property Casualty Corporation, USF&G Corporation, and Hanover Re have begun pilot programmes to trade catastrophic insurance options.[8] Even so, the market remains small and insurers continue to use traditional reinsurance, financing, and securitisation, which deliver tailored coverage in the amount needed with fewer transactions.

Contract issues Besides limited liquidity, one major problem with PCS catastrophic insurance options is that the options are cash-settled based on *aggregate* loss indexes. Consequently, there is basis risk in trading the product. That is, the options work as an adequate hedge only if a company's portfolio of risks closely matches the weightings in the index. While this may work for some companies, it clearly does not for many.

CONTINGENCY FINANCING

Overview In contrast to exchanges that trade reinsurance or options, the capital markets have been more successful in creating vehicles for controlling catastrophe risk. Innovations have taken two primary forms: contingent financing and securitisation. Banks typically are the providers of contingent financing, while investors are the source of funds for securitisation. Contingent financing has now emerged as a major force in the market, while securitisation in gaining momentum.

In contingency financing, the bank simply extends a line of credit to the insurer based on traditional credit analysis. Importantly, *capital access is not conditioned on the occurrence of a catastrophe*. However, the intent of most insurers is to utilise this credit only when there is a catastrophe and insured losses are high. Thus, to the insurer, contingency financing substitutes for reinsurance. But from the bank's perspective, contingent financing is credit risk.

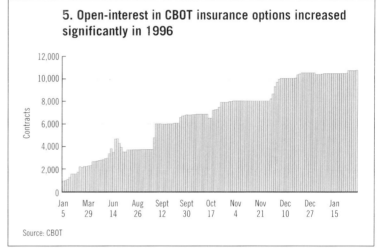

5. Open-interest in CBOT insurance options increased significantly in 1996

Source: CBOT

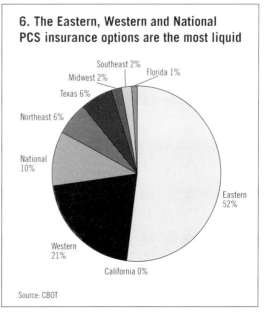

6. The Eastern, Western and National PCS insurance options are the most liquid

Southeast 2%
Florida 1%
Midwest 2%
Texas 6%
Northeast 6%
National 10%
Eastern 52%
Western 21%
California 0%

Source: CBOT

The terms The major reason contingency financing has made inroads into the reinsurance market is competitive pricing. For example, in late 1995 a syndicate of banks extended a line of credit to State Farm totalling US$3 billion. The five-year line of credit was priced 13.5 basis points above Libor, if drawn upon, plus a facility fee of 6.5bps annually. A similar five-year arrangement was put in place by Allstate in June 1995 for US$1.5 billion.

Loan facilities can be priced competitively because they are based primarily on the firm's creditworthiness. This type of assessment is more broad-based and different from traditional reinsurance, in which pricing is based on the probability of a specific event and the potential magnitude of losses. Creditworthiness considers the health and exposure of the entire company, which may have offsetting risk exposures in other businesses.

Another reason contingent debt can be competitively priced is that it is usually provided by a consortium of banks. Because the risk to any one bank in a consortium of banks is small, the banks will accept a lower price than would be the case if only one bank was financing the insurer. This is a benefit of diversifying risk exposures.[9]

The use of contingency financing by quasi-government pools Bank-arranged contingency credit facilities are also being used to fund reinsurance layers for pools such as the Hawaii Hurricane Relief Fund (HHRF), the Florida Windstorm Underwriting Association (FWUA), the Florida Residential Joint Underwriting Association (JUA), and the California Earthquake Authority (CEA).

In the case of HHRF, US$500 million is to be loaned after policyholder deductibles, industry assessments, and reinsurance are used. If the credit facility is tapped, it would be repaid by applying a surcharge to policyholders. Similarly, FWUA received a US$1 billion line of credit in August 1995 that will be used to finance claims. JUA closed a 30-month deal with a bank consortium for a US$1.5 billion credit facility later in 1995. And the CEA used a US$1 billion line of credit as part of the publicly financed portion of its US$10.5 billion catastrophe insurance programme.

Like contingency financing for insurance companies, the use of contingency financing by pools is due to competitive pricing advantages. For example, the original US$500 million HHRF credit facility was later increased to US$750 million at the expense of reinsurance, which carried a rate on-line of 16%, versus a commitment fee of less than 1% annually from the banks.

Contingency security financing: blurred distinctions from straightforward contingency debt In addition to contingent loans, some insurers are using contingency financing in which the financier receives debt or equity securities in exchange for capital. Under this arrangement, fixed-income securities or equities are issued to the financing institution at the insurer's option.

As with plain-vanilla contingency financing, the pricing of this product can be competitive with reinsurance because the recipient of the securities views the transaction as predominantly credit risk and sets prices accordingly. The insurer has access to capital, if it is needed, and the provider of the facility receives securities that may be resold (in some cases). Securities tendered may include notes, bonds, surplus notes, equity, or preferred stock.

Several reinsurance companies such as Risk Capital Re are offering this type of product to their clients. In exchange for accepting credit and/or equity risk, the reinsurer receives an annual commitment fee equal to a percentage of

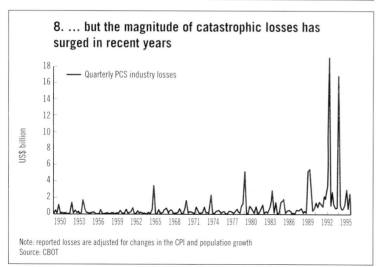

7. The historic probability of large catastrophic losses is small ...

Average loss = US$0.8 billion
Standard deviation = US$2.0 billion
Maximum = US$19.2 billion
Minimum = US$0 billion

Greater than US$6.5 billion

Probability (%)

Loss in US$ billion

Note: Reported losses are adjusted for changes in the CPI and population growth. Based on quarterly PCS data
Source: CBOT

8. ... but the magnitude of catastrophic losses has surged in recent years

— Quarterly PCS industry losses

US$ billion

Note: reported losses are adjusted for changes in the CPI and population growth
Source: CBOT

Table 2. Examples of contingency financing

Recipient	Vehicle	Provider	Amount (US$bn)	Date
Pure contingency financing transactions				
Insurers				
Allstate	Credit facility	Bank syndicate	1.5	June 1995
State Farm	Credit facility	Bank syndicate	3.0	October 1995
Pools				
Hawaii Hurricane Relief Fund	Credit facility	Bank syndicate	0.5	October 1994
			0.75	March 1996
Florida Wind-storm Underwriting Association	Credit facility	Bank syndicate	1.0	August 1995
Florida Joint Underwriting Association	Credit facility	Bank syndicate	1.5	December 1995
California Earthquake Authority	Credit facility	Bank syndicate	1.0	November 1996
Hybrid transactions				
Various insurance companies	Contingent security financing	Risk Capital Re	Ongoing	Ongoing

Source: Press reports

Table 3. Capital market approaches to catastrophe risk

Structure	Characteristics
Traditional reinsurance	Insurer/reinsurer agreement
	Direct payment to insurer if defined event occurs
	An event-risk transaction
Contingent financing	Insurer/bank consortium agreement
	Loan extended to insurer at insurers' discretion
	Insurer pays fee for loan facility
	A credit-risk transaction
Securitisations	
❑ Credit-risk securitisations	Securities issued to investors by a SPV or subsidiary
	SPV holds fixed-income securities and pays investors the returns
	At its discretion, the insurance company may call the SPV's securities and replace them with surplus notes or company debt
	A credit-risk transaction
❑ Synthetic reinsurance	Securities issued to investors by a SPV
	SPV receives premium from ceding insurance company
	SPV holds fixed-income securities and pays investors an enhanced return if the defined event does not occur
	If the defined event occurs, the SPV pays the insurance company a specified amount
	An event-risk transaction
❑ Other structures such as "earthquake" bonds	Third party issues securities to insurance company
	The third party pays returns on the securities
	If a defined event occurs, the insurance company has the right to put the securities back on the third party in exchange for cash
	An event-risk transaction

the capital pledged. In this regard, contingency security financing is similar to plain-vanilla contingency debt financing. But the use of securities is a different twist that makes this transaction something of a hybrid between contingency financing and securitisation. To the extent that the securities involved are equity-like, the financing institutions are taking on more insurance risk instead of purely credit risk.

SECURITISATION: AN EMERGING SOURCE OF REINSURANCE

Overview Securitising insurance risk offers another approach to managing catastrophic risk. It is unique in that it taps a new capital base – including but not limited to institutional investors who are unlikely to participate in this asset loss without some form of securitisation. In this way, securitisation of catastrophic risk represents an innovation that improves capital market efficiency.

For the purposes of this chapter, we define reinsurance securitisation as any transaction that:

❑ involves the issuance of bonds or notes up front to third-party investors; and
❑ provides a means for insurers to access capital, either in the case of a defined event or at their option.

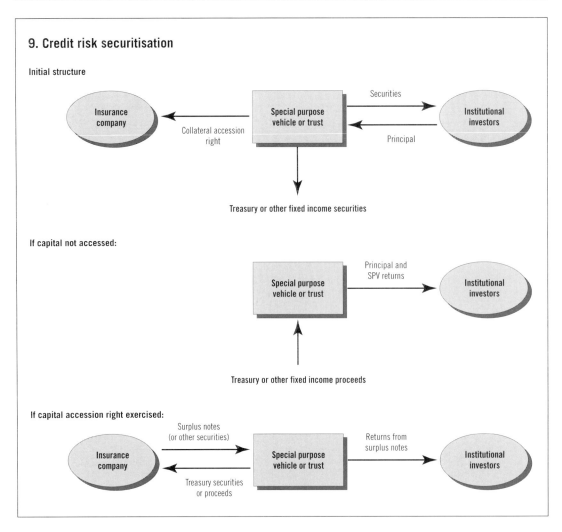

9. Credit risk securitisation

Initial structure

Insurance company ← Collateral accession right ← *Special purpose vehicle or trust* → Securities → *Institutional investors* ← Principal

Special purpose vehicle or trust → Treasury or other fixed income securities

If capital not accessed:

Special purpose vehicle or trust → Principal and SPV returns → *Institutional investors*

Treasury or other fixed income proceeds → *Special purpose vehicle or trust*

If capital accession right exercised:

Insurance company → Surplus notes (or other securities) → *Special purpose vehicle or trust* → Returns from surplus notes → *Institutional investors*

Special purpose vehicle or trust ← Treasury securities or proceeds → *Insurance company*

The securities are usually issued by a special purpose vehicle (SPV) or trust, but may be issued directly by the ceding company. The securities may pay a return that is contingent on the occurrence of the defined event(s), but this is not an absolute requirement.

Both contingent financing and securitisation are similar in that each allows the insurance company to access capital when necessary. But in contingent financing, no securities are issued at the time the arrangement is made and outside investors are not usually involved.

Credit risk versus event risk From the insurance company's perspective, both contingent financing and securitisation provide access to capital if a catastrophe occurs. However, from the providers' perspective, contingent financing usually represents credit risk. On the other hand, securitisation may represent either event risk or credit risk depending on the structure of the transaction.

Reinsurance securities that provide the insurer with capital access if a specific catastrophe takes place entail event risk. Such securities are a direct substitute for reinsurance. In contrast, some

reinsurance securities allow the insurer to access capital *at their discretion*. This feature is similar to a line of credit. Although the insurer is unlikely to exercise its option to access capital unless there is a catastrophe, these securities nonetheless represent more of a credit risk and are priced accordingly.

All reinsurance securitisations are highly tailored transactions of varying sizes, maturities, coupons, event definitions and threshold levels. For this reason, comparisons are difficult and must be done transaction by transaction. The rates on risk vary from a few percentage points above comparable Treasury yields into double digits for greater risk.

TYPES OF SECURITISATIONS
Reinsurance securitisations typically fall into one of three categories (see also Table 3):

❑ *Credit risk securitisations* involve the issuance of notes or bonds to investors through a SPV. The insurer has the right to access the capital of the SPV by substituting surplus notes or other securities at the insurer's discretion. Investors may or may not be other insurance companies (see Figure 9).

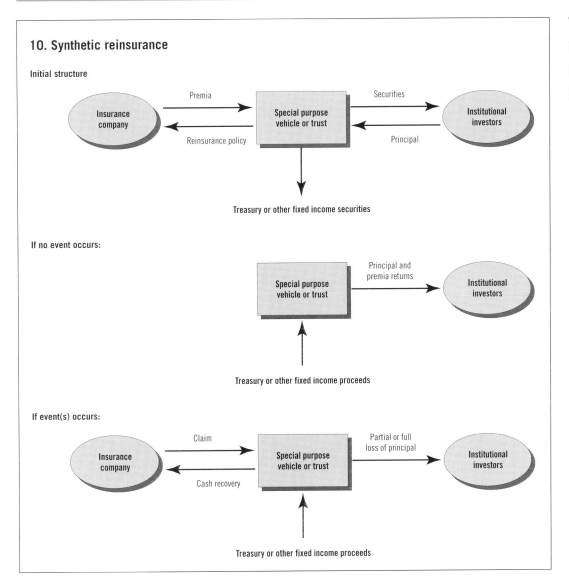

10. Synthetic reinsurance

Initial structure

If no event occurs:

If event(s) occurs:

❏ *Synthetic reinsurance* is exactly what it sounds like – a SPV funded by investors simply replaces the traditional reinsurer. Under this arrangement, the insurance company is paid by the SPV if a defined event occurs. If no event occurs, investors receive the returns on the trust's assets (see Figure 10).

❏ *"Other structures",* a category that includes instruments such as event put or earthquake bonds, in which securities are issued and the investor has the right to put the bonds back to the issuer if a defined event occurs. These are effectively "liquidity bonds." Insurance companies are the most likely buyers of these securities and would redeem them for cash when catastrophe struck and they need capital.

CREDIT RISK SECURITISATION STRUCTURE
For most credit risk securitisations, an SPV such as a trust or special purpose insurance company is used. Most include the following features:

❏ The trust issues securities, such as contingent surplus notes (CSNs) to investors. The trust's capital is used to purchase Treasury securities or other fixed income instruments.

❏ The insurance company receives the right to access the SPV's collateral at its discretion and replace it with surplus notes or other securities.

❏ Investors receive the SPV's returns (less organisation and administrative expenses, of course) and a return of principal, as long as the insurer does not exercise its collateral attachment right.

❏ If the collateral attachment right is exercised (which would most likely occur if the insurer experienced a catastrophe), the investor receives the returns on the surplus notes or other securities transferred to the trust.

In this way, investors are exposed primarily to the credit risk of the insurance company. This is why these types of securities are referred to as credit risk securitisations.

Table 4. Representative reinsurance securitisations

Insurance company or agent	Amount (US$m)	Instrument	SPV	Buyer	Issue date	Maturity	Description
Credit risk securitisations							
Nationwide Mutual Insurance Company	392 senior, 8 junior notes	Contingent surplus notes	Nationwide CSN Trust	Mutual funds and other investors	Feb 1995	2025, callable thereafter	Trust purchases. Treasuries due in 2005. The trust is required to deliver Treasuries to Nationwide through its agent in exchange for Nationwide surplus. Senior trust notes pay coupon of 9.875%; junior trust notes pay 12.22%
Arkwright Mutual Insurance Co	100	Contingent surplus notes	Arkwright CSN Trust	Mutual funds and other investors	May 1996	Callable through 2016	Arkwright may exchange its surplus notes for Treasuries held by the trust. Trust notes pay coupon of 9.625%
Synthetic reinsurance							
AIG (through Benfield Ellinger)	10	Catastrophe-linked bonds	Off-shore reinsurance company	UK fund manager	April 1996		Reinsurance company issues funds to investor. If defined catastrophe losses in any of five geographic areas exceed preset levels, the principal of the trust becomes available to pay claims
USAA	500	Catastrophe-linked bonds	Residential Reinsurance Ltd	Private placement	Forth-coming		Previously marketed as bonds issued by SPV; principal at risk due to single hurricane causing US$1 billion of insured losses to USAA
Other structures							
Hannover Re	100	Portfolio-linked swap	none	Eight North American institutional investors	Nov 1996	5-year programme	Investors' returns linked to the performance of the company on seven classes of insurance risk
St Paul Companies	68.5	Loss-linked notes and preference shares	Georgetown Re	Private placement	Dec 1996	2007 for notes, 2000 for shares	Investors' returns linked to the performance of the company; principal guaranteed for the notes
RLI Corp	50	Catastrophe equity puts	None	Centre Re	Oct 1996	3-year programme	RLI can put up to US$50 million of convertible preferred shares to Centre Re at a prenegotiated rate if there is a catastrophe loss
Winterthur Insurance Co	290	Catastrophe bonds	None	Institutional and retail accounts	Jan 1997	Jan 2000	Convertible bonds, three-year, coupon of 2.25%. Coupon not paid if automobile claims due to bad weather exceed a threshold level

Source: Press reports

Both Nationwide and Arkwright have issued CSNs in which the collateral attachment right allows the insurers to replace Treasury's with surplus notes. Nationwide's catastrophe securities issue was particularly interesting when it was done in 1995, both for its size and novelty at that time. The trust purchased Treasury securities with investors' funds, but if Nationwide exercises its right to substitute surplus notes for Treasurys, investors receive a return dependent on Nationwide's ability to pay on the surplus notes, subject to regulatory approval.

SYNTHETIC REINSURANCE

Synthetic reinsurance includes securities often referred to as "CAT bonds" or "Act of God" bonds. It is similar in some respects to credit securitisations, but it is simpler. Instead of a collateral attachment right, the insurer simply receives a direct payment if a defined event occurs. In this regard, synthetic reinsurance is exactly analogous to reinsurance, except a SPV funded by investors replaces the reinsurer.[10]

The structure of synthetic reinsurance is straightforward:

❏ The insurer pays a fixed premium to the SPV or trust annually over a specific time frame.
❏ The SPV or trust agrees to pay the insurer a fixed indemnity if and when a defined event occurs.
❏ If the defined event occurs, investors forfeit their contribution and the SPV is dissolved, or investors' capital is reduced by the amount of the loss.

If the event does not occur, investors receive the returns on the SPV's investment portfolio, their principal, and a pass-through of the insurance company's reinsurance premia. Because all this is conditional on whether a defined catastrophe occurs, synthetic reinsurance constitutes pure event risk for investors.

This product structure is somewhat analogous to a high-yield bond in that the probability of the defined event – like the probability of default for a risky company – must explicitly be taken into account. This means that the yield on synthetic reinsurance securities is often high – as much as 15–20% - depending on the length of the reinsurance contract, event definition and whether principal is at risk.

EVENT-PUT OR EARTHQUAKE BONDS
Event-put or earthquake bonds offer a unique option feature that distinguishes them from catastrophe bonds. In the case of event-put or earthquake bonds, securities are issued initially by a third party *and bought by insurers*. If a defined event occurs, the insurer has the right to put the bonds back at par to the issuer in exchange for cash. This early redemption feature is similar to the event-driven "loan call" characteristics of contingency financing or the "collateral call" traits of credit-risk securitisations.

Earthquake bonds have been the most common event-put security issued because of the highly uncertain nature and frequency of earthquakes. Transfer of this risk on a stand-alone basis represents a "liquidity financing" solution. Earthquake bonds were issued by various European institutions to Japanese insurers in the early 1990s.

Among the bonds issued, one had a put feature that could be exercised in the event of an earthquake measuring seven or greater on the Richter scale within 100 kilometres of four Japanese city centres. Insurers were attracted to these instruments because they were cash-rich at that time and preferred to invest rather than pay for a line of credit. The bonds allowed them to achieve this objective while simultaneously providing liquidity when it was most critical to their operations. Earthquake bonds have clearly not achieved the popularity of other types of catastrophe bonds, but certainly remain an alternative for insurers.

ADVANTAGES OF SECURITISATION
The securitisation of insurance risk offers appeal because it allows the insurance industry to tap institutional investor capital for the first time. In addition, securitisation offers insurance companies the opportunity to tailor a product to their specific needs, including duration, desired capital structure and trigger criteria when contingencies are involved.

Institutional investors are attracted to insurance securities because of their similarity to high-yield bonds with potentially large returns and their low correlation with the performance of other asset classes. The major challenge remaining for catastrophe insurance securities is to reach critical mass so that institutions can readily participate in the market.

A somewhat related issue is the increased frequency of high-cost disasters, which complicates the pricing of reinsurance securities. The probability of catastrophe must be accurately estimated to avoid over- or under-paying for securitised reinsurance. As institutions become more comfortable with this analytical approach, the use of catastrophe securitisation should expand even more.

State catastrophe funds
Following the large catastrophic events of recent years, California, Florida, and Hawaii created catastrophe funds to act as reinsurers of last resort. The purpose of these funds is to encourage insurance companies to requote business in their states by providing reinsurance financing to insurers who issue policies. California is the most aggressive to date in terms of size and began issuing policies in December 1996.

CALIFORNIA
The January 1994 Northridge earthquake produced US$12.5 billion in insured losses in California, causing major problems for catastrophe insurers in the state and making new policies difficult to obtain. The California Earthquake Administration was formed to take over the bulk of the state's earthquake-insurance market to address the problem.

CEA's charter is to assure the provision of bare-bones coverage on houses, but not on outbuildings, swimming pools, patios, or fences, with a deductible equal to 15% of the insured amount. CEA spent most of 1996 putting together its financing package to support insurers operating in the state. Prior to start-up, CEA was required to obtain financial backing from insurers representing 70% of the state's homeowners insurance market.

THE BERKSHIRE HATHAWAY SURPRISE
CEA originally planned to raise part of its funding through the sale of US$1.5 billion of catastrophe

11. Insurers' layering of risk: the new paradigm

Catastrophe above limits
– no protection

Securitisation – third layer of protection

Contingency financing –
second layer of protection

Traditional reinsurance
– first layer of protection

Self-insurance –
easily affordable risk;
no protection

Size of box shows frequency of use
Magnitude of potential exposure is inversely proportional to size of box

bonds to institutional investors. In November, the CEA backed off this approach and announced that Berkshire Hathaway had agreed to provide US$1.5 billion in reinsurance to CEA at a premium of approximately 10%. According to press statements, this saved CEA US$67.5 million annually since the bonds would have cost CEA as much as 14.5%.

Under the terms of the Berkshire Hathaway deal, CEA will pay premiums totalling up to US$590 million beginning at the end of March and continuing through March 2001. Berkshire Hathaway's reinsurance coverage kicks in when an earthquake or a series of quakes produces more than US$7 billion in insured losses. Other reinsurers are providing up to US$2 billion layer of coverage that will be tapped before Berkshire Hathaway is liable.

IMPLICATIONS OF THE BERKSHIRE HATHAWAY DEAL FOR SECURITISATION
CEA's use of traditional reinsurance instead of issuing catastrophe bonds was a surprise because of the significant gap between Berkshire Hathaway's price and the estimated pricing of the bonds. It would seem that either the bond underwriters got the price wrong or Berkshire-Hathaway did (assuming the difference was actually as wide as reported in the press).

Regardless, the loss of US$1.5 billion in catastrophe bonds represents only a minor setback in the timetable for securitisation, and only delays the ultimate emergence of the market segment a little. Considering potential investors' awareness of Warren Buffett's acumen as an investor, it highlights the credibility of interest in the securities. The recent successful St Paul Re securitisation (US$69 million of notes and preferred shares announced on December 30, 1996) and other deals show that securitisation is alive and well.

HAWAII AND FLORIDA
Hawaii used contingent financing to partially fund its pool beginning in 1994, while Florida set up two catastrophe funds and obtained financing in 1995. Florida is considering a catastrophe bond issue but it is not yet decided whether the bonds would be sold as tax-excempt or taxable securities, or whether some of the bonds would be guaranteed. The form that these securities eventually take could be the next major development in reinsurance securitisation.

Are catastrophe insurance securities a new asset class?

Several research studies published in the past two years present a strong case that reinsurance securities constitute a new asset class.[11] The argument for this is based on the fact that catastrophes occur randomly and are unrelated to movements in returns on other asset classes.

For example, when a catastrophe occurs, the price of *existing* reinsurance securities should decline because the value of the contingent call on capital embedded in their structure rises. This means that reinsurance returns are inversely related to the occurrence of catastrophes. Because catastrophes are obviously uncorrelated suggests that reinsurance security returns will be unrelated to stock and bond returns that move with developments in the economy.

This is supported using two different approaches in studies by Froot, Murphy, Stern, and Usher (FMSU) and Canter, Cole and Sandor. The former uses reinsurance broker data to show the existence of little relationship between reinsurance returns and those of other assets. The latter indicates that PCS losses are essentially uncorrelated with returns on the S&P500.

REINSURANCE AND RETURNS AND VOLATILITY
But the real question is what are the relative returns on reinsurance and how volatile are these returns? Until the FMSU study, there was no answer because of a lack of hard data. But using information from 2,000 reinsurance contracts brokered by Guy Carpenter from 1970 to 1994, FMSU concluded that a portfolio of reinsurance contracts outperformed Treasury bills by 200 basis points with returns that were less volatile than stocks or bonds.

This indicates that, from an asset allocation perspective, the addition of reinsurance securities (or a position carried synthetically on CBOT) would expand the efficient frontier for portfolio investors. Total returns could be increased without any greater risk by adding reinsurance securities to stock and bond holdings.

UNRESOLVED ISSUES

But before running out and loading up your portfolio with reinsurance securities, some caution is in order. First, the FMSU study begins in the 1970s – a period of extraordinarily poor bond and equity returns. This may artificially bias downward other asset returns versus returns from reinsurance. Second, the secondary market for reinsurance securities is small, fragmented and illiquid. It is virtually impossible to construct a balanced portfolio of such securities. Although this will change in the future, it remains an issue for the time being.

Third, it is *prospective* returns that are important in making asset allocation decisions – not historic returns. The explosion in large losses over recent years is likely to increase both return and risk from holding reinsurance securities. This may make the future risk-return profile of reinsurance securities fundamentally different from what it was in the past.

Despite these caveats, the overwhelming evidence strongly indicates that reinsurance securities constitute a new asset class and should be considered as a component of a balanced portfolio. Furthermore, the best time to establish a position in this asset class would be in the aftermath of a catastrophe or catastrophes when returns and perceived risk are high, and when prospective returns in the near future on other securities are low. Some pundits would argue this is precisely the environment we are in at the moment.

Conclusion

Outlook Recent developments in the reinsurance business include exchange-traded options, Catex, contingency financing, and securitisation. These innovations are reshaping the industry and will continue to do so in the future. While it is premature to say that exchange-traded options are here to stay and that Catex will eventually operate, contingency financing and securitisation are a success and their use will continue to expand.

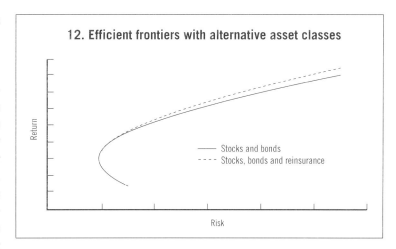

12. Efficient frontiers with alternative asset classes

Many insurance companies and state-operated insurance pools are already using different structures for layering their reinsurance risk exposure. For this reason, we will continue to see future insurance risk managed by establishing a layer of traditional reinsurance, a layer of contingency financing, a layer of catastrophe bonds or other securities, and perhaps a layer of protection carried in PCS options.

Because we are now well into the current reinsurance cycle, with rates declining moderately, competition is intensifying between reinsurers and alternative risk-management vehicles. This skirmishing will persist and returns will decline more or less proportionately with perceived risk. That is, until another disaster pushes up rates again and spawns another cyclical oscillation.

Securitisation Before the current reinsurance cycle ends, securitisation is likely to expand further and there will be more successful transactions. Investor interest is high due to superior returns, the increased flow of information newly available on the performance of the asset class and because of lower prospective returns on stocks, bonds, and other assets.

Catastrophe insurance securities are appealing for the same reason that any asset is – they have a superior risk-to-reward profile. In the past, the major issue for most investors was whether reinsurance securities did in fact expand the efficient frontier. Research published recently now confirms that this is indeed the case.

1 *See "A Structural Financial Alternative to Reinsurance,"* Standard & Poor's Credit Week, *November 13, 1996, pp. 28–30, which lists eight firms in Bermuda with US$5.1 billion in capital:*

Firm	Capital in US$bn
Partner Re Holdings	*1.3*
Mid Ocean Reinsurance Co	*1.0*
Tempest Reinsurance	*0.7*
Renaissance Reinsurance	*0.5*
Global Capital Reinsurance	*0.5*
IPC Holdings	*0.4*
LaSalle Re	*0.4*
CAT	*0.3*
Total	*5.1*

In addition, for a discussion of recent developments in the reinsurance market, see Sara Borden and Asani Sarkar, "Securitising Property Catastrophe Risk," Current Issues, *Federal Reserve Bank of New York, August 1996 and Sumit*

*Paul-Choudhury, "New Cures For Catastrophes?" Risk,
September 1996, p. 13.*

2 *For example, in 1996 Munich Reinsurance Company
announced it would acquire American Re for US$3.3 billion.
This better balances catastrophic risk for the combined entity
since Munich Re's exposure is predominantly international
versus the US exposure of American Re.*

3 *Actually, third parties had recognised the need for
additional risk management prior to Andrew. For example,
CBOT reinsurance contracts had already been developed at
that time and were listed in December 1992.*

4 *Note that our demand and supply chart focuses only on
recent demand shifts and neglects the supply-increasing
effects of innovations. Were these included, supply would
shift out to the right, dampening the price effect.*

5 *Actually, the US$9 billion in new capital that entered the
industry in 1993 began to push rates down. But then the
Northridge earthquake pushed up demand again and rates
reached new highs.*

6 *We use transparency to mean a market in which prices
and other information are fairly open and available to all.
A confidential one-on-one transaction is opaque in that
other market participants do not known the terms of the
transaction or its price.*

7 *In this example, the transaction would provide
US$1 million in protection (US$200 per index point ×
50-point spread × 100 contracts). The insurer would buy the
spread while a reinsurer would do the opposite. For more
detail, see Chicago Board of Trade, PCS Catastrophe
Insurance Options, 1995.*

8 *See* CBOT Review, *Third Quarter, 1996, and "Travellers/
Aetna Set to Move,"* National Underwriter, *July 8, 1996.*

9 *This replicates to some extent the way reinsurance is often
sold to the insurer – it is often priced by a lead underwriter
but placed with a syndicate of reinsurance companies. The
distinction is that in the case of reinsurance, it is event risk
that is diversified instead of credit risk.*

10 *The SPV is sometimes licensed as a reinsurance
company.*

11 *See Michael Canter, Joseph Cole, and Richard Sandor,
"Insurance Derivatives: A New Asset Class for the Capital
Markets and a New Hedging Tool for the Insurance
Industry,"* The Journal of Derivatives, *Winter 1996,
pp. 89–104, reprinted as Chapter 11 of the present volume,
and Kenneth Froot, Brian Murphy, Aaron Stern, and
Stephen Usher,* The Emerging Asset Class: Insurance Risk,
*Special report from Guy Carpenter and Company,
July 1995.*

9

The Exotica Portfolio
New Financial Instruments Make Bonds Obsolete

R. McFall Lamm Jr
Bankers Trust

Recent innovations in financial markets offer fundamentally new risk and return characteristics that render conventional stock and bond portfolio allocations obsolete. Notably, Treasury inflation-protection securities (TIPS) offer virtually the same potential returns as traditional bonds, but with significantly less volatility. In addition, insurance-linked securities produce returns that exceed those of bonds, but with virtually zero correlation versus other financial asset classes.

Our analysis indicates that low-volatility TIPS replace traditional Treasury securities in optimum portfolios, while insurance-linked securities enhance portfolio returns via tremendous diversification benefits. These conclusions hold rigorously under a variety of alternative scenarios. In particular, the inclusion of both instruments in portfolios allows investors to increase exposures to more risky assets with little increase in total portfolio risk. Our own view is that a portfolio with TIPS and insurance-linked securities substituted for Treasury bonds will significantly outperform traditional stock and bond allocations over the near future.

This view is time-dependent, however. That is, we believe there is a general lack of information and understanding of the TIPS and insurance-linked securities markets. As familiarity increases, the advantages of owning these products will be arbitraged away as the knowledge gap is closed and risk-adjusted returns converge. For this reason, early buyers of these assets should benefit disproportionately.

TIPS and insurance-linked securities force a reconsideration of traditional asset allocations

For many years, traditional asset allocation models have embraced equities, bonds and cash as the fundamental portfolio components. The list of acceptable investments has expanded over the last decade to include international equities and bonds, emerging-market securities, asset securitisations and hybrid products combining the characteristics of bonds and equities. Yet many of these asset classes are highly correlated with overall market performance and do not always produce the portfolio diversification benefits desired by portfolio managers (see Figure 1 and Table 1).

NEW ASSET CLASSES

Further complicating investment strategy is the seemingly endless stream of new products promoted as new asset classes. Many have more complex characteristics that make it difficult to evaluate whether they convey the advantages attributed to them. Two such enigmas are Treasury inflation-protection securities (TIPS) and insurance-linked securities. As we shall demonstrate, both have unique attributes and significantly shift the efficient frontier outward.

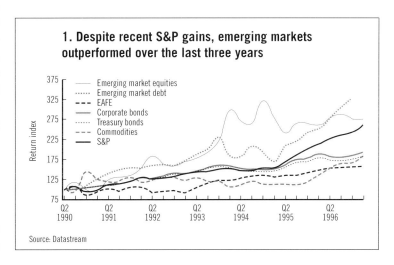

1. Despite recent S&P gains, emerging markets outperformed over the last three years

Return index

- Emerging market equities
- Emerging market debt
- EAFE
- Corporate bonds
- Treasury bonds
- Commodities
- S&P

Source: Datastream

Table 1. Quarterly returns and correlation matrix for selected asset classes, 1991–96

Asset class	Commodities	S&P	EAFE	Emerging-market equities	Cash	Treasury bonds	Corporate bonds	Emerging market debt	Real estate
Return (annualised, %)	7.8	19.2	12.7	30.8	4.5	10.7	11.6	26.8	2.3
Volatility (entire period, %)	27.7	18.1	22.0	65.0	1.1	15.1	13.8	38.4	7.2
Sharpe ratio	0.28	1.06	0.58	0.47	4.13	0.71	0.84	0.68	0.32
Correlation matrix									
Commodities	1.00	−0.53	−0.54	−0.39	0.37	−0.16	−0.22	0.11	−0.18
S&P		1.00	0.46	0.30	0.15	0.44	0.53	0.30	0.25
EAFE			1.00	0.12	−0.13	0.43	0.43	0.17	0.01
Emerging-market equities				1.00	−0.13	−0.18	−0.06	−0.30	0.02
Cash					1.00	0.06	0.05	0.21	0.06
Treasury bonds						1.00	0.97	0.21	−0.33
Corporate bonds							1.00	0.23	−0.32
Emerging market debt								1.00	0.08
Real estate									1.00

Based on compounded quarterly returns from 1991–96.[1] Returns, volatility and correlations for each asset class are based on quarterly total return indexes. EAFE and emerging-market equity returns are based on the corresponding Morgan Stanley Capital Indexes. Treasury bonds, corporate bonds, and emerging-market debt are Salomon Brothers indexes. Commodity returns are based on the Goldman Sachs Commodity Index, while real-estate returns are measured by the NCREIF index. Source of raw data: Datastream.

BROADER ASSET CLASSES

To further increase diversification by reducing correlation, some analysts have argued that the set of admissible assets should be expanded to include commodities.[2] While some portfolio managers have done so, the vast majority have not. For this reason, we also explore the efficacy of including commodities in portfolios as well as TIPS and insurance-linked securities.

2. Inflation expectations implicit in nominal Treasuries and inflation-protected securities

Note: Ignores inflation risk premium
Source: Derived from Bloomberg data for the 2007 TIPS and the 2007 nominal bond

Table 2. Inflation-protected securities issued

Amount US$m	Issuer	Issue date	Yield (%)	Maturity (years)
7,000	US Treasury	January 29	3.45	10
300	Tennessee Valley Authority	February 5	3.46	10
300	Federal Home Loan Bank	February 14	3.15	5
100	Federal Farm Credit Banks	February 14	3.00	5
450	Salomon Inc	February 14	3.88	5
100	Toyota Motor Credit	February 15	3.20	5
200	JP Morgan	February 15	4.00	15
100	NationsBank	February 18	3.25	5
100	Federal Home Loan Bank	February 19	3.37	10
200	Student Loan Marketing Association	February 20	2.90	3
300	Korea Development Bank	March 1	3.40	5
25	Merrill Lynch	March 7	3.00	5
100	Federal National Mortgage Association	March 13	3.14	5
39	City of Orlando	March 27	na	various
8,000	US Treasury	April 8	3.65	9.75

Source: Press releases and Bloomberg

Treasury Inflation-Protection Securities (TIPS)

THE DEBUT

TIPS were first issued in late January by the US Treasury as a vehicle for potentially reducing funding costs.[3] The initial offering was oversubscribed and produced a real yield of 3.45%. Thus, if inflation averages 3% over the note's life, the return to investors will equal 6.55%.[4] At the same time, comparable yields on conventional 10-year Treasury bonds were 6.55%. Consequently, the market was valuing "break-even" inflation at exactly 3% and TIPS buyers acquired inflation protection at essentially no cost.[5]

The major reason buyers secured an apparently equivalent nominal Treasury yield with the added benefit of a zero-premium inflation hedge was because of market uncertainty and lack of information on the product. In addition, inflation is relatively low by historical standards and has been very stable for a decade. Nonetheless, you would think the inflation protection embedded in TIPS should have some discernible value, given the possibility of an inflation burst at any time over the next decade. Extraordinarily, the market appears to be pricing in relatively low and stable inflation (see Figure 2).

Following the first auction, break-even inflation on TIPS declined briefly in secondary-market trading. This made for more credible valuations. In addition, federal agencies and private issuers sold inflation-protected securities of varying maturities adding depth to the market (see Table 2).

THE SECOND AUCTION

A second Treasury auction was conducted on April 9. This produced a real yield of 3.65%, which compared to a nominal Treasury yield of 6.82% and implied a break-even inflation of 3.1%. Thus, the real yield on TIPS has roughly paralleled the apparent real yield on comparable 10-year Treasuries. We conclude that the real yields on the two securities are nearly the same – as long as realised inflation is actually about 3% (see Figure 3).

The amount bid in the second auction was US$18.1 billion – down from the US$37.2 billion bid in the first. Some pundits interpreted this as declining demand for the product. However, this is a misguided interpretation because the first auction contained a huge range of bids to cover extreme uncertainty regarding the ultimate yield. In the second auction, TIPS had traded actively for several months, more market participants understood their behaviour and a real yield had already been established in the market.

TIPS RISK AND VOLATILITY

TIPS initially experienced higher price volatility than nominal Treasury securities over the first month of trading. But volatility then declined to about three-fourths that of nominal bonds (see Figure 4). The early period of volatility should be discounted, however, because high volatility is characteristic of new financial product markets that normally gyrate because of initial market uncertainty. Also, several market participants were purportedly short TIPS following the auction and needed to eliminate their exposure.

WHY TIPS VOLATILITY SHOULD REMAIN CONSISTENTLY LOWER THAN THAT OF NOMINAL BONDS

Theoretically, we expect nominal bonds to be more volatile than TIPS because the price response of either security to changes in real interest rates is nearly the same, while changes in inflation expectations affect only nominal bond prices. Thus, two constantly changing forces drive nominal bond prices, while only one affects TIPS. As long as expected inflation volatility does not sink to zero, the volatility of nominal bond returns should exceed that of TIPS.[6]

THE UK EXPERIENCE

If the record to date of lower volatility for TIPS is not sufficient, the same conclusion is supported by the UK experience. In the UK, returns volatility on index-linked gilts ("linkers") has averaged about two-thirds that of nominal gilts for over a decade. This is strong evidence because of the relatively large size of the market (nearly a fifth of outstanding government debt) and because there have been periods of both rising and falling inflation in the UK over the past 10 years.

In addition, experience in the UK shows that changes in real yields affect nominal securities and linkers in the same way – higher real yields translate into lower prices for both securities. But changes in inflation expectations, as evidenced by fluctuations in break-even inflation, have had no effect on linkers while having a large impact on returns and prices for nominal gilts.

TIPS CORRELATION WITH OTHER ASSET CLASSES

One unique aspect of TIPS is that with stable inflation, their behaviour mirrors that of nominal bonds. That is, both securities converge into being essentially the same product and they are nearly perfectly correlated. However, if inflation changes,

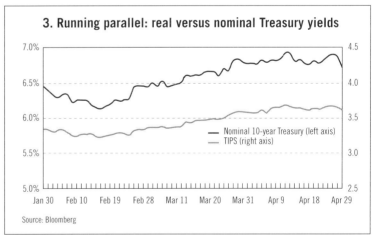

3. Running parallel: real versus nominal Treasury yields

Nominal 10-year Treasury (left axis)
TIPS (right axis)

Source: Bloomberg

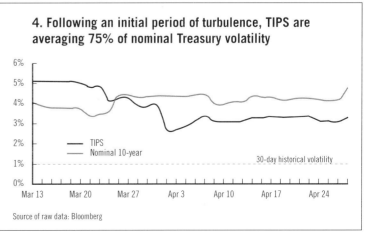

4. Following an initial period of turbulence, TIPS are averaging 75% of nominal Treasury volatility

TIPS
Nominal 10-year

30-day historical volatility

Source of raw data: Bloomberg

this is not true and correlation between the two assets declines. In particular, if inflation rises strongly, the correlation between nominal and real bonds is negative.

This also is illustrated by experience in the UK. From 1988 to late 1990, inflation rose from 4% to more than 10%. Index-linked gilts outperformed nominal gilts, and there was a lengthy period of negative correlation in 1990. Because the structure of linkers and TIPS is nearly identical, we would expect declining correlation between nominal Treasury bonds and TIPS in a rising inflation environment (or to be more accurate – a rising inflation *expectation* environment). Negative correlation would result if inflation surged strongly.

Similarly, we would expect the correlation between TIPS and other asset classes to emulate the behaviour of bonds versus other asset classes in a stable inflation environment. Correlation would diminish to the extent that there are changes in inflation (and inflation expectations).[7]

Insurance-linked securities

SECURITY STRUCTURE
Insurance-linked securities are just coming into their own as a method of satisfying insurers' needs for event risk management. To date, most issues have focused on catastrophe insurance. Eventually, securitisation will expand to include other types of insurance risk, such as mortality, worker compensation and automobile damage.

Insurance-linked securities are generally issued by insurers through special purpose vehicles (SPVs). SPVs act as conduits receiving funds from investors, paying a return and principal (dependent on the occurrence of an insurance event such as a natural catastrophe) and channelling funds to the insurer as required.

If the specified event does not occur, investors receive returns significantly exceeding comparable Treasury rates. If the event occurs, the SPV dispenses funds to the insurer and investors' coupons (and sometimes principal) are reduced accordingly. In one of the more common types of arrangements, investors provide "synthetic" reinsurance since the securities issued substitute for traditional reinsurance.[8]

MARKET SIZE AND EVOLUTION
There have been at least a dozen large insurance-linked securitisations over the past few years with a total value approaching US$2 billion (see Table 3). Most consist of pure insurance risk although some products embed credit risk in

their structure. Issue sizes have ranged from US$10 million to US$400 million.[9] The majority of the issues consist of synthetic catastrophe reinsurance or catastrophe-related structures.

Insurance-linked securities differ from TIPS in that the market is significantly smaller and illiquid. But like TIPS, the structures of the securities are complex. Indeed, few of the insurance-linked securities sold in the market are homogeneous – each issue is highly engineered by buyers' and sellers' needs.

RETURNS ON INSURANCE-LINKED SECURITIES
Insurance-linked securities offer fairly high returns with moderate volatility. An analysis by Froot, Murphy, Stern and Usher (FMSU) for Guy Carpenter found that catastrophe reinsurance outperformed Treasury bills by an average of 2% from 1970–94.[10] This was done with an annual volatility of 5.8%.

In another study, Litzenberger, Beaglehole and Reynolds (LBR) found an excess return of 7.9% for catastrophe reinsurance versus Treasury bills and a returns standard deviation of 19.9% (see Chapter 12). This latter result was obtained by deriving an implicit return on catastrophe reinsurance based on adjusted Property Claim Services (PCS) data. Although the FMSU and LBR studies use different data and methodologies, we can reasonably conclude that reinsurance outperforms Treasury bills, but there is a legitimate question regarding by how much.

RETURNS VOLATILITY ON INSURANCE-LINKED SECURITIES
Using different approaches, FMSU and LBR estimate volatilities for reinsurance of 5.8% and 19.9%, respectively. This is significantly different. But the Sharpe ratio for the former is 0.34 while the latter is 0.39. This is very close. To add another perspective, we used an alternative data source – the Paragon Price Index – which measures catastrophe reinsurance rates (see Figure 5). Our results indicate that the price of reinsurance rose 13% annually over the past five years with a volatility of 17%. This represents an excess return of 8.5% and a Sharpe ratio of 0.50. Long term, since 1984, the index rose on average 8% annually with a volatility of 11%. This is an excess return of 2% and produces a Sharpe ratio of 0.18.[11]

CORRELATION WITH OTHER ASSET CLASSES
The most profound insight from these studies is that insurance-linked securities lack any

Table 3. Representative insurance-linked securitisations

Insurance company or agent	Amount (US$m)	Type of instrument	Issue date	Maturity	Description
Credit risk securitisations					
Nationwide Mutual Insurance	392 senior, 8 junior notes	Contingent surplus notes	Feb 1995	2025, callable thereafter	Trust purchases Treasuries due in 2005. The trust is required to deliver Treasuries to Nationwide in exchange for Nationwide surplus. Senior trust notes pay coupon of 9.875%; junior notes pay 12.22%
Arkwright Mutual Insurance	100	Contingent surplus notes	May 1996	Callable through 2016	Arkwright may exchange its surplus notes for Treasuries held by the trust. Trust notes pay coupon of 9.625%
Synthetic reinsurance					
AIG (through Benfield Ellinger)	10	Catastrophe-linked bonds	Apr 1996	na	Reinsurance company issues bonds to investor. If defined catastrophe losses in any of five geographic areas exceed preset levels, the principal of the trust becomes available to pay claims
USAA	150–400	Catastrophe-linked bonds	Q2 1997	na	Previously marketed as SPV-issued bonds; principal at risk due to single hurricane causing US$1 billion of insured losses to USAA. Now contemplated as principal-protected
Hannover Re	100	Portfolio-linked swap	Nov 1996	5-year programme	Investors' returns linked to the performance of the company on seven classes of insurance risk
St Paul Companies	68.5	Loss-linked notes and preference shares	Dec 1996	Notes – 2007 Shares – 2000	Investors' returns linked to the performance of the company; principal guaranteed for the notes
Reliance National	20–40	Catastrophe-linked bonds	Q1 1997	18-month programme	Investors' returns linked to the performance of the company on five classes of insurance risk for one-year period. Libor-based, issued at discount to par
Other structures					
RLI Corp	50	Catastrophe equity puts	Oct 1996	3-year programme	RLI can put up to US$50 million of convertible preferred shares to Centre Re at a prenegotiated rate if there is a catastrophe
Winterthur Insurance	290	Catastrophe bonds	Jan 1997	Jan 2000	Convertible bonds, three-year, coupon of 2.25%. Coupon not paid if automobile claims exceed a threshold level
Horace Mann	100	Catastrophe equity puts	Mar 1997	3-year programme extendible to five	Horace Mann can put up to US$100 million of convertible preferred shares to Centre Re at a prenegotiated rate if there are one or more catastrophes exceeding US$65 million in aggregate

Source: press reports

significant correlation with other financial assets. This is because catastrophe reinsurance returns vary with the incidence of cataclysmic events – primarily hurricanes and earthquakes. When natural disasters occur, reinsurance prices increase (more than doubling over the most recent cycle, for example). Obviously, weather and the shifting of tectonic plates are unrelated to financial markets (or at least we hope so).

If hope is not enough, available statistical analyses strongly support the supposition. For example, FMSU found that catastrophe bonds have returns correlations of –0.13, 0.07, 0.21, and 0.21 with returns on the S&P500, government bonds, EAFE and international bonds, respectively. None of these was found to be statistically different from zero *even though based on a lengthy sample covering 1970 to 1994*. Similarly, LBR found a statistically insignificant (zero) correlation between catastrophe reinsurance versus equities and bonds between 1955 and 1994.

In yet another related study, Canter, Cole and Sandor (CCS) found a zero correlation between annual changes in the S&P500 and the PCS national index from 1950 (see Chapter 11). We overwhelmingly conclude that insurance-linked securities are so-called zero-beta assets with no correlation with other asset classes.[12]

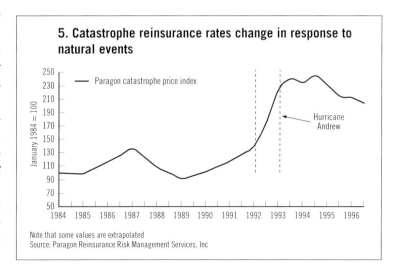

5. Catastrophe reinsurance rates change in response to natural events

Note that some values are extrapolated
Source: Paragon Reinsurance Risk Management Services, Inc

Risk and returns in traditional asset classes

Having now established the basic characteristics of TIPS and insurance-linked securities, we turn to the broader question of how these products fit into a general portfolio of assets with competing attributes. This endeavour is complex because, like TIPS and insurance-linked securities, returns and risk for competing assets are time-dependent. In addition, there are issues in using asset allocation models in that they must be delicately handled and interpreted to produce meaningful results.

OUTPERFORMANCE AND RISK ARE A FUNCTION OF THE TIME PERIOD EVALUATED

Returns for various asset classes show varying degrees of correlation and returns depending on the historical time horizon considered. For this reason, what is a risky high-return asset today may be antipodal tomorrow. This is illustrated by several contemporary asset price bubbles:

❑ Investors in emerging-market equities in the early 1990s were richly rewarded but subsequently punished in the crash following the peso crisis in December 1994.
❑ The fantastic outperformance of the US equity market with relatively low risk over the past two years made investors with significant exposures to markets like Japan appear obtuse.
❑ There was also the fantastic boom and bust in high-technology companies in 1996 that quickly created, and then erased, massive equity market wealth.

Of course, there are many other examples, but the point is that outperformance is relative.

Based on the foregoing, the lesson is that history does not repeat itself – at least in the short run. Of what use then are historical data on asset class performance and volatility? The response is that over longer time frames, fundamental characteristics of market behaviour are revealed.

For example, equities offer higher returns with greater risk than bonds, while real estate and commodities offer diversification benefits. The question is to what extent these characteristics prevail over a strategic asset allocation horizon that is usually relatively short.

GENERAL PROBLEMS WITH THE ASSET ALLOCATION MODELS

Clearly, one must be able to predict returns and risk going forward to construct a superior asset allocation strategy. This is where most asset-allocation models fail and why they are used primarily as supplementary tools instead of as prime drivers of asset allocation. Who can concurrently predict returns, volatility and correlation? And, as events transform return profiles, to what degree should extreme somersaults in weighting be quickly implemented if indicated?

ASSET ALLOCATION MODELS OFTEN LACK ROBUSTNESS

Another problem is that asset allocation models notoriously lack robustness.[13] That is, a small change in forecast return or risk causes a large change in the weight allocated to an asset class. This is why it is imperative to select asset classes for which one is confident of consistent behaviour and comfortable that expected returns will be realised.

There are also issues involved when more asset classes are added to a simple stock and bond portfolio. The real world consists of more complex portfolios and instruments. But after a point, focusing on the incremental benefits of additional assets becomes useless and is a false dichotomy. When more complex portfolios are considered, say with 10 or 15 asset classes, the results blur as it becomes more difficult to shift out the efficient frontier to improve expected performance.

ANALYTICAL APPROACH USED HERE

Despite all this, asset allocation models remain useful for assessing strategies and determining which assets to include in portfolios. In the analysis we report here, we use a straightforward and simple asset allocation model (see Table 4).[14] The questions we address are: *Does the addition of TIPS and insurance-linked securities to portfolios shift out the efficient frontier and, if so, what are the appropriate weights for these asset classes?* We consider a wide range of assets and portfolios, and add our two candidates to the analysis in a variety of situations.

Anticipated returns, risk and correlation

PREMISES

Our basis conclusions are that TIPS now offer about the same returns as nominal Treasuries with significantly lower volatility *as long as inflation is flat*. In addition, if inflation rises, TIPS offer low or even negative correlation with other financial asset classes. Insurance-

Table 4. Returns and correlations for asset classes used in the asset allocation model

Asset class	Commodities	S&P	EAFE	Emerging-market equities	Cash	Treasury bonds	Corporate bonds	Emerging market debt	Real estate	TIPS	Insurance-linked securities
Return (annualised, %)	5	10	12	20	5	7	7.5	10	3	6.8	7
Volatility (entire period, %)	30	20	25	40	1.5	10	11	15	4	7.5	11
Sharpe ratio	0.16	0.50	0.50	0.50	3.33	0.70	0.68	0.63	0.75	0.91	0.64
Correlation matrix											
Commodities	1.00	−0.53	−0.54	−0.39	0.37	−0.15	−0.20	−0.10	−0.20	−0.10	0.00
S&P		1.0	0.46	0.30	0.15	0.44	0.53	0.30	0.25	0.30	0.00
EAFE			1.00	0.12	−0.10	0.43	0.43	0.17	0.15	0.30	0.00
Emerging-market equities				1.00	0.10	0.15	0.15	−0.30	0.10	0.10	0.00
Cash					1.00	0.06	0.05	0.21	0.00	0.00	0.00
Treasury bonds						1.00	0.97	0.21	−0.30	0.50	0.00
Corporate bonds							1.00	0.23	−0.30	0.50	0.00
Emerging-market debt								1.00	−0.10	0.10	0.00
Real estate									1.00	−0.25	0.00
TIPS										1.00	0.00
Insurance-linked securities											1.00

Source: BT Global Economic Research

linked securities offer relatively high returns but with considerable volatility. However, they also exhibit zero correlation with other asset classes.

THE FUTURE VERSUS THE PAST

To make an effective portfolio allocation, one must forecast future returns, volatility and correlations. Rather than take recent history as a guide and blindly extrapolate forward, we use our own longer-term views on market directions for different asset classes as a base case. Our time frame is more or less the next 12 months and our expectations are summarised in Table 5. A brief summary of the logic underlying our prospective outlook follows.

THE MACROECONOMY AND DOMESTIC ASSET PERFORMANCE

Tightening monetary policy combined with near-neutral fiscal policy and a slowing (but non-recessionary) economy late this year will keep real (and nominal) interest rates near current levels.

We expect some softening in rates as the economy slows, however. Inflation persists near its 3% pace of the last decade. Gains in the S&P continue, but earnings growth slows as the economy weakens and the strong dollar cuts into exports.

Outperformance shifts more to EAFE and emerging markets as relative growth improves versus the US. Commodities perform poorly following stellar outperformance over the recent past. Real estate performs better than it has over the last decade but there is no property price explosion.

INTERNATIONAL ASSETS

We expect a shift from relatively strong US economic performance back to the rest of the world, particularly in emerging markets and Europe. Singapore, Thailand, Korea and India pick up steam in Asia following recent problems. Also, Latin America continues strong. However, the fantastic outperformance of Brady bonds ends, although spreads versus Treasuries narrow a little more.

TIPS AND INSURANCE-LINKED SECURITIES

By presuming that inflation holds steady near its current level, there is no significant outperformance by nominal Treasuries. Indeed, we assume TIPS yield only 0.2% below Treasury securities, while averaging a conservative three-quarters of the volatility of nominal Treasury bonds. This is about where TIPS are trading now and produces a Sharpe ratio significantly higher than that for Treasury bonds.

For insurance-linked securities, we make the conservative assumption that yields exceed cash by only 2%, but with a relative volatility that matches emerging-market debt. We also impose the constraint that the asset class is uncorrelated with all other asset classes. For most other assets considered in the analysis, we assume that past correlation relationships continue to hold.

Asset allocation model results

OVERVIEW

We conduct a series of simulations in which we vary our initial assumptions. We specifically change:

Table 5. Summary of anticipated macroeconomic performance and asset class returns

Sector or asset class	Current situation	Outlook (one year horizon)
Macroeconomy		
Economic growth	Strong current expansion above recent trends	Softening by 1998 to below 2.5%
Long rates	High due to strong credit demand	Flat to slightly declining late in the year as the economy slows
Short rates	Rising due to tight Federal Reserve monetary policy	Risk of several Federal Reserve increases
Inflation	Averaging slightly less than 3% but fear of acceleration due to wage pressures	Averaging 3%
Monetary policy	Rather tight with real short rates above 2%	Continuing tight for the balance of the year until signals of much slower growth emerge
Fiscal policy	Deficits declining in actual dollars and as a percent of GDP	Deficits continuing to decline by all measures
Dollar	Very strong at the moment due to relative high interest rate environment	Continued strength in response to interest rate increases and uncertainty over EMU
Asset classes		
Commodities	Prices declining from highs reached last year for energy and metals	Prices declining somewhat due to eventually weakening demand
S&P	A temporary market correction has been reversed	Strong market with episodic volatility
EAFE	Continuing to lag the S&P due to weaker market performance in Japan and Europe	Outperforms the S&P due to lower overseas interest rates and strengthening economic growth
Emerging market equities	Improving strongly versus the trough reached in 1995; Asian emerging markets lagging Latin America	Asian emerging markets catching up with Latin markets as economies improve. Emerging markets again outperform developed markets due to more robust growth
Cash	High returns currently with Federal funds at 5.25% and strong prospects for 5.5%	Stabilising following additional Federal Reserve increases
Long bonds	Relatively strong returns	Returns strengthening again with long rate declines late in the year
Emerging market debt	A lull in returns following the best of any asset class over the past two years	Spreads tightening versus Treasury bonds as credit quality and economies continue to improve
Real estate	Returns continue to rebound from cash in the early 1990s	Returns remain modest due to lower inflation and some expansion in supply
TIPS	An evolving market offering returns near those of comparable Treasury bonds	Performance comparable to that of comparable Treasury bonds but with less volatility
Insurance linked securities	An infant market that offers returns significantly above Treasury securities but with no correlation with other assets	Excess returns versus Treasury securities persist. Zero correlation with other asset classes continues

Source: BT Global Economic Research

❑ the number of asset classes considered;
❑ the inflation assumption (which is the key driver of anticipated returns); and
❑ selected asset class returns and volatilities.

We start with a classic portfolio of stocks, bonds, and cash, then add TIPS and insurance-linked securities. We then proceed to expand the set of portfolio assets to include corporate bonds, commodities, EAFE, emerging-market equities and emerging-market debt (see Table 6).

BASIC SOLUTION FOR DOMESTIC PORTFOLIOS
In this simplest of cases with stocks, bonds and cash as admissible assets, the basic solution puts a heavy allocation to cash because of its high current returns and high prospective returns going forward.

When TIPS and insurance-linked securities are added to the portfolio, the cash allocation declines more quickly to zero for moderate levels of risk. In addition, the equity allocation decreases slightly and *nominal bonds are purged from the portfolio*. TIPS and insurance-linked securities primarily replace bonds but also substitute somewhat for cash and equities at moderate levels of risk. But most important, the addition of TIPS and insurance-linked securities adds a full 0.5% return to the portfolio for the same level of risk versus the three-asset portfolio.

THE BROAD-BASED INTERNATIONAL PORTFOLIO
Turning to a more realistic scenario, we consider nine broad asset classes that most portfolio managers embrace in varying degrees. Specifically, we add corporate bonds, EAFE, commodities, emerging market debt and emerging market equities.

The basic allocation, prior to including TIPS and insurance-linked securities, is vastly superior

Table 6. Optimum asset allocations (%)

(a) For purely domestic portfolios

	Three-asset portfolio				Five-asset portfolio					
Portfolio return	Equities	Cash	Bonds	Portfolio volatility	Equities	Cash	Bonds	TIPS	Insurance-linked securities	Portfolio volatility
5.0	0	99	1	1.5	0	99	0	1	0	1.5
5.5	8	87	5	2.1	4	80	0	9	6	1.8
6.0	18	75	7	3.3	11	64	0	15	11	2.7
6.5	28	63	9	4.5	18	48	0	20	15	3.7
7.0	38	51	11	5.8	25	31	0	24	19	4.8
7.5	48	39	13	7.1	32	15	0	29	24	5.9
8.0	58	27	15	8.4	40	0	0	32	28	7.0
8.5	68	15	17	9.7	57	0	0	17	26	8.4
9.0	78	3	19	10.9	74	0	0	1	25	10.0
9.5	94	0	6	12.4	91	0	0	0	9	12.0
10.0	100	0	0	15.0	100	0	0	0	0	15.0

(b) For broad international portfolios

Return	Commodities	All equities	Cash	Bonds	Corporate bonds	Emerging market debt	Real estate	TIPS	Insurance-linked securities	Portfolio volatility
11 asset classes Including TIPS and insurance-linked securities										
5	0	1	83	0	0	0	9	5	2	1.4
6	2	6	78	0	0	4	0	5	5	2.0
7	5	14	59	0	0	9	0	6	8	3.0
8	9	20	40	0	0	13	0	7	10	4.1
9	13	29	21	0	0	18	0	7	13	5.2
10	16	37	2	0	0	22	0	8	15	6.3
11	18	43	0	0	0	29	0	0	9	7.6
12	17	49	0	0	0	34	0	0	0	9.4
13	11	55	0	0	0	35	0	0	0	12.0
14	4	60	0	0	0	36	0	0	0	15.5
15	0	67	0	0	0	33	0	0	0	18.7
16	0	76	0	0	0	24	0	0	0	22.5
Nine asset classes										
5	0	0	100	0	0	0	0	–	–	1.5
6	2	7	85	0	0	6	0	–	–	2.2
7	6	12	69	0	0	13	0	–	–	3.3
8	9	18	53	0	0	19	0	–	–	4.5
9	13	24	37	0	0	26	0	–	–	5.6
10	17	31	21	0	0	32	0	–	–	6.9
11	20	37	4	0	0	39	0	–	–	8.1
12	17	42	0	0	0	42	0	–	–	9.7
13	10	47	0	0	0	43	0	–	–	12.4
14	4	51	0	0	0	44	0	–	–	15.5
15	0	59	0	0	0	41	0	–	–	18.9
16	0	69	0	0	0	32	0	–	–	22.8

For simplicity of presentation, the three equity classes are combined into one aggregate

to the domestic portfolio results. Returns increase from 2% to over 3% at equivalent levels of risk versus purely domestic portfolios.[15] This clearly illustrates the well-known advantages of international diversification.

Of some surprise is the rather substantial allocation to commodities – despite low expected returns and high volatility. The primary reason for this is that commodities are the only major asset which is negatively correlated with most other asset classes. Thus, commodity returns are worth a lot because of their diversification attributes.

THE BROAD PORTFOLIO PLUS TIPS AND INSURANCE-LINKED SECURITIES
Because of the high expected returns of international and emerging market assets, the addition of TIPS and insurance-linked securities to the broad portfolio increases expected returns only

about a quarter of a percent for equivalent levels of risk. Although this may seem small, an additional 25 basis points is an acceptable outperformance level for many portfolio managers. TIPS and insurance-linked securities displace primarily cash and commodities, but cut into holdings of other asset classes as well.

EXCLUDING CASH FROM THE PORTFOLIO

We do note that our results are somewhat skewed because of high expected returns on cash and international securities in the near future. However, in a series of alternative simulations in which these returns were reduced, the allocation to TIPS and insurance-linked securities rose (as you would expect), producing at minimum 0.25% gains in return for equivalent levels of risk (see Table 7).

TENTATIVE CONCLUSIONS

Our key findings are that TIPS and insurance-linked securities consistently enter the optimum portfolio with significant allocations at low and moderate levels of risk. Clearly, TIPS dominate nominal bonds while insurance-linked securities offer diversification benefits previously proclaimed. One surprise is the sizeable allocation to commodities in many optimum portfolios.

The only way to remove TIPS from optimum portfolios is to decrease their Sharpe ratio by reducing expected return or by increasing volatility. While some reduction might be justified,

reducing the TIPS' Sharpe ratio below that of nominal Treasuries flies in the face of reality given a near 3% inflation expectation and market ignorance of TIPS (which has produced a zero inflation-risk premium). Regarding insurance-linked securities, this asset emerges as a superb diversification tool that appears to have an important place in portfolios.

When do nominal Treasury securities enter the allocation?

REAL VERSUS NOMINAL SECURITY FUNDAMENTALS

As already noted, inflation and inflation expectations are the key to relative returns for TIPS versus nominal bonds. A surge in inflation would push up returns for TIPS and reduce their correlation with nominal bonds and other assets. Thus, if inflation accelerates, inflation expectations rise and the prices of nominal bonds implode. In a rising inflation scenario, clearly TIPS win out over nominal bonds and their weighting in optimal portfolios increases.

In contrast, a decline in inflation (which we assume reduces inflation expectations proportionately) will push up relative returns on nominal bonds since holders receive a higher real income stream than anticipated. Declining inflation also would reduce the correlation between nominal bonds and TIPS, but it would still be positive.

DECLINING INFLATION SCENARIO

How much of a decline in inflation expectations is sufficient for nominal bonds to replace TIPS in optimum portfolios? The answer is somewhat complicated and conditional on the assumptions made. In brief, if we presume inflation and inflation expectations drop 1% from an initial level of 3%, and that Treasuries have a nominal coupon of 6.5% and TIPS a real coupon of 3.45%, then nominal bond returns would rise to approximately 14%.

This is in response to an 8% increase in price plus a coupon of 6.5%. The return on TIPS would fall 1%, to 5.5%. This is substantially less than the nominal bond return.[16] In contrast, if inflation rises instantaneously by 1%, the return on nominal bonds is –1.1% while the return on TIPS rises 1% to 7.5% (see Table 8).

We can solve for the inflation decline necessary to equilibrate nominal bonds and TIPS on a risk-adjusted basis so both have the same Sharpe ratio. It turns out that this is about 0.3% on an

6. Diversification benefits: adding TIPS and insurance-linked securities increases returns at the same risk level

Efficient frontiers

Returns (%)

Volatility (%)

Based on polynomial approximations in the indicated range

——— Stocks, bonds, cash, TIPS, and insurance-linked securities ⎤
- - - - - Nine assets excluding TIPS and insurance-linked securities ⎦ Diversified international portfolios
· · · · · Stocks, bonds and cash ⎤
——— Eleven assets including TIPS and insurance-linked securities ⎦ Purely domestic portfolios

Table 7. Alternative allocations excluding various asset classes (%)

Return	Commodities	All equities	Cash	Bonds	Corporate bonds	Emerging market debt	Real estate	TIPS	Insurance-linked securities	Portfolio volatility
Excluding cash										
5	100	0	–	0	0	0	9	0	0	30.0
6	78	6	–	0	0	5	0	0	10	22.6
7	39	9	–	0	0	8	0	0	44	11.7
8	25	17	–	0	0	15	0	0	44	7.9
9	21	25	–	0	0	21	0	0	33	6.5
10	19	38		0	0	25	0	0	21	6.5
11	18	44	–	1	1	29	0	0	9	7.7
12	17	51	–	1	1	31	0	0	0	9.6
13	15	61	–	1	1	23	0	0	0	12.5
14	12	67	–	1	1	19	0	0	0	16.0
15	10	73	–	1	1	16	0	0	0	19.8
16	8	78	–	1	1	12	0	0	0	23.8
Excluding cash and commodities										
5	–	0	–	9	0	6	53	21	–	2.9
6	–	7	–	5	0	10	48	20	–	3.2
7	–	13	–	0	2	14	37	21	–	3.9
8	–	19	–	0	0	17	26	22	–	4.8
9	–	26	–	0	0	20	14	21	–	5.7
10	–	33	–	0	0	23	3	20	–	6.6
11	–	44	–	0	0	28	0	10	–	7.7
12	–	53	–	0	0	33	0	0	–	9.0
13	–	58	–	0	0	39	0	0	–	10.6
14	–	69	–	0	0	30	0	0	–	12.9
15	–	80	–	0	0	19	0	0	–	16.3
16	–	90	–	0	0	9	0	0	–	20.1
Excluding cash, insurance–linked securities and commodities										
5	–	3	–	0	0	8	63	25	–	3.0
6	–	9	–	0	0	12	53	26	–	3.5
7	–	15	–	0	0	16	43	26	–	4.2
8	–	21	–	0	0	20	32	26	–	5.1
9	–	27	–	0	0	24	22	26	–	6.0
10	–	36	–	0	0	26	11	25	–	7.0
11	–	44	–	0	0	30	1	24	–	8.1
12	–	54	–	0	0	35	0	11	–	9.0
13	–	60	–	0	0	39	0	0	–	10.6
14	–	69	–	0	0	30	0	0	–	12.9
15	–	80	–	0	0	19	0	0	–	16.3
16	–	90	–	0	0	9	0	0	–	20.1

Note that when only cash is excluded, the lower bound of the risk minimisation frontier is reported. This is not optimal and the higher returns would be accepted with lower risk

annual basis. That is, if there is a 0.3% decline in inflation tomorrow that is sustained, then nominal Treasury securities or TIPS would be equally acceptable.

Eliminate nominal bonds?

INFLATION IS UNPREDICTABLE

In our view, no one can truly predict the path of inflation over the long term. You never know what the Federal Reserve might do next – it has recently relied heavily on a Keynesian theory popular in the 1960s regarding the lineage between unemployment and inflation. Furthermore, there may be an extraneous shock (war,

Table 8. Comparative first-year returns on TIPS versus nominal Treasury bonds in response to inflation shocks (%)

Inflation shock	Nominal Treasury			TIPS			Correlation
	Price	Coupon	Total	CPI adjustment	Real coupon	Total	
−1	7.8	6.5	14.3	2.0	3.45	5.5	Positive but declining
0	0.0	6.5	6.5	3.0	3.45	6.5	Colinear
+1	−7.1	6.5	−1.1	4.0	3.45	7.5	Slightly negative
+2	−13.5	6.5	−7.0	5.0	3.45	8.5	Moderately negative
+3	−19.4	6.5	−12.9	6.0	3.45	9.5	Strongly negative

Compares hypothetical impact on 2007 TIPS versus 2007 nominal Treasury assuming an immediate and sustained change in inflation. The initial nominal bond yield is assumed to be 6.5%, while the TIPS real yield is 3.45% and initial inflation (actual and expected) is 3%.

Table 9. Year-to-year changes in the consumer price index (%)

Year	CPI change	Year	CPI change
1983	3.2	1990	5.4
1984	4.3	1991	4.2
1985	3.6	1992	3.0
1986	1.9	1993	3.0
1987	3.6	1994	2.6
1988	4.1	1995	2.8
1989	4.8	1996	3.0

	1983–96		*1991–96*
Mean	3.5	Mean	2.9
Sigma	0.9	Sigma	0.2

Source: BLS

energy, famine, embargo) or a burst of irrational exuberance at any moment (see Table 9).

Despite this caveat, changes in monetary policy typically show up in the price level about 18 months later. For this reason, given the current relatively tight policy of the Federal Reserve, it is hard to make a case for either a strong surge or significant drop in inflation over the near future.

Therefore, it seems rational to include TIPS in portfolios. Even for those who believe inflation will drop from, say, 3% to 2%. TIPS still offer a method of hedging if it does not. Indeed, if one thinks there is a chance inflation can decline to less than 2%, then a weighting to TIPS is still justified. The solution: weight the probability of lower inflation and hold a combination of nominal bonds and TIPS.[17]

Of course, if inflation rises (as some now fear because of labour force pressures), TIPS will outperform nominal bonds. *We conclude that the overwhelming evidence supports the inclusion of TIPS as a substitute for nominal bonds for at least a significant portion of efficient portfolios.*

Some practical considerations

TIPS ALLOCATION

Of course, the market for TIPS is now only about US$15 billion in size and the secondary market is not incredibly liquid (maybe US$50 million daily). But the Treasury plans more auctions this year. The yield curve will eventually be fleshed out and secondary market liquidity enhanced. For this reason, all but the largest portfolio managers should be able to satisfy their appetite for TIPS.

INSURANCE-LINKED SECURITIES

Insurance-linked securities are more problematic. The market is illiquid and small – under US$2 billion (including insurance and credit-linked securities). But more offerings are planned this year. Even so, it will be difficult to include sufficient insurance-linked securities to reach the level of allocations suggested by our analysis. The only solution is to add to portfolios as much as possible.

SKEWNESS OF OUR ASSET ALLOCATION

As a final note, it is reasonable to argue that our asset allocation is skewed to cash and equity markets. But even if one lowers the expected returns on these asset classes, both TIPS and insurance-linked securities have dominating characteristics that bring them into the optimum portfolio, largely at the expense of Treasury bonds.

Exploiting the information gap

NEVER HEARD OF IT

We finally note that a prime reason for the superior portfolio-enhancing characteristics of TIPS and insurance-linked securities is that these assets are more complex and not well understood by the general market. This is evident in news commentaries and erroneous statements by some public fund portfolio managers. With time, this will change as market liquidity grows and as understanding of the dynamics of these products becomes more widespread.

A TEMPORARY OPPORTUNITY

As market learning occurs, the superior risk-adjusted returns on these assets will vaporise. In particular, we expect the Sharpe ratios of TIPS and nominal Treasuries to eventually converge. The same pattern should evolve for insurance-linked securities – their long-term Sharpe ratio

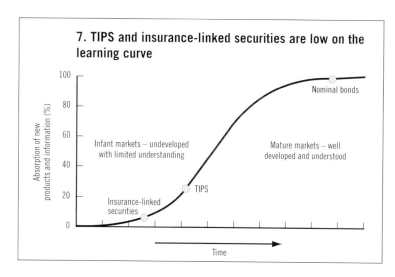

7. TIPS and insurance-linked securities are low on the learning curve

should eventually average about the same as for nominal Treasury securities. For this reason, early participants in these markets will outperform those who stick with classical bond allocations. Life is change.

Summary and conclusion

ELIMINATE NOMINAL BONDS FROM PORTFOLIOS

In brief, we have articulated our view that TIPS and insurance-linked securities can replace nominal bonds in efficient portfolios. Our only reservation is that markets for TIPS are still fairly small and the supply of insurance-linked securities is limited.

The major virtue of TIPS is that they appear to dominate nominal Treasury securities on a risk-adjusted basis. In addition, insurance-linked securities offer limited prospective correlation

with existing asset classes while simultaneously yielding attractive returns versus Treasury securities.

SENSITIVITY ANALYSIS CONFIRMS CONCLUSION'S RIGOUR

These findings are largely invariant with respect to assumed returns and risks for other asset classes. If we increase our Sharpe ratios for domestic securities *vis à vis* international securities, we induce greater allocations to US equities, TIPS and insurance-linked securities, as well as commodities.

The only issue is if we decrease the Sharpe ratio for TIPS. As it converges to that of nominal Treasuries, traditional bonds re-enter the efficient portfolio. We do not expect this to happen soon in the market, however. TIPS offer better prospective portfolio characteristics than nominal bonds, at least until laggard managers discover them.

1 *Returns, volatility, and correlations for each asset class are based on quarterly total return indexes. EAFE and emerging-market equity returns are based on the corresponding Morgan Stanley Capital Indexes. Treasury bonds, corporate bonds, and emerging-market debt are Solomon Brothers indexes. Commodity returns are based on the Goldman Sachs Commodity Index, while real-estate returns are measured by the NCREIF index.*

2 *See, for example, Robert Greer, "What is an Asset Class, Anyway?"* The Journal of Portfolio Management. *Winter 1997, Vol. 23, No. 2, pp. 86–91. Note that for years managed futures funds have attempted to position themselves as an alternative asset class, yet continue to be viewed as on the fringe of legitimacy. The returns of such funds arise largely from profits made on short-term trading in futures markets. However, this activity is fundamentally different from the return earned by carrying a long position in commodities. Such positions earn Treasury returns on balances not deposited as margin, price appreciation in commodities, and rollover yield.*

3 *We discussed this and other issues regarding inflation-protected securities in two previous publications: "US Inflation-Indexed Bonds: An Overview", BT Global Economic Research report, September 6, 1996, and "US Inflation-Protection Notes: Assessing Fair Value", BT Global Economics Research report, November 27, 1996.*

4 *Note that the return on TIPS is multiplicative, not additive. It equals* $(1 + i)(1 + r)$ *where* i *is the real interest rate, and* r *is inflation. In calculating the expected return on TIPS, actual inflation is replaced with expected inflation. The real return is known with certainty while the expected return depends on the inflation assumption. in contrast, nominal cash flows are known with certainty for traditional bonds but real returns are uncertain. Expected real Treasury bond returns thus depend on an assumed inflation rate, diametrically the opposite of TIPS.*

A related issue is taxation. TIPS are taxed on inflation accrual even though it is not received. Treasury bondholders pay taxes only on actual amounts received. TIPS are consequently disadvantaged because of taxation on "phantom profits". For this reason, they are appropriate only for tax-exempt funds, unless short-term trading is the goal.

5 *They also acquired illiquidity risk and the possibility that the CPI could be revised. For clarity of presentation and because these effects are likely small, we ignore them in the discussion.*

6 *The impact on bond prices of changes in real interest rates and inflation is easily illustrated for both TIPS and nominal Treasury bonds. For an inflation-protected security:*

$$P_r = \sum_{j=1}^{n-1} c/(1 + i)^j + (m + c)/(1 + i)^n$$

where P_r *is the price of a "real" inflation-protected security,* c *is the real coupon amount (prior to inflation adjustment),* m *is the real principal due at maturity (also prior to inflation adjustment),* i *is the real interest rate, and there are* n *years of coupon payments. Because inflation does not enter into the formula for determining a real bond's value, changes in inflation have no effect on real bond prices. That is,* $\partial P_r/\partial r = 0$.

Changes in real interest rates do have a significant effect on both real and nominal bond prices:

$$\partial P_r/\partial i = -\sum_{j=1}^{n-1} jc/(1 + i)^{j+1} - n(m + c)/(1 + i)^{n+1} < 0$$

For nominal bonds, price is the discounted present value of future cashflows:

$$P_n = \sum_{j=1}^{n-1} C/(1 + i)^j(1 + r)^j + (M + C)/(1 + i)^n(1 + r)^n$$

where C *is the coupon,* M *the principal, and* r *is expected inflation. Note that we decompose the nominal interest rate* into its real and expected inflation components such that $(1 + t) = (1 + i)(1 + r)$ where t is the nominal interest rate. It follows that:

$$\partial P_n / \partial i = -\sum_{j=1}^{n-1} jC/(1 + i)^{j+1}(1 + r)^j$$
$$-n(M + C)/(1 + i)^{n+1}(1 + r)^n < 0$$

which indicates that nominal bond prices fall when real interest rates rise.

We can further see that $\partial P_r / \partial i > \partial P_n / \partial i$ since

$$\sum_{j=1}^{n-1} jc/(1 + i)^{j+1} + n(m + c)/(1 + i)^{n+1}$$
$$> \sum_{j=1}^{n-1} jC/(1 + i)^{j+1}(1 + r)^j + n(M + C)/(1 + i)^{n+1}(1 + r)^n$$

Because $c < C$, $m < M$, and $(1 + i)(1 + r) > (1 + i)$ it is clear that a change in real interest rates has a larger effect on real bond prices than on nominal bond prices. This difference in general is not large, however.

In addition:

$$\partial P_n / \partial r = -\sum_{j=1}^{n-1} jC/(1 + i)^j(1 + r)^{j+1}$$
$$-n(M + C)/(1 + i)^n(1 + r)^{n+1} < 0$$

which shows that as inflation expectations rise, nominal bond prices decline (the same thing is true for equities by similar logic although if earnings and dividends inflate simultaneously with inflation, there may be no effect).

Of major significance is that varying inflation expectations affect Treasury bond prices while having no impact on TIPS prices. Thus, in the normal course of events, changes in inflation expectations induce volatility in nominal bond prices that is absent from inflation-protected securities. Consequently, nominal bond prices (and returns) should normally be more volatile than TIPS. Only in extreme cases where expected inflation is constant would nominal bond volatility exceed real bond price volatility, and then by only a small amount.

7 Brad Prout, Gary Wyetzner and others contributed to the preparation of this section.

8 We reviewed the evolution of insurance-linked securities in "The Catastrophe Reinsurance Market: Gyrations and Innovations Amid Major Structural Transformation", BT Global Economic Research report, February 3, 1997; reprinted as Chapter 8 of the present volume.

9 The amount issued would have been significantly higher if the California Earthquake Authority had gone ahead with its plan to issue US\$1.5 billion in catastrophe bonds to investors in late 1996. The plan was dropped at the last moment in favour of a reinsurance agreement with Berkshire Hathaway.

10 For more detail on the studies referenced in this section see: R. H. Litzenberger, D. R. Beaglehole, and Craig Reynolds, "Assessing Catastrophe Reinsurance-Linked Securities as a New Asset Class," The Journal of Portfolio Management, Special Issue, Volume 22, pp. 76–86; reprinted as Chapter 12 of the present volume; Kenneth A. Froot, Brian S. Murphy, Aaron B. Stern and Stephen E. Usher, The Emerging Asset Class: Insurance Risk, special report from Guy Carpenter, July 1995; and Michael S. Canter, Joseph B. Cole and Richard L.

Sandor, "Insurance Derivatives: A New Asset Class for Capital Markets and a New Hedging Tool for the Insurance Industry," The Journal of Derivatives, Winter 1996, pp. 89–103; reprinted as Chapter 11 of the present volume.

11 We note that our time horizon is significantly different from the other two studies and that the Paragon index is not a total return index. Also, the Paragon results are numerically based on annual data through 1992 and semi-annual data thereafter. Furthermore, the last five years constitute an unusual pricing period during which reinsurance rates doubled following hurricane Andrew. In addition, it should be mentioned that the Paragon Index excludes the economic exposure of possible actual losses but assumes pricing reflects loss experience.

12 Richard Bernero, Anne McMillen, Eleanor Gibson and others provided assistance on material covered in this section.

13 For a brief review of this and other problems with standard asset models, see Yiannis A. Koskosidis and Antonio M. Duarte, "A Scenario-Based Approach to Active Asset Allocation," The Journal of Portfolio Management, Winter 1997, Vol. 23, No. 2, pp. 74–85.

14 We simply minimise portfolio volatility for given return targets to generate the efficient frontier. In the interest of simplicity, we use actual asset class returns and volatilities – not subtracting out riskless Treasury yields. Mathematically the procedure we follow is:

$$\min \mathbf{b'Vb} \text{ subject to } \mathbf{p'b}=p^* \text{ and } \mathbf{i'b}=1$$

for an arbitrary range of $0 < p^* < p^{max}$ where $\mathbf{V}$ is the $n \times n$ covariance matrix $\mathbf{V} = \mathbf{s'Rs}$. $\mathbf{s}$ is an $n \times 1$ vector of asset class return standard deviations, $\mathbf{R}$ is an $n \times n$ matrix of asset correlations, $\mathbf{b}$ is a $n \times 1$ vector of class weights, $\mathbf{p}$ is $n \times 1$ vector of asset class returns, p^* is the target return, and $\mathbf{i}$ is an $n \times 1$ unit vector. The author is indebted to Paul Schulstad who devised an ingeniously simple computer algorithm to produce these calculations.

15 This reproduces a similar conclusion presented last year in "Emerging Market Equities – Poised To Take-Off Again?" BT Global Economic Research report, May 10, 1996.

We approximate each efficient frontier by polynomials. The expressions for each are included in the following table.

Approximating polynomial coefficients

Assets	b_0	b_1	b_2	b_3	b_4	R^2
3	4.44	0.458	0.0004	−0.0004		0.9982
5	3.93	0.9024	−0.0705	0.0043	−0.0001	0.9982
9	3.15	1.342	−0.0557	0.0009		0.9991
11	3.19	1.458	−0.0689	0.0013		0.9994

Each polynomial is estimated from the following regression equation:

$$r = b_0 + b_1 v + b_2 v^2 + b_3 v^3 + b_4 v^4$$

where r is return and v is volatility.

16 The return of Treasury bonds is simply the change in price of the security plus the coupon yield. The return for TIPS is simply the CPI plus the real coupon.

Treasury bond returns and prices respond significantly to changes in inflation expectations as already shown. If the inflation expectations increase is not large, Treasury bond returns may still be positive if the coupon is large enough to offset the decline in price. Otherwise Treasury returns will decline with an increase in inflation expectations. This is clear since:

$$R_{nt} = P_{nt} - P_{nt-1} + C$$

where R_{nt} is return. Note that $\partial R_{nt}/\partial r = \partial P_{nt}/r - \partial P_{nt-1}/\partial r$. Because $\partial P_{nt}/r < 0$ and $\partial P_{nt-1}/\partial r = 0$, rising inflation creates negative returns if the price decline exceeds C.

17 *Generally, risk-management consultants in the UK recommend at minimum a 5% weighting to index-linked gilts.*

10

Insurance-Risk Securitisation and CAT Insurance Derivatives

Hélyette Geman
University Paris IX Dauphine and ESSEC

The magnitude of insurance-industry losses associated with natural disasters has recently risen in a spectacular manner. Considering only the case of the US, hurricane Andrew in 1991 (US$15.5 billion) and the Northridge earthquake in 1994 (US$12.5 billion) resulted in US$28 billion in *insured* industry losses (for total disaster costs estimated at around US$65 billion) and caused the failure of nine insurance companies. Since the Northridge earthquake (which damaged more than 86,000 structures), two large California insurers have announced that they will no longer write earthquake coverage. The next largest industry loss associated with a natural disaster was caused by hurricane Hugo and amounted to US$2 billion (for a total of US$4 billion losses). Over the five-year period 1988–93, the US insured-industry losses exceeded US$34 billion (expressed in 1993 dollars), more than the cumulative total over the previous 21 years.

The future does not look any more promising: a recent study by Stanford University earthquake experts estimates that a recurrence of the Great Kanto earthquake that devastated Tokyo and Yokohama in 1923 would cause fewer casualties (between 40,000 and 60,000 deaths, in comparison with the 140,000 people killed in 1923); but property damage and economic losses could total US$800 billion–1.2 trillion. This figure is large enough to have an impact on the world financial markets and economies, since the Japanese would withdraw international and domestic investments to rebuild their country.

More generally the US primary-insurance industry has as of today about US$190 billion of standard capital; there is a further US$30 billion in reinsurance and maybe US$10 billion in Lloyd's, which makes less than US$250 billion to cover US property. It is clear that this coverage is far from being appropriate for a US$7 trillion economy. It is therefore natural to look for extra capital in the US$13 trillion (as estimated by the National Underwriter Company) US capital markets. An effective cycle of risk management could be built at the level of global economies: risk of individual agents would be ceded to primary insurers through standard insurance contracts, then partly passed to private reinsurance companies. The remaining risk would, after some securitisation procedure, be transferred to the financial markets, where it would be bought, for an adequate return, by individual or institutional investors (see Figure 1).

The only difficult part of this scheme is the transformation of insurance risk into tradable securities: since the early 1970s, bankers have known how to repackage the loans sold to their customers into collateralised mortgage obligations (CMOs), Government National Mortgage Association (GNMA) pools and other types of mortgage-backed securities. These instruments today represent the second-largest market in volume in the US after the bond market. However, while it is fairly easy to forward the reimbursement cash flows of a loan to an ordinary investor, as opposed to the bank that initiated the loan, it becomes quite difficult to put the responsibility

This chapter was first published in Financial Derivatives & Risk Management, *September 1996. This copyrighted material is reprinted with permission from IFR Publishing.*

102

INSURANCE-
RISK
SECURITISATION
AND CAT
INSURANCE
DERIVATIVES

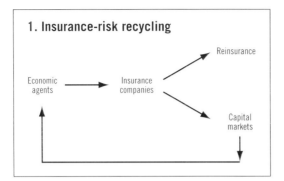

1. Insurance-risk recycling

of the outcomes of an insurance contract into the hands of investors familiar with financial markets but who do not have the expertise or the capital of an insurance company. In comparison the quanto, Asian, barrier and exotic instruments which have lately flourished appear to be easy mechanisms that financial engineering has produced to hedge the different exposures to currency or interest-rate risk faced by firms.

As a result, insurance is one of the few sectors of the economy that has diversified away in the financial markets such a low amount of the industry risk, which is basically retained by a small number of insurers and reinsurers. At the same time the "values-at-risk" have become enormous because of the concentration of expensive buildings, villas, bridges and other structures in regions exposed to natural disasters. Consequently the existing insurance and reinsurance markets experience "overexposure" to catastrophe risk.

Insurance derivatives as a first example of risk securitisation in insurance

In December 1992 the Chicago Board of Trade (CBOT) launched the first insurance derivatives, futures and options. These contracts were meant to offer as an alternative to reinsurance the low transaction costs of futures markets and also the possibility of closing a position (at variance with the long-termed financial reinsurance). The major difficulty to be faced, and which is still valid today, was the non-existence of an identified underlying instrument to which derivatives could be related.

In the first family of the CBOT contracts, the so-called Insurance Statistical Office (ISO) contracts, the key quantity defining the settlement value of the futures contracts (and therefore the payoff of the options written on the futures) was the "loss to premium" ratio observed at maturity on a pool of insurance policies selected by the ISO, an independent statistical firm, from more than 30 insurance companies on the basis of geo-

graphical diversification in the region covered by the contract, diversity of business, etc. The amount of premium collected on the pool was known before the beginning of the trading period; the aggregate amount of losses experienced in the pool during the event quarter was the only random quantity, fully revealed at maturity of the contract.

This key quantity, the aggregate-claim index, became explicitly the underlying variables in the new contracts launched in September 1995. At that time the CBOT introduced an important change on the insurance-derivatives exchange. The contracts were no longer ISO-based, but became PCS (Property Claim Services)-based. One of the goals of this change was to answer some complaints of the insurance industry about the absence of information release by ISO on the already incurred catastrophes during the trading period. In insurance, as much as (and probably more than) in finance, asymmetry of information is very undesirable, especially in a growing market. The new PCS index (aggregate amount of losses) is revised by PCS after the occurrence of an event. The estimate of insured-property damage is obtained by using a combination of procedures, including a general survey of insurers (at least 70% of the market based on premium-written market share), as well as a PCS analysis of census data, tax records and other demographic data. (PCS owns an inventory of buildings, broken down into residential, commercial and industrial buildings, as well as of insured vehicles.) The index is available daily upon request and so determines exactly the values at which positions are closed or initiated, which provides the clarity market participants can expect.

The PCS contracts

Nine types of contracts are offered in terms of geographic specification: one national, four regional (Eastern, Mideastern, Southeastern, Midwestern, Western) and three state (Florida, Texas, California). Take the example of the so-called Eastern September 1996 contracts: the event or "loss period" is the third quarter of 1996 (summer is the season of hurricanes on the east coast of the US). The "development period" may be the six or 12 following months. If we choose the six-month development period, the corresponding contract matures on the day T = March 31, 1997 and the value $L(T)$ of the index – which will determine the pay-off of the expiring options – is the aggregate amount of insured claims related to catastrophes (earthquakes, hurricanes,

103

INSURANCE-
RISK
SECURITISATION
AND CAT
INSURANCE
DERIVATIVES

hail, riots or floods) that took place during the third quarter of 1996 and were reported during that quarter or during the following six months (the development period is meant to allow for a lag between the occurrence of an event and the necessary time to report accurately the amount of claims it generated). For all quarters, contracts of the two types are available: an insurer will choose the one which best agrees with his portfolio of insurance policies and his existing reinsurance coverage.

Besides the region, the loss quarter and the length of the development period, the CBOT offers two types of contracts for the PCS options, the so-called "small cap" versus "large cap" contracts. Small cap options track aggregate industry losses from US$0 to US$20 billion; large cap those between US$20 billion and US$50 billion. The strike price k of the option, as well as the PCS index, are expressed as a percentage of a nominal value of US$100 million; k varies between 0 and 200 for the small cap contracts and between 200 and 500 for big-cap contracts.

Assuming that on July 1, 1996 (date 0) an insurer has bought a six-month-development-period Eastern September 1996 call option with a strike price k = 40 and has paid for this option an amount C(0) (which will be discussed later). If at maturity T = March 31, 1997, the PCS index L(T) is equal to 70, the insurer receives (70 – 40) × 1/100 × 100 million = US$30 million; if the PCS index is equal to 40 or below, the insurer receives nothing (and loses the option premium C(0) he paid at time 0). In all cases the call option payout at maturity is defined (as always) by max{(L(T) – k),0}, where this quantity has to be multiplied by the nominal amount of US$100 million. Obviously an insurer who wants to hedge against an excess of underwriting risk, ie against an excess of potential losses associated with the insurance policies he has sold, will buy call options on the PCS index. The insurer could also sell (although less likely) a put option, in which case he would cash at time 0 the amount P(0) and pay at maturity T the amount max{(k – L(T),0}. US$100 million (which would mean no payment at maturity if the losses registered in the index over the quarter have been very high and his gain P(0) would offset his own losses). As usual, the problem of correlation between an insurer's individual portfolio and the index has to be addressed.

Among the different option strategies which are well known in the financial markets (such as strangle, butterfly, etc), the so-called CAT call spreads have been particularly popular since

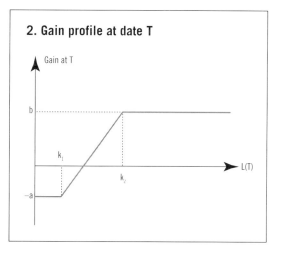

2. Gain profile at date T

catastrophe derivatives started trading. A call spread is the combination of a long position in a call with strike price k_1 and a short position in a call with strike price k_2, with $k_1 < k_2$ and same maturity; k_1 and k_2 are called the attachment points of the call spreads. Since the value of a call is a decreasing function of the strike price, the call spread obviously has a positive value (this value at time 0 is denoted CS(0)). The (algebraic) gain profile at date T of the buyer of a call spread at time 0 is the function of the index value L(T) shown in Figure 2.

The maximum loss is equal to the premium CS(0) with accrued interest. The maximum gain b (obtained of $k_1 \geq k_2$ when both calls are in the money), is equal to b = US$100 ($k_2 – k_1$) million – CS(0)$e^r$T where r denotes the interest rate over the period.

The remarkable property of Figure 2 is that it replicates identically the gain profile obtained by an excess of losses (XL) reinsurance treaty (losses over k_1 up to the level k_2). By no arbitrage, if two positions have the same value "in all states of the world" at time T, ie for all values of L(T), they must have the same value at any time t prior to T. Since insurers and reinsurers know the "market" price of the different layers, these prices can be transferred to the corresponding call spreads.

Pricing CAT options

This paragraph will look at the valuation of a CAT European call, which will obviously give by difference the price of a call spread; the methodology is the same for a CAT put. The problem is as follows: given that at maturity T the payoff of the call is max{(L(T) – k),0}, where L(T) is the index of aggregate insured losses related to events that took place during the loss quarter $[0,T_1]$ and reported during that quarter $[0,T_1]$ or during the development period $[T_1,T_1]$, what is the fair price

INSURANCE-
RISK
SECURITISATION
AND CAT
INSURANCE
DERIVATIVES

C(t) at time t of this call? It is clear that, to determine this value C(t), a crucial choice resides in the modelling of the dynamics of the stochastic process (L(t)) over the trading period $[0,T_1]$.

The model described below was introduced in Geman (1994) and Cummins and Geman (1995). Since the reporting of claims is done continuously on [0,T], the aggregate claim index is written as $\int_0^T S(t)dt$ where (S(t)) is the instantaneous (positive) claim process, which means that during the time interval dt (for instance one day), the new claims added to the index amount to S(t)dt. We can observe that even though actuaries usually represent aggregate losses as a sum, ie as an expression of the type $L(T) = \sum_i X_i$, where the X_i are individual losses, the continuous-time representation is more appropriate for the continuous reporting of claims and agrees with the option-pricing methodology that started with the seminal work by Black and Scholes (1973) and Merton (1973) for standard options and which has been extended in the same type of framework to options on currencies, on bonds, etc. In all these examples the assumption of no arbitrage (that will be made for insurance markets as well) implies the existence of a probability measure Q (so-called risk adjusted) under which the discounted prices of primitive assets are martingales. Q is in fact the actuarial probability under which actuaries compute the premiums of insurance policies. Consequently, it is under the probability measure Q that we are going to describe the dynamics of the instantaneous claim process (S(t)).

To take into account the difference between the two subperiods of the lifetime [0,T] of the option, the instantaneous claim process (S(t)) is assumed to be driven over the interval $[0,T_1]$ by a Poisson-diffusion process, namely:

$$dS(t) = S(t)[\alpha dt + \sigma dW_t] + \kappa dN_t \qquad (1)$$

where:
α, σ and κ are constant, with σ and κ positive
(W_t) is a Brownian motion under Q
(N_t) is a Poisson process whose intensity λ ($\lambda >$ 0) represents the frequency of occurrence of jumps, κ denoting their magnitude.

In the right-hand side of equation (1), the diffusion term is meant to represent the randomness in the reporting of the claims, the Poisson process to represent the big losses associated to catastrophes (all the arguments and the methodology developed here can be immediately extended to a finite number, for instance three

Table 1: Monte Carlo simulation prices of call spreads

$\alpha = r = 0.1$; $\alpha' = 0.15$; $\sigma = \sigma' = 0.5$; $\lambda = 0.5$; $\kappa = US\$4bn$

Time to maturity	CAT 20–40	CAT 40–60	CAT 60–80
0.20	1.70	0.51	0.09
0.35	1.98	0.52	0.10
0.45	1.99	0.55	0.10

Poisson processes with intensities λ_1, λ_2, λ_3, and magnitudes κ_1, κ_2, κ_3 which would represent respectively the major, medium and small-sized catastrophes). A lognormal assumption (without any jump component) as in the Black–Scholes model performs poorly when it is tested on catastrophe historical data.

During the reporting period $[T_1,T]$ the instantaneous claim process (S(t)) may be reduced to a pure diffusion, with drift α' and volatility σ' possibly different from the values α and σ and the dynamics under Q of (S(t)) are defined on $[T_1,T]$ by:

$$dS(t) = S(t) [\alpha'dt + \sigma'dW_t] \qquad (2)$$

We can observe at this point that we have introduced in our model two sources of randomness while we have a whole series of layers of reinsurance – our "primitive" assets – which are traded by insurers and reinsurers. This entails the completeness of the insurance derivatives markets and allows us to write the price of a call option at time t as:

$$C(t) = e^{-r(T-t)} E[max(L(T) - k,0] \qquad (3)$$

Given the complexity of L(T) (integral of a Poisson-diffusion process), it is necessary to run Monte-Carlo simulations to obtain the values of the different calls C(t), and hence of call spreads CS(t). Values of these call spreads for several sets of parameters are provided in Geman (1994) and Cummins and Geman (1995). An alternative modelling of the claim index, closer to the actuarial representation, is proposed in Geman and Yor (1997).

Conclusion

Even though the volume of exchange-traded insurance derivatives is not yet very high, this market is likely to take off rapidly at some point. As of October 1996 the Catex (Catastrophe Risk Exchange) should allow property and casualty insurers, reinsurers and brokers to swap in over-the-counter transactions exposure to natural disasters. For instance, two companies may agree on a partial, reciprocal liability for a defined component of each other's risk, such as US$50 million of New York windstorm exposure for US$100 million of Midwest tornado exposure.

Besides these insurance derivatives and swaps, other insurance-tailored products are being designed by investment bankers and financial institutions that have appreciated the immensity of the insurance markets and the profits at stake in the process of insurance-risk securitisation.

INSURANCE-RISK SECURITISATION AND CAT INSURANCE DERIVATIVES

11

Insurance Derivatives
A New Asset Class for the Capital Markets and a New Hedging Tool for the Insurance Industry

Michael S. Canter, Joseph B. Cole and Richard L. Sandor
AIG Risk Finance; Hedge Financial Products

The property insurance industry has paid out over US$60 billion in losses in the past five years due to increasingly severe catastrophes such as hurricane Andrew (1992, US$16 billion), the Northridge earthquake (1994, US$12.5 billion), hurricane Opal (1995, US$2.1 billion) and hurricane Fran (1996, US$1.6 billion).[1] Some industry experts believe that even larger catastrophes are looming because population and building development continue to increase in highly exposed coastal areas such as California, Florida and Texas.[2] In addition, there may be good reason to believe that such catastrophes will occur more frequently and with greater force in the future because of changes that are taking place in the earth's atmosphere.[3]

At present, however, the insurance and reinsurance industries simply do not have the resources needed to support a major catastrophe. The primary insurance industry in the US has US$239 billion of capital and the reinsurance industry has US$52 billion of capital.[4] Due to various asbestos and toxic hazards that have occurred in the past four years, there is US$26 billion in outstanding environmental liabilities;[5] thus, there is approximately US$265 billion of capital that must service a country with US$25 trillion–US$30 trillion worth of property.[6] As one might expect, this imbalance of supply and demand, coupled with the insurance industry's elevated level of risk and reward potential, has prompted an influx of capital into the reinsurance business. Prior to hurricane Andrew in 1992, not a single reinsurance company specialised in property catastrophe reinsurance; today there are eight Bermuda-based catastrophe

reinsurers with a total capital of US$6.5 billion. The additional capacity that these Bermuda reinsurers have provided, however, is not adequate.

We believe that, for the needed capacity to be achieved, non-traditional forms of reinsurance capacity such as hedge funds, pension funds and commodity funds need to be tapped. For this to occur, insurance risks must be transformed into securities and derivatives that an investor can understand and can therefore include in an investment portfolio.[7] These financial instruments must also be effective hedging and risk management tools that the insurance industry is willing to use. Catastrophe-linked options and bonds are innovations that have the potential to meet these needs, and thereby bridge the gap between the capital and insurance markets.

In fact, this process has already begun. Recently investors oversubscribed to buy the two largest catastrophe bond issues to date – a US$477 million issue by USAA and a US$137 million issue by Swiss Re. In addition, the catastrophe options traded on Chicago Board of Trade (CBOT) have reached an open interest of over 18,000 contracts.

This chapter focuses on the development and use of catastrophe-linked securities and derivatives as an alternative hedging mechanism for the

This chapter was first published in Journal of Applied Corporate Finance, Vol 10, no 3, 1997. *This copyrighted material is reprinted with permission from Stern Stewart Management Services Inc. An earlier version of this article was published in the Winter 1996 issue of* Journal of Derivatives. *The authors would like to thank their colleagues at Hedge Financial for their comments and assistance, particularly Anthony Chiarenza and Dan Newberg.*

insurance industry and as a new asset class for the capital markets. After a brief description of the property reinsurance market, we then show how each of these instruments can be used as a hedging tool. Next we demonstrate that securitised catastrophe risk has the characteristics of a promising new asset class for capital market investors – namely, expected positive excess returns and returns that are uncorrelated with the returns of traditional assets. Lastly we discuss the evolution and performance of these markets to date.

Reinsurance contracts viewed as option spreads

Insurers use reinsurance to reduce the volatility of operating results, to provide financing and to increase capacity (the amount of coverage a company can provide). The primary insurance market is characterised by the sale of insurance policies, such as automobile and homeowner policies, from a primary insurer to the insured. Primary insurers may then "cede" or pass on some or all of their insurance risk to another insurer, called the "reinsurer," which charges a premium for assuming this risk. Reinsurers, in turn, may "retrocede" or pass on portions of their reinsurance risk to other reinsurers, which in this type of transaction are called "retrocessionaries".

A typical reinsurance contract provides the insurer with protection above an agreed-upon dollar amount of losses called the "attachment" or "trigger" point; in this respect, it is very similar to option-based hedging strategies. For example, "a layer of traditional reinsurance" in which the insurer is seeking coverage for US$10 million in excess of US$30 million of losses would require the reinsurer to pay up to, but no more than, US$10 million beyond the initial US$30 million in losses retained by the reinsured. If we think of the insurance company's loss as the "underlying," this traditional "excess-of-loss"

policy is similar to the insurer hedging his risk by buying a call with a strike of US$30 million and simultaneously selling a call with a strike of US$40 million. The long call with the strike of US$30 million enables the insurer to receive the excess loss over US$30 million, while the short call with the strike of US$40 million places a cap on this payment of US$10 million. This combination of being long a call at one strike price and at the same time short a call with a higher strike price is called a "bull" call spread.

As we will demonstrate below, the similarities between reinsurance contracts and call spreads allow for an easy transformation of these insurance risks into bonds and exchange-traded options.

Catastrophe-linked options and bonds: new hedging tools

CONTRACT SPECIFICATIONS OF PCS CAT OPTIONS
On September 29, 1995 the CBOT began trading options contracts based on Property Claims Services (PCS) indexes, which track the aggregate amount of insured losses resulting from catastrophic events that occur in given regions and risk periods.[8] After a catastrophic event occurs, PCS estimates the insured property damage by surveying a wide range of insurers regarding the dollar amount of claims they expect to receive.[9] PCS also uses its own information about the value of the property in the affected counties and, in some cases, conducts its own on-the-ground survey of the damage. Once PCS has made its assessment, it releases an official loss estimate for each of the states affected. The state losses are added to the appropriate regional and/or state indexes (see Table 1 for a listing) so that each index represents the total losses incurred in that region during the risk period.[10]

The risk period for each index is the time period over which losses are aggregated. For an index in which catastrophes are seasonal (as in the case of hurricanes and tornadoes), the risk period is quarterly and the options trade on a March, June, September, December cycle. For regions in which catastrophes are not seasonal (earthquakes), the risk period is annual and only a December contract is traded. Each index is zero at the beginning of its risk period and increases by one point for each US$100 million of insured property damage that occurs in that time period.

Following each risk period, moreover, there is a "loss-development" period of either six or

Table 1. PCS catastrophe indexes

Region	Risk period	Contract months	States covered
Florida	Quarterly	Mar, June, Sep, Dec	FL
Texas	Quarterly	Mar, June, Sep, Dec	TX
California	Annual	Dec	CA
Eastern	Quarterly	Mar, June, Sep, Dec	Includes Northeastern and Southeastern regions
Northeastern	Quarterly	Mar, June, Sep, Dec	ME, NH, VT, MA, CT, RI, NY, NJ, PA, DE, MD, DC
Southeastern	Quarterly	Mar, June, Sep, Dec	VA, WV, NC, SC, GA, FL, AL, MS, LA
Midwestern	Quarterly	Mar, June, Sep, Dec	OK, AR, TN, KY, OH, MI, IN, IL, WI, MN, ND, SD, IA, NE, KS, MO
Western	Annual	Dec	HI, AK, WA, OR, CA, NV, AZ, NM, UT, CO, WY, MT, ID
National	Quarterly, Annual	Mar, June, Sep, Dec, Annual	all 50 states plus Washington DC

12 months. During this time, PCS will update the amount of damage that occurred during the risk period as more information becomes available. For example, if there were storms in Florida in the third quarter of 1997 that caused an aggregate of US$10 billion of damage, the September 1997 Florida index value would be 100. But if during the fourth quarter, PCS determines that the storms actually caused US$12.25 billion of damage, the September 1997 Florida index would be adjusted to 122.5, while the December 1997 Florida index would be unaffected by this change.

Contracts are available for trading throughout the development period; thus, a September 1997 12-month development contract is available for trading until September 1998. The development period is necessary due to the difficulty in making a timely and accurate assessment of the amount of damage that has occurred after a large catastrophic event. The development period thus insures that the indexes are accurate reflections of the damages incurred, and that buyers receive the full benefits of their hedges.[11]

Option contracts are now trading on the five regional, three state and two national indexes listed in Table 1. The owner of a PCS option has the right, but not the obligation, to exercise his option at the pre-specified strike price upon the option's expiration. These options are cash-settled; that is, if the owner of a call option chooses to exercise it, he simply receives a cash payment equivalent to the index dollar value minus the strike dollar value. (An owner of a put contract would receive a cash payment equivalent to the strike value minus the index value.) For example, if a company buys September 10, 1996 Northeast 50 call contracts, it would only choose to exercise its option if the index were to settle at a value higher than 50. Each index point has a cash value of US$200. Thus, if the index settles at 60, the company would receive a cash payment of US$20,000 (cash payment = $(60 - 50) \times 10 \times$ US$200).

Each of the PCS options can be traded as either a "small-cap" or "large-cap" contract. Small-cap options track aggregate insured losses from US$0 to US$20 billion, and large-cap options track losses from US$20 billion to US$50 billion. These caps limit the amount of losses that are included under each contract, and thus turn a seller of an uncovered call into a call spread seller. (In a call spread, a seller sells a call at one strike value and simultaneously buys another call of the same expiration at a higher strike value, thereby limiting his potential loss to the difference between the strike prices of the two options.) Thus, a seller of a December Western 1997 150 call, in essence, is selling a 150/200 call spread (or, in insurance terminology, the US$15 billion–20 billion industry loss layer). If there is an aggregate amount of insured damage in the Western region totalling US$25 billion (250 index points), the seller of a 150 call will need to pay only US$10,000 ((200 – 150) × US$200) for each call spread written – not US$20,000 ((250 – 150) × US$200).

In theory, these caps play an important role because traders would not want to write out-of-the-money calls for a small premium while bearing the risk of unlimited losses. In practice, market participants recognise that even these caps do not provide enough protection against large losses, and they have therefore traded mostly call spreads. The most commonly traded small and large-cap call spreads transfer US$4,000 (or 20 index points) and US$10,000 (50 index points) of risk per spread, respectively.[12] Puts can also be traded on all of the indexes, but they rarely are.

There are, however, no underlying futures contracts listed for trading the PCS catastrophe indexes. This makes PCS options the first contracts ever listed on the CBOT that do not have underlying futures contracts. Further details on the contract specifications are listed in Table 2.

HEDGING EXAMPLES AND POTENTIAL
BENEFITS OF USING PCS OPTIONS
An insurance company may seek to buy a call spread as an alternative to buying a traditional layer of reinsurance. For example, a hypothetical insurance company, Innovative Mutual, has a high concentration of its exposure in Florida and wants to limit its potential worst-case scenario loss of US$120 million to just US$80 million. Innovative Mutual comprises 1% of the industry

Table 2. PCS catastrophe option contract specifications

Method of trade:	Open outcry
Index valuation:	Each index point has a cash value of US$200, and represents US$100 million of insured damage
Premiums:	Quoted in points and tenths of a point
Tick size:	One-tenth of a point, or US$20
Small/large-cap options:	Both small and large-cap options contracts are listed for trading. Small-cap contracts track aggregate estimated catastrophic losses from US$0 to US$20 billion; Large-cap contracts track catastrophic losses from US$20 billion to US$50 billion
Development period:	Six or 12 months
Trading hours:	8.30am to 12.30am Chicago time

in Florida, but has found that because it is "underexposed" (relative to the industry) along the coast, it experiences losses of 80% of its expected market share. Instead of buying a traditional US$40 million in excess of US$80 million reinsurance layer, Innovative decides to buy PCS call spreads by employing the methodology outlined in Table 3.

Thus, Innovative buys 4,000 September Florida 100/150 call spreads.[13] If Innovative paid 7.5 points per spread, a 15% rate-on-line (premium of 7.5 divided by a gross risk exposure of 50), this hedge would cost it US$6 million and provide it with US$40 million of coverage.

Similar strategies could be used by (re)insurance companies to fill in gaps in their traditional reinsurance programmes or to synthetically alter the composition of their risk.[14] For example, if a reinsurance company writes only traditional reinsurance in the east, but would like to receive the benefit of being more geographically diversified, it could sell western and midwestern call spreads. A (re)insurance company could also use the PCS options to swap the layers of risk to which it is exposed. For example, if a (re)insurance company feels it is overexposed to a US$6 billion–10 billion event in the southeast, it could buy southeastern 60/100 call spreads and sell 100/140 call spreads so that it shifts some of its exposure to a higher level. Or, if an insurance company can buy traditional reinsurance only at a retention (strike) level it finds intolerably high, it can use PCS call spreads to purchase coverage at retention levels below its traditional coverage.

For example, suppose Innovative Mutual wanted to purchase a traditional reinsurance coverage of US$40 million in excess of US$80 million in losses, but reinsurance companies were only willing to provide Innovative with reinsurance coverage of US$20 million in excess of US$100 million of losses from US$100 million to US$80 million by buying 4,000 September Florida 100/125 call spreads (following the same methodology outlined in Table 3). Insurance Corporation of Hanover, a wholly owned subsidiary of Germany's Hanover Re, has used PCS options in this way to fill in the gap between its desired retention level and the retention level provided by its traditional reinsurance.[15]

Thus, it is clear that PCS options are an innovation that can be of great use to the (re)insurance industry. But in order for PCS options to succeed, the insurance industry needs to be willing to hedge its risks in a new and different way. As a first step, the insurance industry will need to become familiar and comfortable with the language and use of derivatives, as well as the basis risk involved in using PCS options. Basis risk is the risk that the losses that individual (re)insurance companies incur will not have the anticipated correlation with the losses that the industry as a whole experiences. In the Innovative Mutual example given above, the basis risk is the risk that the losses that Innovative experiences will differ greatly from the anticipated 0.8% (1% × 80%) of industry losses.

It is common in financial markets for hedgers to accept basis risk in exchange for the increase in efficiency and the reduction in credit risk and earnings volatility that comes from using a standardised, exchange-traded contract. The traditional reinsurance market is notorious for its lack of price transparency, abundance of legal work, inefficient transfer of funds, and long and difficult price negotiations. Transacting in PCS options is a much easier process. Price quotes for PCS options are easily accessible via market data vendors, commodities brokers, and the Internet; and when a trade occurs, the involved parties' accounts are automatically credited or debited.

Insurance derivatives may also help primary insurance companies in managing credit risk. When a primary purchases traditional reinsurance, it has the credit risk that its reinsurer may default. There is considerably less credit risk involved in purchasing PCS options because the clearing house guarantees every trade. There has never been a default by a US clearing house and it is unlikely that even a US$50 billion catastrophe

---

Table 3. Calculating a hedge for Innovative Mutual

Objective: Innovative Mutual wishes to hedge US$40 million in exposure above US$80 million in retained losses

Assumptions: Innovative Mutual has a 1% market share in Florida, but experiences (losses of?) 80% of its expected market share

Solution: Buy 4,000 September 1996 100/150 vertical call spreads

Buy calls with strike price =
= (Beginning of company's loss layer/company's market share) * (loss adj. factor)
= (US$80 million/1%) * (1/80%)
= US$10 billion or 100 index points

Sell calls with strike price =
= (End of company's loss layer/company's market share) * (loss adj. factor)
= (US$120 million/1%) * (1/80%)
= US$15 billion or 150 index points

Number of 100/150 spreads to buy =
= Amount of protection needed/US$ amount of protection offered by each spread
= (US$40 million/(150 − 100)) × (US$200)
= 4,000 spreads

could cause such a default. The CBOT has taken the precaution of requiring sellers of PCS calls and call spreads to post margin of 20% of their maximum loss – which is limited by the spread and the caps (see Table 2). In addition, insurance risk is likely to represent only a small portion of the clearing house's risk exposure, so that even if some customers were to default, the clearing-house should have the capital to cover them.

Thus, overall, PCS call spreads are valuable hedging mechanisms that have the potential to increase efficiency and decrease the credit risks and costs that the insurance industry currently experiences when buying reinsurance.

CATASTROPHE-LINKED BONDS

Catastrophe-linked (CAT) bonds are another mechanism that (re)insurance companies can use to gain access to the capacity of the capital markets. A CAT bond constitutes an exchange of principal for periodic coupon payments wherein the payment of the coupon and/or the return of the principal of the bond is linked to the occurrence of a specified catastrophic event. An insurance company that wishes to securitise its risk by issuing a CAT bond will typically establish an off-shore special purpose vehicle (SPV) reinsurer from which it will buy a reinsurance contract. The SPV will then issue a bond that cedes that reinsured risk to the capital markets. In this type of structure, the insurance company pays a rein-surance premium to the SPV, which passes this premium on to the investors in the form of a coupon.[16] In turn, the investors must post the notional amount of the bond (the maximum loss) in trust. All of the funds in the trust are then invested in short-term US Treasuries. The risk being borne by the investors is thus fully collater-alised and eliminates any credit risk issues. If there is an event that causes losses exceeding the attachment point in the geographic region and time period delineated in the bond, the investors will lose a portion or all of their principal. If there are no such trigger events, the investor will have earned the coupon plus the risk-free rate.[17]

An example of a note with this kind of structure is the USAA hurricane note. In June of 1997, USAA, a Texas-based insurance company, established a special purpose reinsurance company called Residential Re, which issued a US$477 million note that has two tranches: US$313 million of A-2 notes that have a coupon of 5.75% plus Libor, in which the principal is completely at risk; and US$164 million of A-1 notes that have a coupon of 2.82% over Libor, in which the

coupon is at risk, but the full return of the principal is guaranteed. A default of these notes will be triggered if there is a hurricane on the east coast between July 1, 1997 and December 15, 1997 that causes over US$1 billion of claims against USAA. A complete default will occur if the damage from any one hurricane causes USAA claims of at least US$1.5 billion. Thus, the buyer of the A-2 notes is effectively writing USAA a US$1 bil-lion/US$1.5 billion call spread, one whereby the investor shares proportionately 62.6% of the maximum loss of US$500 million. This note also includes a development period of six months.

Of the principal of the A-1 notes, approxi-mately half, or US$85 million, will actually be used for reinsurance. If a trigger event occurs, the US$85 million that was at risk will be used to pay USAA's claims. The other US$77 million will be invested in treasury securities (for at most 10 years) until the principal can be returned in full. If there are no trigger events during the risk period, the principal will be returned in full after the initial six-month development period. This kind of structure is designed for entities that can invest only in securities in which the return of principal is guaranteed (AAA-rated notes).[18]

Why would USAA or any other (re)insurance company choose to buy its reinsurance via a CAT bond instead of buying traditional reinsurance? CAT bonds and options were not created to replace traditional reinsurance, but rather to sup-plement it. Property/catastrophe reinsurers cur-rently have a concentrated amount of risk associated with certain perils such as hurricanes on the east coast of the US and earthquakes in California. These reinsurers, therefore, cannot afford to assume any more risk in these regions, even though primary insurers would like to buy more reinsurance coverage in these areas. This is especially true for low frequency, high-severity events – the kind that can be insured by "top-layer" catastrophe coverage.[19] Thus, we believe the needs of insurers present an opportunity for the capital markets to reinsure these hard-to-place risks "synthetically" by means of CAT bonds and CBOT transactions.

The capital markets have the ability to offer large amounts of capacity for catastrophe risks that the traditional reinsurance market simply cannot handle. This ability stems not only from the size of the capital markets, but also from the fact that capital markets' portfolios have virtually no exposure to catastrophe risk. Thus, securi-tised insurance risk offers money managers a new asset class through which they can diversify their portfolios (see the next section). For a reinsurance company, however, the exact opposite may be true – assuming more top-layer risk may further concentrate its risk to catastrophes. After catastrophes occur there are always a number of reinsurers who go out of business and default on their obligations to pay their claims. This credit risk issue is alleviated when a (re)insurance company sells a CAT bond.

(Re)insurance companies may find CAT bonds to be an attractive alternative to PCS options because they have a more flexible structure. In a CAT bond, a (re)insurance company can customise its hedge to be indexed on its own losses, as is done in traditional reinsurance, or it can be indexed on PCS. In addition, a bond can be structured to resemble not only "excess-of-loss" contracts, but also "quota-share" contracts in which investors share proportionately in the gains and losses of the reinsured.

CAT bonds and the SPV structure also provide the issuing insurance company with access to a broader set of investors than PCS options. Some investors, such as pension funds and mutual funds, are restricted from transaction in *derivatives* such as PCS options, but are allowed to invest in *securities* such as bonds or notes. The ability to offer principal-protected tranches of a note increases the investor base even further because there are some investors that can only invest in AAA-rated securities. This larger set of potential investors may be especially important for companies seeking to transfer large amounts of risk to the capital markets.

The biggest disadvantage to issuing a CAT bond instead of hedging through the purchase of PCS options is the cost. Setting up the SPV, getting a note rated and paying investment bankers can be very costly, depending on the complexity of the structure and the size of the deal. For some companies, another drawback of issuing CAT bonds is that proprietary information about a company's potential losses will become relatively public information.

From the investor's viewpoint, the biggest disadvantage of CAT bonds is the loss of leverage. PCS options require only a 20% margin, whereas the CAT bonds require 100% funding of the potential maximum loss. Thus, when an investor sells PCS call spreads, he can invest 80% of his maximum loss in a manner of his own choosing, instead of this money being invested in Treasuries as stipulated in most CAT bond structures. For hedge funds and more aggressive money managers this makes selling PCS call spreads more appealing than CAT

bonds.[20] More conservative investors, however, might prefer assuming securitised insurance risk via a bond because a bond rating will allow them to assess the relative risk and return of these investments versus traditional debt instruments.

Overall, then, the flexibility and security nature of CAT bonds enable (re)insurance companies to buy fully-funded reinsurance from a diverse set of institutional investors.

Securitised insurance risk as a new asset class

In the past, derivatives markets have succeeded only when both hedgers and speculators have found it attractive to participate in a market. This will also need to occur if insurance derivatives are to succeed. As discussed in the previous section, insurance and reinsurance companies – the potential hedgers – have incentives to securitise their risk. If reinsurance companies were the only ones who bought CAT bonds or sold PCS call spreads, some beneficial price discovery would occur, but the more important goal of attracting additional reinsurance capacity would not be achieved. This goal can be achieved only if the capital markets find securitised insurance to be an attractive investment opportunity. We believe that this will be the case because of the new asset class characteristics of insurance risk: expected positive excess returns and portfolio diversification benefits.

We theorise that investors will be able to earn a return in excess of the risk-free rate by selling PCS call spreads and buying CAT bonds due to the imbalance of supply and demand that exists for catastrophe reinsurance. In the language of derivatives, this is called a "net hedger imbalance" – that is, a situation in which the number of hedgers wishing to buy is greater than the number of speculators willing to sell. When this is the case, the hedgers must be willing to pay speculators a spread (or risk premium) over the "true probability of loss" in order to entice them into trading with them.

For example, suppose there are an abundance of insurance companies that need to buy coverage to protect themselves from a US$6 billion–8 billion east coast hurricane. They would, therefore, like to buy September Eastern 60/80 call spreads. Let's assume that the "fair" market value for the call spread is a price of two index points per spread or a 10% rate-on-line. (The rate-on-line is the premium paid divided by the gross amount of risk transferred.) In this case, the "fair" rate-on-line was estimated to be 10% because there has only been one year in the past 10 in which aggregate damage exceeded US$6 billion. If, however, there are more hedgers who want to buy the 60/80 call spreads than there are speculators who are willing to sell 60/80 call spreads, the hedgers will be forced to raise the price they are willing to pay for this coverage. Some hedgers will find that they would rather go without this catastrophe coverage than pay more than 10%, but other hedgers will place a greater utility on hedging their risk, and will decide to pay more than the historical expected value. In today's market, September Eastern 60/80 call spreads, and their equivalent in the over-the-counter market, trade at approximately a 17% rate-on-line, which implies a risk premium of 7%.[21]

In order for capital market participants to be comfortable participating in the securitised insurance market, it is essential that they develop a methodology for pricing insurance risk. Unfortunately, the Black–Scholes option pricing formula does not apply to pricing catastrophe options; therefore other pricing methods must be used. Some market participants have simply relied on historical loss data, inflation rates and demographic adjustments to estimate how often an event can be expected to occur. (This was the methodology used above to determine the 10% rate-on-line for the September Eastern 60/80 call spread.) A more sophisticated approach has been taken by some reinsurance companies which have developed computer models that use data on property values, simulation paths of hurricanes and epicentres of earthquakes to price catastrophe options. Commercial companies like Risk Management Solutions (RMS), Equecat and Applied Insurance Research (AIR) sell access to their catastrophe pricing models. These companies are often hired by the investment banks to estimate the probability of default on a bond. These estimates are prominently displayed in bond prospectuses and are used as a basis for pricing. The rating agencies also use these models, as well as their own asset-backed securities models, to rate catastrophe-linked bonds.[22]

Thus, the pricing of these assets is at the very beginning of its development.[23] But if there truly are positive excess returns to be made from writing PCS call spreads, we expect that Wall Street firms will invest the time and money necessary to model and price catastrophes, just as they have done with mortgage, interest rates and commodities.[24]

It is useful for investors to think of CAT bonds and PCS call spreads in the same way as they think about high-yield bonds. In the high-yield bond market, an investor charges an interest rate that he expects to compensate him for the probability of default. Similarly, when buying CAT bonds or selling PCS call spreads, the investor charges a coupon or option premium that is expected to compensate him for the probability of a catastrophe event. In the event of a default, an owner of a high-yield bond stands to lose the principal of the bond and its future coupon payments. A "synthetic reinsurer" stands to lose the maximum coverage provided by the call spread (or CAT bond) plus the future interest those funds would have earned. For example, someone who sells 250 30/50 Western PCS call spreads at a price of two index points (10% rate-on-line) stands to lose US$1 million plus interest. (Let's assume that the seller posts US$1 million of margin, which earns the risk-free rate.) A similar investment in the corporate bond market is a bond with a principal of US$1 million that pays a 15% annual coupon when the risk-free interest rate is 5%. This comparison is especially analogous if the investor assesses the true probability of default/loss to be 5%.

Some market observers say, however, that this analogy breaks down when one considers that when a bond default does occur, the investor is able to recoup 43% of his principal on average; whereas when catastrophes occur the recovery rate is expected to be considerably lower. This higher probability of losing the entire principal, given that a default does occur, has led to the development of principal-protected tranches in some CAT bond issues.

Those investors who have been participating in the market thus far have diversified this risk of default by creating a portfolio of insurance risks. Just as an investor can buy a portfolio of debt issues to diversify his default risk, an investor can diversify his risk to any particular catastrophic event by buying CAT bonds and selling PCS call spreads across a number of regions and risk periods. Moody's Investor Service has estimated that B-rated corporate bonds have a 10-year cumulative default probability of over 40%.[25] Guy Carpenter, a reinsurance brokerage firm, has estimated that "top-layer" catastrophe reinsurance has a 10-year cumulative default probability of 22%. Guy Carpenter has further estimated that the return on the insurance risk over the past 10 years has been 9.2% over treasuries, while B-rated bonds have only returned 4.63% over treasuries.[26] Thus, the risk/reward ratio of selling catastrophe reinsurance is superior to that of owning certain high-yield bonds. The structural shortage of "top layer" catastrophe reinsurance has enabled this situation to persist.

The returns and risk premiums from buying a portfolio of CAT bonds and selling PCS call spreads are expected to be especially large in the years following a major catastrophe. For example, catastrophe reinsurance rates doubled after hurricane Andrew in 1992. This change in price may have been due to a shift in people's perception of the "true probability of loss." In addition, it reflected a surge in demand from insurance companies and an effort by reinsurance companies to avoid concentrated risk exposure in any one area of the country.[27]

An influx of capacity provided by synthetic reinsurers should cause a reduction in the levels of risk premiums so that prices more closely reflect the "true probability of loss". This should also lead to a reduction in the volatility of reinsurance prices as the reinsurance supply curve becomes more elastic. This would be an enormous benefit to insurance companies (and possibly consumers of insurance), which would no longer have to pay as high a price for reinsurance coverage.

Securitised insurance risks represent a new asset class that portfolio managers can use to further diversify their traditional portfolios of stocks, bonds, cash, and real estate. Intuitively one expects the occurrence of catastrophes and the amount of damage they induce to be uncorrelated with movements in the prices of stocks. To verify this hypothesis, we correlated the yearly percentage change in the S&P500 index with the yearly percentage change in the PCS national index, using data from 1949 to the present. We found the correlation coefficient to be insignificantly different from zero ($\rho = -0.05$, $t = -0.33$, as shown in Figure 1). Thus, options on PCS indexes are expected to be zero-beta assets.

By adding insurance risk to their portfolios, investors can move their portfolios closer to the "efficient frontier." The efficient frontier consists of all the optimal combinations of minimum risk and highest return available to investors, where risk is measured by the standard deviation of returns, and return is measured by the total holding period return for the portfolio over a particular time period. New assets that have low correlation with an existing portfolio and are also expected to earn high returns are extremely valuable because they can simultaneously increase a portfolio's returns and reduce its risk. Guy Carpenter estimates that by adding 2% catastrophe risk to a portfolio of 60% stocks and 40% bonds, the expected return of the portfolio increases by 1.25% and the standard deviation of the portfolio decreases by 0.25%.[28] These kinds of potential benefits are sure to attract the attention of the capital markets.

Alternatively, one can just buy reinsurance stocks to get some access to insurance risk without having to invest the time and money in modelling catastrophe options. The benefits that come from being a synthetic reinsurer, however, cannot be duplicated by owning stock in reinsurance companies. Reinsurance stocks are highly correlated with the general movement in stock prices. We found that a portfolio of 10 prominent catastrophe reinsurers has a beta of 0.83 with the S&P500. Thus, securitised insurance risk offers investors diversification that does not currently exist in the market.

In sum, we believe that the proper incentives are in place for the capital and insurance markets to provide a market-based solution to the national problem of a structural shortage of property catastrophe reinsurance.

The performance of PCS options

PCS options are perhaps the most innovative contract developed by the CBOT in decades. As in the case of many new contracts, however, speculative and hedging interest is developing at a cautious but steady pace. Initial trading in PCS options has not been very liquid, but this was expected due to the learning process that insurance professionals must undergo to familiarise themselves with derivatives, and capital markets professionals to familiarise themselves with insurance risk. The issue of liquidity is more of an issue for capital markets professionals, who are accustomed to being able to enter and reverse trades at a moment's notice. Whether or not PCS options will ever reach this level of liquidity remains to be seen.

In the meantime, investors need to think of themselves as "synthetic reinsurers". As a

1. Catastrophe losses versus S&P500

"synthetic reinsurer", the investor needs to decide how much risk he is willing to take, and for what price, and assume that he is entering an "insurance deal" that will last the duration of the contract, rather then entering a "trade" that can be reversed at any time. One advantage of transacting in PCS call spreads is that an investor's potential losses are pre-defined (no. of contracts × spread × US$200); thus, the investor does not need to worry about what the liquidity of the market will be in the case of a US$50 billion event.

Insurance and reinsurance companies do not put as much emphasis on easily getting in and out of a trade as their capital market counterparties do. Once these companies buy catastrophe coverage, they intend, for the most part, to keep that position for its duration. Liquidity in this respect is not a problem for insurance companies, but they are concerned with the current lack of size of the bids and offers for PCS call spreads. There are market-makers in PCS options who stand ready to make a bid and offer in any contract. Thus far, their bids and offers have ranged from 10 to 250 spreads. The largest trade to date has been a strip trade of 335 of the 40/60 September and December 1996 call spreads, which provided the buyer with a total of US$2.68 million of coverage. There have been a number of other large trades of US$1 million of exposure: 250 of the 80/100 December 1997 Western call spreads, 250 of the 40/60 September 1997 Southeast call spreads, and strip trades of 100 of the September and December 1996 national 200/250 contracts. Although trades of this size are encouraging, it seems that large insurance companies prefer to do transactions that provide at least US$5 million of coverage. If PCS options are to succeed, it will be crucial that (re)insurance companies enter bids of this size and that capital market investors respond with offers of equal size.

At the end of the third quarter of 1997, all 10 of the PCS contracts had traded and the total open interest for those contracts was 18,021 – a 200% increase since the third quarter of 1996. There were a total of 494 trades for an average of 25 call spreads per trade. The total volume of capacity (risk exposure) traded was US$53.6 million. The average rate-on-line for these trades was 11%, with an average exposure of US$108,000.

Although it is difficult to gauge how efficient this market is based on only two years of data, there are some encouraging signs. First, it is worth noting that PCS has been making and releasing

estimates of damage in a timely and orderly fashion. PCS's end-of-risk-period loss totals for the December 1995–September 1997 contracts are shown in Table 4. Second, the sellers of these contracts have made a net profit of US$4.1 million for assuming a total risk of US$42 million. This return of 9.8% over Treasuries, though hardly definitive, is comparable to the average return of 9.2% over Treasuries over the past 10 years.[29] (These preliminary numbers do not include the December and annual 1997 contracts, which are still in the midst of the risk period.) This is a good sign that the market is experiencing pricing similar to what the reinsurance market has seen in the past. Third, there has been increased activity of bids, offers and trades before and during major catastrophic events such as the "blizzard of 1996" and hurricanes Fran and Opal. On September 5, 1996, the day hurricane Fran made landfall, total trading on the CBOT added US$6 million of capacity to the reinsurance market: the September/December Eastern 40/60 call spread strip traded 733 times at prices ranging between 3.4 and 4 index points (17–20% rate-on-line). Offers on the over-the-counter market for similar coverage ranged from 30–35% rate-on-line. Thus, when insurers needed coverage to protect them from an approaching storm, the best price was provided by the capital markets on the CBOT. This is perhaps the most positive sign yet that the necessary building blocks are in place for the CBOT, PCS, the insurance industry and the capital markets to collaborate to create an efficient market for reinsurance risk management.

The evolution of the catastrophe bond market

In 1995 and 1996 insurance companies began to test the securitisation waters. While some of these initial attempts were unsuccessful, each one played a role in educating investors, bankers

Table 4. PCS end of risk period index values

PCS contract	1995 Q4	1996 Q1	1996 Q2	1996 Q3	1996 Q4	1997 Q1	1997 Q2	1997 Q3*
National	26.3	25.6	16.6	20.8	9.0	8.8	9.8	5.1
Eastern	23.5	18.0	3.2	17.6	2.8	3.9	2.8	1.7
Northeastern	1.5	12.0	1.4	1.2	2.2	3.2	0.4	1.1
Southeastern	22.0	6.1	1.8	16.4	0.7	0.7	2.4	0.7
Midwestern	0.5	5.1	11.4	1.3	1.7	4.8	5.7	2.6
Western	2.4	1.1	0.8	2.0	3.8	0.0	0.0	0.8
Florida	14.4	0.6	0.0	0.0	0.2	0.0	0.7	0.0
Texas	0.0	1.4	1.3	0.0	0.8	0.1	1.4	0.0
California	1.1	0.0	0.0	0.0	1.1	0.0	0.0	0.0

* The development period has not been completed

and insurance companies about the securitisation process. A comparison of some of these deals is outlined in Table 5.

In 1996, both USAA and CAT Ltd attempted to issue bonds indexed on their company's losses, while ACE tried to issue a bond indexed to PCS's determination of the amount of damage incurred by the entire insurance industry. The coupons on these issues varied from 1.5% to 5% over the risk-free rate. The most common reason given for the failure of these bonds was that there was not enough time to fully educate investors about the underlying risks before the start of the hurricane season. Nonetheless, the biggest impediment to investors buying these bonds seemed to be that they did not know how to model and price the risk. Although companies like RMS, AIR and Equecat estimated very low default probabilities relative to the coupons being offered, investors remained reluctant to buy. Another fear of investors was that even if they could model and price the risk, they doubted whether it was going to be possible to acquire a diversified portfolio of insurance risks.

Some market observers thought that the insurance derivatives market would get the impetus it needed from the US$1.5 billion California Earthquake Authority (CEA) offering that was to come to market at the end of 1996. Instead, the deal was pulled because Warren Buffet's insurance company, National Indemnity, came in and offered better terms through a traditional reinsurance programme. To some observers this left the impression that traditional reinsurance was more efficient and better priced than what the capital markets could offer. More sceptical observers felt this was an attempt by Warren Buffet to protect National Indemnity's franchise on the "super cat" business. In the end, bankers made the best of a disappointing situation by using Warren Buffet as a perfect example of a capital markets person who includes catastrophe risk in his equity and bond portfolio.

In late 1996 and early 1997, the market saw its first successes with placements of bonds and notes that covered a variety of catastrophes (see

Table 6). Hanover Re entered into a US$100 million CAT note with Citibank in December of 1996, which involved a portfolio of catastrophe risks: Japanese earthquake; Australian and Canadian earthquake and wind storms; aviation disasters worldwide, and European wind storms. The Winterthur bond, the first publicly placed CAT bond, was issued to cover potential losses from a hailstorm in Switzerland that would cause damage to at least 6,000 cars. Reliance entered the market by issuing a note that involved a risk transfer of US$450 million of various aviation, marine, satellite and property catastrophes. St Paul Re issued a multi-year US$68 million bond that allows investors to share in the losses and gains (ie, quota share) of St Paul's worldwide property catastrophe business. Together these deals stimulated enough interest to set the stage for the much larger issues that were to follow.[30]

In June 1997, USAA issued its US$477 million hurricane note to 62 different investors. An important element in the success of the USAA note was the involvement of the rating agencies. Once the note was given a rating, it became easier for investors to assess whether they were being compensated for the risk they were being asked to assume. The A-2 tranche of the USAA note is rated BB and pays 575 basis points over Libor, whereas the average BB corporate note pays 200 basis points over Libor. Thus, relative to other notes determined by the rating agencies to be of similar risk, the USAA CAT note pays a substantial premium to investors. By paying this premium today, USAA believes it is helping to jump-start a market that could develop into a valuable alternative source of reinsurance capacity.

On the heels of the success of the USAA bond came the US$137 million Swiss Re earthquake bond, which was bought by approximately 20 investors. The bond was structured into three different tranches: the class A notes paid 2.50% plus Libor and were 40% principal protected; the class B notes paid 10.5% and were principal unprotected; and the class C notes paid 12% and were principal unprotected. The notes will default if there is an earthquake in California that causes industry-wide insured property damage (as estimated by PCS) of the following amounts: over US$18.5 billion of damage, but less than US$21 billion, will cause a loss of 33% of the capital at risk; US$21 billion or more, but less than US$24 billion, will cause a loss of 66% of the capital at risk; US$24 billion or more will cause the entire capital at risk to be lost. The class C notes will default if there is a California quake that

Table 5. Unsuccessful CAT bonds

	ACE Ltd	USAA '96	CAT Ltd
Underwriter:	Goldman Sachs	Merrill Lynch	Morgan Stanley
Size:	US$25 million	US$500 million	US$50 million
Region:	US	Texas, Gulf coast and east coast of US	Northeast of US
Perils covered:	Hurricanes, earthquakes	Hurricanes	Hurricanes
Underlying index:	PCS	USAA's losses	CAT Ltd's losses
Trigger:	US$25 billion	US$1 billion	US$55 million
Coupon:	T-bills + 5.5%	Libor + 300bp	6.72%

Table 6. Early CAT bond successes

	Hanover Re	Reliance	St Paul Re	Winterthur
Underwriter:	Citibank	Sedgwick Lane Financial	Goldman Sachs	CS First Boston
Size:	US$100 million	US$40 million	US$68.5 million	US$280 million
Region:	Japan, Australia, Canada, Europe, and worldwide aviation	Aviation, marine, satellite and worldwide property	Worldwide	Switzerland
Perils covered:	Earthquake and wind	All perils	All perils	Hail
Underlying Index:	PCS, SIGMA	SIGMA	St Paul's losses	# of Winterthur's cars damaged in one storm
Trigger:	Various	Various	Various	6,000 cars
Coupon:	NA	NA	100% of available net income	2.25% plus convertible into 5 shares

causes US$12 billion or more of insured property damage. Once again, the key component to the success of these bonds was the ratings they received: the class A notes were rated BBB– and the class B notes were rated BB.

In sum, we believe that the events of the past year have brought the financial and insurance markets one step closer to convergence. The USAA and Swiss Re bonds were watershed events in the insurance derivatives market. They attracted investors' attention because of their price, rating and size. In order to sustain this momentum, the investment banks and insurance derivative boutiques will need to convince more insurance and reinsurance companies to securitise their risk. Their goal should be both to structure valuable hedging instruments for insurance companies and to create a variety of products so that investors can construct a diversified portfolio of insurance risks. In the belief that this broad range of products will become available a number of money management firms are establishing funds that will invest solely in insurance derivatives.

Conclusion

If a US$50 billion catastrophe were to occur in the US, approximately 20% of the capital of the primary and reinsurance industries would be wiped out. A loss of this magnitude would obviously be a devastating blow to the insurance industry. To the capital markets, however, such a loss is almost routine. It has been estimated that the total value of the capital markets is US$19 trillion, and that the average daily standard deviation of the market is US$133 billion. Thus, what is needed is an efficient instrument through which the capacity of the capital markets can be funnelled to the insurance market.

We believe that the PCS catastrophe options and catastrophe-linked bonds are vehicles that can be used to accomplish this task. In this essay we have shown that PCS options are not only effective hedging mechanisms and risk management tools for the insurance industry, but they also offer efficiency and price discovery that are lacking in today's market. CAT bonds are an attractive way for (re)insurance companies to transfer their risk because it allows for the flexibility of traditional

Table 7. Recent CAT bond successes

	Swiss Re	USAA
Underwriter:	CS First Boston	Goldman Sachs, Merrill Lynch, Lehman Brothers
Size (Tranche):	A: US$62 million (40% protected)	A-1: US$164 million (100% protected)
	B: US$60 million (0% protected)	A-2: US$313 million (0% protected)
	C: US$15 million (0% protected)	
Region:	California	Texas, Gulf Coast and east coast of US
Peril covered:	Earthquake	Hurricane
Risk period:	2 years	1 year
Coupon:	A: Libor + 255 bps	A-1: Libor + 282 bps
	B: 10.5%	A-2: Libor + 575 bps
	C: 12.0%	
Underlying index:	PCS	USAA's Losses
Trigger:	A: US$18.5 billion, US$21 billion, US$24 billion	A-1: US$1 billion
	B: US$18.5 billion, US$21 billion, US$24 billion	A-2: US$1 billion
	C: US$12.0 billion	
Estimated probability of default:	A: 1.0%	A-1: 0.0%
	B: 1.0%	A-2: 1.0%
	C: NA	

This information is based upon data believed to be reliable, but since it has not been independently verified, Centre Financial Products Limited does not warrant, guaranty, or make any representations as to its accuracy

reinsurance, but eliminates the credit risk in traditional reinsurance. If PCS options and CAT bonds are successful at transferring risk to the capital markets, the insurance industry will benefit in the long run through increased reinsurance capacity – which, in turn, will cause lower and less volatile reinsurance rates.

On the other side of the equation, we have provided evidence that insurance risk is a new asset class that should draw the attention of portfolio managers seeking to diversify their risks and increase their returns. We also reviewed the performance of the PCS options contracts to date and found that the size of trades, open interest, and responsiveness of the market are promising. Last, we discussed the over-the-market for catastrophe bonds and described how this market has evolved from a buzzword to the point where a number of sizeable deals have come to fruition.

Thus, the foundation for a bridge between the capital and insurance markets has been built and continues to develop. The exchange hopes in the future to offer insurance derivatives on health, auto, casualty, marine, aviation, and international property catastrophe insurance claims. In the over-the-counter market, investment banks such as Goldman Sachs, Morgan Stanley and Bankers Trust have set up groups to specialise in marketing insurance risk products such as catastrophe bonds. There have also been numerous (re)insurance companies that have set up "financial products" subsidiaries to investigate how their companies can use insurance derivatives. Thus, it seems that the worlds of finance and insurance are converging, and that, as part of this convergence, the insurance industry may change the way it chooses to hedge its risk for the first time in over 300 years.

1 *Property Claims Services.*

2 *Sara Borden and Asani Sarkar, "Securitising Property Catastrophe Risk,"* Current Issues, *Federal Reserve Bank of New York, August, 1996.*

3 *United Nations Conference on Trade and Development (1995).*

4 *This reinsurance figure includes the US$26 billion in capital of Berkshire Hathaway. Source: Reinsurance Association of America.*

5 *Eric Simpson, Dolson Smith and Cynthia Babbit, "P/C Industry begins to Face Environmental and Asbestos Liabilities,"* Best Week Property/Casualty Supplement, *January 29, 1996.*

6 *This is our estimate based on data provided by Dun & Bradstreet and Claritas.*

7 *The idea of securitising risk was first suggested in an article by Robert Goshay and Richard Sandor, "An Inquiry into the Feasibility of a Reinsurance Futures Market,"* Journal of Business Finance, *Vol. 5 No. 2, 1973, pp. 56–66.*

8 *Previously, the CBOT listed a catastrophe contract on an index provided by Insurance Services Office (ISO). This index was based on the losses of 25 companies, which represented 23% of the property insurance industry. The reliability of the ISO index became a concern when the industry's losses from the Northridge earthquake were not adequately reflected in the index. The PCS indexes are a much broader reflection of how an event affects the insurance industry.*

9 *PCS will change its estimate if the actual dollar amount of claims differs from its original estimate. PCS defines a catastrophe to be an event that causes more than US$25 million of insured losses to personal property, vehicles, boats, and business interruption. Prior to 1997 an*

event qualified as a catastrophe if it caused more than US$5 million in damage. PCS losses do not include losses involving uninsured property, including publicly owned property, utilities, agriculture, aircraft, and property insured under the National Flood Insurance Program (CBOT, PCS Options User's Guide, 1995).

10 *PCS is a division of American Insurance Services Group, Inc., a not-for-profit organisation that has been estimating insured property damage from catastrophes since 1948. The PCS indexes are already widely used by reinsurance companies as an index for over-the-counter deals between reinsurance companies.*

11 *The majority of the contracts traded have been in the 12-month loss development contracts. The importance of this feature is exemplified by the Northridge earthquake, which PCS first estimated caused US$2.5 billion of damage, then adjusted this estimate up in the following months until it finally was determined to have caused US$12.5 billion of damage.*

12 *The margin requirement for the seller of a call spread varies before, during, and after the risk period. Prior to the risk period the seller of a call spread must post margin of US$200 per spread. During the risk period the seller is required to post a margin of the maximum of US$200 per spread, the mark to market value of the spread, and 20% of the maximum possible loss. The margin required during the development periods is just the mark to market value of the spread, unless the CBOT margin review group anticipates that PCS may make a substantial revision to an index. The buyer of a call spread need only post margin equal to the premium he pays to the seller.*

13 *Hurricane season is from June 1 to November 30, but the majority of intense hurricanes have occurred in the third quarter of the year (see Table 4.) Thus, Innovative Mutual chooses to hedge its risk using the September contract.*

14 *We use "(re)insurance" throughout this article to denote reinsurance and/or insurance companies.*

15 CBOT Review, *Third Quarter 1996.*

16 *If the coupon is at risk, the SPV will place the coupon in a trust for the investors until the term of the bond is complete.*

17 *This type of SPV structure allows the insurance company to securitise its risk, but still receive reinsurance accounting treatment. The establishment of the SPV offshore is usually done for regulatory, tax, and efficiency purposes. The SPV also serves a purpose for the noteholder because it separates the risks he is reinsuring from the other risks on the reinsured's books.*

18 *For a detailed discussion of the USAA bond, see the Harvard Business School case study by Kenneth Froot and Mark Seasholes, "USAA: Catastrophe Risk Financing," Case #N9-298-007, September 5, 1997.*

19 *See Kenneth Froot, "The Limited Financing of Catastrophe Risk: An Overview," Harvard Business School and NBER Working Paper, April, 1997, for a discussion and evaluation of the possible causes of the current lack of reinsurance purchased and supplied for high-severity, low-frequency events.*

20 *An alternative structure is a CAT swap, in which the returns are still linked to the occurrence of an insured event, but there is no exchange of principal. Instead, the investor would receive his premium upfront and, depending on his credit rating, would use a letter of credit to guarantee his obligation. This structure enables the investor to invest the notional of the swap in a manner of his own choosing throughout the term of the swap, instead of this money being invested in Treasuries as stipulated in most CAT bond structures.*

CAT swaps have very low transactions costs because the ISDA master swap agreement can be used to execute all transactions. Swap transactions, however, are expected to be limited to index-based trades due to the due diligence that would be needed to assess traditional claims.

21 *Kenneth Froot and Paul O'Connell suggest that the price of reinsurance generally exceeds "fair value" because of reinsurers' high costs of capital. See Froot and O'Connell, "On the Pricing of Intermediated Risks: Theory and Application to Catastrophe Reinsurance," NBER Working Paper Series, Paper #6011, April 1997.*

22 *For a discussion of how ratings agencies go about rating cat bonds, see Fitch Special Report, "Structured Finance and Catastrophic Risk," February 3, 1997, and Lehman Brothers Fixed Income Research, "Introduction to Catastrophe-linked Securities," May 23, 1997.*

23 *In addition, a theoretical model of CAT options was formulated by David Cummins and Hélyette Geman in a*

paper published in 1995. Although the authors were unable to find a closed-form solution to the problem, they used Monte Carlo simulations to price the options. See J. David Cummins and Hélyette Geman, "Pricing Catastrophe Insurance Futures and Call Spreads: An Arbitrage Approach," Journal of Fixed Income," March 1996, pp. 46–57; reprinted as Chapter 4 of the present volume.

24 *See Robert Litzenberger, David Beaglehole and Craig Reynolds, "Assessing Catastrophe Reinsurance-Linked Securities as a New Asset Class," Journal of Portfolio Management, Special Issue, December 1996, pp. 76–86; reprinted as Chapter 12 of the present volume.*

25 *Lea Carty and Dana Lieberman, "Corporate Bond Defaults and Default Rates, 1938-95," Moody's Investors Service, January 1996.*

26 *See Kenneth Froot, Brian Murphy, Aaron Stern and Stephen Usher, "The Emerging Asset Class: Insurance Risk," Guy Carpenter & Co.*

27 *Kenneth Froot and Paul O'Connell show that supply shifts are more important in explaining reinsurance pricing after a catastrophe than revised actuarial valuation. See Froot and O'Connell, "The Pricing of US Catastrophe Reinsurance," NBER Conference on The Financing of Property/Casualty Risks, Working Paper, March 1997.*

28 *CBOT conference on Zero-Beta Investing, Comments by Stephen Levy, Guy Carpenter, June 1996.*

29 *It is customary to express the profit on an insurance risk in terms of the return that would have been earned on a portfolio of Treasury notes equal in value to the entire insured risk. The total return is the interest and premium received, less the losses paid out, relative to the risk amount.*

30 *Insurance companies have also accessed the capital markets in an indirect fashion through contingent-surplus notes. Arkwright Mutual Insurance Co and Nationwide Insurance Enterprise have raised US$100 million and US$400 million, respectively to establish trusts to issue the notes. The trusts invest the money in Treasuries which can be accessed by the insurers at any time over a 20-year period for any reason including funding catastrophe losses. In exchange for the right to access these treasuries the insurers pay the investors 2.75 and 2.2 percentage points above treasuries. If the insurers need to use the funds in the trust, they will issue a surplus note (an IOU) to the investor, which pays them their expected rate of return over treasuries. Thus, the payment is the same as it was prior to the funds being drawn upon, but now it is exposed to greater credit risk. Thus, in a contingent-surplus note structure, catastrophe risk is only assumed by the capital markets indirectly.*

12

Assessing Catastrophe Reinsurance-Linked Securities as a New Asset Class

Robert H. Litzenberger, David R. Beaglehole and Craig E. Reynolds

Goldman, Sachs & Co; Deutsche Bank

Assets that have low correlations with stock and bond indexes are potentially attractive additions to diversified portfolios. And stock and bond indexes are generally uncorrelated with insurance losses associated with catastrophic events.[1]

The securitisation of catastrophic insurance risk would allow investors to combine reinsurance-linked securities with the traditional asset classes, thereby pooling catastrophic risk with other economic exposures of the capital markets. Given the current pricing of reinsurance, we believe these reinsurance-linked securities would offer attractive risk/return opportunities to investors when included in diversified stock and bond portfolios.

Most insurance coverage involves individual events that have a significant economic impact on a single insured entity but are small relative to the reserves of the insurance company providing the coverage. The insurance company is able to pool such independent risks and charge premiums based on its administrative costs and its actuarial assessments.

Natural catastrophes such as hurricanes and earthquakes involve many more insured entities, and have the potential for very large aggregate claims. Unlike the typical "high-frequency, low severity" risks that insurance companies are easily able to manage, such "low-frequency, high-severity" risks present particular difficulties.

Insurance companies take divergent approaches to managing such risks. Many companies purchase catastrophe (CAT) reinsurance that will reimburse them for natural catastrophe-related claims over a threshold amount. Some very large insurance companies feel that the CAT reinsurance market does not have the capacity to offer them sufficient protection, and they hold very substantial capital in lieu of reinsurance.

In recent years, two natural catastrophes, hurricane Andrew in 1992 and the Northridge earthquake in 1994, have eaten into the capital of primary underwriters, reduced the capital of many reinsurance companies, and diminished underwriting capacity in the reinsurance market. The resulting increase in demand and decrease in supply of CAT reinsurance has caused large rate increases at the same time as the capacity of many reinsurance companies has been reduced.

This fundamental difficulty of managing "low-frequency, high-severity" risks – whose aggregate exposure levels may amount to multiples of the level of capital available in the current reinsurance markets – has led insurance companies to seek new ways of managing their exposures to major catastrophes. Securitising catastrophic risks in the form of instruments accessible to the broad capital markets would allow insurers to manage these types of risks better while at the same time offering an attractive new asset class of significant potential size to investors. This chapter explores these possibilities.

This chapter was first published in Journal of Portfolio Management, *Special Issue, December 1996. This copyrighted material is reprinted with permission from* Institutional Investor *and the authors.*

122

ASSESSING
CATASTROPHE
REINSURANCE-
LINKED
SECURITIES
AS A NEW
ASSET CLASS

We first discuss traditional reinsurance contracts, the market for catastrophic contracts, and actuarial pricing of such contracts. Then we examine the securitisation of reinsurance and general approaches to the valuation of this new asset class, and analyse the attractiveness of the asset class. A comparison of a hypothetical reinsurance-linked debt security with high-yield debt is quite promising.

Traditional reinsurance contracts

Traditional CAT reinsurance is designed to protect the primary insurance carrier against the losses that result from a momentous event, such as an earthquake, hurricane or other major catastrophe. Such reinsurance can be broadly categorised into two types:

❑ *pro rata* coverage against a fixed percentage of losses; and
❑ *excess of loss* protection for a fixed amount of losses above a specific threshold, or *attachment point*.

Both types of reinsurance are ordinarily purchased for one-year terms.

An excess of loss programme typically involves a series of layers that cover a company's actual losses from single or multiple catastrophe events. For example, a 10/30 excess loss layer would provide indemnification for the first US$10 million (the limit) in losses over US$30 million (the attachment point) associated with a single event.[2] In return for this coverage, the company pays an up-front premium, which is quoted as a percentage of the limit. This percentage fee is known as the rate on line (ROL).

ACTUARIAL VALUE
The actuarial assessment of a given excess of loss coverage is similar to the valuation of an option spread on a common stock. Specifically, we may express the actuarial value of the coverage as the expected value of losses above the attachment point less the expected value of losses above the sum of the attachment point and the limit.

The first component is the actuarial value of an option on a forward contract based on the losses with a strike price equal to the attachment point. The second component is the actuarial value of an option on a forward contract based on the losses with a strike equal to the sum of the attachment point and the limit.

Reinsurance has also been offered in the form of a lump sum paid in the event that an attachment point is reached. We can value this coverage as a binary call option that pays a fixed amount if a pre-specified strike is exceeded. We refer to this type of reinsurance contract as *binary coverage*.

IMPACT OF RECENT LOSSES
The principal providers of CAT reinsurance have historically been reinsurance companies and Lloyds syndicates, which are unlimited liability partnerships of wealthy individuals ("names"). The large losses experienced in US catastrophes in recent years have reduced the surplus levels of many primary insurers and reinsurers, and diminished the wealth of Lloyds names. Over the past six years, cumulative losses from major catastrophic events were US$35 billion, which is about 18% of the total surplus of the US insurance industry.

Hurricane Andrew alone caused US$15 billion of insured losses when it swept through Florida and Louisiana in 1992. According to a report by the Insurance Services Office (ISO), Florida's 1992 total insured losses for catastrophe-related lines were nearly seven times the corresponding total direct premiums earned in that year.[3] Moreover, Florida's insurance costs from hurricane Andrew exceeded the US$14.6 billion in total direct premiums earned in Florida in the *seven years* from 1986 through 1992 for the corresponding lines of coverage.

These events have resulted in significant increases in the cost of CAT reinsurance. The greater demand relative to supply is evidenced by an increase in both the average attachment point for coverage and the average ROL. In 1992, US insurers provided approximately US$10 billion in catastrophe coverage; they bought a total of US$8 billion in catastrophe reinsurance coverage above the US$2 billion in coverage they retained. In 1993, the ISO projected that catastrophe reinsurance retention would double.

For the top 20 clients of the largest reinsurance broker, Guy Carpenter, from 1989 to 1995, the average ROL increased from 7.93% to 15.09%, while the average attachment point for a single catastrophe increased from US$1.14 billion to US$2.57 billion in industry losses.

A ROLE FOR THE CAPITAL MARKETS
The Federal Emergency Management Agency (FEMA) estimates that if the 1906 San Francisco earthquake had occurred in 1988, insured damages would have been US$38 billion.[4] The same intensity of earthquake in the Los Angeles area in 1988 would have resulted in US$50 billion of

ASSESSING
CATASTROPHE
REINSURANCE-
LINKED
SECURITIES
AS A NEW
ASSET CLASS

insured damages.[5] And, according to an ISO estimate, had hurricane Andrew hit Miami, the insured losses would have exceeded US$40 billion.

The magnitude of such "low-frequency, high-severity" CAT losses, while large relative to industry reserves and capital, is dwarfed by the size of the US capital markets, which the National Underwriter company estimates at almost US$13 trillion. If reinsurance-linked securities were recognised as an asset class, and included as a component of investors' diversified portfolios of stocks and bonds, insurers and reinsurers could be better able to manage such volatility effectively. Given the current price of CAT reinsurance, we believe that these securities, when combined with traditional asset classes, would provide attractive risk/return opportunities to investors.

Securitisation of reinsurance premiums and exposures

We now explore approaches to the valuation, pricing and assessment of reinsurance-linked securities. The development of these securities is in its initial stages, so our discussion is at a general level only as to the new asset class. The assessment of any particular offering of securities that may be developed will depend on its structure and terms.

Traditional CAT reinsurance involves detailed analyses of the underwriting risk of the primary insurer, because the indemnification is based on its specific loss experience rather than on aggregate industry losses. Securitisation of specific CAT exposures is possible, but investors would need to analyse the insurer's specific exposures and underwriting procedures in relation to a particular transaction structure. Accordingly, it is likely that reinsurance premiums and exposures would be securitised primarily through indexes of industry-wide catastrophe losses.

For example, in designing a CAT loss option contract, the Chicago Board of Trade (CBOT) chose to use the index of aggregate US catastrophe losses, which Property Claim Services (PCS) has been compiling since 1949. Nevertheless, securitisation based on specific company experience is also possible.

When a securitisation is based on a particular company's book, it is important to avoid the possibility of adverse selection and to assure a strong economic incentive for careful underwriting. Adverse selection is avoided by having predefined cession rules where the exposures passed on to the security-holders depend only on the firm's underwritings, and the firm is not allowed to "cherry pick" the exposures it retains for itself. Requiring the firm to maintain a large share of each of the risks that it partially transfers to the security-holders is essential to maintain the economic incentive for careful underwriting.

PROBABILITY ASSESSMENTS

To assess securities linked to reinsurance, investors require analysis of the distribution of possible future values. There are two basic approaches to forming such probability assessments. One is to use forward-looking computer simulations based on scientific information on hurricanes, earthquakes and other natural catastrophes. The other is to use historical data to assess the distribution of future insurance losses from natural catastrophes.

Both approaches rely on simplifying assumptions to infer a probability distribution of future CAT insurance losses. Obviously, the valuation of hypothetical CAT insurance-linked securities is highly sensitive to these assumptions. Future valuations placed on such securities may reflect probability assessments that differ substantially from those produced by the historical analysis used for the valuation examples given here.

Forward-looking simulations The first approach requires a vast amount of data regarding seismology, weather patterns and insured value exposures. Several consulting firms have specialised in such simulations, including Applied Insurance Research, EQECAT, Risk Management Solutions and Towers Perrin. Such analysis, where available and applicable, has the potential to provide valuable information in assessing risks.

The simulations use computers to apply randomly generated hurricane and earthquake scenarios to data on property types, location and insured values. This process thus provides a "ground-up" assessment of the probability distributions of specific levels of insured losses employing a wide range of historical, meteorological, seismological and economic information. Such modelling capabilities are applicable to and available for certain natural catastrophes, such as earthquakes and hurricanes.

This approach is limited by the available recorded histories of hurricanes and earthquakes and the many subjective judgements and assumptions needed to build the simulation models. We use historical data to analyse a simplified security that is indexed to the PCS loss index, but results of forward-looking simulations could be quite different.

ASSESSING
CATASTROPHE
REINSURANCE-
LINKED
SECURITIES
AS A NEW
ASSET CLASS

Analysis of historical CAT loss data Both insurance losses and premiums are affected by population growth, development, changes in insurance coverage and inflation in building costs. Therefore, our analysis of historical CAT losses uses a historical time series of loss ratios (LRs). The LR is measured as the PCS aggregate loss index divided by a sum of earned premiums on lines of insurance that pay claims related to natural catastrophes.[6] Even these ratios have increased over time, because the underlying premiums reflect non-CAT as well as CAT coverage.

Population growth and related development have been greater in California and Florida, just where earthquakes and hurricanes are more likely. The combined population of these two states as a percentage of the US population increased from 10% in 1956 to 18% in 1994. Concurrent with an increase in the population density of areas with higher exposure to natural catastrophes, there has been an increase in the market penetration of CAT insurance coverage.

To account for both the increase in the population of high-risk CAT areas and the increase in the market penetration of CAT coverage in these areas, we regress the logarithm of the LRs on the logarithm of the ratio of California plus Florida population to US population in a given year. The coefficient is an estimate of the elasticity of the LR with respect to an increase in the combined populations of California and Florida relative to total US population. An elasticity coefficient greater than unity indicates increases in the penetration of CAT coverage in these higher-risk areas. For the period from 1956–94, we find the estimated coefficient to be 2.83. We use the resulting regression results to adjust the time series of LRs.

Table 1 presents the LRs and the adjusted historical loss ratios (AHLRs) for the sample period. We plot the time series of LRs and AHLRs in Figures 1 and 2. Unlike the LRs, the AHLRs do not display any time trend.

Because immense natural catastrophes occur very infrequently, the range of loss ratios implied by an analysis of 39 years is likely to vary from what would be obtained by analysis of a longer period. Statistical inference based on a parametric characterisation of the probability distribution of future loss ratios permits the estimation of the parameters of a continuous probability distribution from the limited sample of observations.

The lognormal distribution, frequently used in financial economics, has well-known properties. If we approximate the AHLR distribution as log-

Table 1. Property Claim Services: reported industry catastrophe losses as percentage of weighted sum of prior year's earned premium

Year of catastrophe	Unadjusted	Adjusted
1956	2.181	9.904
1957	2.178	9.138
1958	0.792	3.123
1959	1.205	4.614
1960	5.193	16.929
1961	4.322	13.404
1962	5.057	14.863
1963	0.704	1.956
1964	5.030	13.212
1965	19.169	48.583
1966	1.930	4.818
1967	4.922	12.032
1968	1.846	4.436
1969	4.286	10.011
1970	4.815	11.022
1971	1.742	3.950
1972	2.259	5.028
1973	3.275	7.005
1974	5.052	10.472
1975	3.670	7.060
1976	1.493	2.800
1977	2.045	3.733
1978	2.920	5.148
1979	7.310	12.452
1980	4.225	6.875
1981	2.402	3.790
1982	5.062	7.683
1983	7.347	10.768
1984	4.304	6.009
1985	6.281	8.391
1986	1.714	2.187
1987	1.710	2.080
1988	2.523	2.938
1989	13.389	14.850
1990	4.826	5.212
1991	8.035	8.415
1992	38.668	39.923
1993	8.887	9.041
1994	23.965	23.965

normal, we can use the Black–Scholes option pricing formula to price CAT options.

In Figure 3, we compare the frequency distribution of the natural logarithm of the AHLRs with a normal distribution. The frequency distribution shows that years with logarithms between 3.75 and 4.05 occur more often than would be predicted by a lognormal distribution. We can attribute this result to only two events: hurricane Andrew and hurricane Betsy. These two events in the limited 39 years of data are sufficient to reject statistically the assumption of lognormality. This illustrates the difficulty of estimating the probability of low-frequency events based on small samples, and explains why the imputed probability for extremely large loss ratios may be quite different under these approaches.

The use of historical realised AHLR as a discrete probability distribution is referred to as a *bootstrap*. In the discussion that follows, we contrast results produced by a bootstrap to those based on the lognormal approximation.

VALUATION OF A HYPOTHETICAL SECURITISED REINSURANCE CONTRACT

To illustrate the securitisation of reinsurance premiums and exposures, we first consider a one-year debt security with an embedded binary CAT option. Assume that the security has an above-market annual coupon of 15.14%, or 1,000 basis points over the one-year Treasury. The repayment of principal is indexed to the LR. For an LR less than 20%, the bondholder receives a repayment of the entire principal; for an LR greater than 20%, one-half the principal payment is lost.

This security may be divided into two components:

❑ long a bond with an above-market coupon of 15.14%; and
❑ short a binary call on the LR with a strike of 20% and a payout amount of US$50.

The present value of the differential between the above-market coupon of 15.14% and the market coupon of 5.14%, US$9.63, is the implicit reinsurance premium (IRP).

We calculate the implicit rate on line of 19.25% by dividing the IRP by the maximum payout of US$50. The IRP and the implicit ROL can be compared with the actuarial value of the exposure.

The actuarial value of that exposure is the expected forward value of a binary option on the LR with a strike, K, equal to 20%. The expected forward value of a binary option with a strike of K, BOption[K], is simply the probability of LR exceeding K, or prob[LR > K], times the option's payout, P.

Under the assumption that the natural logarithm of LR is normally distributed, we may express the probability of LR being less than K in terms of the cumulative normal evaluated at a z value where LR = K. That is:

$$prob[LR < K] = N[z_k]$$

where $z_k = (log[K] - u)/\sigma$, and u and σ are the mean and standard deviation of log[LR]. Since probabilities sum to one:

$$prob[LR > K] = 1 - N[z_k]$$

Since the normal distribution is symmetric:

$$1 - N[z_k] = N[-z_k]$$

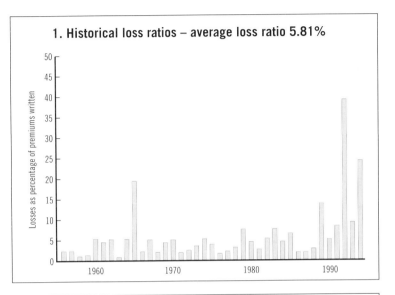

1. Historical loss ratios – average loss ratio 5.81%

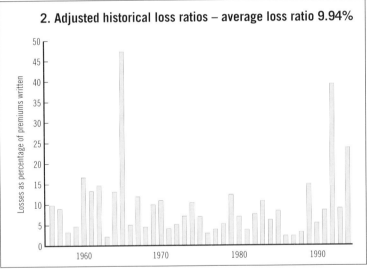

2. Adjusted historical loss ratios – average loss ratio 9.94%

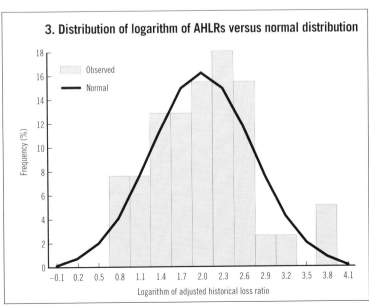

3. Distribution of logarithm of AHLRs versus normal distribution

126

ASSESSING
CATASTROPHE
REINSURANCE-
LINKED
SECURITIES
AS A NEW
ASSET CLASS

Thus, under the assumption of lognormality, the forward value of the binary option is:

$$\text{Boption}[K] = N[-z_k] \times P$$

The mean of the logarithm of our time series of AHLRs is 2.0, with a standard deviation of 0.74. Thus, z_k is equal to $(\log[20] - 2.0)/0.74$. As $\log[20]$ is equal to 2.995, $z_k = 1.35$. Evaluating the standard cumulative normal at –1.35 gives a probability of exceeding 20% equal to 8.92%. As three of the 39 AHLRs exceed 20%, a bootstrap gives a probability of 7.69%.

The differences in these estimated probabilities illustrate the difficulty associated with inferring the probability of a low-frequency event from limited historical data. An alternative approach based on forward-looking simulations could produce very different results.

Multiplying these probabilities by the maximum loss of US$50, and discounting at the one-year Treasury rate of 5.14%, we find that the present value of the reinsurance embedded in the bond is US$4.24 under lognormality and US$3.66 using a bootstrap.

Dividing the present value of reinsurance by the maximum exposure of US$50 gives a break-even ROL of 8.48% for the lognormal case and 7.31% for the direct historical data. The implied ROL of 19.25% exceeds the break-even ROL by 10.77% under lognormality and by 11.94% using the bootstrap. The differences between the implied ROLs and the break-even ROLs represent estimates of the premium paid to investors for bearing the CAT reinsurance-linked risk.

We now consider the securitisation of reinsurance premiums and exposures in a one-year debt security with an embedded CAT call option spread. Assume that the security has an above-market annual coupon of 18.14%, or 1,300bp over the one-year Treasury. The repayment of principal is indexed to the LR. For an LR less than 20%, the investor receives a repayment of the entire principal; for an LR between 20% and 30%, the fraction of principal lost is $(LR - 20\%)/(30\% - 20\%)$; and for an LR greater than 30%, the entire principal payment is lost.

This security may be divided into two components:

❑ long a bond with an above-market coupon of 18.14%; and
❑ a CAT call option spread consisting of a short position of 10 calls with a strike of 20% and a long position of 10 calls with a strike of 30%.

The second component is analogous to an excess loss reinsurance contract on the LR × US$1,000 with an attachment point of US$200 (ie $0.2 \times$ US$1,000), a maximum limit of US$300 (ie $0.3 \times$ US$1,000), and a maximum payout of US$100 (ie US$300 – US$200).

The present value of the differential between the above-market coupon of 18.14% and the market coupon of 5.14%, US$12.51, is the implicit reinsurance premium. We calculate the implicit ROL of 12.51% by dividing the implicit reinsurance premium by the maximum payout of US$100. We can compare the implicit ROL with the break-even ROL based on the actuarial value of the exposure.

The actuarial value of that exposure is the difference between the expected forward values of 10 CAT call options with strikes of 20% and 10 CAT call options with strikes of 30%. Thus, the value of the options embedded in the CAT note is:

$$1,000 \times (\text{Call}[20\%] - \text{Call}[30\%])$$

The expected forward value of a call option with a strike of K, Call[K], is simply the product of the probability of LR exceeding K, prob[LR × K], and the difference between the expectation of LR conditional on LR exceeding K, $E[LR \,|\, LR > K]$ and the strike K:

$$\text{Call}[K] = \text{Prob}[LR > K] \times [E[LR \,|\, LR > K] - K]$$

As in the binary option valuation, $\text{Prob}[LR > K] = N[-z_k]$ where $z_k = (\log[K] - u)/\sigma$. For Call[20%], $z_k = (\log[20] - 2.00)/0.74$; thus $z_k = 1.35$ and, evaluating the cumulative normal of z_k, $N[-1.35] = 8.92\%$. Therefore, the probability of the LR exceeding 20% is 8.92%.

Using a bootstrap, $\text{Prob}[LR > K]$ is the fraction of times when the LR exceeds K. For Call[20%], three of the 39 observations exceed 20%, which yields a probability of the LR exceeding 20% equal to 7.69%.

If the LR is lognormally distributed with mean u and variance σ^2, then the conditional expectation of the loss ratio is:

$$E[LR \,|\, LR > K] = e^{u + \sigma^2/2} \times N[-z_k + \sigma]/N[-z_k]$$

Note that this term is the unconditional expectation of LR, and the ratio of the two cumulative normal terms is equal to the ratio of the conditional to the unconditional expectation of LR.[7] With mean 2.00 and variance 0.74, the $E[LR > K]$ is N[–1.35 + 0.74]/N[–1.35], which equals 29.6%.

127

ASSESSING
CATASTROPHE
REINSURANCE-
LINKED
SECURITIES
AS A NEW
ASSET CLASS

Using a bootstrap, the $E[LR \mid LR > K]$ is equal to the mean of all observations that are greater than the strike of 20%. The three observed AHLRs that exceed 20% are 48.58%, 39.92%, and 23.97%. Therefore, $E[LR \mid LR > K]$ is 37.49%.

Using these probabilities and conditional expectations, we find that the value of Call[20%] is US$0.0086 under lognormality and US$0.0134 using a bootstrap. Using exactly the same procedure, we find the value of Call[30%] to be US$0.0033 under lognormality and US$0.0073 using a bootstrap. With these call values, the forward value of the options embedded in the CAT bond, which equals 1,000(Call[20%] − Call[30%]), is US$5.27 under lognormality and US$6.14 using a bootstrap.

Discounting the actuarial forward value at the one-year Treasury rate and dividing by the maximum exposure of US$100 gives a break-even ROL of 5.01% under lognormality and 5.84% using the bootstrap technique. The implied ROL of 12.51% exceeds the break-even ROL by 7.5% under lognormality and 6.67% using a bootstrap.

Catastrophe reinsurance as an asset class

Natural catastrophes such as hurricanes and earthquakes reduce private wealth just as do economic losses on diversified portfolios of stocks and bonds. As we have noted, a substantial portion of this exposure is borne by private corporations (privately held reinsurance companies) and small numbers of wealthy individuals (Lloyds names). This inefficient sharing of risk has resulted in high reinsurance rates and has motivated many primary reinsurance companies to maintain very large exposures and to cease issuing new or renewal policies in selected areas

A more efficient risk-sharing procedure would allow the capital markets to spread the risk among large numbers of investors to whom this exposure is a very small portion of their total portfolio risk exposure. The crisis in the reinsurance market resulting from losses associated with recent catastrophic events has caused the very high ROLs relative to the actuarial risk assessment and has created, potentially, highly attractive returns in this asset class.

A BLACK–LITTERMAN ASSET ALLOCATION APPROACH

We now consider the attractiveness of this new asset class using an approach based on the capital asset pricing model, suggested by Black and Litterman (1991). Consider the addition of a new security to an existing portfolio. The addition would be attractive if and only if it increases the portfolio's Sharpe ratio, ie the ratio of excess return (expected return above the riskless interest rate) to standard deviation of return. A portfolio with a higher Sharpe ratio would offer more attractive risk/return opportunities when combined with borrowing or lending. A higher Sharpe ratio would result from a small increase in a security's weight if and only if the security's ratio of excess return to its beta with the existing portfolio exceeds the existing portfolio's excess rate of return.

As the security's portfolio weight is increased, the beta with the enhanced portfolio also increases. The new asset class would still be an attractive incremental portfolio investment if its ratio of excess return to beta with the enhanced portfolio exceeds the enhanced portfolio's excess rate of return.

The expected excess return on the enhanced portfolio is $R_e = wR_n + (1 - w)R_o$, where R denotes excess rate of return (expected rate of return above riskless interest rate); e, n, and o are subscripts denoting the enhanced portfolio, the new asset, and the old portfolio; and w is the portfolio weight, given the new asset.

If the new asset is uncorrelated with the old portfolio, the beta with the enhanced portfolio, β_{ne}, is:

$$\beta_{ne} = \frac{w\sigma_{R_n}^2}{w^2\sigma_{R_n}^2 + (1-w)^2\sigma_{R_n}^2}$$

Under these conditions, the inclusion of the new asset (portfolio weight = w) with an existing portfolio (o) would be attractive if:

$$\frac{R_n}{\beta_{ne}} > wR_n + (1-w)R_o$$

This reduces to a hurdle rate for the new asset; ie,

$$R_n > [R_o(1-w) + wR_n]\beta_{ne}$$

Over the sample period, March 1955 through December 1994, the correlations of the AHLRs with the returns on the S&P500 index and a government bond index were 0.058 and 0.105, respectively. These numbers imply that the correlation with the securities embedded with the CAT exposure option is slightly negative, because the return on these securities varies inversely with the AHLRs.

ASSESSING
CATASTROPHE
REINSURANCE-
LINKED
SECURITIES
AS A NEW
ASSET CLASS

Since these correlations are small and statistically insignificant, we assume a zero correlation for our analysis. Note that a negative correlation would produce a lower hurdle rate.

Over the sample period, the average excess rate of return and standard deviation were 0.4% and 9.4%, respectively, for government bonds, and 5.7% and 14.4% for the S&P index. According to *Stocks, Bonds, Bills, and Inflation* (1996), the correlation between the S&P index and government bonds was 0.278 over the same period.

CAT NOTE EXAMPLE

We now consider the one-year debt security with an embedded call option spread on the PCS index of aggregated CAT losses in the US. We estimate the parameters of a lognormal distribution from the historical AHLRs, and find that this investment has an expected excess return of 7.94% and a standard deviation of return of 19.9%.[8]

Applying the Black–Litterman analysis, we estimate that investors holding a portfolio corresponding to the S&P500 index would find it attractive to hold 1% of their portfolios in the CAT investment, provided the excess return of the CAT is at least 11bp over the short rate. If the expected excess return exceeds 22bp over the short rate, they would find a holding of 2% attractive.

Applying the same analysis to investors holding a bond portfolio, we find that an excess return of 3bp would make a 1% holding of CAT notes attractive, while an excess return of 5bp would make a 2% holding of CAT notes attractive. If investors held an equal percentage of their capital in stocks and bonds, the break-even excess returns for them to hold 1% and 2% of the CAT note are 13bp and 27bp, respectively. When we compare this with the offered return of 794bp, the CAT note is clearly attractive.

Now consider the threshold excess return for the binary CAT note we have discussed. The results shown in Table 2 indicate that catastrophe reinsurance bonds at the ROLs shown, if we extrapolate from historical loss experience, are sufficiently attractive to warrant inclusion in a diversified bond or balanced fund.

Multi-year securitised reinsurance compared with high-yield debt

Most reinsurance today is written for single-year coverage. The securitisation of multi-period reinsurance provides an innovative alternative to single-year coverage, allowing issuers to lock in the cost of reinsurance for an instrument's life. Another advantage to issuers is that, when CAT coverage is embedded in a bond, the reinsurance contract is effectively collateralised up-front. The massive size of the capital markets and the attractive risk/reward opportunities offered by this new asset class have the potential to vastly increase reinsurance capacity.

To illustrate a multi-period securitisation, we consider a hypothetical 10-year bond with an embedded binary structure similar to the structure considered so far. Over the life of the bond, the investor receives a coupon of 14.57%, or 900bp over Treasuries. If, in any calendar year, the loss ratio exceeds 20%, the bond expires, with the investor receiving one-half of the principal.

We use two approaches to generate the distributions of returns for the multi-period CAT bond. We first simulate 10,000 scenarios of 10 consecutive loss ratios by taking random draws from a lognormal distribution with the same mean and standard deviation as the AHLRs. If in any given year the randomly drawn AHLR exceeds the binary strike of 20%, the CAT bond loses half of its principal. We assume that we reinvest all received coupons in Treasuries and that, if the bond exceeds the binary strike of 20%, we reinvest the recovered amount in Treasuries at current forward interest rates. After each scenario, we compute the annualised return of the bond. We then analyse the distribution of the annual rates of return over the 10-year horizon.

In the second approach, rather than use draws from a lognormal distribution, we randomly select, with replacement, a sequence of 10 AHLRs. This approach is called bootstrapping. Figures 4 and 5 display the distributions of the possible rates of return.

Because of its high coupon rate and principal exposure, the CAT bond is analogous to a high-

Table 2. Threshold excess returns for one-year CAT notes

	Weight of CAT note in enhanced portfolio	Type of embedded CAT exposure	
		Excess of loss (bp)	Binary (bp)
S&P500 index	1%	11	22
	2%	22	44
Bond	1%	2	4
	2%	4	8
Balanced (50% stock/50% bond)	1%	13	27
	2%	27	53
ROL		12.51%	19.25%
Offered return		7.94	10.85

129

ASSESSING
CATASTROPHE
REINSURANCE-
LINKED
SECURITIES
AS A NEW

yield bond. An investor in a high-yield bond pays for the bond up-front, and receives a high coupon in return for taking on the risk that the debt issuer will default. In the event of default, the investor can sell the bond and recover a portion of the principal amount, which averages about one-half of the principal.

For example, the average coupon rate on a 10-year single-B rated bond was 10.7%, based on market conditions on January 17, 1996. According to Moody's, the median price of such a bond is US$46.56 immediately after a default event. Thus, the maximum principal exposure on our hypothetical CAT bond is similar to that of a single-B bond.

To compute the annual rate of return for the single-B bond over a 10-year horizon, we assume that we reinvest all received coupons in Treasuries and that, if the bond defaults, we reinvest the recovered amount in Treasuries. We compare the distribution of returns on a single-B bond (Figure 6) with the distribution of returns on our hypothetical CAT bond.

The average rate of return on a single-B bond is 5.61%, while the average rates of return from simulations using lognormality are 7.47% and 7.88%, based on the bootstrap. The minimum return on the CAT bond is 0.6%; the minimum return on a high-yield bond is –1.38%.[9]

We can make an even stronger statement than this. In the example above, for any chosen comparative return level, the probability that the return on the CAT note will exceed that return is always greater than the probability that the single-B bond will exceed that return. The CAT note dominates the single-B bond stochastically in the sense that any rational person, who prefers more wealth to less wealth, will choose the CAT note over the single-B bond. If credit risk and catastrophe risk are uncorrelated with an existing portfolio, then some combination of the CAT note and the existing portfolio will also dominate a combination of the single-B bond with the existing portfolio.

Conclusion

Securitised CAT reinsurance is a potentially attractive new asset class, because current pricing of CAT reinsurance can provide compelling expected returns on securitised reinsurance. The addition of small amounts of securitised reinsurance to diversified portfolios would enhance the risk/reward opportunities of investors. Under current market conditions, we believe the potential returns offered by properly structured

catastrophe notes could be attractive relative to other securities.

We have focused on products that are linked to a single aggregate nationwide catastrophe index. If this market develops and a richer variety of products are offered, investors will be able to customise a portfolio of reinsurance risks.

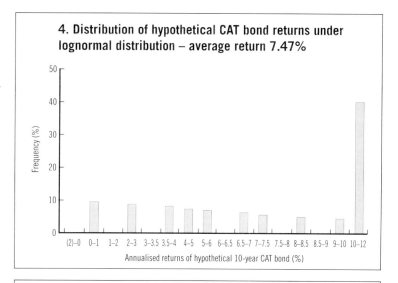

4. Distribution of hypothetical CAT bond returns under lognormal distribution – average return 7.47%

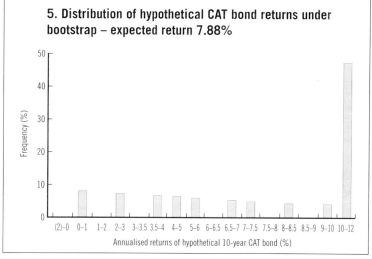

5. Distribution of hypothetical CAT bond returns under bootstrap – expected return 7.88%

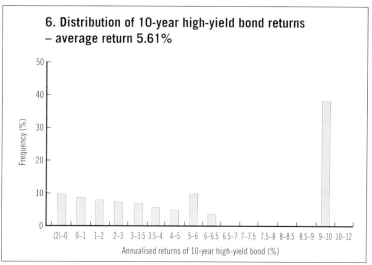

6. Distribution of 10-year high-yield bond returns – average return 5.61%

ASSESSING
CATASTROPHE
REINSURANCE-
LINKED
SECURITIES
AS A NEW
ASSET CLASS

1 *See Froot et al (1995).*

2 *These policies frequently include a requirement to repurchase the coverage at the original premium after it is used for one catastrophic event (the reinstatement charge).*

3 *See "The Impact of Catastrophe" (1994).*

4 *See "Higher Chance for Big Quake" (1988).*

5 *See "Earthquake Losses" (1988).*

6 *We calculate the premium base as the sum of 100% of Fire & Allied Lines, 95% of Farm Owners' Multiperil, 90% of Home Owners' Multiperil, 100% of Commercial Multiperil, 70% of Inland Marine, 37.5% of Private Passenger Automobile Physical Damage, and 40% of Commercial Automobile Physical Damage (premiums from A.M. Best). This weighting scheme is the same as that used by the Chicago Board of Trade in historical simulations of its early ISO-based futures contract.*

7 *The conditional expectation is given by the Black model for the pricing of the forward, when the forward price is substituted for the unconditional expectation (see Black, 1976, p. 177). The expectation in the current model is based on the actual distribution rather than the martingale distribution, however, and risk aversion may result in the conditional expectation differing from the forward.*

8 *We have already discussed the expected payoff of a traditional reinsurance excess of loss layer. The standard deviation of the return, as shown calculated for a maximum reinsurance payout of US\$100, can be calculated for an attachment point $K_1 = 20\%$ and a limit $K_2 = 30\%$ as:*

$$\sigma = \frac{1,000}{K_2 - K_1} \sqrt{E[R^2] - (E[R])^2}$$

where:

$$E[R^2] = |(K_2 - K_1)^2 N(-z_4) + K_1^2(N(z_3))|$$
$$- 2K_1 E[I] |N(z_6) - N(z_5)|$$
$$+ (E[I])^2 e^{\sigma^2} |N(z_8) - N(z_7)|)$$

$E[R]$ *is the expected reinsurance payout for a maximum reinsurance payout of US\$10. Here σ is the standard deviation of the logarithm of the PCS ratio, u is the mean of the logarithms of the PCS ratios, $z_3 = (\ln(K_1) - u)/\sigma$, $z_4 = (\ln(K_2) - u)/\sigma$, $z_5 = z_3 - \sigma$, $z_6 = z_4 - \sigma$, $z_7 = z_5 - \sigma$, and $z_8 = z_6 - \sigma$.*

9 *Simulation may also be used to calculate option-adjusted spreads on CAT bonds.*

BIBLIOGRAPHY

Black, F., 1976, "The Pricing of Commodity Contracts," *Journal of Financial Economics*, 3.

Black, F. and R. Litterman, 1991, "Global Asset Allocation with Equities, Bonds, and Currencies," Goldman, Sachs & Co.

Froot, K.A., B.S. Murphy, A.B. Stern and S.E. Usher, 1995, *The Emerging Asset Class: Insurance Risk*, Guy Carpenter & Co.

"Higher Chance for Big Quake," *The New York Times*, July 7, 1988.

Industry Research Council (formerly the All-Industry Research Advisory Council), 1988. "Earthquake Losses Under Workers Compensation and General Liability".

Insurance Services Office (ISO), 1994, "The Impact of Catastrophe on Property Insurance," ISO Insurance Issues Series.

Ibbotson Associates, 1996, *Stocks, Bonds, Bills, and Inflation*, Chicago: Ibbotson Associates.

13

A Note on Pricing PCS
Single-Event Options

Michael J. Tomas III
Chicago Board of Trade

The insurance market has seen a great number of changes recently, as capital market participants have brought in a ready pool of investment funds generated through new products and structures. These alternatives allow insurance and reinsurance companies to tap into additional capital to back up ever-increasing commitments. Exchange-traded options, securitisations (CAT bonds) and contingent financing solutions are some of the forms these alternatives are taking.

One of the early participants in this growing market was the Chicago Board of Trade (CBOT), which introduced insurance futures and options in 1992. In 1995, the CBOT diversified its product offering by launching the Property Claim Services (PCS) catastrophe insurance options. The contract has shown steady growth, with currently more than 10,200 open interest positions across all contracts.

Building on the success of the PCS options, the CBOT plans to list PCS single-event catastrophe options in June 1998.[1] These options will be based on the occurrence of single catastrophes, rather than the aggregation of catastrophes, as with the current insurance options. One difficulty facing users of this market is pricing these securities. Traditional option model distributional assumptions are inappropriate and alternative methods must be developed.

In this article we discuss a pricing model for the new PCS single-event catastrophe options. Numerical examples are provided, as well as a discussion of the inputs to the model. We start with a brief overview of the new contracts.

The nature of PCS single-event catastrophe options

The new PCS single-event options differ from those already listed on the CBOT. The earlier options are based on indexes of aggregate losses as compiled by PCS. Canter, Cole, and Sandor (1996) give a comprehensive description of these instruments and their use. The PCS single-event catastrophe options are per-occurrence options, and not based on aggregate indexes.

Options are listed on the sequential occurrence of insured industry catastrophic loss single events, defined as earthquakes or atmospheric events (hurricane, tropical storm, windstorm), in the following regions: National, Western, California, Eastern, Northeastern, Southeastern, Midwestern, Texas, and Florida. The National contract covers both earthquake and atmospheric events. Western and California cover earthquake events. The remaining regions cover atmospheric events. Each loss event tracks PCS estimates for insured industry losses resulting from catastrophic single events in the area, during the loss period covered, and pays US$10,000 if the single-event loss exceeds the strike price.

This chapter was originally published in Derivatives Quarterly, *Spring 1998. This copyrighted material is reprinted with permission from Institutional Investor. The author is grateful to Sylvie Bouriaux and Mark Holder of the Chicago Board of Trade, Amy Morgan of Bradley University, Rick Hernandez of Hedge Financial Products and Dan Rosenbaum of Risk Management Solutions for their helpful comments. The views stated are those of the author and do not necessarily reflect those of the Chicago Board of Trade or its staff.*

Otherwise, the option expires at zero value (making this a binary option). Each point in the single-event loss corresponds to US$100 million in insured industry catastrophic losses.

The same events that are aggregated to form the PCS indexes are used for the single-event contracts. However, they are not aggregated but maintained as individual estimates in the order of occurrence. The sequencing of the events is very important to the nature of the contract. As with the earlier PCS contracts, there is a loss period (six months for atmospheric option contracts and one year for earthquake or combined option contracts), and a development period (12 months following the end of the loss period). These options have European exercise. Strikes for these options are in five-point (US$500 million) increments.

For instance, a 1998 California single-event contract would be based on insured industry losses occurring between January 1, 1998, and December 31, 1998, and expire on December 31, 1999. A 1998 Florida single-event contract, for the first half of the year, would be based on insured industry losses occurring between January 1, 1998, and June 30, 1998, and expire on June 30, 1999.

Each option is for a particular single event in the sequence, at a particular strike. For instance, an option buyer could purchase a first-event 40 Florida December call. In this case, the buyer's option would be in the money if at least one atmospheric event during the loss period (July 1–December 31) exceeded 40 points. Or, for instance, an option buyer could purchase a second-event 30 Southeast December call. In this case, the buyer's option would be in the money if at least two atmospheric events during the loss period exceeded 30 points (each event exceeding 30 points).

Since the options are governed by a dual condition, event sequence and strike, one party's "first" event may be different from another's. For example, assume party A purchases a first-event 40 Florida call and a second-event 40 Florida call. Party B purchases a first-event 20 Florida call, and a second-event 30 Florida call. Three atmospheric events occur during the loss period: a 25-point event, a 45-point event and a 35-point event, in that order. Party A will have its first-event option exercised, based on the 45-point event, while its second event will not be exercised. Party B will have its first-event option exercised, based on the 25-point event, and its second-event option exercised based on the 35-point event.

Pricing single-event options

The nature of the single-event option, with its dual trigger (strike and event based on catastrophe losses) and binary payout (US$10,000), make standard option models inappropriate for pricing these options. Most standard option pricing models make assumptions regarding the type of movement the underlying instrument follows. In the case of the Black and Scholes (1973) model, the underlying is assumed to follow a geometric Brownian motion process (a continuous process). Because of the way the model was derived, it was possible to form hedge portfolios with the underlying security so that risk-neutral pricing could be used. Cox, Ross, and Rubinstein (1979) derive a model in discrete time in which a similar hedging argument is used. Black–Scholes and Cox–Ross–Rubinstein are classified as arbitrage models. Other arbitrage models specifically derived to price catastrophe index options exist. Cummins and Geman (1995), Geman (1996), and Chang, Chang and Yu (1996) are examples of these.

Cummins and Geman (1995) developed an arbitrage model using an Asian option approach to pricing the original CBOT insurance futures contract (which was based on the Insurance Services Office (ISO) index). Geman (1996) developed a model for contracts based on the PCS indexes, in which the index for a particular region, during the loss period, is based on a jump-diffusion process. During the development period the process is assumed to follow a diffusion process. Chang, Chang and Yu (1996) use a transformation method to convert a compound Poisson process into a pure diffusion process. Unfortunately, the transformation results in an option with a random maturity.

These models were all designed to price index options, where a series of events are aggregated. Modifications would need to be done to price single-event options. Assumptions necessary to maintain arbitrage pricing, such as complete markets and an underlying hedging instrument, may not hold up, however.

Another approach that can be used for pricing is the actuarial method. This has long been popular in the insurance industry for measuring and pricing various forms of insurance risk. A good description of the general methodology can be found in Panjer and Willmot (1992). This approach is quite intuitive and will be used to derive a simple model for the new PCS single-event options.

In the actuarial approach to modelling insurance, the nature of the risk to be covered by the

133

A NOTE ON
PRICING PCS
SINGLE-
EVENT
OPTIONS

insurer can be viewed as having two parts:

❏ the frequency of unexpected events; and
❏ the severity of financial impact, or size of the claims.

Combining the frequency and the severity of the claims over some specified period results in the aggregate or total claims the insurer is liable for. The insurer, in order to hedge its exposure, must assign a value to its portfolio of expected total claims, known as the premium (or risk premium) and usually set to cover the expected total claims plus expenses. Expenses include components such as broker commissions, contingency margins and management fees.

The general approach taken by actuarial models is to look at factors affecting the frequency and severity of claims and attempt, through distribution and model assumptions, to assign a value to the risk premium. This approach is used for a variety of insurance types such as life, automobile, fire and natural disasters.

Using the actuarial approach we can specify a simple pricing formula for a first-event option at a particular strike as:

$$\text{Price} = \text{US\$10,000exp}(-rt)\text{Prob}(\text{Event}_1 > X) \quad (1)$$

where r, t, Event_n and X are the risk-free rate, time to maturity, first event to exceed the strike, and the strike, respectively. This is simply the present value of US$10,000 times the probability that an event occurs with a loss greater than the strike. This can be extended to the nth event at a particular strike as:

$$\text{Price} = \text{US\$10,000exp}(-rt)$$
$$\times \text{Prob}(\text{Event}_n > X \mid$$
$$\text{Event}_1, \text{Event}_2, ..., \text{Event}_{n-1} > X) \quad (2)$$

where r, t, Event_n and X are the risk-free rate, time to maturity, nth event to exceed the strike, and the

strike, respectively. The nth event to exceed the strike is conditional on $n-1$ events having exceeded the strike level. In the insurance industry this price is known as the "pure premium".

This is very similar in spirit to the idea of certainty equivalent cash flows in capital budgeting. In this case the probability accounts for the risk, similar to a certainty equivalent factor (see, for instance, Copeland and Weston (1988) for a description), thus the risk-free rate can be used to discount the expected cashflow. The most difficult element to obtain in this pricing model is the probability of an event exceeding the strike level.

Suppose we wish to price single-event 1998 California earthquake options. To do so we will need information on the various probabilities of losses exceeding strike prices by the event number. For example, suppose we wish to price the second event to exceed 20 (US$2 billion in insured industry losses). The price of such an option can be written as:

$$\text{Price} = \text{US\$10,000exp}(-rt)$$
$$\times \text{Prob}(\text{Earthquake}_2 > 20 \mid$$
$$\text{Earthquake}_1 > 20) \quad (3)$$

Alternatively (assuming the events are independent), we can write this as:

$$\text{Price} = \text{US\$10,000exp}(-rt)$$
$$\times \text{Prob}(\text{Two Earthquakes} > 20) \quad (4)$$

In order to price the various strike and event combinations, a model for the probability of earthquakes in California could be used to create a set of probabilities as displayed in Table 1. A discussion of where and how these probabilities can be generated follows.

The probabilities would adjust through time due to shortening maturity, and due to events occurring. For example, if an earthquake occurs and causes US$1.1 billion in damage (11 on the index) the new probabilities would adjust to those in Table 2.

Table 1. California 1998 earthquake probabilities

Strike	First event	Second event	Third event	Fourth event	Fifth event
5 (US$500m)	P(1 event > 5)	P(2 events > 5)	P(3 events > 5)	P(4 events > 5)	P(5 events > 5)
10 (US$1bn)	P(1 event > 10)	P(2 events > 10)	P(3 events > 10)	P(4 events > 10)	P(5 events > 10)
15 (US$1.5bn)	P(1 event > 15)	P(2 events > 15)	P(3 events > 15)	P(4 events > 15)	P(5 events > 15)
20 (US$2bn)	P(1 event > 20)	P(2 events > 20)	P(3 events > 20)	P(4 events > 20)	P(5 events > 20)
25 (US$2.5bn)	P(1 event > 25)	P(2 events > 25)	P(3 events > 25)	P(4 events > 25)	P(5 events > 25)
...	...	...	...	...	...

This table contains a partial listing of probabilities for the California earthquake contract. Initially first and second-event call options will be listed for trading, with strikes from 5 to 500 in five-point increments

134

A NOTE ON
PRICING PCS
SINGLE-
EVENT
OPTIONS

Table 2. California 1998 earthquake probabilities

Strike	First event	Second event	Third event	Fourth event	Fifth event
5 (US$500m)	occurred (P = 1)	P(1 event > 5)	P(2 events > 5)	P(3 events > 5)	P(4 events > 5)
10 (US$1bn)	occurred (P = 1)	P(1 event > 10)	P(2 events > 10)	P(3 events > 10)	P(4 events > 10)
15 (US$1.5bn)	P(1 event > 15)	P(2 events > 15)	P(3 events > 15)	P(4 events > 15)	P(5 events > 15)
20 (US$2bn)	P(1 event > 20)	P(2 events > 20)	P(3 events > 20)	P(4 events > 20)	P(5 events > 20)
25 (US$2.5bn)	P(1 event > 25)	P(2 events > 25)	P(3 events > 25)	P(4 events > 25)	P(5 events > 25)
…	…	…	…	…	…

This table contains a partial listing of probabilities for the California earthquake contract. Initially first and second-event call options will be listed for trading, with strikes from 5 to 500 in five-point increments

NUMERICAL EXAMPLES

Suppose on January 1, 1998, we wished to price a first-event California 150 strike call option (the first earthquake event to exceed US$15 billion in industry losses in California). Assume that the probability of such an event for 1998 is 1.5%. The option has a one-year period and a one-year development period; the option will settle on December 31, 1999. Additionally assume that the two-year Treasury rate (on a continuously compounded basis) is 5.25%. The price of the option would be calculated as:

$$US\$135 = US\$10,000e^{(-0.0525 \times 2)}(0.015) \quad (5)$$

As a second example, suppose on January 1, 1998, we wished to price a second-event National 200 strike call option (a second earthquake or atmospheric event to exceed US$20 billion in industry losses). Assume that the probability of two such events (events exceeding US$20 billion) for 1998 is 0.1%. Again the option has a one-year loss period and a one-year development period. Using the same assumption for the two-year Treasury the price of the option would be calculated as:

$$US\$9 = US\$10,000e^{(-0.0525 \times 2)} (0.001) \quad (6)$$

Probabilities

The probabilities used as inputs to the model are the keys to its accuracy. There are essentially two methods to estimating these probabilities:

❑ historical data; and
❑ modelled data.

In the first method, historical data on insured industry losses is used to estimate the probabilities of exceeding certain trigger levels in the regions defined. Given the time-frame necessary to get a reasonable number of sample points for estimation (catastrophes occur far less frequently than changes in stock prices, for instance), a

minimum of two adjustments need to be done to the data series:

❑ adjust for population; and
❑ adjust for inflation.

Even if proper adjustments for demographics and property values can be done, however, there may not be sufficient data to get good estimates for the probabilities of large catastrophes, as they have occurred so rarely through history.

Another alternative is to employ modelling to estimate the severity of damage given particular catastrophes at various magnitudes. Several firms have developed an expertise in catastrophe modelling and provide this type of information as part of their services. Examples include Applied Insurance Research (AIR), Earthquake Engineering International (EQE) and Risk Management Solutions (RMS). These firms collect and maintain data at the county, state, and regional level on industry exposures, company specific exposures, local underwriting practices, building inventories and construction codes. They then employ sophisticated software to simulate structural damage of existing homes and businesses under a variety of natural disasters. These simulations can provide the probabilities of losses exceeding user-defined dollar or event thresholds for a variety of regions, including those defined in the PCS contracts. Unlike historic data, where so few events have occurred, simulations can generate a more complete picture of pricing probabilities.

Conclusion

The PCS single-event options are conceptually quite different from most existing exchange-traded options. Despite their unique features a relatively simple model can be employed to price them. The main challenge of this approach lies in acquiring the proper probability information. However, this information is calculated by a variety of firms in the industry. The model outlined is a function of the time to maturity, the risk-free rate, and the

135

A NOTE ON
PRICING PCS
SINGLE-
EVENT
OPTIONS

probability of exceeding the strike level for the number of events contracted. For hedgers and investors this model can provide a simple way to benchmark the value of these options.

1 *The CBOT received CFTC approval but has yet to launch these contracts.*

BIBLIOGRAPHY

Black, F. and M. Scholes, 1973, "The Pricing of Options and Corporate Liabilities", *Journal of Political Economy*, 3, pp. 637-59.

Canter, M., J. Cole and R. Sandor, 1996, "Insurance Derivatives: A New Asset Class for the Capital Markets and a New Hedging Tool for the Insurance Industry", *Journal of Derivatives*, 4 (Winter) , pp. 89-104; reprinted as Chapter 11 of the present volume.

Chang, C., J. Chang and M. Yu, 1996, "Pricing Catastrophe Insurance Futures Call Spreads: A Randomised Operational Time Approach", *Journal of Risk and Insurance*, 63(4) , pp. 599-617.

Copeland, T. and J. Weston, 1988, *Financial Theory and Corporate Policy*, third edition, Addison-Wesley.

Cox, J., S. Ross and M. Rubinstein, 1979, "Option Pricing: A Simplified Approach", *Journal of Financial Economics*, 7, pp. 229-63.

Cummins, J.D. and H. Geman, 1995, "Pricing Catastrophe Insurance Futures and Call Spreads: An Arbitrage Approach", *Journal of Fixed Income*, 4(4), pp. 46-67; reprinted as Chapter 4 of the present volume.

Cummins, J.D., C. Lewis and R. Phillips, 1996, "Pricing Excess-of-Loss Reinsurance Contracts Against Catastrophe Loss", Conference on The Financing of Property/Casualty Risks, November 21-3.

Geman, H., 1996, "Insurance-Risk Securitisation and CAT Insurance Derivatives", *Financial Derivatives and Risk Management*, September, pp. 21-24; reprinted as Chapter 10 of the present volume.

Panjer, H. and G. Willmot, 1992, *Insurance Risk Models*, Society of Actuaries.

14

The High-Yield Bond Market
Catastrophe Bonds versus Defaultable Bonds

Hélyette Geman
University Paris IX Dauphine and ESSEC

This chapter argues that in the fundamental subject of financial risk analysis, some valuable lessons may be drawn from insurance. In particular, we show that the genuine hazards generated by global capital markets and illustrated by the events of summer 1998 create a market incompleteness that is not fully addressed by existing models of defaultable bonds. In contrast, the long experience of risk premium analysis in the insurance and reinsurance industry, as well as the existence of historical data on natural disasters, render the valuation of catastrophe bonds less perilous than that of defaultable bonds.

Over the past 15 years, insurers have come under increasing pressure to move to more imaginative financial operating strategies. After having been sheltered for decades from the reality of market forces, they must adapt to a situation in which performance and company value are based on the price of common stock, itself determined by the law of supply and demand. Insurers still lag behind other industries in managing capital. A review of debt and equity issues raised in the past two decades demonstrates the weakness of insurers in accessing US debt markets (see Figures 1 and 2).

The industry's access to capital has been restrained by the limited secondary trading in insurance debt markets. Few portfolio managers and participants in the capital markets feel they can justify the cost of a fixed-income analyst specialising in the insurance industry. This has negatively affected the spreads for insurance issues for some time.

Recently, however, insurers and reinsurers have capitalised on the convergence of the insurance

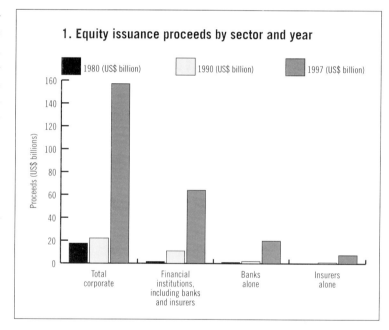

1. Equity issuance proceeds by sector and year

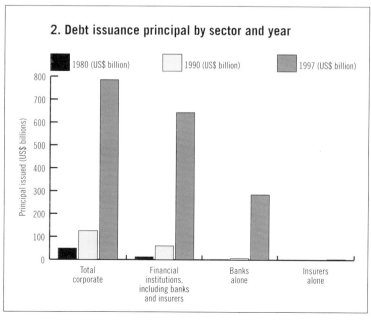

2. Debt issuance principal by sector and year

and capital markets by employing financial engi-neering solutions to raise capital and reallocate underwriting capacity. Catastrophe bonds, con-tingent surplus notes and other insurance-linked securities are proliferating as substitutes for and complements to traditional reinsurance. Insurance markets, like credits markets, trade in discrete event risk, in contrast to equity and commodity markets in which price volatility is more continuous.

Pricing catastrophe bonds

Catastrophe bonds, sometimes called "Act of God" bonds, are bonds issued by an insurance or rein-surance company. Such bonds were first issued by the state of California when insurance companies decided, after the Northridge earthquake of 1994 generated insured losses of US$12.5 billion, not to write any more earthquake coverage. The coupon (and part of the principal, depending on the tranche) is not paid if some well-specified event such as an earthquake of a given magnitude on the Richter scale with an epicentre in a designated geographical zone or if a sinistrality index in a des-ignated geographical area such as the Property Claim Services index reaches a certain threshold during a specified period.

To describe the cashflows attached to a cata-strophe bond, let us consider an instrument of this type, supposing it has no optional features such as callability or convertibility (as in the Winterthur 1995 catastrophe bond issue). Denot-ing by A the principal, C the coupon payment, p the probability of occurrence of the trigger event during the coupon period (a semester or a year), N the maturity of the bond (in unit periods) and ℓ the loss ratio – meaning that the final payment after the catastrophic event is $(1 - \ell)(A + C)$ – the contingent bond payments and their associ-ated probabilities are described in Table 1.

In terms of cashflow payments, catastrophe bonds look very much like defaultable bonds; how-ever they provide better portfolio diversification and are easier to price, for the following reasons:

❑ the correlation between catastrophe bond return and market return is very close to zero, hence the diversification effect is outstanding;

❑ the fraction of the principal at risk is not a ran-dom quantity as in the case of defaultable bonds, but fully specified at issuance; and

❑ the hazard rate, ie the probability of an event over the next accounting period, can be derived from observable variables provided by weather and meteorology departments.

Let us recall that, if we model the event occur-rence by a simple Poisson process – which has been, since Lundberg's work in 1903, the central model for insurance losses – the hazard rate is identical to the intensity λ of the Poisson process, implying that the probability of an event occuring in the interval $[t, t + dt]$ is equal to λdt and the probability of no event up to time t is $e^{-\lambda t}$.

In the so-called reduced form models for the valuation of defaultable bonds, default is also rep-resented by an unpredictable stopping time. The insurance terminology, "hazard rate", has been adopted by most authors (Madan and Unal, 1993; Duffie and Singleton, 1994, and many others). In the case of catastrophe bonds this hazard rate λ is adjusted deterministically over time in the light of meteorological information. In the risky debt mar-ket, λ_t evolves stochastically over time (as recent world events have shown) and the recovery rate $(1 - \ell)$ is also a random variable; intensity and magnitude of losses for defaultable bonds may be exogenous or derived from some equilibrium model. One central result, derived by arbitrage arguments, is that the credit spread over Treasury bills may be written as $s = \lambda.\ell$, ie, the hazard rate times the loss ratio. Hence the value at time t of a cashflow ϕ to be paid at time T is

$$V(t) = E_Q\left[\phi \exp\left(-\int_t^T (r(u) + \lambda.\ell)du\right)/F_t\right] \quad (1)$$

In the case of deterministic parameters λ and ℓ, an intuitive proof of the expression of the spread in terms of λ and ℓ can be obtained by writing in two different manners the value at date t of a risky dollar to be paid at time $t + dt$. The first one involves a risk-adjusted discount factor, namely a spread s added to the (locally risk-free) short-term rate $r(t)$; the other a proba-bility-weighted average of the payouts dis-counted at the risk-free rate, ie:

$$\frac{1}{1 + (r + s)dt} = 1.(1 - \lambda dt) + (1 - \ell)\lambda dt$$

$$(2)$$

Equation (1) is very elegant and in total conti-nuity with the actuarial methodology described

Table 1. Contingent payments on specimen catastrophe bond

Period	No-default payment	Probability	Default payment	Probability
1	C	$1 - p$	$(1 - \ell)(A + C)$	P
2	C	$(1 - p)^2$	$(1 - \ell)(A + C)$	$p(1 - p)$
.../... j	C	$(1 - p)^j$	$(1 - \ell)(A + C)$	$p(1 - p)^{j-1}$
.../... N	C + A	$(1 - p)^N$	$(1 - \ell)(A + C)$	$p(1 - p)^{N-1}$

above; but it raises some questions. The equivalent martingale measure Q is not unique since the completeness of the defaultable bond market is questionable, in particular when the intensity λ is supposed to be stochastic. The identification of the two key parameters, λ and ℓ, is very difficult, under any probability measure and in particular under the measure Q since it should incorporate the risk premiums.

Financial institutions may not have a database big enough to extract reliable estimators. Rating agencies, which provide not only credit ranking but also migration probability matrices for different grades of bonds, may be working on quicksand as well, since there is no precedent for today's globally integrated financial markets. Lastly, when the loss ratio ℓ and/or the intensity λ are stochastic, the use of the T-forward neutral probability measure Q_T (see Geman, 1989), which is a powerful tool to price random cashflows under stochastic interest rates, does not provide an immediate answer because of the lack of independence of the level of interest rates and the credit spread $\lambda\ell$ (ie, between current interest rates and default occurrence).

In a somewhat circular theoretical argument, equation (1) is most popularly used to infer the value of the spread as a function of the maturity of the bond and rating of the firm. This methodology obviously assumes that markets price credit in a coherent manner, ie that the markets understand the risk and know the recovery value. The recent shrinking of emerging markets departments in a number of institutions hints that this assumption may not necessarily be well founded. The question of how to price therefore remains open. The fundamental lesson derived from option theory is that the only safe answer lies in the price of the (self-financing) hedging portfolio. If no hedge can be found, the existence of an arbitrage price is not obvious. The valuation of the security thus requires either the use of the utility function of a representative agent or of a risk-minimisation criterion appropriate for the type of incompleteness at stake. In all cases, prudent reserves are relevant.

Equation (1) applies to catastrophe bonds in a much safer manner because of the greater reliability of the estimation of the key parameters. Data have been accumulated over time. The treatment of such data has received renewed attention in the past few years because of the crucial role they play in the valuation of catastrophe derivatives (traded on the Chicago Board of Trade or in over-the-counter transactions). Historical data on insured losses are used to estimate the probabilities of exceeding certain trigger levels in a defined area. Adjustments for changes in demographics and property values need, however, to be made. It is important to notice that, at variance with the random evolution over time of creditworthiness in the financial markets, these adjustments are deterministic. Several engineering firms have developed a real expertise in providing loss estimates. These firms collect and maintain data at the zip code, county, state and regional level on industry exposures, building inventories and construction codes. They then employ sophisticated software to simulate structural damage to existing homes and businesses from a variety of natural disasters in different regions.

Let us take as an example the recent catastrophe bonds issued by Swiss Reinsurance on behalf of the insurance company Tokio Marine. The coupon (or the principal, for some riskier tranches) is nullified or reduced if the magnitude of a seismic event on the Richter scale in the Grand Kanto area of Japan reaches a given threshold. The available information on the dollar (or yen) amount of losses generated by an earthquake in terms of the distance of its epicentre from major cities is bewildering in its quality. As for the probabilities of such seismic events occuring, these have been studied in departments of civil engineering by academics who were already using Monte Carlo simulations in a standard manner 30 years ago.

Consequently, the price at time t of a catastrophe bond can be written as

$$V(t) = E_Q\left[\sum_{k=1}^{n} \phi_k \exp\left(-\int_t^{t+k} r(s)ds\right) 1_{I_k < A}/F_t\right] \quad (3)$$

where:

❏ the cash flows ϕ_k, $k = 1, \ldots n - 1$, represent the fixed coupon payments at dates $t + k$ and ϕ_n includes the principal repayment (if a coupon of the type Libor plus basis points is paid, a swap may be added to the structure to recover the fixed-coupon framework);

❏ I_k is the loss index over the year $(t + k - 1, t + k)$ and A the trigger level; and

❏ Q is the risk-adjusted probability measure whose unicity depends on the number of "primitive assets" available in the market to which the index is related, compared with the number of sources of randomness in the index representation. For instance, in the case of the CBOT insurance derivatives, Geman (1994) proposed to extract from layers of reinsurance the construction of the probability measure Q.

We can observe that, using the reasonable assumption of independence between interest rates and natural risks, equation (3) can be reduced to

$$V(t) = \sum_{k=1}^{n} B(t,t+k)\phi_k E_Q[1_{I_k<A}/F_t] \quad (4)$$

and no choice of interest rate model is necessary. If the coupon ϕ_k is not fixed but depends on the Treasury yield curve observed at date $(t+k)$, the same formula prevails with ϕ_k replaced by $E_{Q_{t+k}}(\phi_k)$.

The only quantity that remains to be evaluated is:

$$Prob_Q[(I_k < A)/F_t]$$

and this obviously requires the specification of the index I and its dynamics over the period $(t+k-1, t+k)$.

Whether the index I is an aggregate loss index or another measure of a catastrophic event, it should be represented by a stochastic including a jump component. (This modelling may also be appropriate for temperature indexes, such as those measured by the National Weather Service in the US and to which heating and cooling degree-days weather derivatives are tied.)

The dynamics of I under the probability measure Q may be described by the stochastic differential equation

$$dI_t = I(t^-)[\alpha dt + \sigma dW_t] + k\, dN_t \quad (5)$$

where
❑ α and σ are constants accounting for the diffusion part of I, ie for the small moves;
❑ (W_t) is a Brownian motion under Q;
❑ (N_t) is a Poisson process with intensity λ, where λ denotes the frequency of the jump; and
❑ (N_t) accounts for the big moves of the index.

The solution of equation (5) is the Doléans–Dade exponential which takes a simpler form when (W_t) and (N_t) are assumed to be independent, namely I(t):

$$I(t) = e^{X(t)}\left[S(0) + k\int_0^t e^{-X(u)}\right] \quad (6)$$

where

$$X(t) = \left(\alpha - \frac{\sigma^2}{2}\right)t + \sigma N(t)$$

The values of parameters α, σ, λ, k can be derived (see Cummins–Geman, 1995) from the market prices of insurance derivatives, traded on the Chicago Board of Trade and in OTC transactions. The computation of the probabilities $Prob_Q(I < A)$ requires Monte Carlo simulations of the trajectories of the index I as described in equation (5), since an exact closed-form solution only exists today for the cases of a pure diffusion $(k = 0)$ or a pure jump $(\alpha = \sigma = 0)$. These quantities incorporated in equation (4) give the price of the catastrophe bond.

Among many other points that could be discussed, an important one needs to be emphasised: that the market value of a catastrophe bond (credit risk in these instruments is mostly eliminated by investing the proceeds of the bond issue in Treasuries through a special purpose vehicle) does not depend on the *size* of the issue. This is another key difference with sovereign or corporate debt for which the number of outstanding bonds may have an impact on the probability of default, hence on the bond value.

Conclusion

This chapter argues that actuarial and stochastic modelling together with the fundamentals of financial economics are the necessary tools to address the valuation of high-yield bonds. Not surprisingly, catastrophe analysis carries common features in the case of defaultable bonds and catastrophe bonds. The former problem may be more difficult, however, because the overwhelming recent changes in the capital markets may overpass in magnitude the evolution of weather patterns and nature-related events. Moreover, in the case of catastrophe bonds, the data series necessary to estimate the parameters have, in principle, been accumulated for centuries. Hence, from different perspectives, the catastrophe bond market is less severely "incomplete" than the defaultable bond market.

BIBLIOGRAPHY

Ané, T. and H. Geman, 1997, "Order Flow, Transaction Clock and Normality of Asset Returns", *The Journal of Finance*, forthcoming.

Cummins, J.D. and H. Geman, 1995, "Pricing Catastrophe Insurance Futures and Call Spreads: An Arbitrage Approach", *Journal of Fixed Income*, March, pp. 46–57; reprinted as Chapter 4 of the present volume.

Diebold, F.X., T. Schuermann and J.D. Stroughair, 1998, "Pitfalls and Opportunities in the Use of Extreme Values Theory in Risk Management", manuscript, The Wharton School.

Duffie, D. and K.J. Singleton, 1994, "Modeling Term Structures of Defaultable Bonds", manuscript, Graduate School of Business, Stanford University.

Embrechts, P. and H. Schmidli, 1994, "Modelling of Extremal Events in Insurance and of Finance", *Mathematical Methods of Operation Research*, 39.

Geman, H., 1989, "The Importance of the Forward Neutral Probability Measure in a Stochastic Approach to Interest Rates", ESSEC working paper.

Geman, H., 1994, "Catastrophe Calls", *Risk*, 7(9), pp. 86-9.

Hill, B.M., 1975, "A Simple General Approach to Inference About the Tail of a Distribution", *Annals of Statistics*, 3.

Lamarre, M., B. Townsend and H.C. Shah, 1992, "Application of the Bootstrap Method to Quantify Uncertainty in Seismic Hazard Estimates", *Bull. Seis. Soc. Am.*, 82(1).

Leadbetter, M.R., G. Lindgren and H. Rootzen, 1983, *Extremes and Related Properties of Random Sequences and Processes,* New York: Springer-Verlag.

Madan, D. and H. Unal, 1993, "Pricing the Risks of Default", *Review of Derivative Research*, University of Maryland.

Pye, G., 1974, "Gauging the Default Premium", *Financial Analysts Journal*, January–February.

15

The Perfume of the Premium II

Morton Lane and Oleg Movchan
Gerling Global Financial Products; UBS Brinson

Shortly after the introduction of insurance derivatives and the commencement of their trading at the Chicago Board of Trade (CBOT), we began to analyse catastrophe options by looking at the "implied loss distributions" embedded in the traded prices. The results were recorded and described in the proceedings of the 1995 Bowles Symposium at Georgia State University in Atlanta, Georgia, under the title, "The Perfume of the Premium".

Our attempt was to examine those traded prices "which [were] high enough to bring forth sellers and low enough to induce buyers". Or, in the words of the old adage, prices where the perfume of the premium overcomes the stench of the risk. Within these traded prices were implicit market assumptions about loss distributions and risk. Our task was to try to make those implicit assumptions explicit: to reveal the "market actuary".

The analysis followed a procedure familiar to the conventional options market. Namely, rather than estimate volatilities and calculate consistent prices (using, say, the Black–Scholes model), take the traded prices and extract the volatilities consistent with those prices (ie find the implied volatility).

The exercise was complicated by the fact that:

❑ the trade data was sparse;
❑ the underlying (aggregate catastrophe loss) did not trade;
❑ this underlying rose monotonically over time; and
❑ the probability distribution was extremely long-tailed.

Some of these problems were addressed by characterising the implied loss distribution as a gamma distribution, rather than the lognormal familiar to conventional options traders. (It could not, therefore, conveniently be characterised by a single parameter.)

The exercise was useful and allowed us to gauge where the market might price and trade covers not yet transacted. Also, it allowed year-to-year and month-to-month comparisons of pricing risk over time. Our analysis showed that for such a small market, it was a remarkably accurate barometer of the price changes that were taking place in the underlying reinsurance market.

But, truth to tell, the CBOT market has never progressed to the point of building a deep liquid market where such insights could be of much trading value. As of this writing, only about US$100 million of risk has been transferred via the exchange.

It is all the more surprising then to see several competitor exchanges – the Bermuda Commodities Exchange (BCOE) and the Catastrophe Risk Exchange (Catex) – begin to have some trading success. (See the relative growth illustrated in Figure 1.)

The nascent success of these exchanges has re-energised our interest in extracting implied loss distributions from market data and is the *raison d'être* for this chapter. The new exchanges present some important new insights as well as challenges to the business of extracting risk information from insurance and insurance derivative pricing.

This chapter therefore lays out some of the issues involved, our solutions, and the insights gained from market prices at mid-1998.

This chapter was first published in Derivatives Quarterly, *Spring 1995. This copyrighted material is reprinted with permission from Institutional Investor.*

Derivatives versus insurance pricing

Underscoring all the modelling that goes into the price of derivatives and other capital market instruments is the idea that prices are calculated from expected values and this is tantamount to prices being arbitrage-free. This means, for example, that the price of a 40/60 call spread, plus the price of a 60/80 call spread is identical to the price of a 40/80 call spread (otherwise arbitrage would be possible). This property is humorously summed up in a recent cartoon (see Figure 2).

Insurance pricing on the other hand is more mysterious. It remains a fact that the word insurance does not even appear in the index of most finance texts. Furthermore, insurers do not speak the same language as finance officers.

The insurance translation of a call spread, which we earlier referred to as the 40/60 spread would be the US$2 billion × US$4 billion aggregate layer. Insurers would not necessarily price this layer at its expected loss but rather at

expected loss plus a "load" commensurate with their perception of risk. Furthermore, it would not necessarily be the case that the cost of the 2 × 4 layer plus the 2 × 6 layer is the same as the 4 × 4 layer. Mathematically this can be demonstrated if one takes a load relative to risk. Also, in practice, brokers often represent horizontal layered solutions as cheaper than syndicated (or vertical) coverage.

These observations about insurance refer to individual perceptions of pricing, but what of the whole market? Well, to date it has not been a traded market: so how could it be arbitrage-free? Nor is it a transparent market. Prices are known only to insiders and then usually incompletely. (At the insurance – as opposed to reinsurance – level, the situation is complicated even further by heavy price regulation.)

The development of insurance securitisation and derivatives in a transparent market promises to change things. That is why it is so important to understand these early attempts to develop exchanges. In what follows, we assume that the two known principles of the existing markets, expected value pricing and arbitrage-free pricing, will prevail in these new insurance markets. Our analytical models are built on these foundations.

The loss process

Before turning to the exact instruments traded at the three exchanges, it is important to understand the nature of the underlying losses being traded.

Insurance companies write a variety of retail policies to individual homeowners and business owners all over the US. A fire, say in one house here, and in another there, causes losses to the company. Ideally, over time, the sum of these losses (indemnity payments) to the homeowners is less than the premiums collected and the company experiences a profit to reward the shareholders.

Problems arise when concentrations of losses occur due to, say, an earthquake, a hurricane, a tornado or a riot. Such concentrations of loss are called "catastrophic" and these "CAT" losses are the ones that primary companies try to reinsure against. It is this risk that is being traded in the new exchanges, although catastrophe reinsurance itself is by no means new.

It is often difficult to statistically characterise these risks. A tornado or wind-burst can cause a US$20 million industry insured loss – a small CAT – while a hurricane can and has caused a US$20 billion insured loss. Estimates of future

1. Risk transfer outstanding

Catex*
US$6,000,000

CBOT
US$50,000,000

December 1997

BCOE
US$17,260,000

CBOT
US$59,748,000

May 1998

CBOT
US$61,308,000

August 1998

*Assumes an average trade size of US$2 million

2. An arbitrage-free transaction

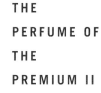

possible hurricane losses now range from US$60–100 billion.

The range (ie severity) of possible CAT losses is huge and must be characterised by a long-tailed distribution. At the same time such losses are, thankfully, infrequent. Only a few losses over US$5 billion have occurred in the past 20 years. Even counting the smaller CATs, the number is between 20 and 30 per year, with some years having very few.

In what follows, we emulate insurance market convention and characterise the uncertainty of catastrophic losses by a frequency and severity distribution. In our case, for analytic convenience, severity is characterised by a gamma distribution, and frequency is characterised by a Poisson distribution. The process might be thought of as in Figure 3.

The object of the chapter is to gauge the parameters of implied frequency and implied severity distributions from the prices traded at the CBOT, BCOE, and Catex.

The traded instruments

At the CBOT, the option contract is based on the sum of all catastrophes (large and small) that occur in a specified territory over a specified period of time. The underlying index is the aggregate of CAT losses as defined by Property Claims Service (PCS), an independent third-party loss assessor, for all perils it considers to be catastrophic in nature. The focus of our attention will be the national annual aggregate contract for all CAT losses in the US.

A most important feature of CBOT options is that the loss recovery to the buyer is proportionate to the amount by which the losses exceed the strike (or trigger). This feature is in sharp contrast to the contracts traded at the other two exchanges. At the BCOE, contracts are listed on aggregate losses, first loss, and second-loss-event covers (although as of this writing, only first loss contracts have traded for the national contract). The options pay off the moment the underlying losses exceed the strike. Furthermore, they pay off in full. They are binary options, not conventional proportionate-payout options. Part of the challenge of extracting implied loss distribution information is gauging the interplay between single events and the aggregation of such events.

The options traded at Catex are also binary options, though they need not be. Catex is not really an exchange in the accepted sense of the word (there is no clearing, no margining, nor standardisation of contracts). Rather it is an electronic notice board where insurance portfolios can be traded. One particularly popular form of cover listed on this exchange is an "industry loss warranty" (ILW – also known as "original market loss warranty" or franchise cover). Under this, the cover has two triggers:

❑ one based on indemnity payments incurred by the buyer; and
❑ one based on the level of losses incurred by the industry as a whole.

The presence of an indemnity trigger means that insurers can treat the ILW as insurance in their underwriting book.

CBOT and BCOE options are clearly derivatives that must be accounted for in the investment part of the balance sheet. In any case, the indemnity trigger in ILWs is typically set very low so as to be easily satisfied. The principal value of the contract falls on the second industry trigger. Therefore, the ILW contract is priced to all intents and purposes as if it were a derivative based solely upon industry loss. As such, the ILW's price can be compared with the other derivatives at CBOT and BCOE.

Trades that took place at the Catex during the middle of 1998 are listed in Table 1.

We remarked earlier that reinsurance prices were opaque. Catex prices still are not well distributed, but they are available to subscribers to the system. Notice in the list of prices there are two transactions for losses in excess of US$20 billion. One, on May 29, 1998, traded at a 6.50% rate-on-line. The second on June 1, traded at 10%

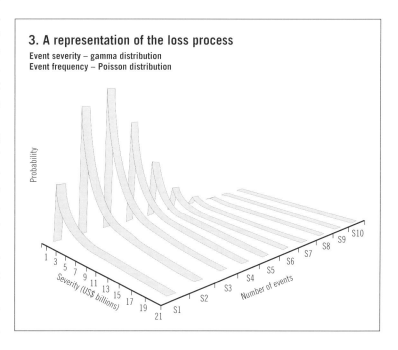

3. A representation of the loss process
Event severity – gamma distribution
Event frequency – Poisson distribution

146

THE
PERFUME OF
THE
PREMIUM II

Table 1. Catex transaction listing

Catex trades (mid-1998)

Trade date	Report number	Region	Peril	Line of business	Exposure	Type	Limit retention	Premium rate-on-line (%)
May 7	39	US possessions	All	Property	Second event @ US$10bn	ILW	na	4.25
May 29	44	US	Wind	Property	First event @ US$20bn	ILW	na	6.50
May 29	45	US	All	Property	First event @ US$10bn	ILW	na	18.00
June 1	46	US	All	Property	US$20bn	ILW	na	10.00
June 24	48	US	All	Property	US$1m (US$25bn)	ILW	na	5.00
July 1	56	US	All	Property	First event @ US$25bn	ILW	na	5.50

Table 2. Catastrophe exchanges

	CBOT	BCOE	Catex
Forum	Open outcry	Electronic	Electronic notice board
Clearing	"AAA" Clearing Corporation	Clearing house	None: notice board
Product	PCS options	BCOE options	Various ILW policies
Geographic regions	US	US	Potentially worldwide
Geographic detail	State, region, nation	Zip code	As specified
Insured Property	Commercial, private	Homeowner	As specified
Perils	All perils	Atmospheric perils	As specified
Index	PCS	GCCI	As specified
Index value	US$billion of loss ÷ 10	Varies by contract	Variable
Index source	Insurer/ground survey	Insurer paid loss records	Variable
Contract periods	Quarterly or annually	Semi-annually	Variable
Contract	Aggregate	First event	As specified
		Second event	
		Aggregate	
Contract Size	Option spread × US$200	US$5,000	Variable
Premium cash value	Index points = US$200	US$ amount	Variable
Type	Proportional	Binary	Variable
Settlement period	6 months	Partial, full, first update	Variable
	12 months	second update, third update	

Table 3. CBOT catastrophe options (PCS Index)

Lower strike	Upper strike	Cover structure	Cover type	Bid price	Last price	Ask price	Points	Rate-on-line (%)
40	60	Call spread	Aggregate loss	11.0			11.0	55.00
60	80	Call spread	Aggregate loss	6.0	9.5	10.0	7.5	37.59
80	100	Call spread	Aggregate loss			8.0	5.7	28.39
100	120	Call spread	Aggregate loss	3.5		6.0	4.4	22.08
100	150	Call spread	Aggregate loss			12.0	9.4	18.76
120	140	Call spread	Aggregate loss	1.0		6.0	3.5	17.46
250	300	Call spread	Aggregate loss	0.5		2.5	1.9	3.84
100		Call	Aggregate loss			20.0	14.7	14.75
150		Call	Aggregate loss	4.0		7.5	5.4	10.74
180		Call	Aggregate loss	0.4		1.8	1.8	9.06

rate-on-line. The two trades differed in only one respect. The June 1 trade covered "all perils". The May 29 trade covered only losses caused by wind (ie hurricanes) and did not cover earthquakes – the only realistic peril besides hurricanes that might cause a US$20 billion loss in the US. So it can be inferred that, at the US$20 billion level, the risk of earthquakes is assessed at around at around a 3.5% rate-on-line. The balance of price allocated to earthquakes versus hurricanes increased with the attachment point so that at US$50 billion it

might be 50% of the risk, but at US$5 billion it might only be 20% because of the increased frequency of eligible hurricanes at that level.

For these perhaps tenuous reasons, we leave the May 29 trade out of our consideration. However, to make the cross-exchange point, we leave in the BCOE contracts that are strictly "wind-only" or atmospheric exposures. These contracts are also strictly homeowners only, although in what follows they will be compared to industry-wide losses (ie including commercial losses).

Table 4. BCOE catastrophe options (GCCI Index)

Strike price	Equivalent US$ loss trigger	Cover structure	Cover type	Bid price (US$)	Last price (US$)	Ask price (US$)	Theoretical price Points (US$)	Theoretical price Rate-on-line (%)
100	60,781,685,651.21	Binary	Single loss		175.0		2.3	0.05
15	9,117,252,847.68	Binary	Single loss	400.0		806.0	682.0	13.64
20	12,156,337,130.24	Binary	Single loss			600.0	457.6	9.15
25	15,195,421,412.80	Binary	Single loss	237.0			312.6	6.25
30	18,234,505,695.36	Binary	Single loss			400.0	216.5	4.33

Table 5. Catex transactions (US$ loss)

Lower strike	Upper strike	Cover structure	Cover type	Bid price (%)	Last price (%)	Ask price (%)	Theoretical price Points (%)	Theoretical price Rate-on-line (%)
10,000,000,000		Binary	Second loss		4.25		1.02	1.02
20,000,000,000		Binary	Single loss	9.50	10.00		4.69	4.69
22,500,000,000		Binary	Single loss			9.00	3.50	3.50
25,000,000,000		Binary	Single loss		5.00	8.00	2.63	2.63
10,000,000,000		Binary	Single loss		18.00		16.16	16.16

Table 2 lists the exact contract specifications and Table 3 lists the bid-offers and last trades that occurred around mid-1998. These prices are denominated in the price convention of each exchange (the PCS Index at the CBOT, the Guy Carpenter index at the BCOE, and in rate-on-line at Catex.

Other caveats/qualifiers

Although we are seeking to compare prices on different instruments (aggregate versus first event, etc) for a similar underlying risk (catastrophes in the US), the comparison is not always exact (witness the discussion of wind versus all-perils). Two other important adjustments must be kept in mind when inputting data into the model and these involve time.

The PCS national annual contract at the CBOT considers the aggregate exposure for the whole of the calendar year. By mid-year only six months of exposure are left, so the prices are for the remaining period of exposure. But it is also true that by mid-year catastrophes have already happened – in particular winter storms and Midwest tornadoes. In fact, by mid-1998, nearly US$4 billion of small losses had been accumulated. CBOT prices must therefore been viewed as prices for the remainder of the year, conditioned by the fact that US$4 billion of losses have already happened.

BCOE July contracts are for the exposed period, July–December, and therefore do not cause any special time problems for a mid-year analysis.

Catex prices are however typically negotiated on a 12-month basis so that a mid-year rate-on-line of say 20% represents the price for two periods:

the latter-half of 1998 and the first half of 1999. Now, as we have seen, higher attachment exposures typically can only occur in a single event, by hurricane or earthquake. Furthermore, hurricanes typically happen only during the latter half of the year between July and October. In dividing the price of an annual ILW between two periods, in order to compare with other prices, we therefore have to load for the seasonal exposure effect and put most of the price into the latter half of 1998. Guided by the May 29 and June 1 traded comparisons (and throwing in considerable judgement), we made our comparative analysis using 75% of the Catex prices as the component relevant to the latter-half of 1998 and relevant to a comparison to CBOT and BCOE prices.

Finally, in what follows, model prices are compared to traded prices on a consistent basis, rate-on-line. As already noted, each market has different pricing conventions and they are displayed here in tables respecting those conventions. However, optimisation takes place using rates-on-line.

The fitting model

The columns on the right of Tables 3, 4 and 5 contain bid prices, last traded prices and offered prices – for or about the middle of 1998 – on each of the three exchanges. The data is recognisably sparse, but it is faithful to what is available.

Our objective is to find the parameters of our chosen severity distribution (the gamma class) and the chosen frequency distribution (the Poisson class) which best explain the prices in these exhibits. The gamma distribution is a two-parameter distribution α, β whose mean is $\alpha\beta$

and standard deviation is $\beta\sqrt{\alpha}$. The Poisson distributions is a single-parameter distribution λ whose mean is λ and whose standard deviation is $\sqrt{\lambda}$. So the fitting model is to choose α, β, λ to "best explain prices".

Best explain prices is interpreted to mean choosing α, β, λ that generate prices that are :

❑ lower than known offers;
❑ higher than known bids; and
❑ closest to actual traded prices.

The optimisation is two-tier. First, get inside the bid-offer spread. Second, get closest to actual trade prices. The two-tier effect is achieved by attaching (ideally non-Archimedean) weights to each of the two objective functions. Closest is defined as the absolute value of the difference between the actual traded price and the theoretical (or fitted) prices.

The constraints on this optimisation procedure are simply the definitions of the distance between actual prices and the theoretical prices. The algebra of deriving the theoretical prices is laid out in the Appendix. For the "algebraically challenged," consider the following rationale for the CBOT prices.

First consider the possible severity distribution for an *individual* event – this is the fitted gamma. It is shown in the Appendix that the *sum* of such individual events is also gamma. If the number of events were known, say 10, then we would know the distribution of the sum of those 10 events. However, the number of events is unknown; it is randomly drawn from a Poisson distribution – the fitted frequency distribution. Therefore, the probability of the gamma distribution over all possible number of events. Its analytic form is shown in the Appendix (Equation (A7)). This is the distribution used to fit the expected value of options prices at the CBOT.

Satisfyingly, the mean of this aggregate distribution is the expected value of an individual event (severity mean) times the expected number of individual events (frequency mean). So much for the distribution used to calculate expected values of all the price-articulated calls and call spreads at the CBOT.

A similar rationale must be used to derive the binary prices at BCOE and Catex from the same source distributions. Once again, the algebra is provided in the Appendix; the hopefully more intuitive explanation follows.

The probability of *any* event exceeding a particular binary trigger, when the number of events

and their sizes are unknown, is simply 1 minus the probability that *none* of the events exceeds the trigger. This distribution is known as the exceedance distribution. The probability of a *particular* event exceeding the trigger is 1 minus the cumulative probability from the severity distribution. Given that the severity distribution is gamma, then it can be shown that if the frequency is Poisson, then the exceedance distribution can be given convenient analytic form as shown in the Appendix (Equation (A10)). And it can be demonstrated that the expected number of events above the trigger is the expected number of all events, multiplied by the probability that an individual event is above this trigger.

The expected price of the binary option uses this exceedance probability distribution. Since the binary option pays out in full above the trigger, but pays out nothing below, the expected value is simply the cumulative probability above the trigger using the exceedance distribution.

Clearly, the choice of α, β and λ to achieve the fitting objectives, subject to the traded options price constraints described above, is a highly non-linear problem. However, computers can perform such searches using fairly standard subroutines. Assuming such searches are performed to test whether the optimal solutions are global rather than local, we can calculate the implied severity and frequency distributions for the second half of 1998.

Output

THE PARAMETERS
The net result of all of our structurings and optimisations, given the prices in Tables 3, 4 and 5, is three numbers:

$$\alpha = 0.188721$$
$$\beta = 11.2$$
$$\lambda = 2.23$$

These are the implied parameters extracted from mid-year prices. What do they mean?

Let us start with initiatives. We can make the following statements:

❑ the market expects 2.23 events for the remainder of the year;
❑ individual events are expected to average US\$2.114 billion in size. (Derived from $\alpha \times \beta$ or 11.2×0.188721); and
❑ total losses for the remainder of calendar 1998 are expected to be US\$4.713 billion. (Derived

Table 6. Event history

Year	Number of events (Second half of year)	Average size of event (Second half of year)
1988	15	58,739,804
1989	12	990,457,040
1990	13	189,851,826
1991	9	468,965.571
1992	17	1,601,503,906
1993	15	141,227,406
1994	20	89,004,626
1995	12	415,863,087
1996	15	210,487,733
1997	8	100,700,000
Average	13.6	US$437.7 million
Average aggregate		US$5,953.3 million

Table 7. Standard deviation – history and implied

	History	Implied
Standard deviation Individual events size	US$2.095 billion	US$4.866 billion
Standard deviation Aggregate loss size	US$7.728 billion	US$7.922 billion

from the average size of events or $2.23 \times US\$2.114$ billion.)

These insights can be compared with historical experience. Table 6 shows the number of events experienced in the second half of each year for the previous 10 years.

Clearly implied probabilities show that the market is priced as if it expects fewer events but larger ones than in recent history. In contrast to this seeming underestimate of frequency, the market is priced to expect fewer aggregate losses than in recent history. Recall that the past 10 years include hurricanes Andrew and Hugo. (The Northridge earthquake took place in the first half of the year.) The market seems to be priced consistent with a preoccupation with large events rather than with lots of little cats.

Other insights emanate from the parameters. Prices depend not only on means but the tails of the distribution. One imperfect way to capture this is through standard deviation. The comparison with history is laid out in Table 7. Once again the market appears to get the overall picture right (volatility of the aggregates) but it tends to overestimate the variability of individual events.

Finally, a less intuitive observation confirms the trend. Historically (over the past 10 years) about five out of 136 events (3.68%) were greater than US$2 billion. The implied parameters suggest a probability of 23.7% that events will exceed US$2 billion. The market is more cautious than history.

THE PRICES

The prices by our model are given in the right columns of Tables 3, 4 and 5. For each of the three exchanges the following observations are in order.

CBOT Whoever paid 9.5 for the 60/80 call spread probably paid too much (see Table 3). The consistent price was 7.5. On the other hand, the 1.8 offer for the 180 call was probably the best buy from all of the offers (if one sought coverage at that level).

BCOE The fitted prices threaten neither the listed bids nor the listed offers. This is just as well considering that these contracts are for atmospheric risks only. The only trade that is listed (the 100 single loss at US$175) is clearly overpriced to a fitted price of US$2.30. Either the buyer ignorantly paid way too much or the inaugural trade was entered into simply for its advertising effect (see Table 4).

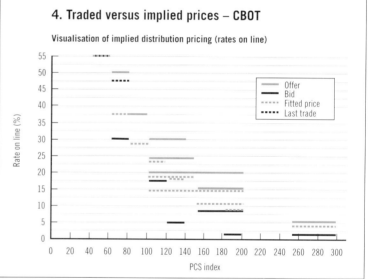

4. Traded versus implied prices – CBOT

Visualisation of implied distribution pricing (rates on line)

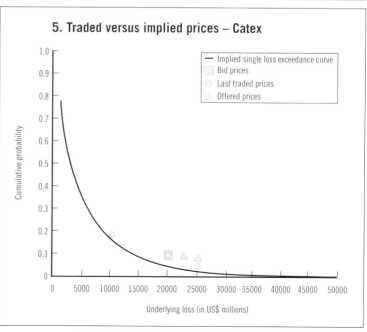

5. Traded versus implied prices – Catex

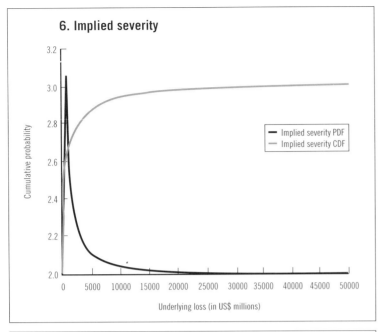

6. Implied severity

- Implied severity PDF
- Implied severity CDF

Cumulative probability (y-axis): 2.0, 2.2, 2.4, 2.6, 2.8, 3.0, 3.2

Underlying loss (in US$ millions): 0, 5000, 10000, 15000, 20000, 25000, 30000, 35000, 40000, 45000, 50000

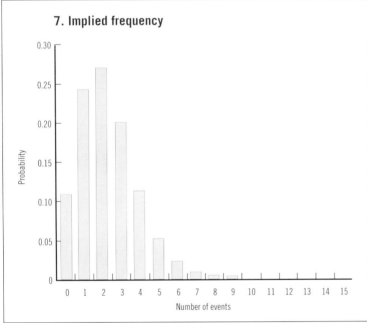

7. Implied frequency

Probability (y-axis): 0, 0.05, 0.10, 0.15, 0.20, 0.25, 0.30

Number of events: 0, 1, 2, 3, 4, 5, 6, 7, 8, 9, 10, 11, 12, 13, 14, 15

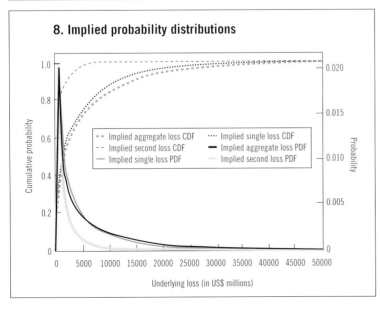

8. Implied probability distributions

- ░ Implied aggregate loss CDF
- ···· Implied single loss CDF
- -- Implied second loss CDF
- ▬ Implied aggregate loss PDF
- ── Implied single loss PDF
- Implied second loss PDF

Cumulative probability (left y-axis): 0, 0.2, 0.4, 0.6, 0.8, 1.0

Probability (right y-axis): 0.005, 0.010, 0.015, 0.020

Underlying loss (in US$ millions): 0, 5000, 10000, 15000, 20000, 25000, 30000, 35000, 40000, 45000, 50000

Catex The most substantive trades have taken place on Catex (see Table 5). These are, after all, real reinsurance trades. Here our implied prices consistently underestimate the Catex prices. This is least obvious at the US$10 billion level (16.16% versus 18%) and most obvious at US$20 billion (4.69% versus 10%). Based on these overpricings, risk-takers should definitely write ILWs rather than CAT options at the CBOT.

To illustrate these prices, consider Figures 4 and 5. Figure 4 shows the various different call spreads, in rate-on-line terms, against the PCS Index range they cover. Generally, the fitted prices lie within the bid-offer ranges. In Figure 5 the implied exceedance curve is plotted against the observed prices at Catex. The implied curve is consistently below the traded prices suggesting that Catex trades are a better "write" than the CBOT and vice versa.

ARBITRAGE POSSIBILITIES

Earlier we suggested that Catex prices were expensive relative to the CBOT. The aggressive arbitrager should jump over all such possibilities to seek out low-risk profit. However, the market is sparse at this point and no true arbitrage presents itself. (Prices seem to indicate that lifting the 180 call offered at the CBOT at 9% and writing the US$20 billion ILW on Catex at the 9.5% bid is a locked-in arbitrage. However, this disappears with the time adjustment.)

Notwithstanding this, the suggestion of cheapness and dearness can be used to improve the risk-reward of particular trades – as in the following example. Consider writing the US$20 billion ILW for a (seasonally adjusted) 7.5% rate-on-line. The implied pricing suggests that there is a gain of US$75,000 per US$1 million of exposure against a 0.075 probability of losing US$1 million.

Contrast this with an alternative trade. Write US$6.6 million of the US$20 billion ILW and buy US$6.6 million of the 200/250 call spread at an implied price of 6.36%. The sizes are chosen so that the net premium received is the same as the previous trade: US$75,000. The upside is therefore the same. The risk on the downside, however, is greatly reduced. Maximum loss would take place when only one single loss of US$20 billion occurred during the remainder of the year. At that point, the aggregate would be 240 (remember, it is already at 40) and the net loss would be US$1.32 million. However, the chance of exactly one further loss of *exactly* US$20 billion is 0.04%. Trade two is clearly a superior trade.

Table 8. Implied rates-on-line

Aggregate excess covers	Market rate-on-line (%)	Single ILW covers	Market rate-on-line (%)
2 × 6	37.59	6	21.15
2 × 8	28.39	8	15.89
2 × 10	22.08	10	12.12
5 × 15	10.74	15	6.40
5 × 20	6.26	20	3.51

The trade constructed is not a true arbitrage, but it is an improved risk-reward trade and thereby demonstrates the utility of using implied pricing to detect improvement opportunities.

THE IMPLIED DISTRIBUTIONS AND THEIR PROBABILITIES

Figures 6 and 7 show the implied severity and implied frequency distributions for the derived parameters already discussed. Figure 8 shows the corresponding cumulative density functions (CDFs) and probability density functions (PDFs) for the aggregate, first-loss, and second-loss covers, consistent with traded prices. These curves

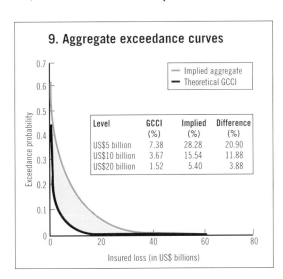

9. Aggregate exceedance curves

Level	GCCI (%)	Implied (%)	Difference (%)
US$5 billion	7.38	28.28	20.90
US$10 billion	3.67	15.54	11.88
US$20 billion	1.52	5.40	3.88

Insured loss (in US$ billions)

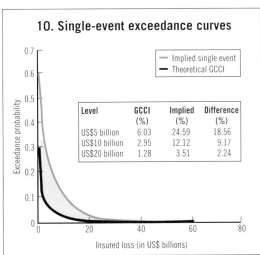

10. Single-event exceedance curves

Level	GCCI (%)	Implied (%)	Difference (%)
US$5 billion	6.03	24.59	18.56
US$10 billion	2.95	12.12	9.17
US$20 billion	1.28	3.51	2.24

Insured loss (in US$ billions)

can be used to predict where the market might trade different covers (see Table 8).

What is remarkable here is that our procedure has taken us from observed prices on particular covers to implied distributions to fitted prices for any cover. All this without recourse to an actuary!

THE IMPLIED VERSUS HISTORICAL EXCEEDANCE CURVES

A final piece of information to be sifted from our analysis is how implied exceedance curves compare to geophysical exceedance analysis. Unfortunately, modelling companies specialising in such geophysical exceedance analysis are proprietary and do not make their data publicly available. General comparison is impossible. Nevertheless, in an effort to be more transparent, the BCOE has provided exceedance curves for the Guy Carpenter Index – compared down to the zip code level. These are attempts to measure the "true" underlying risk using history and geophysical modelling. Figure 9 shows these curves contrasted with the implied curves. Clearly, the implied curves are of the correct general shape. They are also above and to the right of the geophysicals. The shaded area represents the difference between the two approaches. This area represents the likelihood of earthquakes (remember the BCOE is atmospheric and homeowners only) plus any implied profits. Clearly, the difference between the two curves is large – reflecting both earthquake risk and the "load" that is used to calculate profit.

Finally, note that Figure 10 illustrates the prices that the market would have to charge for *binary* aggregate covers if they were to be consistent with other prices. To date, *binary* aggregates have not been traded on the national contract on any exchange.

Conclusion

The objective of this chapter is to make explicit that which is implicit in the traded prices around mid-1998. The result is a huge amount of statistical insight into prices. No actuary was needed to produce the implied probabilities, though a knowledge of statistics was necessary to characterise the underlying loss process. The results are extremely encouraging and the methodology will be useful if and when the deep and liquid market in insurance derivatives fully develops.

It is true that our analysis has been built on thin data and confined to a particular restricted class of distributions. It is also true that different optimising routines and models could have produced other results. We accept such criticism but also plead that further improvements can wait until another day. Given the present status of trading, the analysis is more than adequate to the task.

What has been achieved is this. Without examining statistics and without the help of actu-ary or geophysical modeller, we have examined prices and revealed the loss distributions believed by the market as a whole. We have revealed the "market actuary" and can introduce him to the company actuary to expose where opportunities lie.

Appendix: Formulas used in the model

Severity and frequency distributions

Gamma distribution

$$f(x) = \frac{1}{\Gamma(\alpha)\beta^\alpha} x^{\alpha-1} e^{-x/\beta}, \ x > 0; \ \alpha > 0, \ \beta > 0 \tag{A1}$$

Poisson distribution

$$p_t(n) = P(N_t = n) = \frac{(\lambda t)^n}{n!} e^{-\lambda}, \ n = 0,1,2\ldots \tag{A2}$$

Aggregate loss, single loss and second loss distributions

DERIVING THE AGGREGATE LOSS DISTRIBUTION

By an *aggregate loss* we mean a total loss calcu-lated as a sum of all individual losses due to eligi-ble events. Since neither number of the losses during the risk period nor the severity of those losses is known, the aggregate loss is traditionally modelled as a random *sum* defined as

$$S_t = S(t) = \begin{cases} 0, N_t = 0 \\ \sum_{i=1}^{N_t} X_i, N_t > 0^{t \in |0,T|} \end{cases} \tag{A3}$$

Here (X_i), $i = 1,2,\ldots$ are severities (magni-tudes) of individual losses and N_t is the number of losses up until time t. In this case the segment [0, T] constitutes the risk period.

The main assumptions underlying such a model are:

❑ the random variables (X_i), $i = 1,2,\ldots$ are inde-pendent and identically distributed (ie they con-stitute an iid-sequence, as it is often said); and
❑ random variables $N, X_1, X_2, X_3, \ldots$ are mutually independent (ie frequency of individual events does not depend on their severity).

We derive a general form of a distribution of an aggregate loss, given that distributions of severity and frequency of individual losses are known.

Using the law of total probability, we have the expression for the cumulative distribution func-tion of the aggregate loss distribution:

$$F_{S_t}(x) = P(S_t \leq x) = \sum_{n=0}^{\infty} P(S_t \leq x | N = n) P(N = n)$$

$$\sum_{n=0}^{\infty} P(X_1 + \ldots X_n \leq x) P(N_t = n) \tag{A4}$$

By the same token, one can easily obtain the following form for the probability density func-tion of the aggregate loss:

$$f_{S_t}(x) = P(S_t = x)$$

$$= \sum_{n=1}^{\infty} P(X_1 + \ldots + X_n = x) P(N_t = n) \tag{A5}$$

Therefore, in order to calculate the probability distribution of aggregate losses, one has to know the probability distribution for the sum $\sum_{i=1}^{n} X_1$ for any given n. Sometimes, if the distribution of the sum is known, the formula is just plugged into (A4) and (A5) and everything boils down to calculating the sum of the functional series on the right-hand side of (A4) and (A5). Note that both series uniformly converge on any compact subset of the support of the severity distribution and, therefore, can be approximated with any arbitrary accuracy by taking sufficiently many terms in the series. However, in most cases, the situation is not so simple, and one has to rely on certain numerical methods to approximate the distribution of $\sum_{i=1}^{n} X_1$. In the case of gamma dis-tribution, the desired distribution has a simple analytical form, which can be easily derived using the moment-generating function tech-nique. Simply speaking, the sum of n indepen-dent random variables having a gamma distribution with parameters α and β also has a gamma distribution with parameters αn and β. Therefore, if we assume the Poisson distribution for the frequency of individual events, then the aggregate CDF has the following form

$$F_{s_t}(x) = e^{-\lambda t}$$

$$+ \sum_{n=1}^{\infty} \int_0^x \frac{1}{\Gamma(\alpha n)\beta^{\alpha n}} y^{\alpha n-1}e^{y/\beta}dy \frac{(\lambda t)}{n!} e^{-\lambda t}$$

(A6)

The corresponding PDF is

$$F_{s_t}(x) = F_t(x) = \sum_{n=1}^{\infty} \frac{1}{\Gamma(\alpha n)\beta^{\alpha n}} x^{\alpha n-1}e^{x/\beta} \frac{(\lambda t)}{n!} e^{-\lambda t}$$

(A7)

It is easy to check that the expected value of S_t is $E[S_t] = \lambda t\alpha\beta$, which corresponds to the general result that $E[S_t] = E[N_t]E[X]$, where X is generic notation for the severity random variable.

DERIVING THE SINGLE LOSS DISTRIBUTION

This distribution concerns itself with the following question: What is the probability that no eligible event during a specified risk period causes a loss that exceeds some level?

Denote by $F(x) = Pr(X \leq x)$ the cumulative distribution function of the severity of individual losses and let $f(x) = F(x)$ be the corresponding density. Let us also denote by $F_I(x)$ the cumulative distribution function and $f_I(x) = F_I(x)$ is the density of single loss. As before, $p_t(n)$ denotes the probability density function of the frequency of individual losses. If exactly n events occur, then the conditional probability that all losses are less than or equal to x given that there were n events, is

$$Pr(max(X_1, ..., X_N) \leq x \mid N = n)$$

$$= [P(X \leq x)]^n = [F(x)]^n$$

(We have independent events and the probability of each event is $P(X \leq x) = F(x)$.)

Then, using the law of total probability, we have the marginal probability of all losses not exceeding x

$$Pr(max(X_1, ..., X_N) \leq x) = F_I(x)$$

$$= \sum_{n=0}^{\infty} Pr(max(X_1, ..., X_N) \leq x \mid N = n)Pr(N = n)$$

$$F_I(x) = \sum_{n=0}^{\infty} |F(x)|^n p_t(n)$$

(A8)

Accordingly,

$$f_I(x) = F_I(x) = \sum_{n=1}^{\infty} n|F(x)|^{n-1}f(x)p_t(n)$$

(A9)

It is not difficult to derive an analytical expression for the single loss distribution under the Poisson frequency assumption. We have

$$F_I(x) = \sum_{n=0}^{\infty} |F(x)|^n \frac{(\lambda t)^n}{n!} e^{-\lambda t}$$

$$= e^{-\lambda t}\sum_{n=0}^{\infty} \frac{|\lambda tF(x)|^n}{n!} = e^{-\lambda t|1-F(x)|}$$

Thus,

$$F_I(x) = e^{-\lambda t|1-F(x)|}$$

(A10)

Finally, note that the *expected number of eligible events causing losses greater than* x can be conveniently expressed as

$$\lambda t[1 - F(x)]$$

In our model, $F(x)$ is assumed to be a gamma cumulative distribution function. It is clear, however, than this argument is very general, and one might derive similar expressions for other assumptions about frequency of individual losses.

DERIVING THE SECOND LOSS DISTRIBUTION

The same line of argument as before leads to the following equation for the second loss distribution (frequency of individual loss is again assumed to have a Poisson distribution).

$$F_{II}(x) = e^{-\lambda t[1-F(x)]}(1 + \lambda t[1 - F(x)])$$

(A11)

This equation gives the probability that at most one event is greater than x.

Calculations of expectations for various underlying losses and payoff structures

In this section we derive equations needed to calculate expected values for some specific options based on the loss distributions described previously. In particularly, we focus upon two main categories: call and put spread options traded at CBOT based upon an aggregate index and single loss and second loss binary options traded at BCOE.

EXPECTED VALUE CALCULATION FOR CALL AND PUT SPREADS

The payoffs of these instruments could be written in the following form:

$$A_{Call}(S) = min[max(S - X_L, 0), X_U - X_L]$$

(A12)

$$A_{Put}(S) = min[max(X_U - S, 0), X_U - X_L]$$

(A13)

In this case S is a random variable describing an aggregate loss distribution. Thus, we are going to use representation (A7) assuming a gamma distribution with parameters α and β for severity of individual losses and a Poisson distribution with intensity parameter λ for their frequency.

First, we derive the expected value formula for call spreads. The corresponding formula for the put spreads is derived in absolutely the same fashion.

Suppose first that we want to compute the expected payoff of the call spread on an individual event. In our situation, it is $E^{\alpha,\beta}[\Lambda_{Call}(X)]$, where X has a gamma distribution with parameters α and β. We have

$$E^{\alpha,\beta,\lambda}[\Lambda_{call}(S)]$$

$$= \int_0^{+\infty} \min\left|\max(x - X_L, 0), X_U - X_L\right| f_{\alpha,\beta}(x)dx$$

$$= \int_{X_L}^{X_U} (x - X_L)f_{\alpha,\beta}(x)dx + \int_{X_U}^{+\infty} (X_U - X_L)f_{\alpha,\beta}(x)dx$$

$$= \int_{X_L}^{X_U} xf_{\alpha,\beta}(x)dx - X_L\int_{X_L}^{+\infty} f_{\alpha,\beta}(x)dx$$

$$+ X_U\int_{X_U}^{+\infty} f_{\alpha,\beta}(x)dx$$

$$= \alpha\beta\int_{X_U}^{X_U} \frac{x^{(\alpha+1)-1}}{\Gamma(\alpha+1)\beta^{\alpha+1}} e^{-x/\beta} dx$$

$$- X_L\int_{X_U}^{+\infty} f_{\alpha,\beta}(x)dx + X_U\int_{X_U}^{+\infty} f_{\alpha,\beta}(x)dx \qquad (A14)$$

Therefore,

$$E^{\alpha,\beta}[\Lambda_{Call}(S)] = \alpha\beta[F_{\alpha+1,\beta}(X_U) - F_{\alpha+1,\beta}(X_L)]$$
$$X_U[1 - F_{\alpha,\beta}(X_U)] - X_L[1 - F_{\alpha,\beta}(X_U)] \qquad (A15)$$

The similar equation for put spreads is

$$E^{\alpha,\beta}[\Lambda_{Call}(S)] = X_U[F_{\alpha,\beta}(X_U)] - X_L[1 - F_{\alpha,\beta}(X_L)]$$
$$- \alpha\beta[F_{\alpha+1,\beta}(X_U) - F_{\alpha+1,\beta}(X_L)] \qquad (A16)$$

In order to calculate the expected value of the aggregate call spread, one needs to use probability distribution function given by (A7). However, applying the expectation operator to the payoff formula, we see that it can penetrate through the integral sign and we get

$$E^{\alpha,\beta,\lambda}|\lambda_{Call}(S)| = \sum_{n=1}^{\infty}\left[\int_0^{\infty} \Lambda_{Call}(S)f_{\alpha n,\beta}(s)ds\right]p_t(n) \qquad (A17)$$

where the integral inside the summation is nothing else but $E^{\alpha n,\beta}[\Lambda_{Call}(\bullet)]$ and can be computed using formula (A14). The case of the put spreads is handled by the same token.

EXPECTED VALUE CALCULATION FOR BINARY OPTIONS

It is well known that the price of a binary option is equal to the amount of the payoff multiplied by the probability of the option being in-the-money. Thus, to calculate the corresponding expected values, one only needs to get exceedance probabilities for the option strike prices. These probabilities are represented by the upper tail of the corresponding cumulative distribution function. For a CDF it is given by the equation

$$F(x) = 1 - F(x) \qquad (A18)$$

Actuaries and other applied statisticians often call this function a survivor function. Thus, for instance, single-loss binary option at BCOE with a strike price of 15 pays US$5,000 if a single event measured by GCCI exceeds the T = US$9,117,252,847 level for the entire US in the corresponding time period. If the probability of exceedance is $F_I(T) = 15\%$, then the price of one option contract is US$5,000 × 0.15 = US$750. The rate-on-line for the contract is clearly, 15%. The same line of argument analogously applies to the second-loss binary contracts.

16

Insurance-Linked Securities

Gail Belonsky, David Laster and David Durbin[1]
Swiss Re

In the past two years approximately US$2 billion in worldwide insurance and reinsurance capacity has been created through the issuance of capital market instruments including:

❑ over-the-counter swaps;
❑ exchange-traded and over-the-counter options; and
❑ private placement bonds.

Although still small in comparison to 1997 worldwide reinsurance industry premiums of US$125 billion, this new class of "insurance-linked" securities (ILSs) has broken new ground in the insurance and financial markets. By bridging the insurance and capital markets, ILSs are creating a range of attractive investment opportunities previously unavailable to those outside the insurance industry. The securities also constitute a potential new source of competitively priced insurance coverage, especially at times when such coverage is in short supply. Insurance and capital market participants who recognise the potential of these securities and position themselves accordingly will help shape the market's development and will stand to profit the most from it.

This chapter explores the prospects for ILSs by focusing on two key questions. First, how might the structures of these instruments evolve over the next few years? A careful review of the ILS deals to date holds some clues. Second, how important will ILSs be to the insurance and reinsurance markets? Ultimately, the success of these securities will depend on not just their level of issuance, but on the extent to which they improve the efficiency of insurance and reinsurance markets.

The plan of the chapter is as follows. First, we consider how insurance-linked securities work and describe some deals that have already come to market. Next, we explain how these securities facilitate a mutually beneficial transfer of risk, allowing issuers to tap into new sources of funds and investors to diversify their portfolios and boost risk-adjusted returns. We then examine the modelling and quantification of catastrophe risk, both processes vital to the pricing of ILSs. Finally, we offer some insights into how the market for these securities might develop in coming years.

How insurance-linked securities work

The majority of ILS transactions to date have involved catastrophe bonds, commonly called "CAT bonds", whose coupon and principal payments depend on the performance of a pool or index of natural catastrophe risk. Insurance-linked securities such as CAT bonds can be structured to hedge the risks of many types of institutions, ranging from global corporations to local insurers, from whose perspective the securities behave like a reinsurance contract.

Consider, by way of example, a simple one-year structure collateralised by a bond issue that provides capital to cover losses in the event of a hurricane (Figure 1). The illustrated transaction involves three parties: investors, the cedant and the issuer. Investors purchase bonds from the issuer, a special purpose reinsurance vehicle (SPV)

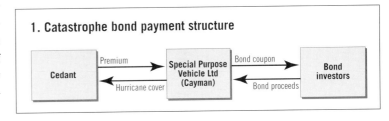

1. Catastrophe bond payment structure

that simultaneously enters into a reinsurance contract with the cedant. The SPV is typically structured as an independent charitably-owned trust that is licensed as a reinsurer in an offshore location such as the Cayman Islands or Bermuda. Its sole purpose is to engage in the business relating to the securitisation. This exclusive focus on a single transaction minimises the risk to which the SPV exposes its counterparties.[2] Thus, the SPV resembles a single-parent captive that is created to serve the reinsurance needs of its parent.

Figure 2 depicts the timing of cashflows in a typical transaction. The funds provided by the bond investors are initially deposited in a trust account with restrictions on how its assets are invested and when they can be withdrawn. The investment earnings on this initial deposit as well as the premium the cedant pays for insurance coverage are periodically (often, semi-annually) paid to investors as a bond coupon. In the typical structure, there is a possible extension period following the maturity date, called the "loss development period", during which the amount of losses payable under the cover is determined. If there have been no qualifying events during the year, the principal amount is returned to the bond investors with their final coupon payment. If there has been an event, the amount due to the cedant under the coverage definition is paid at the end of the loss development period and any balance of the funds goes back to investors as a return of principal.

The simple structure depicted in Figure 1 can be modified. Often, there is a reinsurance company acting as an intermediary between the cedant and the SPV. This reinsurer can retain some risk before retroceding to the SPV. An insurance company may, for example, recover on the basis of its own losses, while the reinsurer enters into a contract with the SPV based on an index of losses. In another variation, a bond issue can have one or more classes that are guaranteed to return to investors some percentage of principal, a feature known as *defeasance*. These bonds can be structured so that investors receive the guaranteed portion of the principal at the regular maturity date if no catastrophic loss occurs. If a loss does occur, the full principal is repaid, but at a later date. This delayed repayment is funded by zero coupon securities that the issuer purchases at the maturity date using the guaranteed portion of the bond proceeds.

CAT bond structures involve an offshore issuer, management agents and trustees, as well as other parties. An alternative way to transfer catastrophe risk is through a swap transaction, in which a series of fixed, predefined payments is exchanged for a series of floating payments whose values depend on the occurrence of an insured event. The swap, by design, offers benefits on both sides, permitting a cedant to lay off insurance risk to a counterparty better equipped to manage it. The cedant can enter into the swap directly with counterparties or through a financial intermediary (Figure 3). In some jurisdictions, the counterparties need not be insurers. New York State insurance regulators ruled in the summer of 1998 that insurance-linked swaps whose payments are not based on the cedant's actual losses are financial contracts and can therefore be entered into by non-insurers.

Examples of specific deals

Three transactions executed over the past 18 months – an index bond, a physical trigger bond and a physical trigger swap – illustrate how deals can be structured so that their payments are based on indices rather than actual losses. Basing a deal on an index rather than a book of business allows the cedant to protect proprietary information from disclosure to competitors and makes the deal more transparent to investors. Index-based deals also raise fewer investor concerns about adverse selection (the fear that an insurer is trying to cede precisely those risks that it privately deems the most problematic), moral hazard (the problem that ceding risk might alter the behavioural incentives of the primary insurer) and unsound underwriting practices. These advantages must be weighed against the advantages of indemnity-based deals, which are based on a book of business. Indemnity-based deals resemble other risk

2. Catastrophe bond cashflow timing

Closing
– Investors pay bond proceeds
– Reinsurance coverage begins

Six months after closing
– First bond coupon payment

Maturity date
– If no events have occurred, bond principal is returned to investors
– If a hurricane has occurred, bond maturity is extended
– Second bond coupon payment

Extended maturity date (if necessary)
– Reinsurance payment to cedant
– Remaining amount returned to bond holders
– Remaining bond coupon payment

3. CAT swap payment structure

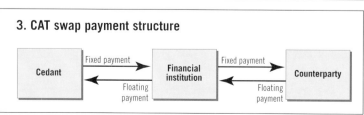

management techniques already in place and are not subject to basis risk – the risk of a mismatch between a firm's book of business and the index to which a particular transaction is linked. If the mismatch in an index deal is substantial, the cedant might remain exposed to the risk against which it sought to hedge. To date, index-based transactions have comprised 20% of the market, as measured by risk capital raised.

INDUSTRY INDEX BOND

In a transaction completed on July 16, 1997, a SPV named SR Earthquake Fund Ltd simultaneously issued US$137 million notes and entered into a US$112.2 million contract with Swiss Re based on an industry-wide index of California earthquake losses. The index was based on the largest insured loss from a single earthquake over the two-year risk period, as determined by Property Claim Services (PCS), a leading provider of loss estimates for the insurance industry.

In response to the varying risk appetites among investors, the bond issue was divided into four classes, or "tranches". The first two classes (A-1 and A-2) are the first insurance-linked notes ever to be rated investment grade (Baa3 by Moody's and BBB– by Fitch) based on their expected loss as measured by a catastrophe loss probability model. Only 60% of the bond principal is at risk; the remainder is invested in Treasury notes maturing before the end of the two-year risk period. A-1 pays a fixed interest rate of 8.645%; A-2 has a floating rate equal to three-month Libor plus 255 basis points. Class B notes (rated Ba1 by Moody's and BB by Fitch), which have 100% of principal at risk, pay a fixed interest rate of 10.493%. If a qualifying earthquake occurs in California during the risk period, these three classes suffer loss of principal because the issuer would have to pay funds on the level of insured losses, as estimated by PCS (Table 1). Class C notes (not rated), whose coupon is 11.952%, entail greater risk. They lose all principal if the largest California earthquake exceeds US$12 billion of insured losses.

The annual expected principal loss is 0.46% to Class A-1 and Class A-2 noteholders, 0.76% to Class B noteholders, and 2.40% to Class C holders.[3] The maximum losses to the US$62 million of Class A-1 and A-2 notes provide US$37.2 million of coverage to Swiss Re. In addition, the US$60 million of Class B notes and US$14.7 million of Class C notes provide further coverage to Swiss Re in those amounts.

The use of the PCS loss index benefited both the reinsured and the noteholders. Because Swiss

Re writes residential and commercial earthquake coverage that closely mirrors the California market, using the PCS loss index exposed Swiss Re's capital to minimal basis risk. In exchange for that risk, the company was able to limit the amount of information it disclosed about its book while minimising any potential adverse selection and moral hazard issues for investors. The parties to the transaction were comfortable using this index over the two-year period. If the risk period were significantly longer, however, the issuer would have sought a mechanism that would allow the effective coverage to vary in response to changes in general conditions and its own exposure to the California insurance market.

Another issue especially relevant to earthquake bonds is the development period. Before the Northridge earthquake in 1994, many industry participants would have estimated the period between the occurrence of a natural disaster and the bulk of the loss claims at six months for earthquakes and slightly less for hurricanes. Northridge, however, was very different. The original PCS estimate for claims was US$7.2 billion after six months and did not develop to the full insurance loss estimate of US$12.5 billion until 20 months after the event.

Reinsurers accept the trickling in of claims over time; investors, however, have collateralised the potential loss payout and would like the flexibility to reallocate their principal to other assets once the risk period is over. (Investors receive the full premium only during the risk period; during the development period, they receive interest rates pegged at either the Libor rate or at Libor plus a nominal spread.) Once the principal is returned to investors, however, it cannot be retrieved. To strike a balance between returning principal too soon (before all losses have been accounted for) and holding it too long (which would reduce the return to investors), a stratified extension period was developed that has been used as a standard for payouts on several subsequent index transactions. Over the development

Table 1. Payout schedule for SR Earthquake Fund issue

PCS estimated insured losses from largest earthquake	Classes A-1, A-2 principal loss*	Class B principal loss*	Class C principal loss*	Annual probability of loss this magnitude (%)
US$12.0 billion or greater	0	0	100	2.40
US$18.5 billion or greater	20	33	100	1.00
US$21.0 billion or greater	40	66	100	0.76
US$24.0 billion or greater	60	100	100	0.52

* as % of original principal

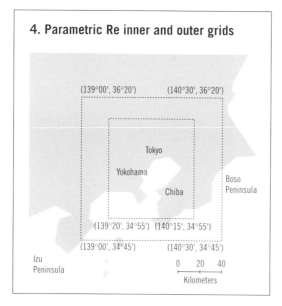

4. Parametric Re inner and outer grids

(139°00', 36°20')   (140°30', 36°20')

Tokyo

Yokohama

Chiba   Boso
                     Peninsula

(139°20', 34°55') (140°15', 34°55')

(139°00', 34°45')   (140°30', 34°45')

Izu
Peninsula

0   20   40

Kilometers

period, which is one year at maximum, the latest estimate of insured losses is periodically compared to an increasing benchmark level. If losses build steadily, the trust account keeps the money on deposit. If the losses stabilise below predetermined trigger levels, additional principal is returned to investors.

PHYSICAL TRIGGER BOND

Tokio Marine, a major writer of Japanese earthquake policies, faced different challenges when purchasing coverage for its earthquake exposure. The company wanted to lock in reinsurance capacity at a fixed price over 10 years, which would facilitate an increase in its underwriting activity. Because the company planned to amortise its issuance costs over the life of the deal, the long risk period also reduced the prospective annual cost of the transaction. (Issuance costs are a one-time expense as compared to the annual costs of reinsurance, such as brokerage fees.) Determining which policies to model for an indemnity transaction would have been difficult because Tokio Marine's book of business was

expected to change over time. Another difficulty was the absence of a generally accepted reporter of loss estimates in Japan. (More generally, the lack of industry loss reporting outside the US makes it difficult to arrange index transactions based on non-US risk.) Finally, even if a reporter of loss estimates did exist, the prospect of the insurance environment changing over the course of a decade created additional uncertainty.

To overcome these obstacles, a first-of-its-kind transaction finalised on November 9, 1997 was structured on the basis of a true physical index. The potential losses in the transaction, which involves a bond issuance by Parametric Re Ltd (a Cayman Island SPV), are based on the magnitude of earthquakes in and around Tokyo (Figure 4). The reinsurance cover, written by Parametric Re, was contingent on the magnitude of earthquake activity in the region as measured by the Japan Meteorological Agency (JMA). An earthquake registering a JMA magnitude of 7.1, for example, would have a recovery of 25% if the earthquake were to occur in the inner grid but zero were it to occur in the outer grid (Figure 5). The bonds issued by Parametric Re were divided into two classes, units and notes. Notes with a face value of US$80 million were fully exposed to earthquake risk (rated Ba2 by Moody's and BB by Duff and Phelp's). Units worth US$20 million risk (rated Baa3 by Moody's and BBB– by Duff and Phelp's) were comprised of US$10 million of defeasance certificates unexposed to earthquake risk and US$10 million of notes exposed to earthquake risk.

A major advantage of the magnitude trigger is that it permits standardisation: a single trigger can be used in multiple transactions. If other companies issue magnitude trigger bonds based on the same index, investors will be able to re-use their analyses of the original transaction. Traditional indemnity-based transactions, by contrast, require investors to analyse each company's book of business. Transactions based on a magnitude trigger also offer investors greater certainty and objectivity. Moreover, because payouts depend on a quickly determined, well-defined standard rather than the settlement of actual claims, investors can receive their funds more quickly.

PHYSICAL TRIGGER SWAP

On April 1, 1998, Mitsui Marine arranged coverage through a swap transaction based on the same earthquake parameters as the Parametric Re bond offering. The insurer wanted to develop

5. Parametric Re loss trigger

Percentage loss of original face amount of notes

100%

81%

63%

44%

25%   Outer grid

25%

85%

70%

55%   Inner grid

40%

25%

7.1   7.2   7.3   7.4   7.5   7.6   7.7

an alternative source of reinsurance capacity for a portion of its Japanese earthquake exposure. Because the amount of coverage it sought was US$30 million, and because of timing constraints, a swap was determined to be the best alternative. As a general rule swap executions involve fewer intermediaries and less documentation, usually resulting in quicker, more cost-effective transactions.

Periodically, Mitsui Marine pays a premium, which is in turn paid to counterparties. Because the notional amount of a swap is not always on deposit with a bank, the deal can expose the cedant to credit risk, just as would be the case for a reinsurance contract. To reduce this risk, the counterparties can be required to pledge collateral.

Natural catastrophe risk analysis[4]

A basic prerequisite for the securitisation of insurance risk is a reliable estimate of expected losses and the likelihood of different loss outcomes. For a peril such as fire, estimates of the expected losses to a portfolio of insured objects are usually based on claims statistics from past years. Historical losses are indexed to current price levels and adjusted to reflect changes in the amount of exposed values. This method is often inapplicable, however, to natural catastrophes. Because the return periods for significant claims can be decades or even centuries, there is usually no representative claims experience for a given portfolio of catastrophe risks. It is difficult, moreover, to index past loss events because the geographical distribution and the quality of the insured objects may change considerably over time. Complicating matters further, many catastrophe-prone areas in the US have experienced rapid increases in population.

One way to develop estimates of the risk from earthquakes or windstorms despite these difficulties is to simulate a representative set of events that might affect a portfolio of risks. For each of the simulated events, insured losses and the frequency of occurrence are estimated. The simulation results are then used to construct an "artificial loss experience", which substitutes for an actual history of losses. The simulations take into account four elements:

❏ hazard;
❏ vulnerability of the insured properties;
❏ distribution of the insured values with respect to location and risk class; and
❏ insurance conditions applying to the original cover.

Hazard refers to how often earthquakes or windstorms of a given intensity can be expected to occur in a particular region, irrespective of the coverage in place. A hazard model is based on historical records of past events and scientific information specifying the perils. Regarding earthquakes, tectonic and palaeoseismic information can be used to improve estimates of recurrence rates. Moreover, the attenuation of earthquake waves from a fault rupture has to be modelled and geological data are needed to consider local site effects amplifying or damping the amount of ground shaking. Regarding storms, wind models characterising the propagation of hurricanes and the spatial distribution of wind speed have to be compiled. After a tropical cyclone has made landfall, natural surface roughness from mountains or manmade roughness created by large cities have to be considered to avoid overestimating wind intensities.

Long-term average recurrence estimates might be inadequate for assessing the risk of a certain event occurring over a short period of time such as a few months. One reason is that the probability of a specific earthquake fault rupturing in the near future depends on the time elapsed since the last event. In the case of atmospheric perils such as hurricanes, analysts must consider short-term changes in occurrence probabilities due to changes in climate.

Vulnerability relates to the degree of destruction that an insured property or a portfolio of insured objects is expected to sustain from an earthquake or windstorm of a given intensity. Analysis of past catastrophe losses permits the quantification of relationships between natural hazard parameters (eg earthquake magnitude or hurricane wind speed), specific risk characteristics (eg line of business, type of buildings) and the expected damage. These relationships can then be applied to portfolios lacking specific loss experience.

The *distribution of insured values* with respect to risk characteristics and geographical zones (eg counties, towns or even individual sites) is central to the analysis of natural catastrophe risks. This information allows one to assess what values are affected by a given event and to consider aspects of site-specific hazard and vulnerability.

The total amount of insured loss arising from an event is also heavily influenced by the *insurance conditions* – like deductibles or limits – that apply to the original cover. If many of the losses that a natural disaster causes are less than the deductible, the total insured loss is significantly reduced.

Finally, additional factors such as underinsurance (a level of coverage less than actual replacement costs), claims handling practices, moral hazard and the sharp increases in building costs that occur in the wake of a disaster should carefully be considered.

Setting up such a natural catastrophe model involves estimating a wide variety of parameters based on incomplete data and knowledge. Given the level of uncertainty inherent in such an exercise, a thorough analysis requires simulations based on many alternative parameter estimates to test for robustness. These simulations, because of their complexity, can only be carried out with the help of computer programs. Based on the representative set of simulated events and their estimated occurrence frequencies, the probability of each loss level is computed. This is summarised in a "loss frequency" or "exceedence probability" curve. These curves provide estimates of expected annual losses as well as the probabilities of attachment for different reinsurance layers.

The loss frequency curve in Figure 6, for example, provides the following information:

❑ a loss amounting to 0.8% or more of the total portfolio values should be expected about once every 10 years (annual frequency 0.1);
❑ a loss ratio of 20% or more will occur on average once every 140 years (annual frequency 0.007); and
❑ some degree of damage can be expected to occur every five years.

Swiss Re and a few other reinsurance companies first developed natural catastrophe risk assessment programmes in the 1980s. Reinsurers bear a

significant share of insured catastrophe losses and therefore have a vital interest in understanding the risks. More recently, a few specialised catastrophe consulting firms have begun providing similar tools to the insurance industry. Several large corporations with heavy risk concentrations have also developed their own models.

Issuers' perspective

Insurance-linked securities offer several potential benefits to issuers, including attractive pricing (whether now or in the future), additional reinsurance capacity, credit enhancement, and greater leverage. We discuss each of these in turn.

PRICING

Insurance-linked securities can provide a viable alternative to traditional reinsurance, although the cost advantage will vary throughout the insurance underwriting cycle. In some periods, such as after a major disaster, industry capital may be in short supply, pressuring insurers and reinsurers to boost premiums to rebuild surplus. At other times, when there is excess capacity in the industry, insurers might aggressively compete for business by lowering their rates. The status of the cycle is thus a major determinant of the attractiveness of ILSs. If, moreover, the timing of the insurance cycle varies by line of business, so too will the potential cost savings associated with securitisation. The tighter the market for a particular line of reinsurance business becomes, the more compelling will be the case for securitisation in that line of business.

Standardisation and transparency also affect pricing. As the market matures, some types of contracts will become easier to standardise, bundle and explain to investors. Standardisation simplifies issuance and reduces transaction costs. As investors grow comfortable with particular ILS structures, moreover, they will require less explanation for each particular deal. The more transparent the securities are, the lower the premium issuers will need to pay. The yield spread between ILSs and Treasury securities should therefore narrow over time, just as they have for other financial instruments such as mortgage-backed securities.

The maturation of the ILS market should also improve its liquidity. If there is no secondary market for a particular instrument, it will attract only a limited clientele – namely, investors prepared to buy and hold until maturity. Issuers will therefore have to pay a liquidity premium above

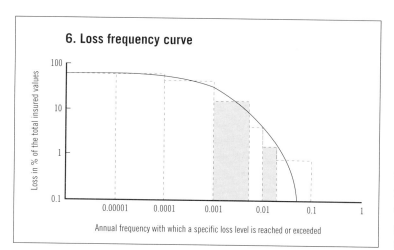

6. Loss frequency curve

Loss in % of the total insured values

100

10

1

0.1

0.00001   0.0001   0.001   0.01   0.1   1

Annual frequency with which a specific loss level is reached or exceeded and beyond the risk premium. Once a more attractive secondary market for the securities develops, ILSs will become more attractive to a broad range of investors, who will therefore require a lower rate of return to hold them.

A final point for potential issuers to note is that in weighing the costs of securitisation, what matters is not just today's cost of reinsurance, but also tomorrow's cost. Assembling the data and documentation needed to issue ILSs typically requires several months. If the reinsurance market firms up, such as after a major catastrophe, issuers will face considerable delay in making their initial entrance into the ILS market because many others will be trying to do the same. Firms with prior experience at issuing ILSs will have a much easier time accessing the market. Thus, even if issuing ILSs is somewhat more expensive than conventional reinsurance, the transaction might ultimately prove cost-effective because it affords the issuer the opportunity to enter the ILS market more readily in the future.

OTHER CONSIDERATIONS
Capacity Another advantage ILSs offer issuers is that they provide additional reinsurance capacity. Some very large insurers, for example, feel that the catastrophe reinsurance market lacks the capacity to provide them with adequate protection against major events. Their response is to hold a substantial buffer of extra capital in lieu of reinsurance. Other firms face a separate concern: when the market tightens, reinsurance contract attachment levels rise in response, effectively providing less coverage. In this context, the ILS market has begun to offer additional reinsurance capacity in the late 1990s, just as the Bermuda market began to do in the late 1980s and early 1990s.

Credit quality Purchasers of reinsurance seriously consider counterparty risk because the situations in which the coverage is most needed are often times of industry distress. This is why insurers generally purchase reinsurance from several companies simultaneously. Reinsurance capacity varies in credit quality. According to a tabulation by Standard & Poor's, less than half of the global reinsurance contracts written in 1996 were by AAA-rated reinsurers; more than a quarter of contracts were issued by firms rated A or below (Figure 7). ILSs can be structured to minimise counterparty risk. When issuing catastrophe bonds, for example, a firm can specify that the principal be invested in highly rated investment-grade securities to be held as collateral in a SPV.

Arrangements such as this may provide greater credit quality than conventional reinsurance.

Leverage One of the traditional uses of reinsurance is to permit a direct insurer to leverage its balance sheet and its underwriting expertise so that it can underwrite more risk with a given level of capital. A mature ILS market might offer some direct insurers even greater latitude to employ leverage. An insurer could, for example, pursue a strategy of underwriting a certain type of policy – be it homeowners, auto or term life – in large volumes, packaging these policies and selling them to an intermediary. This strategy might appeal to firms whose competitive advantage in marketing and processing applications enables them to earn a satisfactory return on underwriting. Indeed, a mature ILS market might stimulate the formation of such firms.

Finally, there are *strategic reasons* for some firms to issue ILSs. A company's risk manager, or credit rating agency, may be uncomfortable with its level of exposure to a particular peril. In response to such concerns, an additional layer above traditional reinsurance can provide an extra margin of safety. Early participation in the market will signal to investors and policyholders that a company is proactive, innovative, and willing to assume a leadership role. If, moreover, the ILS market evolves so that there are profitable niches for various participants, the first firms to issue the securities will be in the best position to learn how the process works and to determine what role they might play in the market.

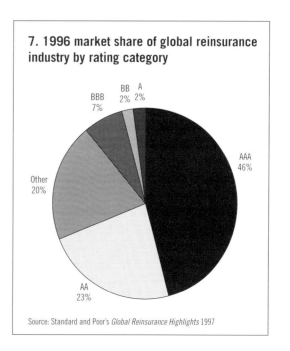

7. 1996 market share of global reinsurance industry by rating category

Source: Standard and Poor's *Global Reinsurance Highlights* 1997

Investors' perspective

Insurance-linked securities can offer investors attractive returns while providing a way of reducing the overall risk of their portfolios.

MARKET YIELDS

Insurance-linked securities offer investors the opportunity to earn high expected returns, for several reasons. In their early stages of development, ILSs will be priced to yield a "newness premium". Catastrophe bonds with a given credit rating, for example, have yielded a spread over Libor that is higher than that of other comparably rated fixed income securities (Figure 8). If the securities become more accepted by investors, the newness premium would disappear or at least shrink, causing the securities to appreciate in value.

Even after the market has matured, investors will still have opportunities to earn high returns. Experts who can discern which ILS issues are undervalued will be able to profit from their specialised knowledge. Profitable opportunities will also arise when a tight reinsurance market causes the industry to conserve its scarce capital by pricing coverage at abnormally high levels. In such high rate environments, issuers will be willing to compensate investors more generously than under normal market conditions, raising the expected return from investing in ILSs.

DIVERSIFICATION OPPORTUNITIES

Because, as empirical analyses have shown, the occurrence of insurance-linked events is uncorrelated with the returns to stocks and bonds, investing in ILSs reduces the overall risk of a diversified portfolio. Indeed, if ILSs represent a limited share of an investor's overall holdings, their inclusion reduces portfolio risk by almost as much as the purchase of a risk-free security. Thus, an ILS need only earn an expected return slightly above the risk-free rate to improve the risk–return profile of a portfolio.

To demonstrate this point, consider a hypothetical ILS structure that pays an agreed-upon yield if no catastrophe occurs but suffers a total loss of principal in the event of a catastrophe, whose probability can be estimated. The greater the probability of catastrophe, the higher the variance of returns to the security.[5] This probability therefore determines the extent to which holding the security reduces overall portfolio risk.

To illustrate, let us compare four securities: a risk-free security (such as a Treasury bill) and three ILSs whose percentage probabilities of total loss of principal are, respectively, 0.5, 1.0, and 2.0. How effectively does each security reduce risk when added to a portfolio of risky assets?

As is well established in the finance literature, adding a risk-free security to a risky portfolio causes a linear reduction in the risk of that portfolio, as measured by the standard deviation of returns (Figure 9, solid line). Thus, a 10% allocation to a risk-free security reduces portfolio risk by 10% (point A), a 20% allocation reduces portfolio risk by 20% (point B), and so forth. As Figure 9 shows, each of the three ILSs provides nearly as much portfolio risk reduction as does the risk-free asset for allocations of 10% or less. For larger allocations, however, the risk reduction facilitated by these securities is substantially weaker. Because ILSs are still a new and unfamiliar asset class, we will concentrate on cases in which investors allocate less than 10% of their portfolios to them.

One way to express the amount of portfolio risk reduction achieved by investing in an ILS is

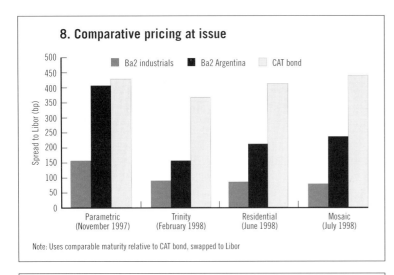

8. Comparative pricing at issue

Note: Uses comparable maturity relative to CAT bond, swapped to Libor

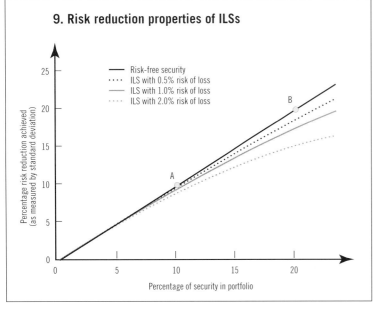

9. Risk reduction properties of ILSs

as a proportion of the portfolio risk reduction realisable through investing the same funds in a risk-free security. Thus, allocating 5% of a portfolio to an ILS securitising a catastrophe risk whose probability of occurrence is 1% reduces portfolio risk by 97.4% as much as would allocating the same funds to a risk-free security (Table 2, Panel A). More generally, for asset allocations of 1–10%, the three ILSs realise anywhere from 89.0–99.7% of the risk reduction achievable by investing in a risk-free security.

This, in turn, has implications for the spread above the risk-free rate that an investor will require in order to be indifferent between holding an ILS and a risk-free security. Taking the same example, a 113 basis-point spread would provide a sufficient incentive for investors to allocate 5% of their portfolios to the ILS (Table 2, Panel B).[6] Of this amount, 100bps would compensate for the expected loss while 13bps would compensate for the marginally smaller amount of risk reduction achieved.

These calculations suggest that ILSs pay investors a premium that more than compensates for the risk of loss. For example, Class A securities of the SR Earthquake Fund issue had a risk of loss of less than 1% yet paid an annual yield of 255bps over Libor (see above). Thus, investors received a spread above the risk-free rate that was far higher than our calculations indicate. The discrepancy was even greater than this comparison suggests, moreover, because our calculation assumed a total loss of principal in the event of a major earthquake, whereas the security's potential loss was capped at 60%.

The difference between the actual and theoretical spread likely reflects several considerations, including newness and liquidity premiums (previously discussed), as well as compensation for model and parameter uncertainty. Model uncertainty reflects our inability to known how faithfully the catastrophe model being used to rate a transaction captures all of its relevant risks. Parameter uncertainty is a concern because even if a model is conceptually perfect, it might still be mis-estimated owing to insufficient data.

To summarise, investors who substitute ILSs for a portion of their holdings in Treasury securities can achieve a higher expected return on their portfolios for a given level of risk. The high coupons that ILSs pay reflect several distinct factors, which should become less relevant as the market for these securities matures.

One final point to note is that the analysis assumes that an investor buys just a single ILS issue. In actuality, many investors will assemble diversified portfolios of these securities, thereby reducing their risk exposure to any particular event. If buying a single ILS represents an attractive opportunity, owning a diversified portfolio of several such securities would be better still.

Potential non-CAT lines of business

The discussion so far has focused on the securitisation of catastrophe risks. What other types of insurance risk might be amenable to securitisation? To gain some perspective, let us first note some of the qualities that typically characterise asset-backed securitisation transactions:

❑ historical basis for pricing or quantitative analysis of future income;
❑ segmentation of business lines;
❑ regulatory or tax advantage;
❑ general industry motivation to transfer a portion of risk; and
❑ need for capital combined with high cost of capital for general corporate risk.

Catastrophe-linked securities satisfy all but the regulatory or tax advantage (the same advantage is accomplished by an existing vehicle, reinsurance) although the other characteristics may only be satisfied weakly. One of the stronger motivations is the industry need to handle large, infrequent catastrophes. While other lines of insurance, such as marine and aviation, have been covered through securitisations, the coverage has been small relative to catastrophe coverage obtained in the market.

Another insurance risk that has been securitised in significant size is life insurance. The transactions to date have been motivated by a need for capital to finance acquisitions of existing books of business. Securitisation may work well for life

Table 2. Risk reduction facilitated by investing in an ILS

Portfolio allocation to ILS (%)						
Panel A: Reduction achieved relative to a risk-free security				Panel B: Yield spread above risk-free rate needed to compensate investor for added risk (in basis points)		
Percentage probability of catastrophe				Percentage probability of catastrophe		
	0.5	1.0	2.0		0.5	1.0	2.0
1	0.997	0.995	0.990	1	51	103	205
5	0.987	0.974	0.947	5	57	113	226
10	0.972	0.945	0.890	10	64	128	255

Note: Figures in Panel B assume that risky portfolio earns expected return of 5% above risk-free rate

insurance because many of the risks that would cause a mismatch between assets and liabilities (policies) are risks that are well understood. The securitisation raises money based on the present value of the merging surplus of the business. Other risks embedded in the surplus include mortality and lapse risk, both of which have a historical basis for analysis. Each transaction differs based on the type of policies included. More of these types of transactions should occur in the future.

Several other lines of business seem well suited for securitisation. Workers' compensation and auto insurance are often mentioned because of their historical pricing basis. Mortgage insurance and residual value insurance have both been securitised in the last year. Asbestos and pollution are additional, albeit more challenging, potential lines of business. Although there have been many historical surprises in the loss development of these risks, some of the uncertainty in development patterns has been reduced. Further, the size of future claims in the industry remains quite large, making it an attractive candidate for securitisation. Credit insurance, a large European line, is very well suited for securitisation because of the existence of capital markets pricing comparables. Finally, securitisation may also be attractive for some of the high-severity, low-frequency types of political risks that are now being integrated into coverage.

How might the market evolve?

Although the issuance of insurance-linked securities has begun in earnest, the extent to which the market will grow over the next decade and beyond remains uncertain. We can, however, gain insight into this new market by considering the development of other financial innovations. Especially instructive is the emergence of a market for mortgage-backed securities (MBS) as well as other asset-backed securities that combine the repackage individual cash flows. Drawing in part on this history, we offer a few observations.

"EARLY ADAPTERS"
Just as the success of a new consumer product often depends upon the acceptance of "early adapters" (trend-setters inclined to try something new) so too have ILSs had some natural constituencies in the early going: mutual funds, investors with industry knowledge and hedge funds. The number of participants in these categories seems poised to increase. One such set of investors is yield-conscious bond fund managers. Bond funds, of which there are now thousands,

have become a commodity product. Because funds within a given subcategory hold very similar securities, managers seeking to differentiate themselves from their peers actively seek new instruments that provide some pick-up in yield. Insurance-linked securities, in limited quantities, might fit the bill.

Another class of early investors includes firms and individuals with institutional knowledge of insurance markets. The securities offer insurers and reinsurers a simple way of entering a particular market (line of business or region) without building costly infrastructure. Similarly, individuals who have worked in the insurance field, whether as underwriters, actuaries, or security analysts, might open asset management boutiques investing exclusively in these instruments. Finally, hedge funds, which have flexibility to invest in a wide range of assets, could also take more of an interest in these securities.

LUCRATIVE NICHES SHOULD EMERGE IN THE ILS MARKET
A major accomplishment of the MBS market is that it reduced the costs of underwriting a mortgage by permitting a more efficient allocation of capital and division of labour through specialisation. Before the market developed, banks would typically make mortgage loans, carry them on their books and service them for the life of the loan. Although they might occasionally swap or sell off a block of loans to another bank, this was a cumbersome activity. Today with the advent of the MBS market, a bank typically makes a loan and then sells it to an agency, such as Fannie Mae or Freddie Mac, which in turn bundles the mortgages, offers credit enhancement and services the loans.

A similar development may be in store for insurance-linked securities. Today, primary insurers generally sell policies, invest the premiums, service the policies and manage the liability. In coming years, an established market for insurance-linked securities would allow different industry players to assume more focused roles. Some firms can become "virtual insurers", marketing policies by direct mail or phone and then immediately selling off the policies once the sale is made (banks, for example, might find this role attractive).

Other firms might be the securitisers, purchasing policies from a variety of direct insurers, packaging them in ways that appeal to investors (perhaps offering credit enhancements) and then reselling them. Major reinsurers or firms with experience in securitising assets might be naturals for the role. A third market niche would involve servicing the individuals policies – collecting premiums and processing claims, for which a service fee can be collected. Firms with efficient, low-cost back-office capabilities might be especially suited to the role.

Finally, firms that can effectively sell ILSs to clients will stand to earn commissions or placement fees. Investment banks, retail brokers and reinsurers are candidates for this role. In short, a lesson to be learned from other financial innovations is that there is money to be made by those who successfully specialise in particular securitisation-related activities rather than doing everything themselves.

CATALYSTS FOR MARKET DEVELOPMENT
Potential catalysts for market development include the occurrence of a catastrophe, a major stock market downturn, the increased participation of the ratings agencies, and favourable regulatory treatment.

As many observers have noted, a major catastrophe or series of catastrophes could accelerate the market's development. After such an event, some insurers might fail, capital would become scarcer, premiums would rise and new sources of insurance capacity would be sought. It was just these sorts of shocks that facilitated the growth of the Bermuda market in the late 1980s and early 1990s.

Another type of event that might accelerate the development of the ILS market is a plunge in securities prices, which would have several implications. Insurers and reinsurers would suffer losses on their investments, straining their surpluses and pressuring them to raise premiums in response. Investors, whose expectations have been coloured by an extraordinary 15-year bull market in US equities, would grow disillusioned, reduce their equity holdings and look elsewhere for new investment opportunities.

The involvement of credit rating agencies and regulators can also stimulate the development of the ILS market. As they have begun evaluating deals, the rating agencies have increased the credibility of the securities in the eyes of investors who lack the experience or resources to investigate the details of the security. By assigning ratings to the deals and explaining their evaluation methodologies to the investment community, the rating agencies provide a simple way to compare the risk of different ILSs while inviting comparisons between ILSs and other fixed-income securities.

Regulatory reaction to the new securities is important for two reasons. First, if regulators indicate that the risks underlying the securities are adequately disclosed, more investors would feel comfortable owning them. Second, depending on how insurance and banking regulators classify the securities, their owners will receive more or less favourable treatment with respect to taxes and capital requirements. A favourable tax ruling on a particular mortgage-backed structure known as "REMICs" made it a preferred alternative for many issuers and investors in that market.

DEAL STRUCTURE
To win widespread acceptance, the securities must find a proper structure or paradigm. As previously noted, insurance risk can be packaged in a variety of forms. Although each alternative form is merely a different way of dividing the same pool of risk, how the risk is parcelled out determines what types of investors will find the securities attractive. Insurance risk packaged as a bond will appeal to a different class of investors than it would if packaged as an option or swap. The choice of structure also has legal, regulatory and tax consequences.

Because there is no scientific way to determine which financial product design will prove most popular, underwriters will need to experiment with a variety of structures in order to discover which ones appeal most to investors as well as issuers.

PROSPECTS
The potential scale of the ILS market is substantial. Under conservative assumptions, domestic US ILS issuance could reach US$10 billion per year within the next decade. The current scale of the US property-casualty market offers a rough sense of the potential markets for ILSs.

For example, in 1997 net written premiums were US$45 billion for multiple peril insurance, US$129 billion for commercial and personal automobile insurance, US$23 billion for workers' compensation and US$60 billion for all other lines. If over the next decade securitisations grew to 5% of multiple peril, 2% of automobile, 1% of workers' compensation and 2% for all other lines (including the longer-tailed liability lines), they would total US$6.3 billion, assuming no growth in direct premium volumes. Annual premium growth of 3–4% over the next 10 years would bring this to between US$9 billion–10 billion in the US alone, or four to five times the recent US$2 billion annual pace of issuance. Thus, while still a relatively small piece of the overall insurance market, it seems quite plausible that ILSs will grow to become an important risk-financing tool.

An interesting question is the extent to which these securities will create new financing possibilities, as opposed to substituting for more traditional insurance and reinsurance financing. If securitisation starts to replace traditional insurance financing, insurers and reinsurers will need to either develop expertise in a particular area – be it ILS structuring, risk assessment, or sales and distribution – or face the prospect of declining market share and obsolescence.

1 *Swiss Re New Markets owes special thanks to Edouard Schmid of Swiss Re's Risk and Reinsurance division for his contributions.*

2 *Bermuda allows reinsurance companies to apply for protected cell status that permits the segregation of contracts.*

3 *Expected principal loss is defined as the average of all possible outcomes, weighted by their respective probabilities.*

4 *For a further treatment of this subject, see the Swiss Re publication* Natural Hazard and Event Loss.

5 *More formally, if the investor earns a return of* r^* *in the event of no catastrophe and* $(r^* - 1)$ *if a catastrophe does occur, then the security has an expected return of* $E(r) = q(r^* - 1) + (1 - q) r^* = r^* - q$, *where* q *is the probability of a catastrophe occurring. The security's variance of returns, it can be shown, will equal* $Var(r) = q(1 - q)$ *which, as noted, is an increasing function of* q.

6 *This calculation assumes that the portfolio of risky securities earns a risk premium of 5%. The results are very similar for other values of the risk premium.*

17

Pricing Mother Nature

Eric Briys
Merrill Lynch

Bad weather costs money. This fact has tempted financiers to revive the old idea that nature risks can be priced and exchanged outside the traditional insurance and reinsurance markets – namely on the financial markets.

Numerous institutions including investment banks, reinsurance companies and direct insurers are currently developing a new asset class, so-called weather-linked assets (also called insurance-linked securities). The most common of these assets are weather-linked bonds. This article describes how to price them and how to value the spreads between different bonds.

Weather-linked bonds and other such assets can help to mitigate the effects of the wide spectrum of hazards generated by Mother Nature. In his masterly piece on the history of climate since 1000, Le Roy Ladurie (1983) reports that 1316 had been very wet with some rather unexpected consequences. Inhabitants of Tournai, a wealthy town in what is now Belgium, were forced to drink their execrable local wine because French vineyards had been ruined by heavy rainfall.

On a more modern note, in the UK subsidence risk comes second only to windstorms in terms of costs to insurers over the past decade. Although buildings are constructed to receive support from the ground, a drought propensity across the UK coinciding with shrinkable clays is the cause of a significant subsidence peril to these buildings.

The new weather-linked asset class is often described as the next milestone in portfolio management. Indeed, it is claimed that weather-linked bonds offer outstanding risk-return characteristics.

The common conclusion, based upon historical analysis, is that an investment in a weather-linked bond, after adjusting for risk, tends to outperform an investment in, say, US Treasury bonds. For instance, according to research from

AIG Combined Risks, part of US insurance and financial services conglomerate American International Group, if an investment in natural catastrophe-linked bonds with principal fully at risk had been available for the last 25 years, its return would have been four times that of Treasury bonds with a lower volatility.

Weather risk in the Middle Ages

Transforming weather risks into instruments which can then be traded can be traced back at least seven centuries – however new and cutting-edge some investment bankers may deem the practice.

In 1298, a Genoese merchant, Benedetto Zaccaria, structured an interesting deal with two Genoese bankers, Ballano Grilli and Enrico Suppa. Zaccaria had to send 30 tons of alum from Algues-Mortes in France to Bruges in what is now Belgium. The only way to deliver such a heavy quantity of alum was to hire a ship.

Zaccaria knew that sea navigation was a very risky venture and the odds that the vessel would never reach its final destination were fairly high. Unexpected storms and other hazards could send it and its valuable freight to the bottom of the ocean, and even if the seas were quiet, there was always the danger of buccaneers and corsairs preying on merchant shipping. In both cases, the freight would be lost and the merchant would eventually face bankruptcy.

With the help of Grilli and Suppa, Zaccaria designed a contract to shift the risk away from his business. Zaccaria sold the alum to Suppa and Grilli on the spot at an agreed price. The alum was then loaded on the vessel that headed to Bruges. If the vessel reached Bruges safely, Zaccaria was committed to buying the alum from Suppa and Grilli. He then sold it to his local client. The price at which Zaccaria could repurchase was obviously much higher than the price of the initial transaction. If things went wrong and the alum were lost during the voyage, Zaccaria wouldn't owe anything to Suppa and Grilli.

In other words, Suppa and Grilli granted Zaccaria an option to default on the repurchase transaction provided the feared event occurred. A modern economist would simply say that the three Genoese businessmen had come up with a non-linear risk sharing rule. Viewed from Zaccaria's standpoint, the risk sharing rule is convex: he was long an option to default.

Zaccaria's loan was a weather-linked security: Grilli and Suppa extended a natural hazard-linked loan to Zaccaria, and through this loan, the risk of sea perils was securitised.

Pricing weather-linked bonds

One can develop a simple continuous-time model for valuing weather-linked bonds. The scope is restricted to weather risks that are non-catastrophic. In other words, one can focus on Wiener type of uncertainty rather than Poisson type of uncertainty (that is, normal instead of jump type of uncertainty).

Although a more realistic pricing setting would incorporate both interest rate risk and natural hazards or insurance risk, we will concentrate on the simpler case of constant interest rates. In other words, the only source of uncertainty stems from natural hazards or some other insurance risk.

This uncertainty is usually captured by a suitable index. The return on the weather-linked bond is pegged to this index. The index is either an official one, such as a meteorological index, or a customised index reflecting (or causing) the contingency to be covered (see Simpson, 1997).

A trigger level is defined that remains active during the exposure period. If this trigger is hit by the index the issuer of the bond is allowed to default.

Hereafter, the index and the trigger level are labelled $I(t)$ and K (as of time t) respectively. The bond payout depends on the value of the index. The bond is a zero-coupon bond of maturity T and face value F. It is characterised by an exposure period maturing at time $T' \leq T$. If the index does not exceed[1] the trigger level K during the exposure period, the investor is sure to receive the face value F.

If, however, Mother Nature decides otherwise – the so-called "qualifying event" – the investor loses part of the face value of the bond and

receives only $(1 - \alpha)F$ where α denotes the write-down coefficient applied to the bond. In practice, the period between the end of the exposure period and the maturity of the bond is used for accurately assessing the value taken by the index during the exposure period.[2]

We assume that the index is governed by a continuous-time stochastic process. In the case of meteorological data, the assumption of "on-line" data is rather reasonable. Indeed, a primary task of meteorological offices is to release reliable on-line data on temperature, such as degree-days measured by the National Weather Service in the USA; wind speed, measured on the famous Beaufort scale[3]; and river water level or rainfall.

The index $I(t)$ is assumed to be driven by a geometric Brownian motion:

$$\frac{dI}{I} = \mu dt + \sigma dz$$

where μ denotes the instantaneous expected change in the index and σ its instantaneous standard deviation. The nature uncertainty is captured by the increments of a standard Wiener process $z(t)$.

We denote by $T_{I,K}$ the first passage time of $I(t)$ through the constant trigger level K:

$$T_{I,K} = \{\inf(t \geq 0; 0 < t \leq T' I(t) = K)\}$$

Some weather-linked bonds are characterised by a payout pegged to aggregate (or average) values. A new stochastic process has thus to be defined. If $I(s)$ denotes the instantaneous claim level, aggregate claims are given by

$$A(t) = \int_0^t I(s)ds$$

The first passage time is then defined with respect to $A(t)$.

We could also consider an event in the spirit of Parisian-style options. In this case, the event is described as the one where the index is above the trigger and stays there for a given amount of time. For example, if the index measures the temperature level the corporation issuing the bond will try to hedge a persistent drought.

The index $I(t)$ is usually a non-traded variable. Hence, it is impossible to invoke the Black and Scholes (1973) pricing methodology directly to value the weather-linked bond. Indeed, this methodology requires that the underlying sources of uncertainty be spanned by traded assets. Our setting involves a stochastic process that does not represent the price of a traded asset.

Therefore we have to introduce the market price of risk of this non-traded source of uncertainty. Let λ be the market price of risk of the underlying index $I(t)$. What we can assert is that changing the drift of $I(t)$ from μ to $\theta = \mu - \lambda\sigma$ and then acting "as if" investors were risk-neutral gives the proper value for the weather-linked bond.

Let Q denote the probability measure under which Mother Nature drifts at the rate $\theta = \mu - \lambda\sigma$. The price as of time $t = 0$ of the insurance linked zero-coupon bond is thus given by the discounted value of future expected cashflows under the "risk-neutral probability" Q:

$$D_0 = E^Q \left[\begin{array}{l} \exp(-rT) \\ (F1_{T_{I,K} > T'} + (1 - \alpha)F1_{T_{I,K} \leq T'}) \end{array} \right]$$

The terms of the previous expression can be reshuffled so that the probability distribution of the first passage time of $I(t)$ through the constant barrier K appears explicitly as the key factor driving the pricing process:

$$D_0 = \exp(-rT)F(1 - \alpha Q_{T_{I,K} \leq T'})$$

where

$$Q_{T_{I,K} \leq T'}$$

is the one-sided risk-neutral first passage time distribution of the index $I(t)$ through the barrier K.

The explicit computation of the risk-neutral first-passage time distribution yields the following closed-form solution for the insurance linked bond:

$$D_0 = F \exp(-rT)\left(1 - \alpha\left(N(d_1) \right.\right.$$

$$\left.\left. + \left(\frac{I_0}{K} \right)^{1 - 2\theta/\sigma^2} N(d_2) \right) \right)$$

$$d_1 = \frac{Ln(I_0/K) + (\theta - \sigma^2/2)T'}{\sigma\sqrt{T'}}$$

with:

$$d_2 = \frac{Ln(I_0/K) - (\theta - \sigma^2/2)T'}{\sigma\sqrt{T'}}$$

$$\theta = \mu = \lambda\sigma$$

In this pricing formula, $N(.)$ denotes the normal distribution function.

Valuing weather bond spreads

A whole term structure of weather-linked spreads can be calculated. For the sake of simplicity and without loss of generality, we let $F = 1$ and consider the spread values as of time $t = 0$. We denote by Y_0 the yield of a weather-linked bond whose maturity is T:

$$Y_0 = -\frac{1}{T} LnD_0$$

Using the closed-form pricing formula for D_0 yields:

$$Y_0 = r - \frac{1}{T} Ln\left(1 - \alpha\left(N(d_1) + \left(\frac{I_0}{K} \right)^{1 - 2\theta/\sigma^2} N(d_2) \right) \right)$$

The weather-linked spread S_0 is defined as the difference between the yield Y_0 and the yield of an otherwise riskless zero-coupon bond. The weather-linked spread is thus given by the following equation:

$$S_0 = -\frac{1}{T} Ln\left(1 - \alpha\left(N(d_1) + N(d_2)\left(\frac{I_0}{K} \right)^{1 - 2\theta/\sigma^2} \right) \right)$$

These results are useful when it comes to benchmarking weather-linked bonds against US Treasury bonds. Indeed, they cast some doubt on the validity of a straight comparison between an investment in weather-linked bonds and an investment in US Treasury bonds. To be convincing such a comparison requires that the respective performance be measured at the same risk level.

The proper definition of risk is a rather difficult task. The standard deviation of time-series returns is often used as a risk measure. Guy Carpenter and Co (1995) claim that a 5% investment in insurance-linked assets increases the expected return of a 60/40 equity/bond portfolio by 1.25%, while decreasing its standard deviation by 0.25%. This figure should be taken with extreme care. The relevance of such statistics is rather dubious for assets whose returns are truncated. Indeed, the distribution of return on an insurance-linked bond is highly skewed. Once the trigger is hit, the game is over.

Comparing weather bonds with US Treasury bonds

Comparing time-series sample statistics of realised returns between weather-linked bonds and US Treasury bonds could easily lead the analyst to the wrong conclusions about which product offers the better deal.

The same point that Ambarish and Subrahmanyam (1989) raised about corporate bonds applies to weather-linked bonds. They showed that "the time-series sample means and standard deviations (of returns on corporate bonds) would generally be poor estimators of the *ex ante* expected return and the standard deviations of return." A weather-linked bond can be viewed as a portfolio of two assets: a long position on an otherwise equivalent default-free bond and short position on a binary option. A binary option has a discontinuous payout profile and pays out a fixed amount if the underlying satisfies a predetermined trigger condition but nothing otherwise.

The portfolio weights of these two components can be expressed in terms of the risk neutral first passage time distribution.

Let us assume that the face value F is equal to 1 and that the percentage principal at risk α is equal to 1. The portfolio weights of the two components are thus respectively given by the following expressions:

$$\theta_P = \frac{1}{1 - Q_{T_{I,K} \leq T'}}$$

$$\theta_D = \frac{Q_{T_{I,K} \leq T'}}{1 - Q_{T_{I,K} \leq T'}}$$

These portfolio weights evolve stochastically over time. Their respective values track the movements of the first passage time probability distribution. Consequently, in the same way that the expected return on a corporate bond is highly non-stationary, the expected return on a weather-linked bond is also highly non-stationary. The same holds true for the standard deviation of return, which is plagued by an identical problem. This implies that the investor will be confronted with significant difficulties when it comes to interpreting statistics on the supposed over-performance of weather-linked bonds.

1 *We assume that the index may hit the trigger from below. We could have looked at the related case where the trigger is hit from above. A typical case would be a rain index trading the risk of a low rainfall level.*

2 *This is easily done for a weather-related index, but more difficult for a loss-related index.*

3 *The Beaufont scale ranges from 0 to 17. A value between 0 and 1 corresponds to a wind speed of 0 to 5 km/h, namely a still weather vane. For values between 12 and 17, the wind speed is above 118 km/h. Severe damages to constructions usually occur for values of 10 and above.*

BIBLIOGRAPHY

Ambarish, R. and M.G. Subrahmanyam, 1989, "Default Risk and the Valuation of High-Yield Bonds, a Methodological Critique", working paper, Salomon Brothers Center for the Study of Financial Institutions, New York University.

Black, F. and M. Scholes, 1973, "The Pricing of Options and Corporate Liabilities", *Journal of Political Economy*, 81, pp. 637-54.

Guy Carpenter and Co, 1995, "The Emerging Asset Class: Insurance Risk", Special Report, July 1995.

Le Roy Ladurie, E., 1983, "Histoire du Climat Depuis l'an Mil", Flammarion, Paris.

Simpson, M., Dec 1996/Jan 1997, "Weather Derivatives Shelter from the Storm?" *Energy & Power Risk Management*.

WEATHER DERIVATIVES

18

Weather Derivatives and Hedging Weather Risks

Sailesh Ramamurtie
Southern Company Energy Marketing

Any attempt to discuss in full the impact of weather on the activities of individuals and institutions in economies such as those of the US and western Europe would occupy several volumes. In this chapter, our objective is more modest: to elaborate on some of the weather phenomena that have a significant effect on the risks and rewards realised by participants in the energy sector. We will then discuss the instruments that can give a measure of protection against the impact of weather events deviating from the norm.

It is important to note which aspect of weather we are interested in. Different aspects of weather range from temperature levels during the day (or night), through relative humidity levels at different points during the day (or night), to the levels of rainfall or precipitation during different months or seasons. Each of these is important in terms of its effect on the value generation prospects of any economic activity. The degree of importance will vary with the type of the activity and/or the time at which the activity is undertaken or is being examined.

For example, the highest daily temperature plays a very important role in the power sector, especially in load forecasting in summer. An index of weather patterns in a location where the load has to be supported is a critical input and is tracked by all the participants in the power sector. Similarly, the amounts of precipitation, snow melt etc are very important in terms of power planning and supply forecasting in areas where the primary power sources are hydrological. For instance, in Scandinavian countries and the Pacific north-west of the US, the water levels in the various catchment areas play a significant role in determining the power situation.

Other weather phenomena, such as hurricanes and tornadoes, also play a role in determining the risks of a given activity, but these events are much more difficult to forecast, track and insure against – except through some form of catastrophe insurance.

In the next section, we will focus on the primary weather phenomena that impact on different sectors of an economy. We will then discuss some of these as they affect the energy sector. Here we will not focus on weather events such as hurricanes, whose impact on the production of fuels such as natural gas and crude oil is very significant. Rather, the discussion will focus on the impact of deviations from the norm of factors such as temperature or humidity.

Elements of weather phenomena

When we contemplate weather, we instinctively think about whether it is hot or cold, humid or dry, raining or not, sunny or cloudy. We also like to know what changes in any of the above mentioned factors we can expect in the near future. At different times, we may want to know what events are likely, depending on the season and our location, or a location we have some interest in. In this chapter we focus on measurable phenomena, which have an economic impact on the participants and which drive them to undertake certain activities to limit the negative impact of weather events.

The weather phenomena we will examine relate to daily and hourly temperatures, hourly and daily humidity levels, daily and seasonal patterns of rain and snowfall, and the clustering of weather events around distinct geographical regions or locations. Examples of such events range from warm and cold fronts to hurricane paths.

WEATHER
DERIVATIVES
AND
HEDGING
WEATHER
RISKS

The temperature measurements range from the hourly to daily low, average and high readings at a particular location deemed to be representative of a given homogeneous region. For instance, in the case of a metropolitan area like Atlanta, the temperature readings may be obtained at the Hartsfield International Airport. The same is also true of the humidity and precipitation measurements.

Insurable and non-insurable risks

Not all the business risks arising from adverse weather conditions can be fully or even partially hedged or insured against. To cite a few examples, business losses arising from extreme weather events – such as a tropical storm shutting down drilling operations or damaging platform or rig – cannot be hedged against using a weather derivative. Some form of business interruption insurance and catastrophic insurance may sometimes be available, with corresponding deductibles.

It must be noted that insurability is a function of the measurability of the phenomenon against which protection is being sought. Whether or not such protection will be available depends upon the measurability of the relationship between the weather event and the economic activity that is to be insured. We know that high temperatures affect the revenue stream, but have not yet established a statistically robust relationship between actual temperatures and the revenue (or cost) streams. Obtaining insurance at an affordable price thus becomes a guessing game. For a large variety of businesses, arriving at the nature of the relationship between weather events and economic streams is problematic – if not downright impossible.

In short, weather variables typically affect the volume of output and/or input of a business that is subject to weather risks in a non-linear fashion. This impact is rendered more complex by the interaction between the volumes of commodities involved and the realised prices in the market.

Two other aspects play an important role in the availability of protection against weather phenomena. The first is that those offering such protection must have a sufficiently large and diversified pool of insurable transactions to afford them sufficient revenues for risks being shouldered. This is essentially true of protection against catastrophic events, which are the primary area of interest for insurance companies. The second factor is that the weather phenomenon must be easily measurable, independently

verifiable and transparent enough for binding contracts to be written. This is especially true of weather events such as precipitation or temperature realisations, against which financially settling options or swap contracts are typically written at selected locations against verifiable readings supplied by reliable information sources. The events that fall into this category may be termed non-catastrophic events. It is in this area that weather trading activity in the energy sector is growing most rapidly and catching the interest of a variety of players.

Weather risks and the energy sector

In this section, we give brief descriptions of the different types of weather risks borne by participants in the energy sector.

PRIMARY ENERGY PRODUCERS

Starting from the primary production of energy commodities, we have oil and natural gas producers, which face two types of risks. One is the catastrophic risk arising from extreme weather events that result in loss of production, against which corresponding insurance contracts afford protection. The other type arises not from extreme events, but from variations in weather conditions – such as temperature in consumption regions – that affect the volume of production that can be lifted at economic rates. This risk is a function of the volume of output that is subject to demand-side risk.

ENERGY TRANSPORTERS

Transporters of energy face identical risks to those faced by producers. Pipelines may also have to shut down in extreme weather conditions. Transporters are also subject to major swings in demand because of weather conditions that do not fall into the category of extreme events. For instance, a milder than normal winter can drastically reduce the amount of gas flows through pipelines and have a significant impact on revenues.

Risks faced by producers and transporters of oil are similar, except that in addition to pipelines, there are other forms of transport: ships and barges, rail and other surface transport such as trucks. The risks are thus further magnified by the interaction between the weather events in the production areas and those in the consumption areas.

SECONDARY ENERGY PRODUCERS

The next set of players is the power producers or utilities that transform energy from hydrocarbons

175

WEATHER
DERIVATIVES
AND
HEDGING
WEATHER
RISKS

into electricity. As in the case of the transporters, power producers face weather risks on several fronts. The first is the energy availability risk arising from weather events in the supply chain. The next is the weather risk that affects the operability of the power plants themselves. This can range from shutdowns due to extreme weather conditions, such as tornadoes, to less extreme but above-normal temperatures affecting plant operating efficiencies. On the demand side, there is the demand variability that arises from weather conditions departing from the norm.

To cite a few examples, a below-normal temperature pattern in summer can result in a significant reduction in load, and hence in revenues. On the other hand, above-normal temperatures in summer can adversely affect the extent of demand that has to be met at pre-contracted prices, resulting in opportunity losses. Further, above-normal temperatures in summer can also have a significant impact on emission levels, with corresponding impact on the cost of the necessary emission credits. A concomitant increase in demand for power with an increase in the demand for the fuel elsewhere due to weather conditions can result in a complex interaction of fuel prices and loads with a significant impact on profitability for a power producer.

ENERGY CONSUMERS

The final set of actors in the energy chain is made up of middlemen and retail customers. The middlemen are oil, gas and electricity distribution companies. Consumers range from residential customers to large industrial and commercial establishments. Distribution companies typically have substantial physical assets and hence their ability to withstand wide demand variations resulting from severe weather changes is rather limited. Moreover, they are often heavily regulated, which further inhibits the actions they can take to mitigate the adverse impact of weather on their revenue streams. There is thus a natural incentive for them to protect themselves with weather hedges.

Large retail customers form a natural constituency for weather derivative contracts. This is possible because their exposures to extreme weather events are usually covered by some form of catastrophic insurance, which includes weather as a subset of insured variables. Smaller retail customers' demand is extremely weather-sensitive, but their price sensitivity is low relative to the volume sensitivity and hence no demand for protection against weather events affecting energy cost is foreseen.

Approaches to managing or mitigating weather risk

There are two approaches taken to mitigate or manage weather risk exposures. In the first, the business identifies the catastrophic weather events that have an impact on its revenue stream and arranges catastrophic insurance coverage. A typical example would be a business interruption insurance policy that covers, among other things, a loss of revenue due to plant/business shutdowns resulting from extreme weather events. This type of coverage is quite common and is offered by a variety of insurance companies.

The other type of risk mitigation seeks to provide protection against variances in the revenue streams resulting from weather events that are not extreme but are deviations from the norm. An example would be a power utility that has pre-committed to sell power at a fixed price based on some normal load expectations and is concerned about load or volumetric variability around the expectations. Such a utility would employ a weather derivative as a hedge.

Consider the case of a local (gas) distribution company (LDC). It has to meet its retail customers' needs with very limited scope for passing on any additional burdens from serving such needs. Thus, in the event of a colder than normal winter, for instance, the LDC would have to bear the extra costs of incremental gas demands. It will also have to bear the costs of a reduction in demand in a milder than normal winter. In either case, the LDC is facing volumetric demand variability that is a function of the weather (temperature). A typical weather hedge in such an instance would be winter temperature option, which pays a certain sum whenever the realised temperatures over an observation interval deviate from a pre-committed level. We will explain the structure of such a weather protection in the next section.

Providers and instruments

Insurance companies are the primary source of protection against extreme weather events. They provide coverage against catastrophic events that result in stoppage of economic activity. They typically collect premia from a large collection of entities with the corresponding diversification benefits. To withstand substantial claims resulting from weather calamities that affect a large proportion of their portfolio, these companies often lay off a part of the risk with other insurance firms, or reinsurers. The instruments are standard insurance policies with the attendant deductibles, extent of coverage, tenor etc, varying with the

176

WEATHER
DERIVATIVES
AND
HEDGING
WEATHER
RISKS

nature of the business and the types of weather risks insured.

Protection against non-extreme deviations from the norm is provided by both traditional insurance companies and a variety of non-traditional actors, such as energy trading companies or utilities. The coverage is usually structured as a derivative contract with a specified tenor and extent of coverage in return for a fixed premium. The difference from an insurance contract lies in the fact that there is no deductible and also that the pricing does not strictly follow the actuarial approach characteristic of insurance contracts. Typical instruments include cumulative degree-day options, swaps, precipitation options and collars. Weather protection is also often embedded in energy commodity contracts. We give examples of such protection in the following section.

Market structure and trading

In this section we describe the principal types of weather derivatives that are traded in the energy industry. We also give some examples of typical transactions undertaken by utilities, LDCs and energy trading companies. The primary instruments are options, which are typically based on cumulative temperatures realised over specific time intervals at specified locations; swaps, and most recently futures contracts, are also based on accumulated temperatures at specified locations. Before we give examples of the instruments, we define what are called cooling degree days (CDDs) and heating degree days (HDDs). These are the primary observables on which temperature derivative contracts are based and traded in the market.

Cooling degree day (CDD). This is a summer measure of how hot it is on any given day at a specific location.

$$\text{CDD for a given day} \equiv$$
$$\text{Max [Average temperature for the day} - 65°F, 0]$$

Thus, if on June 12, 1999, the average temperature in Atlanta was 88°F, the number of CDDs for that day in Atlanta equals 33. If the average temperature for May 9, 1999 is 63°F, then the CDDs for that day equal zero.

Heating degree day (HDD). This is a winter measure of how cold it is on any given day at a specific location.

$$\text{HDD for a given day} \equiv$$
$$\text{Max [65°F} - \text{Average temperature for the day, 0]}$$

With this definition of HDDs and CDDs we can also get a measure of the cumulative CDDs and HDDs over different intervals of time, typically covering the summer season from April to October and the winter season from November to March. The cumulative degree-days over a time interval are simply the sum of the respective degree-day values for each of the days in that interval.

The futures contracts being proposed by the Chicago Mercantile Exchange cover monthly intervals at select cities.

Whereas derivative instruments could be traded on the actual daily temperatures or actual accumulated temperature values, the convention has been to trade in terms of the derived degree-day values.

The principal characteristics of instruments based on degree-days are that, first, they are always based on a single location or collection of locations. These locations are typically where the National Weather Service has a temperature measurement set-up. Such locations are given codes called WBANs, and daily temperature readings (as well as other weather data readings) at these locations are reported and widely disseminated by the NWS and other private agencies.

The next aspect of weather derivatives is that they are financially settled. As the underlying is not a traded asset with a market price, a dollar multiplier is used to convert the degree-day number into a dollar value. The multipliers are based on trading demands and there is no specific standard, with levels ranging from US$100 for futures contracts on the CME to US$50,000 for more liquid and heavily traded over-the-counter (OTC) contracts.

The third aspect to note is the tenor. The CME futures are monthly contracts, with the variable being the accumulated degree-days over the month. In the case of OTC instruments, the most liquid contracts are seasonal contracts covering the winter and summer seasons. Multiple-year contracts may be traded but typical contracts cover a single season.

Finally, given the relative immaturity of the market and the difficulty in arriving at a reasonable valuation methodology, it is a feature of almost all OTC instruments that they have dollar payout caps.

We give below several examples of weather instruments designed to meet different energy hedging needs:

EXAMPLE 1: SEASONAL CDD FLOOR
This is a put option that pays if the index drops below the strike. The buyer's liability is limited to

177

**WEATHER
DERIVATIVES
AND
HEDGING
WEATHER
RISKS**

the premium paid and settlement is at end of the period. The floor also has payout limits. Say an energy company wishes to hedge against a cooler than normal summer, but retain the benefit of a hot winter. Its estimated weather sensitivity is US$15,000/CDD. The company decides to purchase a CDD floor.

The company buys a put as follows:

Weather location:	XYZ Airport (WBAN#77777)
Contract term:	July 1, 2000–September 30, 2000
Index strike:	1,900 CDD
Unit price:	US$15,000 per CDD
Premium:	US$525,000
Settlement:	At end of contract term, if strike exceeds index, buyer receives difference times unit price
Payout limit:	US$4.5 million

EXAMPLE 2: WINTER HDD PUT OPTION

The objective here is to obtain protection of throughput. A utility is concerned that a mild winter will have an adverse impact on revenues, since demand and asset utilisation will suffer. It decides to buy a winter HDD put option with the following features:

Location:	Chicago O'Hare WBAN#94846
Index:	Cumulative HDDs
Term:	November 1, 1999–March 31, 2000
Strike:	5,200 HDD
Unit value:	US$5,000 per HDD
Premium:	US$500,000
Payout limit:	US$2 million

Based on historical temperature data for the location, the utility obtains the following possible payout profiles:

Valuation strike: 5,200 HDD
1961–90 normal: 5,298 HDD

	CDD	Payout
1970 average:	5,227 HDD	US$0
1980 average:	5,195 HDD	US$25,000
1990 average:	5,123 HDD	US$385,000
Winter 1997/98:	4,572 HDD	US$2 million (maximum)
Break-even:	5,100 HDD	US$500,000

EXAMPLE 3: CDD SWAP

In this example an independent power producer is seeking to guarantee a constant revenue stream throughout the summer season. He ensures this through the sale of a summer CDD swap with the following characteristics:

Location:	Houston Hobby WBAN#12918
Index:	Cumulative CDDs
Term:	July 1–August 31, 2000
Strike:	1,150 CDD
Unit value:	US$5,000 per CDD
Payout limit:	US$2 million

Together with the assumptions listed below, the summer CDD swap sale should result in the payoff patterns shown in Table 1, depending on whether it is going to be a normal summer, a hot summer or a cold summer next year.

The swap sale guarantees that a minimum or floor stream of revenues is realised.

EXAMPLE 4: TEMPERATURE CONTINGENT DAILY POWER CALLS

In this example, a utility finds that it can obtain summer peaking protection by buying daily summer calls for firm power. Unfortunately, the high underlying prices (>US$50/MWh) and excessive daily option volatilities (>100%) make these peaking options very expensive to buy. With temperature-contingent daily power calls, the utility finds that it can reduce its premium. With such a hedge in place, it will exercise the option only when the day-ahead forecast high temperatures exceed a predetermined level. The seller of such an option takes the utility's behaviour into account and is thus in a position to offer protection at a lower cost compared to the daily power calls.

EXAMPLE 5: PEAKER START-UP COST INSURANCE

In this example, a utility wants insurance against having to cover start-up costs of an old inefficient peaking unit, which is run for system reliability as opposed to economic reasons. The unit has high start-up costs and is needed only when loads go up because of extremely high summer temperatures – exceeding 98°F, for example. Suppose that the startup cost is US$10,000. Then the utility will buy a summer temperature call that pays US$10,000 when the forecast daily temperature exceeds 98°F.

Valuation

There are two principal approaches to pricing weather contracts, arising as a natural consequence of the participants in this market. The first is the actuarial or insurance method. In this approach, typically the expected loss from

---

Table 1. Payoff patterns for summer CDD swap

Case	Capacity factor	CDD	Toll revenue	Swap payment	Net revenues
Expected – normal summer	50%	1,150	US$446,400	0	US$446,400
Hot summer	70%	1,190	US$624,960	<100,000>	US$524,960
Cold summer	40%	1,130	US$357,120	100,000	US$457,120

Assumptions:
Tolling fee = US$3 per MW
300MW plant capacity
992 on-peak hours for July 1–August 31, 2000
Guaranteed heat rate of 8,000 with indexed gas and power off-take provision

WEATHER
DERIVATIVES
AND
HEDGING
WEATHER
RISKS

affording a degree of coverage is estimated on the basis of the statistical distribution of outcomes. The premium is set in the context of a large portfolio of identical and independent risks. The product is valued in such a way that the insurer obtains a return equal to the actuarial value of the risk being taken. The valuation principle is straightforward, the exposure or loss for each outcome is estimated and a corresponding probability of occurrence is obtained from a sample of historical observations.

The other approach is based on modern option pricing theory. It is assumed that a valuation technique akin to that employed for pricing options and other claims on market assets, such as stocks and bonds, can be employed. There is a critical distinction that is not to be underestimated here. The option valuation method used for financial instruments works because of several assumptions. The most important of these is the feasibility of constructing a replicating portfolio using the underlying asset and the risk-free security to mimic the value dynamics of the option or the derivative claim.

In the case of weather derivatives, though, the underlying is not a traded instrument. A proxy market asset must be available, to be used in a dynamic trading strategy that can mimic the value dynamics of the weather derivative or claim. The problem is rendered even more difficult when all that is available is the empirical/statistical distribution of the weather variable.

There are pros and cons of both approaches. The insurance approach is straightforward and is based on the statistical distribution. But it needs a larger diversified portfolio to make the pricing approach reasonable. This is extremely unsatisfactory from the viewpoint of an entity such as an energy trading company. The option paradigm seems a natural candidate, where the law of large numbers need not hold. The downside is that a hedging strategy is not often feasible. In practice, traders often use option pricing models using statistical distributions, but hedge their bets by employing sizeable spreads.

Conclusion

In this chapter we have attempted to give a survey of the types of weather-related risks that are borne by industry participants in the energy area. We have classified weather events as either extremal events, for which insurance-type protection is usually obtained, or other weather events which are not extremal, but nevertheless represents deviations from the norm. Protection against the latter is often obtained through OTC weather-based contracts such as degree day options and swaps. We have given examples of the types of institutions that seek such protection, as well as the agents that offer such products as a part of their set of risk management tools. Finally, we touch briefly upon the modelling approaches that have been employed to value weather products.

19

Weather Derivatives
Hedging Mother Nature

Lynda Clemmons, Vincent Kaminski and Joseph H. Hrgovcic

Enron

Weather derivatives cannot tame Mother Nature, but they do offer companies the chance to temper the economic consequences of her behaviour. Take Bombardier Recreational Products, the Canadian-based maker of Ski-Do snowmobiles. For most of its history the company endured the up-and-down impact that fluctuating snowfall patterns had on its sales and profits. But in 1998, following a record-warm winter brought on by El Niño conditions, the company took the offensive. To entice potential customers into Ski-Do showrooms, it offered to pay US$1,000 rebates to buyers in 19 US cities if the snowfall in their areas failed to equal at least half the average snowfall over the past three years.

If snowfall was sparse, the rebate programme would leave the company with a hefty price tag. To limit this risk, Bombardier entered into what was at that time a novel agreement with Enron Capital & Trade Corp. Bombardier paid a premium to Enron, depending on the total number of snowmobiles sold and the cities in which the machines were sold. In turn, Enron agreed to reimburse Bombardier for any rebates it had to pay out on the snowmobiles. The programme was a spectacular success for Bombardier, which saw its snowmobile sales increase by 80%, more than offsetting the cost of the contract.

Contracts of this type, where payments are determined by weather conditions, are known as weather derivatives. They are becoming increasingly common in industries whose profits are adversely affected by weather, and are one of the most rapidly growing sectors of risk management. While these innovative financial products cannot undo adverse weather conditions, they offer companies the chance to temper the economic consequences.

Of course, protecting business income against extreme weather is not new. Companies have long purchased insurance policies to protect themselves against large losses from meteorological events such as tornadoes, floods and hurricanes. But it has only been within the past two years that derivatives have allowed companies to hedge against weather that is not necessarily catastrophic, but which could still devastate a quarterly earnings report or cripple seasonal cashflow. Imagine a ski resort facing a dry winter, a winter-wear retailer concerned about a warm Christmas selling season, or a utility company forced to buy high-priced energy during a hot summer.

A basic weather derivative embodies features of both stock options and futures contracts. All can be purchased for a fraction of the value they may ultimately provide to the buyer. Just as the end value of an option or futures contract is tied to the price of some underlying commodity, so too is the end value of a weather derivative tied to some facet of the weather: temperature, rainfall, snowfall, even humidity or cloud cover. Settlement of a weather derivative is made in cash when the contract expires, just as is done with a futures contract. Moreover, weather derivatives do not require the cumbersome, lengthy and sometimes intrusive verification of damages required by insurance contracts.

Rapid acceptance

The first weather derivative, a temperature-related power swap between Enron and Florida Power and Light, was transacted in August 1996. Since then, more than 1,800 contracts worth about US$3.5 billion have been written. While most of these deals have taken place in the US, several have been transacted in Europe, where Enron completed the first deal last August. Some industry experts believe that trading volume in the weather risk management market could eventually exceed the volume of all futures and options contracts traded around the world.

The basis for that belief is simple: weather materially affects a large number of industries, including agriculture, energy, retailing, travel leisure and entertainment. Furthermore, the weather risks that one industry faces usually offset those of another. Now that weather derivatives are widely available, it makes little sense that a heating oil company in the north-east US should be exposed to the losses associated with mild winters, when nearby manufacturers are exposed to the opposite weather extremes. By swapping their risks, each can safeguard its sales and profits from the particular set of weather conditions that it finds unprofitable. The resultant stability is an especially attractive prospect for publicly traded companies, whose shareholders crave earnings consistency and are quick to punish offenders by driving down the stock price.

It is worth noting that some companies have in the past tried to hedge their temperature exposures by trading in the commodities markets. A heating oil company, for example, might try to hedge against weak demand for its product by selling heating oil futures. Theoretically, if demand is weak, fuel prices will slump and lost sales will be offset by gains in the short position in the futures market. The problem with this strategy is that it is not a direct hedge. Heating oil futures are a play on the price of fuel rather than on volume of sales. Other factors could keep fuel prices high even during a brief period of weak demand.

The challenge for companies wishing to use weather derivatives is to quantify the extent to which weather conditions have an impact on their profits, and to construct a cost-effective hedge that will prevent extraordinary losses. A proper weather risk management programme identifies the correlation between certain types of weather and profit margins based on historical weather data and corporate financial statements, then shields those margins from adverse conditions.

Anatomy of a deal

Most of the weather derivatives transacted to date have been tied to temperature over the course of several consecutive months – specifically, temperature as measured by *degree days*. In meteorological parlance, a degree day is the difference between a reference temperature (typically 65°F or 18°C) and the mean temperature for a given day (defined as the average of the daily maximum and minimum temperatures). During the heating season, meteorologists calculate heating degree days by subtracting the mean daily temperature from the reference temperature. During the cooling season, they calculate cooling degree days by subtracting the reference temperature from the days' mean temperature. By convention, no degree days are counted when the calculation would produce a negative number. Therefore,

$$hdd = \max(65 - Tavg, 0)$$
$$cdd = \max(Tavg - 65, 0)$$

For example, if the average temperature on five successive days is 60, 66, 67, 65 and 62, the cumulative number of heating degree days for this interval would be $5 + 0 + 0 + 0 + 3 = 8$ while

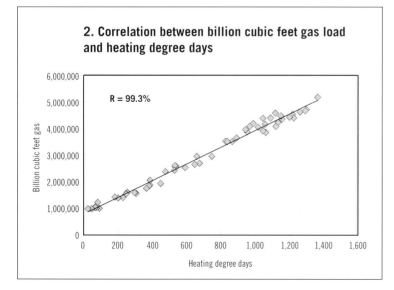

1. Correlation between monthly power load and heating degree days

R = 96.4%

2. Correlation between billion cubic feet gas load and heating degree days

R = 99.3%

the number of cooling degree days would be $0 + 1 + 2 + 0 + 0 = 3$.

Degree days are a popular proxy for energy use because they closely track the extent to which consumers use their heating systems or air conditioners. Studies have shown that correlation between gas and power use and heating degree days can be as high as 97%. Figures 1 and 2 illustrate the relationship between heating degree days and electricity and natural gas consumption respectively, by the customers of two actual US utilities. As one can see, the relationships are statistically highly significant. This makes degree days an especially useful indicator for weather derivatives that are purchased by utility companies and big consumers of power, such as heavy industries.

In the absence of any official exchange to provide official temperature data, the US weather market owes its rapid growth to the National Weather Service's well-regulated network of measurement stations, at which maximum and minimum temperatures (as well as precipitation, wind speed and numerous other parameters) are recorded daily. Occasionally, a weather station does become inoperative for a day or more, so that provisions must be made in any weather deal stipulating the use of suitably transformed temperatures from nearby stations whenever the primary weather data is unavailable. Also, actual temperatures for a given day (usually published on the following day) are first classified as provisional, and are not considered final for up to several months later, allowing the NWS time to perform checks on the data. In most cases, however, the discrepancies between the provisional and final data are very small in number and magnitude. Initial transfers of payments are typically made five days after the end of the accumulation period, and there is an adjustment, if necessary, three months later.

The Chicago Mercantile Exchange plans to establish futures contracts based on monthly degree days in several major cities, and has proposed supplementing the NWS with a third-party service provider that would be charged with releasing official weather data for the purposes of contract settlement. However, given that the primary weather source of any third-party provider would still be the NWS, the idea has met with some resistance.

Structures

Weather options are simple analogues of their equity market counterparts. Consider a heating degree day put. Suppose Gas Corp, a utility company, determines that the average number of heating degree days in its service area during the past 10 years was 5,330 a season. It also knows that budgeted revenues for a heating season with that number of heating degree days is US$50 million, based on the millions of British thermal units of energy that will be sold. The company is able to estimate that each heating degree day deviation from the average depresses revenues by US$12,500.

The company compares how its stock price has behaved in relation to its earnings over time. Its managers conclude that investors are generally willing to live with short-term revenue shortfalls of up to 10% when they are weather-related. Since each heating degree day deviation results in a loss of US$12,500, the company calculates that it could avoid adverse consequences to its stock price as long as temperatures are no more than 7.5% warmer than normal during the forthcoming heating season (in other words, as long as there were no less than 4,930 degree days).

To cap its exposure to temperatures at that level, Gas Corp could purchase a weather derivative. The market-maker would agree to pay US$12,500 for every heating degree day less than 4,930 (the "strike"). Gas Corp would then have established a floor under its weather-related losses, but would retain 100% of any increase in revenues it might enjoy if temperatures are colder than the strike.

Flexibility equals popularity

One of the reasons for the rapid increase in the use of weather derivatives is that they can be tailored to users' precise needs. Most contracts have been structured along the lines of the example cited above – linked to degree days. It was nevertheless fairly easy for Bombardier to purchase an options contract tied to snowfall, which has a much more direct impact on its business. Contracts also can be written in terms of maximum and minimum temperatures, degree days whose baselines temperatures are not 65°F, rainfall, stream flow, or any combination of those indicators.

Derivative contracts can also be structured to avoid the need for any front-end payments. Consider our earlier example. Suppose that Gas Corp was willing to forego any windfall profits associated with extraordinarily cold weather if it could also escape any revenue shortfalls associated with warmer than average temperatures –

and thereby forego a front-end premium. In that case, the market-maker could structure an options swap that provides the following:

❑ the market-maker would pay US$12,500 to Gas Corp for every degree day less than 5,330; and
❑ Gas Corp would pay US$12,500 to the market-maker for every degree day in excess of 5,330.

The result is that whatever the actual weather conditions, Gas Corp will achieve volume-related revenues associated with the target of 5,330 heating degree days. If temperatures are colder than average, the company should be able to finance the payments to its counterparty with the extra volume-related revenues those temperatures generate.

Note that this swap could also be structured so that neither party would pay anything to the other unless the actual number of heating degree days varies by more than some predetermined percentage, say 5%. In this case, Gas Corp would still ensure a degree of earnings stability, albeit within a fixed band, or *collar*.

Pricing: the market-maker's challenge

Although weather derivatives share features with options and futures, the structures are not identical. The statistical processes followed by temperatures are quite different from those governing price movements. Accordingly, the Black–Scholes model, which has become ubiquitous in pricing options, is not entirely satisfactory.

To compensate, some market-makers have incorporated elements of the actuarial approach to pricing characteristic of the insurance industry. In a nutshell, this approach is based on the assessment of probabilities of different climatic outcomes, as determined from historical data, and supported by weather forecasts to the degree of these forecasts' supposed accuracy. The price charged depends on the estimate of the probabilities of different outcomes, the level of interest rates, and the size and diversity of the market-maker's portfolio.

In many cases, the valuation challenges of weather derivatives can be met by combining the actuarial and options-model approaches. Since some commodity prices are sensitive to weather conditions, for example, positions in those commodities can be used to offset, if only imperfectly, the risks of weather derivatives.

More details of the pricing process cannot be addressed in an article of this scope – and most market-makers are in any case loathe to divulge detailed information about their pricing methodology for competitive reasons. Suffice it to say that traders rely on Monte Carlo simulations that create thousands of possible weather scenarios, together with a number of climatic forecast techniques, to arrive at a price that is customised to the types of deals in their portfolio. Most importantly, the resulting cost to the buyer is but a fraction of the potential savings if the weather works against its business model. So long as that remains true, the weather derivatives market will continue to grow and to be an increasingly important part of the risk manager's toolbox.

20

A Weather Risk Management Choice
Hedging with Degree-day Derivatives

Robert Dischel
WxPx.com

In the past two years the weather risk market has grown from a single over-the-counter (OTC) contract to hundreds of contracts each season, with a total notional amount estimated at a few billion dollars. Before the end of this year, we might see the issuance of two weather derivative-linked bonds, and now we have exchange-traded weather futures to supplement the OTC market (Arditti *et al*, 1999). The fledgling market has taken off.

Some assert that this new market has the potential to grow to a notional size of trillions of US dollars, and that it will one day reach into every sector of the world economy. This could happen if the market broadens the scope of the products it offers.

Most articles in newspapers and journals, and most presentations at conferences and seminars, have focused on temperature based degree-day derivatives. It would be unfair to call the market a temperature derivative market, yet most transactions have been based on degree-days. But that serves only one sector where there is interest.

The agriculture, hydropower generation, leisure, retail and transport sectors, to name but a few, are waiting for well-structured and fairly priced contracts on precipitation (rain or snow) and temperature in combination with precipitation. (A few precipitation contracts have been completed, but they are a small fraction of the total.) The problem is one of market immaturity. The next big frontier is precipitation, and we will see a breakthrough in the first year of the new millennium.

There are at least two reasons for the focus on degree-day derivatives. First, the weather market is a child of the power market. It was born of the need for power providers to protect revenue from weather variations. The demand for power for heating or cooling is clearly related to outdoor temperature. This is why the industry developed the ubiquitous degree-day concept to measure heating and cooling demand.

Second, temperature is seen by the market as a more manageable weather parameter than precipitation. For one thing, temperature is continuous in the environment. Weather fronts are not real discontinuities, but relatively sharp and continuous changes over short distances.

Rainfall, on the other hand, is clearly discontinuous. At any moment at any specific location, it is either raining or it is not. And we all know it can rain on one side of the street and not on the other. These realities and perceived measurement challenges cause uncertainty that has factored market prices. The market will have to resolve these issues to enhance the widespread use of precipitation derivatives. Some day soon we will be able to write about how to price precipitation volatility.

For now, we will restrict this chapter to weather risk management with degree-day derivatives, as we understand it can be done today. We describe weather risk hedging with degree-day derivatives as five overlapping concepts. Each might be considered a step in a weather risk management programme.

The first step is to answer the question – is there a need for weather risk management? This requires a hedger to quantify the relationship between the weather and revenue. For example, it may be obvious to many that consumer demand for electricity for air conditioning, and for electricity and gas for heating, are both temperature-dependent. The pattern of demand, however, differs with demographic and climatic differences. To demonstrate some of these differences we present below the electricity demand curve for three distinct climate zones in the US.

The second step is to define the characteristics of past weather that we need to be able to estimate the probabilities of future weather. While 50 or 100 years of weather history may seem a lot when compared to our life experience, it is a short climate record. In addition to the expected season-to-season temperature volatility seen everywhere, most locations in the past few decades have either warmed or cooled, or both. This is why we must be careful about how to use this non-stationary historical time series to calculate future probabilities.

The third step is to estimate future weather probabilities. Here we acknowledge that a brief few decades of weather history do not describe climate and recognise that we must model the future probabilities with our selections from the past. There are a few models from which to choose.

Fourth, we use the modelled weather probabilities to compare various hedging strategies. Knowing how revenue and derivative payouts vary with temperature is only part of building a risk management strategy. It is essential to value these payouts with the probability of their occurrence. Only when we have the probability distribution (probability density function) of payouts can we calculate derivative prices and make hedging comparisons. Specifically, we will look at the benefits and costs of two alternatives – a

long put position and a short swap position – for protecting revenue against a mild winter, each combined with a long call to protect against an extreme season.

Fifth, we evaluate the effects that forecasts have on market perceptions and the merit of using weather forecasts to alter our view of future weather probabilities.

Heating, cooling and outdoor temperature

Wherever it is available, people use power for heating and cooling, and use it more as temperatures become more extreme. In Figure 1, we show the residential demand for electricity over a recent decade for three locations in the US with distinctly disparate climates.

In Figure 1 we consider only the simplest view of outdoor temperature and power demand. For example, we used only monthly average values. Although we believe this is sufficient for the issues we discuss, any serious study of weather-induced revenue variations would consider a finer time resolution.

Also, we have not corrected the data for the demand for lighting that comes with increased darkness in colder months, when people spend more time indoors. Nor have we tried to separate the temperature effect on power demand from the effect of other weather parameters, such as wind, humidity or snow cover.

In discussion we focus on the range of average monthly temperatures at each location and particularly on the temperatures where the demand curve is at a minimum or flattens. It is argued that these temperatures mark the transition between cooling and heating seasons, revealing the habits of residents in demanding power. Specifically, we want to compare these transition temperatures to the transition temperature of 65°F so common in degree-day derivatives.

The rightmost curve in Figure 1 is for south-east Florida. This part of Florida has a sub-tropical maritime climate. The Atlantic Ocean with its Gulf Stream is to the east, and the Gulf of Mexico is to the west. Surrounded by sub-tropical ocean, Florida's climate is mild in comparison to other locations in the US. In the brief period of this analysis, the average monthly temperature in south-east Florida ranged from a low of about 64°F (18°C) to 84°F (29°C).

The transition from the cooling to the heating season occurred at around 74°F (23°C). Residents of south-east Florida turned up their air conditioners when temperatures were higher

1. Residential electricity sales

y-axis: % of annual average use (0, 50, 100, 150, 200)
x-axis: Fahrenheit (14, 23, 32, 41, 50, 59, 68, 77, 86)

Legend: ○ South-east Florida ▪ South-east Wisconsin ▲ South-east Washington

Data sources: US National Climatic Data Center, US Department of Energy

than about 74°F, and turned up the heat when temperatures were below it.

Of these three curves, the one that reaches into the coldest temperatures is for south-east Wisconsin. Wisconsin is near the Canadian–US border but central to the continental landmass. It is far from the direct influences of both the Atlantic and Pacific Oceans. Lake Michigan is to the immediate east. The range of monthly averages is extreme, when compared to the two other sites, because it is far from the moderating effect of the oceans.

In winter in south-east Wisconsin average monthly temperatures fell to 17°F (-9°C), colder than the other two sites. In summer they reached 75°F (24°C), almost as warm as in Florida. The residents of south-east Wisconsin did not turn up the electric heat (they depend more on gas heat) until the outdoor temperature fell below 50°F (10°C), and turn on the air conditioners at around 65°F (18°C).

The third curve is for south-east Washington state. It is about as far away from Florida as is possible within the 48 contiguous states. Washington state is in the north-west corner of the US, at the extreme western end of the Canada–US border. The Pacific Ocean is immediately to the west, and the Rocky Mountains are to the east.

The region we selected in south-east Washington state is east of the Cascade Mountains. The region's climate is dominated by maritime weather systems modified in passing across the mountains.

Winters in south-east Washington state during the period of this record were chilly but not extreme: the coldest month was 23°F (-4°C). Summers were mild, with no monthly average temperature exceeding 73°F (23°C). Residents did not use much electricity for air conditioning, but turned up their heating when monthly temperatures fell below 60°F (16°C).

Even in this limited view of only three sites in the US, we see that transition temperatures marking the energy seasons are varied. They can be as low as 50°F for heating or as high as 74°F for cooling. Obviously the concept of 65°F degree-days, while sometimes useful, does not encompass all the consequences of the cooling and heating seasons everywhere.

Temperature and weather-sensitive revenue

We build a fictional site from real places to help us isolate some events and explore certain issues. We call the site Frozen Falls because it gets very cold there. The climate at this site is common to the interior of the continent along the Canadian–US border (similar to south-east Wisconsin, for example). A fictional company, Hot Air Gas Company (HAGC), provides gas for heating in the region surrounding Frozen Falls. HAGC and a related fictional company, Frozen Falls Fuel Company, were the subjects of risk management studies reported in two previous articles (Dischel, 1999b; 1999c).

Frozen Falls winters are generally cold and gas sales for heating rise as temperatures decline. Customers in the region turn up the gas heat when the outdoor temperature falls below 65°F and generate strong revenue for HAGC. Revenue margin – the difference between revenue from sales and the cost to the company of providing the gas to consumers – is not always good, however.

First, there are years with extremely mild winters, weak gas demand and low revenue. Second, there are years with extremely cold winters with extreme demand. The demand can be so strong as to exceed the company's supply. In extreme winters, the competition for limited gas supplies in extreme cold can drive open market prices to exceed sales prices (see Figure 2). If HAGC must buy at these times to meet demand, margin is reduced and can even become negative.

In Figure 3 we show the dependence of revenue and revenue margin on temperature. This data was drawn from the historical records at HAGC to quantify the company's natural weather exposure. Revenue rises as temperature falls, until it is so cold that customers cannot even generate more heat. At this point the revenue curve flattens. In contrast, the revenue margin curve reflects the strong sales in near normal winters and the declining revenue margin in either mild or extreme winters, as described in the preceding paragraph.

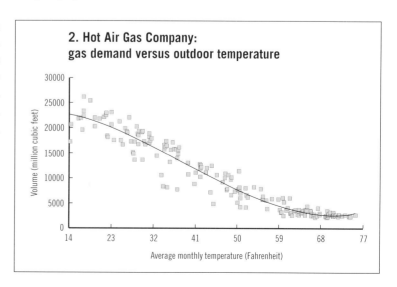

2. Hot Air Gas Company: gas demand versus outdoor temperature

Volume (million cubic feet) vs Average monthly temperature (Fahrenheit)

It is in Figure 3 that we see the company's implied bet on the weather: average and near-average winters generate positive net revenue, but warmer-than-average winters and extreme colder-than-average winters result in reduced, even negative, revenue. How likely this is to occur has yet to be discovered.

Selecting historical data

The data on which weather contracts will be settled are the future measurements made during the agreed strike period at an agreed location, which is almost always a government meteorological site. In pricing and risk management analysis, however, the focus is on the historical data record. Here lie opportunities, as different players take different views of history.

The initial step in any weather derivative analysis is to get the longest and best record of historical weather data available for the site on which the contract will be written. Only some of the historical data may be used in pricing, but all of it is needed. It is essential to know what happened in the past to estimate the probabilities of the future.

It is also important to know the geographical setting of the measurement site. Proximity to bodies of water, and valleys and mountains, for example, are factors that can have great impact on local weather. Demographic changes, specifically urban development, are also important, as discussed below. It is critical to know the site's meteorological characteristics well.

Importantly, the available data record length can be as short as a couple of decades or longer than a century, depending on the measurement site's history. The uncertainty caused by short historical record lengths will be reflected in

prices. Long record lengths may also cause uncertainty if the long-term average has recently changed.

Typically, we spend too little time working through the difficulties in the meteorological data – difficulties that are larger than data missing from the record or discovering that a weather station has moved. Value-added vendors of meteorological data review the government data records and offer repaired data sets. Perhaps a more critical step is to decide what portion of the available historical record to use in a pricing analysis.

If one accepts history, as it is, the choice of record length for estimating the temperature level and volatility for the near future seems to fall into one of three groups. Each has its merits and its flaws. The choices, with a brief statement of their supporting arguments, are as follows:

❑ Use only the most recent decade or two of data. Climate patterns shift and many sites have trends in the data (usually warming), therefore only the most recent data is representative of the near-term future. Even if there is a long-term trend to higher or lower temperatures, nature is persistent. That means that nature is not so chaotic as to depart abruptly in the next few years from the events of the most recent few years.

❑ Use all the available data. More data is better, and the full record contains all the events of the past that may recur. One cannot ignore the extremes of the past just because they have not happened in the past decade or two.

❑ Use some intermediate record length – one that neither leaves out the extremes of the past because it is too short, nor goes back so far that history outweighs what may be a trend for the present. Sometimes 30–50 years is a good compromise.

(An alternative, discussed later, is to accept history as an information set, to be moulded with good judgement into a better statement of the past than the untouched record.)

Warming in cities and at airports around the world is a well-documented result of progressive urban expansion. Paved environments and buildings absorb more sunlight than the natural environment they replaced. Additionally, expanding populations with changing lifestyles use automobiles more and demand more air conditioning. (In fact air conditioning demand is a phenomenon of only the past few decades.) Both of these activities generate more heat in the city (Dischel, 1998c; Portman, 1999).

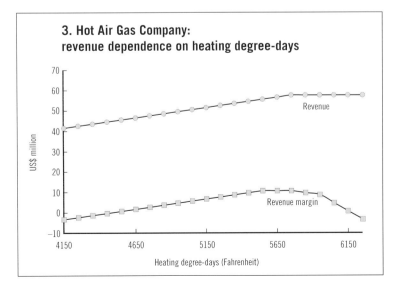

3. Hot Air Gas Company:
revenue dependence on heating degree-days

The changing reflectivity of cities as they evolve, and the changing lifestyles of the populations, have had an impact on cities. Neither impact is likely to go into reverse. If this is not complicated enough, consider that this local event is imposed on the equally well-documented rise in average earth temperature during the past century.

The scientific community explores the reasons for local and global trends, and tries to discern the relative magnitude of each. The weather market issue does not in the short term depend on scientific opinion. The issue remains – many cities have warmed.

Measurements made during the past 100 years or even 50 years may not reflect the events of the next few years in any simple way. We do not need to know why things have changed, only that they have. Then we need to accept the facts and deal with them. We must search for corrective lenses through which to view history to make it useful for weather pricing. Shaping the historical data is one way to do this.

We have previously shown (Dischel, 1998c; 1999e) that the conventional method of calculating the standard deviation of temperature may not be a good measure of temperature volatility for the near future. Consider the time series of seasonal temperatures in New York City in Figure 4. All seasons have warmed over the last century in this record.

Winter has the largest temperature increase of the four seasons and shows the largest year-to-year variability. Clearly, an average over all years in this winter record (33.5°F/0.8°C) is very different from the average of the most recent 20 years (35.4°F/1.9°C). We might have chosen 10 or 30 years or some other period, but 20 years is a common market measure (Gakos, 1999).

It is difficult to calculate a valid volatility measure if there is a trend in the data. We show this in Figure 5, in which we used different portions of the record to calculate the standard deviation. Different record lengths, not surprisingly, produce different temperature volatility – especially in this record because of the trend to higher temperatures.

Volatility for short averaging periods is unsteady in Figure 5 because the numbers of points in these periods are too few to provide valid statistics. A decade or two of seasons is just too small a sample size to calculate a valid volatility measure. Yet, in a record with a trend, as this one has, the volatility of the longer periods is not valid either, and the presence of the trend contaminates the calculation.

We are free to shape history and use it as we wish: history is what happened, not what will happen. Our focus is on the future. There are many ways to shape history, and we develop one that holds to these two apparently conflicting concepts:

❏ Use all the data to estimate the volatility. Every data point contains valuable information – none should be overlooked.
❏ Choose the averaging period that may best reflect the degree-day level of the near future. If you believe that a recent trend in the data will not reverse, then capture the levels of recent decades. If you think that recent decades are only a small part of a larger cycle, then use more of the data.

To make these concepts compatible, we need to deconstruct the past and reconstruct it – to build a "new" history. For New York City, we

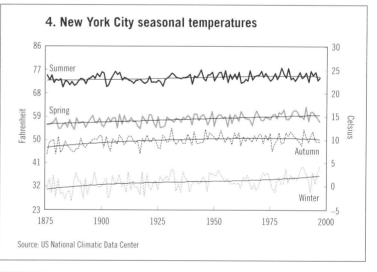

4. New York City seasonal temperatures

Source: US National Climatic Data Center

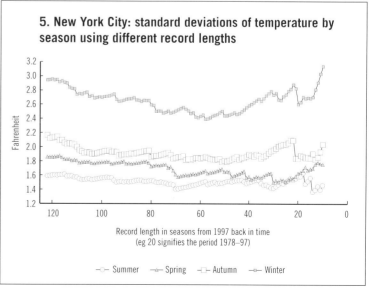

5. New York City: standard deviations of temperature by season using different record lengths

Record length in seasons from 1997 back in time
(eg 20 signifies the period 1978–97)

–□– Summer   –△– Spring   –□– Autumn   –○– Winter

reconstruct the full 122 years of history as it would have occurred if the current population had been in New York and lived the way it does now for the full period of record.

Because we believe the volatility has changed less over the century than has the average temperature, we de-trend the data to get an improved measure of volatility (see Figure 6). That is, we calculate a trend for the 122 winters and subtract the trend from each point in the series.

If we apply this to any of New York's seasons we find that a linear upward sloping trend is a good fit. We then calculate the volatility of history about this trend. That is, we calculate the departures of history from the trend, rather than from a fixed average, to get a difference series. We calculate the volatility of the difference series. We then reconstruct history by selecting a recent level as the long-term flat average and add each point in the difference series to this level.

We calculate the volatility of the de-trended temperature history as the standard deviation of these differences from the trend. We see the stabilising effect this has on the longer period standard deviations in Figure 6.

Trends in Tucson and Phoenix degree-day history

We know that the history of weather at a particular site reveals characteristics peculiar to that site. Sites close to each other sometimes experience different weather, not just at any moment, but also on the average. This is a source of basis risk in the weather risk market that results from local geographical features, and perhaps from those influences generated by man. We see this clearly in Figure 7 for Phoenix and Tucson, Arizona.

In the figure, we present the daily minimum and maximum temperatures in Tucson and Phoenix averaged over a summer cooling season. The cooling season we chose is June, July, August and September. The seasonal average of maximum temperatures in Phoenix (top line) and Tucson (second from top) both start and end the period higher than they were in the middle 1960s to the early 1970s, in what might be suggested is part of a cycle. The series of minimum temperatures in Tucson (bottom line) is more or less flat, while minimum temperatures in Phoenix (second from bottom) ended the period 9°F (5°C) higher than they were at the beginning. (See Gall *et al*, 1991 for this important information.)

In Figure 8, we present the sequence of daily midpoint temperatures averaged over the same summer cooling season. The midpoint temperature, known in this market as the average temperature, is the temperature midway between a day's minimum and maximum temperatures. This sequence of seasonal midpoint temperatures, or

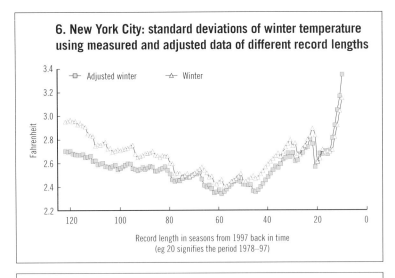

6. New York City: standard deviations of winter temperature using measured and adjusted data of different record lengths

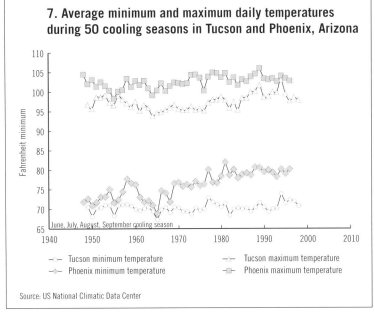

7. Average minimum and maximum daily temperatures during 50 cooling seasons in Tucson and Phoenix, Arizona

Source: US National Climatic Data Center

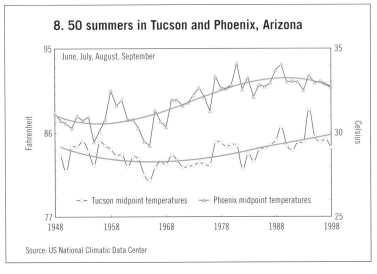

8. 50 summers in Tucson and Phoenix, Arizona

Source: US National Climatic Data Center

its associated degree-days, is usually the starting point for a weather derivative analysis.

Phoenix warmed more than Tucson and the weather trend in Tucson is different from the trend in Phoenix. Quite different regional features surround these two nearby environments. Phoenix is in the Salt River Valley (elevation 1,110 feet/ 338 metres) and Tucson is at the foot of the Catalina Mountains (elevation 2,584 feet/789 metres).

The reasons for the warming, however, might be related to human activity. Tucson's population grew by almost a factor of 10 in the past five decades (see Figure 9). Phoenix's population grew even faster. The scale of urban impacts grew with the population in both cities.

Often, air temperature is at a minimum just after sunrise, exactly at the hour when night-time radiative cooling is about to be exceeded by the warming from increasing daylight. A day's maximum temperature usually occurs in mid-afternoon, for the reverse reason, when the heating effect of decreasing daylight yields to radiative cooling. While a day's midpoint temperature is often close to the temperature averaged over 24 hours, there will be days when it is not, particularly if regional weather events overrun the radiation effects. This might occur, for example, during the passage of a weather front.

Phoenix midpoint temperatures (see Figure 8) rose because both minimum and maximum temperatures rose (see Figure 7), but Tucson midpoint temperatures rose because Tucson maximum temperatures rose. We know that urban areas generate and retain more heat than when the environment was less developed. It is possible that the robust urban development in these two cities has displaced the radiative balance, shifting the maximum temperatures to later in the day and elevating minimum temperatures.

We chose to analyse temperatures and degree-days in Tucson for a few reasons. Tucson is actively traded in the OTC market and is among the cities for which the Chicago Mercantile Exchange will support weather futures contracts. Also, the trend in Tucson temperature history is not flat (see Figure 8) making the data, as measured, troublesome for accurate pricing in most models.

Tucson cooled from about 84°F in the early 1950s to about 82°F in the late 1960s, where temperature fluctuated little for a decade. Then in the late 1970s it began to warm to today's temperatures that average around 85°F, with what may be greater volatility than in the earlier 40 years. It is a challenging location for a weather derivative analysis and demands further exploration.

Burn analysis for Tucson

The presence of a trend in the temperature data raises the issue of how much data to use in a pricing analysis. To evaluate the impact on option prices of choosing different record lengths, we employ a method sometimes called burn analysis (Dischel, 1999e).

Burn analysis is probably the simplest pricing method for weather derivatives and is easy to implement. It asks and answers the question: "What would the buyer of this financial structure have received in each of the past years for which we have weather data?" The average of these payments is an indication of where the security might be priced. It is an estimate of the "fair" price – neglecting for the moment a seller's premiums, supply and demand pressure, and opinions on weather forecasts (none of which can be neglected when trading).

(Burn analysis is important to do, yet it does not describe enough of the future possibilities. We believe that a more fundamental model should also be employed, one that produces a richer distribution of possible future events. We describe such a model in later paragraphs.)

A fair degree-day swap is one that is based only on the average of the measured data and leaves aside all weather forecast and other biases. Usually the statistics are different for different historical record lengths, and swaps based on different records have different strikes, but we will come to this shortly.

As an example, we look at a cooling degree-day swap (CDD swap) for Tucson for the strike period June, July, August and September. If we want an indication of the range where this swap might trade, we could select an analysis record length of 20 years of data (a common but controversial market practice). We then calculate the

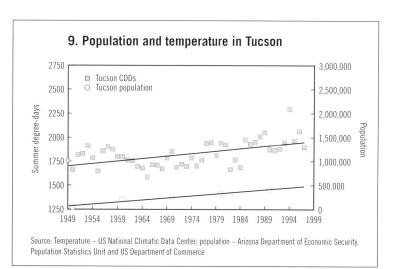

9. Population and temperature in Tucson

Source: Temperature – US National Climatic Data Center; population – Arizona Department of Economic Security, Population Statistics Unit and US Department of Commerce

20-year average as 2,408 degree-days and the standard deviation as 157 degree-days.

The cooling degree-day fair swap strike could be rounded to a strike of 2,400 CDDs. A call and a put keyed to the fair swap, and with a half-standard deviation rounded down to 75 degree-days, might be structured as in Table 1.

(In the market, the swap would trade to one side or the other of the average, depending on market parameters, and the call and put strikes would be shifted accordingly. For example, this swap might trade in the range 2400 +/-75 degree-days. This is the average plus and minus half of a standard deviation. The application of the burn analysis is indifferent to strike levels, while resulting prices clearly are not.)

In Figure 10 we show the 50-year history of what payments would have been for the call and put based on a 20-year level and a strike period of June, July, August and September and defined in Table 1.

Looking at only 20 years of burn analysis, from 1979 to the present, there would have been three times when the put would have paid, and three times when the call would have paid. However, in the first half of the 20 years, 1979–88, the call

would not have paid at all. In the most recent 10 years the put would not have paid at all. The swap strike falls at the midpoint of this trending period. The call would never have paid before 1989, but the put would have paid many times.

Clearly there is a problem here. The level of historical CDDs meanders, mostly upwards, and this is not reflected when looking only at the recent 20 years. For 35 years, at least, there has been a general warming in Tucson. We illustrate how troublesome this is for the market in the following hypothetical example.

If five hedgers, each with a different view on the appropriate choice of record length, were to value the structures as defined above, then the "fair" prices each would calculate are shown in Table 2. The disparate prices in the table are the result of the disparate views of history. This can explain at least some of the differences in price indications and the wide bid/ask spreads seen in the market. Different views often make for healthy and actively traded markets, yet the widely different views seen here can be an unhealthy consequence for this market. If, as happens all too often, a potential buyer and a seller are both tenacious of their individual views, prices cannot converge and some deals never get done.

SHAPING HISTORY AND RECALCULATING THE BURN ANALYSIS

If we deconstruct and reconstruct Tucson weather history, specifically the time series of degree-days, we can get new "fair" values for each of our hedgers (see Dischel, 1999e for more details). The new swap strike based on 20 seasons as above would be recalculated as 2,415 CDDs, and the standard deviation would be about 140 CDDs. The new call and put attachment strikes (half of the standard deviation) would narrow to 70 CDDs off the swap strike.

Our same five hedgers, holding to their views on record length but also accepting a revised history, would calculate the "fair" prices as shown in Table 3 from the payment history as shown in Figure 11.

The wide range of prices for the call option seen in Table 2 has narrowed considerably. The five-year and 10-year hedgers' call prices are still off our "20-year market", but transactions are more likely between anyone with a 20-year view or longer. Using more complex models than the simple burn model might tighten the market even more.

Every modeller understands that using data that poorly represents the phenomenon being

Table 1. A call and put keyed to the 20-year fair swap

	Call	Put
Strike in degree-days (at 1/2 standard deviations off the average)	2,475	2,325
Payment rate (US$ per 65°F degree-day)	10,000	10,000
Payment cap (US$)	1.5 million	1.5 million

Table 2. Burn analysis with different historical record lengths

Based on a 20-year average of the *original* data	5-year	10-year	20-year	30-year	50-year
Call "fair" price (US$)	350,000	325,000	162,500	108,333	65,000
Put "fair" price (US$)	0	0	169,000	475,333	596,800

(Option structure based on the 20-year record length as in Table 1, but burn analysis based on the indicated point of view)

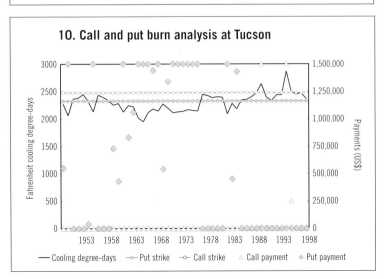

10. Call and put burn analysis at Tucson

Cooling degree-days — Put strike — Call strike — Call payment — Put payment

studied diminishes the value of a model. The simple burn analysis using the "untouched" historical data causes this kind of problem. Shaping the data, as we did, neither violates statistical rules nor offends good judgement, and may offer a better solution.

While we struggle to enhance our weather risk modelling tools, we can put an equal effort into managing the meteorological data. We have shown why weather data, as measured, may not be appropriate for our models. Yet, not wanting to raise a problem without proposing a solution, we have proposed one alternative treatment of the meteorological data to deal with the trends seen in measurements at many locations. There must be more alternatives.

Some practitioners fit a distribution, normal, lognormal or other, to the historical data. Unfortunately we do not have space in this chapter to explore this.

A stochastic temperature model

A risk management programme requires more than the price of a security. A security's probable payout distribution is also necessary. This and the absence of a commodity or security underlying the weather derivative is why Black–Scholes modelling is not useful in weather risk analysis (Dischel, 1998a; 1998b). We propose a model that simulates time series of temperature in future seasons. To do this, we look into the past to see the future. We believe that the time series of temperatures observed at a site over a meagre few decades is one possible sequence from the distribution that also governs the future. We use the observed historical sequence to define the characteristics of the population from which the future sequence will be drawn.

We have described this model in several articles. The most recent descriptions can be found in *Energy and Power Risk Management* (Dischel, 1999b) and *Applied Derivatives Trading* (Dischel, 1999c). There we described a mean-reverting two-parameter model of temperature and temperature changes. There was an error in the principle equation in each of these papers. Fortunately, McIntyre and Doherty (1999), interpreted the equation correctly when they described it in an application to London's Heathrow airport. As they stated, it is similar to Vasicek's model for interest rates, which we first read of in Hull (1993).

In our earlier articles we proposed a two-parameter temperature model. We did so because we believe that the temperature distribution and the distribution of day-to-day changes in temperature

are different – that their averages and standard deviations evolve differently over time. The equation that best describes the two-parameter model is:

$$dT = \alpha[\Theta(t) - T(t)] + \gamma dm_1 + \delta dm_2 \qquad (1)$$

As before, T is the temperature that varies over time, t. The parameter Θ is the time-varying daily temperature averaged over many years for each date. This average reflects the inevitable march of the meteorological seasons that lag the solar cycle. Θ is the gravitational nucleus to which the simulated temperature reverts in the absence of randomness.

In the recent articles we wrote this equation a little differently from in the earlier articles. We replaced the standard deviations of the historical distributions and the Wiener processes with the drawings from the actual distributions $\gamma dm_1 + \delta dm_2$. We emphasise that we have moved away from the notion that the model imposes a normal or some other distribution. We make no assumption about the shape of the distributions – rather we bootstrap the future distribution from the actual history of temperatures.

In practice however, we have only used a one-parameter model as did McIntyre and Doherty (1999).

The model we exploit is a descendant of equation (1). It is formatted for computer programming as a forward-stepping, finite difference equation. This one-parameter temperature model

Table 3. Burn analysis with different historical record lengths, based on adjusted data

Based on a 20-year average of the *adjusted* data	5-year	10-year	20-year	30-year	50-year
Call "fair" price (US$)	300,000	300,000	194,000	197,666	190,400
Put "fair" price (US$)	198,000	139,000	191,000	162,333	197,200

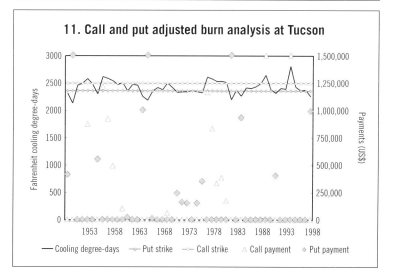

11. Call and put adjusted burn analysis at Tucson

yields very acceptable fair values. The finite difference form can be reduced to:

$$\hat{T}_{n+1} = \alpha\Theta_{n+1} + \beta\hat{T}_n + \gamma\Delta T_{n,n+1} \qquad (2)$$

The circumflex on $\hat{T}$ signifies that it is the simulated or projected temperature. The subscript n indicates a point in time, say today, and $n+1$ indicates the next period, say tomorrow. The random selection of forward temperature change is ΔT. We solve for α, β and γ, imposing $\alpha + \beta = 1$, and $\gamma \le 1$. There is a delicate balance to be found between the role of mean reversion and

the influence of γ. We have so far, only a simple-minded trial and error approach in a non-linear optimisation to find the values of α and γ that make the simulated distribution fit the historical distribution. We usually try to match the average and standard deviation of the simulations to our de-trended history, and often use the historical in degree-day distributions to solve for α and γ.

Comparing hedging alternatives

Viewing an example might be helpful.

We show the historical temperature record for Frozen Falls in Figure 12. Although it is based on real data, it has no strong trend. Not all sites do. Some might even see in this time series the suggestion that it cooled a bit in the first 25 years and then warmed: perhaps it is part of a cycle. We used data from the Frozen Lake airport to calculate 50 years of November through March heating seasons. We see that, at this location, there is almost a perfect correlation between average temperature in a heating season and the collection of 65°F degree-days in that season.

We show the histogram of degree-days for the actual 50 seasons in Figure 13.

Figure 13 is a shaggy histogram and it cannot be fit with a smooth curve. However, it might be a subset of a reasonable-looking distribution. We just do not know. Fifty years of history is too small a sample to fill in the gaps. No one would expect the real distribution to look like this histogram: nature is more consistent.

We use the 4,500 daily temperatures in 30 winter seasons to prime the stochastic model. We simulate 6,000 winter temperature seasons, each with its own path, constrained by the model rules but driven by a random sequence. We convert each daily temperature into degree-days, and collect the degree-days on each path into one season. With 6,000 simulated seasons we are able to produce a modelled distribution that has believable features.

To project a possible future season we begin at a date well in advance of the period of interest. We take the starting date's average temperature, Θ, as the starting temperature. We can calculate a Θ for November 1 as follows. In Table 4, in the row marked Nov 1 (which would have 30 temperatures for November 1 if all the data were shown), we can average the row of temperatures across all years. Although only five years are shown in the table, the data actually extend to the present.

The other two values we need to march forward one day are the next day's Θ, and a selection from ΔT. With these three values we simply step

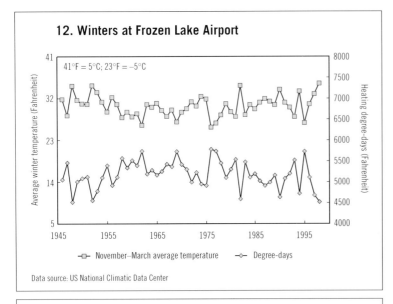

12. Winters at Frozen Lake Airport

41°F = 5°C; 23°F = −5°C

— □ — November–March average temperature   — ◇ — Degree-days

Data source: US National Climatic Data Center

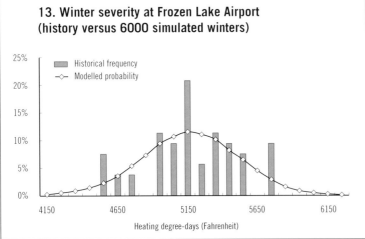

13. Winter severity at Frozen Lake Airport (history versus 6000 simulated winters)

▨ Historical frequency
— ◇ — Modelled probability

Heating degree-days (Fahrenheit)

Table 4. Frozen Lake airport, Fahrenheit temperatures

Number of years = 30		1968	1969	1970	1971	1972	1973
302	Oct 30	37.5	42.0	49.5	61.5	34.0	47.5
303	Oct 31	39.5	48.5	53.5	62.0	33.5	49.0
304	**Nov 1**	**50.0**	**57.5**	**56.0**	**51.5**	**42.5**	**46.0**
305	*Nov 2*	*53.5*	*56.5*	*55.0*	*59.0*	*54.0*	*48.5*
306	Nov 3	45.5	49.5	49.0	47.0	47.5	42.0
307	Nov 4	44.0	44.5	43.5	40.5	42.5	39.0
308	Nov 5	45.5	39.5	40.5	45.0	40.0	35.0
309	Nov 6	42.0	37.0	43.0	45.5	47.5	33.0

forward one day at a time. The array of ΔT (n + 1,n) is the difference found by subtracting the upper row in bold face from the row below (in italics).

To project the temperature for November 2, we randomly select a value from the array, weight it by gamma, and add it to the weighted average of today's temperature and tomorrow's Θ. We repeat the sequence until we have completed a season. We then repeat the entire process, beginning with a different random seed, to get another projected season.

Normally, we simulate thousands of seasons, that is, thousands of temperature paths, each with one temperature for each day of the season. The ensemble of seasons is forced to be consistent with the historical record. One such requirement was described above.

From the ensemble of seasons we can calculate the expected value of temperature, or any parameter derived from temperature, as the average of that parameter in all seasons. Likewise, we can also calculate the probability density function for any temperature-based parameter. In this example we believe we have sufficiently specified the distribution of possible future degree-days with 6,000 paths.

The histogram of the actual degree-days and the distribution of modelled probabilities differ significantly in Figure 13. The modelled distribution is flatter and smoother, and peaks in only one band of degree-days. It is not quite symmetric, as it leans a little to colder seasons. It includes extremes beyond those recorded in history but at believably low probabilities.

Price and probable payout

With a probability density function for winter's severity such as the one in Figure 13, we are able to add another dimension to HAGC's risk management analysis by recasting the revenue information in Figure 3 with its probable occurrence. We redraw these two curves, probability and revenue, in Figure 14, and multiply them (convolve them) to get the probable revenue by winter's degree-days (weighted by 10 in Figure 13 to fit the left vertical scale). This adds a new dimension to understanding the company's uncertain revenue. It shows not just which winter conditions are likely to be troublesome, but also provides a measure of the magnitude of each outcome to the ensemble of possible outcomes in an uncertain future. It is not a replacement for Figure 3, but rather an extension or supplement to it.

There is little new about this approach other than that we are applying it to weather data. Multiplying cashflows by probabilities is a com-

mon way of evaluating any contingent cashflow. We have used it to evaluate contingent insurance liabilities, callable bonds, mortgage-backed securities, and many financial derivatives. Many readers will recognise this as a usual and essential piece of the value-at-risk (VAR) analysis applied elsewhere in finance.

HAGC's revenue is clearly a contingent cashflow as it depends on the weather. To estimate its value we add up the pieces of the probable revenue calculation across the weather spectrum (integrate the area under the probable revenue curve). If, for example, HAGC tried to sell this winter's revenue in advance of winter, potential buyers would estimate it by convolving the revenue function by its probabilities. Its unbiased value is about US$6.4 million.

As stated earlier, HAGC's revenue turns downward in both mild and extreme winters. We look at three of the many possible derivative structures to demonstrate how the company can protect itself, almost perfectly, from revenue shortfalls. We look at two hedging positions that offer protection from mild winter shortfalls, a long HDD put and a short HDD swap, and a long call for protection from extreme winter shortfalls.

For simplicity of discussion, we calculate the average and standard deviation of 50 Frozen Falls winters at 5,175 HDDs, and 375 HDDs, respectively. The swap is struck at the average of 5,175 HDDs and the put has an attachment strike of 4,900 HDDs, a fraction of a standard deviation below the average. Both of these structures pay at the rate of US$10,000 per degree-day and are capped at US$3 million (300 degree-days). The call is struck at about two standard deviations above the average of winters, at 5,950 HDDs. It pays at a rate of US$30,000 per degree day and is capped at US$9 million (also 300 degree-days).

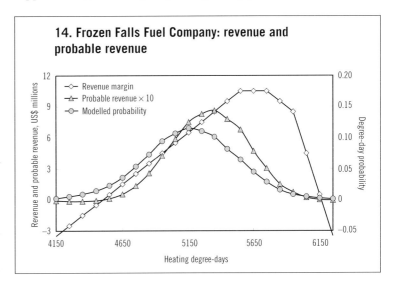

14. Frozen Falls Fuel Company: revenue and probable revenue

We calculate the fair values of the put and the call by integrating the probable option payouts as we earlier integrated the probable revenue. We estimate the put fair price at US$370,000 and the call fair price at US$40,000. (As we said, the fair price is only a modelled indication of where an option might trade in an unbiased market without premiums.)

Recent seasonal forecasts and the weather market

In 1997, for the first time in history, the weather forecasting community correctly predicted the pattern of weather impacts in the US resulting from an El Niño event. The affected US population quickly accepted this forecast ability as something more than it is. This led some participants in the weather risk market to be too confident in current seasonal forecasts and weigh them too heavily in their risk management decisions. This mistaken confidence created trading opportunities for other participants who understood better that forecasts are statements of probability, not of certainty.

El Niño is an oceanic phenomenon that has not been completely explained. Its most obvious characteristic is a warming of the equatorial Pacific Ocean surface. El Niño is preceded by a change in the intensity and sometimes direction of the otherwise persistent trade winds over the equatorial Pacific Ocean. Collectively, the temporary change in the atmosphere and ocean are called the El Niño southern oscillation or ENSO for short. There are theories why ENSO happens on an irregular multi-year cycle, but it has not yet been explained to the scientific community's satisfaction.

It is very important to recognise that not all El Niño and ENSO events affect the US and global weather patterns in the same way. The direction of the weather impact seems to depend on other atmosphere–ocean factors that we have only recently related to ENSO weather. Useful predictions are possible in only some of these combinations and this may remain the case in the near future. That is, in some El Niño events, we will know that we can be confident of the weather impact, in others we will know that we should not be confident.

This is an important distinction. We can watch the development of an El Niño months in advance of the event without knowing how it will affect the world's weather. That is, the predictive skill for the oceanic event far exceeds the ability to predict the weather.

Buoyed by successes in recent decades in understanding ENSO cycles, and wanting to stretch its record of success into the future, the ocean/weather forecast community hopes to predict better the world pattern of weather, season by season, as much as a year in advance. However, no one respects more the complexity of atmosphere, ocean and land exchanges than does this scientific community, and no one understands better the need for caution about the certainty of forecasts.

We need look only at the past few years to see the potential hazard of having too much confidence in a forecast (see Dischel, 1998d).

In the late summer of 1998 it became clear that the strongest El Niño of this century was ending and the eastern Pacific Ocean was returning to a more normal condition of cold water upwelling. This was watched carefully to see if the ocean would swing to El Niño's opposite phase, La Niña. When the beginning of the La Niña phase was detected, some rushed to predict La Niña weather for the continental US (colder than normal winter in the upper Midwest, for example). Some in the market placed a bet on the forecast La Niña weather, but while La Niña did occur, the forecast weather was not borne out on the scale expected. November 1998 broke records for high temperatures.

The expanded ocean-atmosphere observation programmes and the expanding historical evidence of worldwide ENSO weather connections will advance our seasonal forecast skill. We will begin to have more confidence in ENSO-related weather forecasts. In the meantime, it is important to remember that there has been only one solid ENSO weather forecast – the El Niño impacts of 1997–98. Betting on forecasts that have a one-point track record is like sitting on a one-legged stool – it is a balancing act.

15. Winter severity at Frozen Lake Airport (history versus 6000 simulated winters)

Using forecasts in pricing derivatives

Because weather forecasts are uncertain we should treat them as the probability statements that they are. We would like to combine the forecast with the probabilities we calculate from our pricing models. There are a few methods of doing this. We described one that is consistent with our pricing model in Dischel (1998c).

We structured our pricing model to revert to a long-term mean of temperature, Θ. If we move this long-term mean in line with the forecast, and rerun our simulation, we can shift the model's projected probabilities to reflect the forecast. We show in Figure 15 the results of three model simulations, each reflecting a different forecast for the winter in Frozen Falls.

For example, to estimate the effect on the probabilities of a forecast for a moderately warm winter (defined as halfway between normal and very warm), we might:

❏ calculate Θ as the long-term average for a normal winter, and another Θ for the set of winters 25% warmer than normal winter;
❏ average every point along both Θ curves to create one that reflects a moderately warm winter; and
❏ then use this elevated Θ curve to constrain the simulations as before.

The result of this simulation of a warmer than normal winter is the probability distribution in Figure 15 marked "warmer". In the same way, selecting the set of winters that were 25% colder than normal, we could calculate the probabilities of a forecast for a moderately cold winter. The result of the simulation of a moderately cold winter is the probability distribution marked "colder." The third distribution in Figure 15 is the outcome that is expected for a normal winter.

Final comments

A weather market risk analysis is an intensely quantitative analysis, yet only a few have applied the resources needed to carry it out. It is understandable that some people have little experience and are not sure where to begin – it is a very new activity. We hope this chapter helps them begin.

This new market challenges the skilled derivative analyst because there is no commodity or security underlying a weather derivative, depriving him or her of a cherished model. The market challenges the meteorologist who knows that climate changes, has changed and will continue to change, and yet the market must decide where the climate is headed. History needs to be fixed, better models developed. The forecasters are present but the market wants accuracy in forecasts beyond the forecasting community's current ability. We will see much activity around future El Niño and La Niña events, and some will believe more than they should.

Forecasts for specific periods change over time, as they should. This evolution of forecasts is desirable especially since the time to the forecast period shortens whilst we use the new information on the current state of the environment as it becomes available. For those who choose to take a weather market position based on a weather forecast it is essential to stay up-to-date as the forecast evolves. Recognising, however, the limited liquidity in today's weather market, one might have to hold the position until expiration, whatever the new forecast.

We have heard it said that a full risk analysis is not necessary. Some players believe that if the market offers the opportunity a good trader will find it. Yet others say that it is only important to follow the forecast. These views might survive in today's market because of market inefficiencies – but that will not last long.

As more players are drawn in to the market by its obvious utility and potential, the quantitative skill level will rise. The market will learn how to price those whimsical weather uncertainties and to provide useful, though not perfect, instruments for the hedger and the investor.

In the meantime, participating in the weather market continues to be an exciting experience – for professional reasons and partly because there is an armchair storm-chaser in each of us.

BIBLIOGRAPHY

Arditti, F., I. Cai, M. Cao and R. McDonald, 1999, "Whether to Hedge", *Weather Risk – An Energy & Power Risk Management and Risk Special Report*, September.

Dischel, B., 1998a, "Options Pricing – Black–Scholes Won't Do", *Weather Risk – An Energy & Power Risk Management and Risk Special Report*, October.

Dischel, B., 1998b, "Weather Risk – La Niña Volatility", *Energy & Power Risk Management*, November.

Dischel, B., 1998c, "The Fledgling Weather Market Takes Off – Part 1: Weather Sensitivity, Weather Derivatives and a Pricing Model", *Applied Derivatives Trading*, November.

Dischel, B., 1998d, "The Fledgling Weather Market Takes Off – Part 2: Weather Data for Pricing Weather Derivatives", *Applied Derivatives Trading*, December.

Dischel, B., 1999a, "The Fledgling Weather Market Takes Off – Part 3: Seasonal Forecasts and the Weather Market", *Applied Derivatives Trading*, January.

Dischel, B., 1999b, "At Last: A Model for Weather Risk", *Energy and Power Risk Management*, March.

Dischel, B., 1999c, "The Fledgling Weather Market Takes Off – Part 4: Weather Risk Management at the Frozen Falls Fuel Company", *Applied Derivatives Trading*, April.

Dischel, B., 1999d, "The Fledgling Weather Market Takes Off – Part 5: The D1 Stochastic Temperature Model for Valuing Weather Futures and Options", *Applied Derivatives Trading*, April.

Dischel, B., 1999e, "Shaping History", *Weather Risk – An Energy and Power Risk Management and Risk Special Report*, September.

Gakos, P., 1999, "Fooling Mother Nature", *Weather Risk – An Energy & Power Risk Management and Risk Special Report*, September.

Gall, R., K. Young, R. Schotland and J. Schmitz, 1991, "The Recent Maximum Temperature Anomalies in Tucson: Are They Real or an Instrumental Problem?", University of Arizona, Tucson, Arizona, July.

Hull, J., 1993, *Option, Futures and Other Derivative Structures, Second Edition*, Prentice Hall.

McIntyre, R. and S. Doherty, 1999, "An Example from the UK", *Energy & Power Risk Management*, June.

Portman, D., 1999, "Reading Between the Lines", *Weather Risk – An Energy & Power Risk Management and Risk Special Report*, September.

21

The Bermuda Triangle
Weather, Electricity and Insurance Derivatives

Hélyette Geman
University Paris IX Dauphine and ESSEC

Deregulation of electricity markets, well under way in the US, has created for utilities and gas producers there an environment of severe competition. European utilities will probably face the same kind of pressures once the European Union directives on gas and electricity deregulation become effective throughout the continent, after the United Kingdom and the Nordic countries. The variability in revenues resulting from weather conditions that utilities have long faced is now augmented by the effect on earnings of new entrants to the power market.

A well-known and important result in the economic theory of insurance establishes that, under reasonable assumptions of risk-aversion, an economic agent exposed to two sources of risk, one hedgeable, the other unhedgeable, will choose a higher coverage on the first risk than he would have if the latter did not exist. An illustration is provided by the development of the weather derivatives market in the US over the past two years, coinciding with the emergence of new shocks affecting the revenues of utilities.

The Chicago Mercantile Exchange (CME) introduced on September 29 standardised weather futures and options, which are traded on Globex, the exchange's electronic platform. In the past, weather derivatives have been sold by energy and insurance companies, mostly through the intermediation of a broker, since these were only over-the-counter (OTC) contracts. Other weather-related instruments, the so-called catastrophe options, were launched by the Chicago Board of Trade (CBOT) as early as December 1993. However, catastrophe options require, like most insurance products, a demonstration of loss and evidence of the link between this loss and one of the well-defined catastrophic events (eg earthquake, hail, tornado, flood) triggering the Property Claims Service (PCS) option index increments. Weather derivatives, in contrast, require no evidence of this type, since the option payout is expressed in terms of a meteorological index. These contracts can be combined in such a way that the risk exposure is reduced in accordance with the company's attitude toward risk.

Description of weather contracts

Many forms of weather options – such as precipitation, snowfall or windspeed options – are available, covering a single year or several years. But the biggest volume so far has been observed in degree-day options, which are related to daily average temperatures. More precisely, cooling and heating degree-days are defined as follows:

$$\text{Daily CDD} = \max (\text{daily average temperature} - 65° \text{ Fahrenheit}, 0)$$
$$\text{Daily HDD} = \max (65° \text{ Fahrenheit} - \text{daily average temperature}, 0)$$

and are meant to represent the deviations from a benchmark temperature of 65°F. Classically, a CDD (or summer) season includes months from May to September. HDD season months are from November to March.

Moreover, to represent the magnitude of the seasonal demand for electricity dedicated to air conditioner cooling, the aggregation effect is reflected by the following payout of the CDD option at maturity:

$$CDD(T) = \text{Nominal amount.max}$$
$$\times \left(\sum_{t=1}^{n} \max(0, I(t) - 65) - k, 0 \right) \quad (1)$$

where n denotes the number of days in the exposure period as specified in the contract, I(t) is the average daily temperature registered at date t in the specified location and k is the strike price of the option expressed in degrees Fahrenheit. Hence, a cooling degree-day derivative is nothing but an Asian call option written on a daily CDD as the underlying source of risk.

In the same manner, the payout of a heating degree-day option at maturity is:

$$HDD(T) = \text{Nominal amount.max}$$
$$\times \left(\sum_{t=1}^{n} \max(0, 65 - I(t)) - k, 0 \right) \quad (1')$$

ie the payout of an Asian put option written on heating degree-days.

We can notice that for both CDD and HDD derivatives, the option value is highly non-linear with respect to the temperature index, property which bears a number of consequences, in particular for risk analysis (whether it is Value-at-Risk or a better risk indicator).

In the case of the option contracts recently introduced by the CME, the nominal amount is US$100, a relatively small number meant to create liquidity (the number of degree-days during the months of January or July may be of the order of 1,000). The final settlement price is defined by the HDD or CDD (cumulative) index of the contract month as calculated by Earth Satellite Corporation (Earth Sat), an international service firm; and at this point contracts exist for eight cities in the US: Atlanta, Chicago, Cincinnati, Dallas, New York, Philadelphia, Portland and Tucson.

In the case of the insurance derivatives, the CBOT has used the services of independent statistical firms dedicated to insurance data – Insurance Services Office (ISO) initially, PCS since September 1995 –to provide the final (and also intermediary) values of the catastrophic loss indexes associated with the nine regional derivatives contracts. In the same manner Earth Sat has been designated by the CME to define the degree-day indexes. Earth Sat has developed remote sensing and geographic information technologies. The data it has provided over time have proven very accurate when compared with the

data of the US National Climatic Data Center (NCDC). The Globex electronic trading platform will not only allow transactions over 24 hours but also provide price transparency, which is particularly important for small investors that do not have meteorology departments within their firms.

The CME degree-day futures contracts trade, like the degree-day options, for each calendar month. This is a feature they share with all electricity futures contracts traded in the US or Europe, which has the merit of nullifying the calendar *basis risk* when hedging weather derivatives with electricity derivatives. The terminal value F(T) of a futures contract at maturity is defined as:

$$F(T) = \$100$$
$$\times \left[\sum_{j} \text{degree-days measured on day j by Earth Sat} \right]$$

Hence, F(T) will be very high if the weather conditions have been extreme during the month of analysis. Economic actors whose revenues are hurt by these extreme temperatures will hedge their risk by buying, at a date t prior to maturity (an appropriate number of) futures contracts at the price F(t), hence cashing at maturity T the amount F(T) − F(t) (positive if weather conditions have been more extreme than anticipated), which will offset their operating losses.

Several other observations are in order at this point :

❑ The balance sheet of a power utility or gas producer can be managed using classical derivative contracts written on underlying equities, interest rates or exchange rates. But these instruments, useful as they are, do not provide protection against *volumetric risk* – the uncertainty in revenues related to changes in demand for gas and power because of weather patterns. Storage cannot be a solution, because of the nature of the underlying commodity, but weather derivatives (or volumetric energy derivatives, as we will discuss later) can be structured to smooth the cash-flow profile. Market players are generally reluctant to publicise transactions, because this would indicate to competitors what risks they view as particularly dangerous to their earnings.
❑ The fact that nearly all degree-day contracts are tied to National Weather Service (NWS) data guarantees transparency and largely excludes the possibility of manipulation of the index. These

properties are crucial to users that may be legitimately concerned about the possibility of being taken advantage of by a sophisticated counterparty. The contract sites are US government sites and the final settlement of the option occurs when the NWS publishes the official record, generally a few weeks later. Moreover, the NCDC maintains the US archive of weather data (where historical time series can be obtained) and also provides access to the World Meteorological Organisation.

The three communities carefully watching the growth of the weather derivatives market in the US are – in line with the pricing and hedging arguments made in this chapter – power marketers, power producers and insurance/reinsurance companies. The agricultural community is another obvious potential player but has not yet been extensively involved in such transactions. More generally, it is estimated that 80% of all businesses are exposed to weather risk – whether they be involved in construction, retail, tourism or other sectors – and that about US$1 trillion of the US$7 trillion US economy is weather-sensitive.

❑ To create a liquid market through the existence of potential buyers and sellers, the derivative contracts are often capped, ie the option payout is defined as the right-hand side of (1) as long as it is no greater than a fixed threshold U, hence limiting the option seller's exposure to this number.

Keeping in mind the algebraic gain profile at maturity of an option buyer (seller), the gain profile of a capped call option at maturity is shown in Figure 1.

We can observe that a capped call option is nothing but a *call spread* (ie the combination of a long and short call options with different strikes). It was emphasised in Geman (1994) that call spreads, the most popular insurance derivatives, have a gain profile identical to the purchase

of an excess of loss reinsurance contract. Hence they can be valued by incorporating the insurance risk premium embedded in such contracts into the option price. And it is not surprising to find that the most sophisticated (re)insurance companies are in the forefront of weather derivatives transactions.

Pricing CDD and HDD options

The pricing of degree-day options is probably one of the hardest problems still to be solved in option pricing. Among the difficulties that must be addressed are the following:

❑ The options have an Asian-type payout, leading to greater mathematical complexity than with classical options. These difficulties arise from the fact, that in the fundamental reference model of a lognormal distribution for the underlying state variable S:

$$\frac{dS(t)}{S(t)} = \mu dt + \sigma dW_t \qquad (2)$$

(μ and σ are constants), the dynamics described do not extend to a sum nor an arithmetic average. Hence, the Black–Scholes formula definitely does not apply to Asian options and other answers need to be found. Geman–Yor (1993) use Bessel processes (which have the merit of being stable by additivity and of being related to the geometric Brownian motion through a time change) to obtain an *exact* analytical expression of the Laplace transform in time of the option price. The Greeks are obtained with the same accuracy thanks to the linearity of the operator's derivation and Laplace transform.

Another possible way of pricing Asian options is to use Monte Carlo simulations. A single simulation of the index value over the whole period (0,T) provides one set of simulated daily values. These values, incorporated in formula (1), give in turn one *realisation* of the payout of the CDD derivative. The average of these realisations over a number of Monte Carlo simulations gives an approximation of the option price. Geman–Eydeland (1995) show that, because of the smoothness of the Asian payout, a good approximation is obtained by a relatively low number of runs (eg 10,000), but the same accuracy for the Greeks (delta, gamma, vega) necessitates a higher number of simulations.

❑ The evolution over the lifetime [0,T] of the option of the underlying source of risk I(t) needs to be properly modelled, taking into account

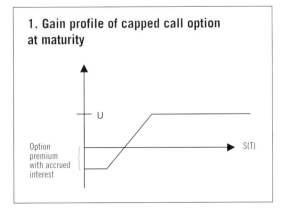

1. Gain profile of capped call option at maturity

seasonal effects over the year, stationarity of some seasonal patterns across a period of several years and possible changes in the parameters over time. Local warming in a city or at an airport site may be the result of global warming, or it may be the product of expanding urbanisation or even part of some secular climate cycle. Given the importance of accurate modelling of the state variable in the option price, one has not only to analyse the temperature data series available from the NCDC but also to use a survey of alterations in the built environment. This information has recently been systematically collected by insurance and reinsurance companies, sometimes with the help of specialised software companies. In the US, government agencies represent a very rich source of information (see for instance Figures 2 and 3); in fact, all the graphs in this chapter come from publicly available data.

Let us model the temperature index as an extension of the geometric Brownian motion.

Representing the randomness of the world economy by the probability space (Ω, F_t, P), where Ω denotes the set of states of nature, F_t the filtration of information available at time t and P the statistical probability measure, we model the dynamics of the average daily temperature I(t) by the stochastic differential equation:

$$\frac{dI(t)}{I(t)} = \mu(t,I(t))dt + \sigma(t,I(t))dW_t \qquad (3)$$

where the drift $\mu(t,I(t))$ may be mean-reverting to capture seasonal cyclical patterns, with a level of mean-reversion possibly varying with time to translate the global warming trend; and where the volatility σ should not be constant, since there seems to be a consensus on the greater volatility over time of temperature, for a number of natural or man-made reasons. However, it may be viewed as admissible to take for σ either a deterministic function of time $\sigma(t)$ or to make σ stochastic but depending only on the current level of the temperature index, ie a function $\sigma(t,I(t))$. In both cases, there is no other source of randomness than the Brownian motion W(t), which will avoid *incompleteness* of the weather market and non-uniqueness of the option price.

❑ We know that the next step in the Black–Scholes–Merton proof is the construction at date t of a portfolio to be held up to date (t + dt) and comprising one call C_t and $\partial C_t/\partial S_t$ shares. This portfolio, being riskless over the period [t, t + dt], has to provide, by no-arbitrage arguments, a return equal to the risk-free rate r. This leads to the well-known partial differential equation satisfied by the call price:

$$\left.\begin{array}{l} \dfrac{\partial C_t}{\partial t} + rS_t\dfrac{\partial C_t}{\partial S_t} + \dfrac{1}{2}\sigma^2 S_t^2 \dfrac{\partial^2 C_t}{\partial S_t^2} - rC_t = 0 \\[1.5em] \text{with the boundary condition C(T) =} \\ \text{max } (0,S(T) - k). \end{array}\right\} \qquad (4)$$

In the case of options on interest rates such as caps, floors or bond options – which raise, at various levels, more difficulties than equity options – the introduction of a portfolio is still feasible, using in all cases bonds as substitutes for interest rates. The same argument cannot be extended to the case of weather derivatives, since weather is not a traded asset and there is no "basic" security such as a stock or a Treasury bond whose price is uniquely related to a temperature index.

❑ The Feynman–Kac theorem establishes that there exists a probability measure Q defined on (Ω,F_t) such that the solution to the partial differ-

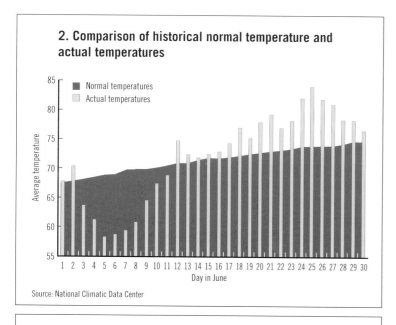

2. Comparison of historical normal temperature and actual temperatures

Source: National Climatic Data Center

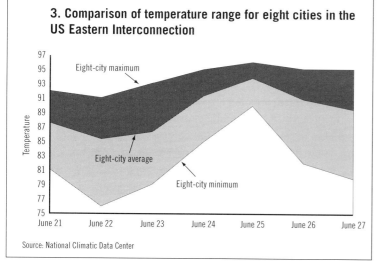

3. Comparison of temperature range for eight cities in the US Eastern Interconnection

Source: National Climatic Data Center

ential equation (3) with its boundary condition can be written as

$$C(t) = E_Q\left[e^{-r(T-t)}\max(S_T - k, 0)/F_t\right] \qquad (5)$$

This probability measure Q, called risk-adjusted, allows us to price an option as the expectation of its terminal payout. It is obviously not equal to the statistical probability measure P, under which data are collected, and its identification is generally not straightforward. (Its uniqueness is insured by "market completeness", which is obtained when the number of sources of randomness is no larger than the number of basic risky securities traded in the economy.)

Some authors have proposed to compute the weather derivative price as the expectation (ie the sum of possible payouts weighted by their probabilities of occurrence) of its terminal value properly discounted. To do this, they would resort for instance to the Monte Carlo simulations discussed earlier. This expectation is computed under the statistical probability measure P (meaning that the weights mentioned above do not reflect any correction for risk-aversion), as if no risk premium was involved. For instance, Cao and Wei (1999) use a Lucas equilibrium framework approach to conclude that a zero market price of risk should be associated with weather derivative values, justifying "the use of the risk-free rate to derive these values as many practitioners do in the industry".

This assertion is questionable, since weather conditions have a significant impact on the whole economy. To take an extreme example, consider the summer 1999 heat wave in Chicago, during which 130 people died. Among the many losses attached to this event, there is a loss in human capital that is clearly not offset in an economic sense. The assumption of the weather risk-neutrality of a so-called representative agent is not fully credible. As far as weather market participants are concerned, their view on the matter is clearly expressed by the large bid–ask spreads observed until recently on derivative prices (sometimes 100% of the bid price).

The difficulty of identifying a (unique) probability measure Q, like the impossibility of delta-hedging a weather derivative or the non-existence of a hedging portfolio comprising the weather derivative and other securities and totally *riskless*, are different expressions of the same issue. This is the *incompleteness* of the weather derivative market, which also affects

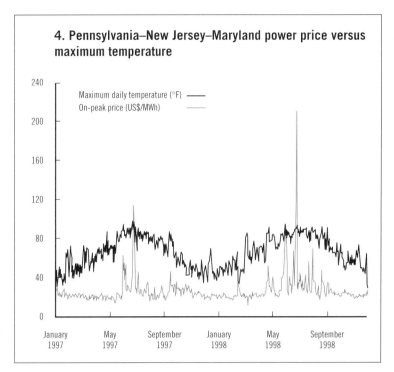

4. Pennsylvania–New Jersey–Maryland power price versus maximum temperature

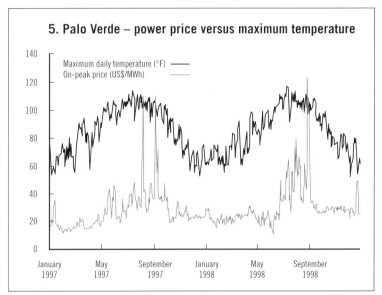

5. Palo Verde – power price versus maximum temperature

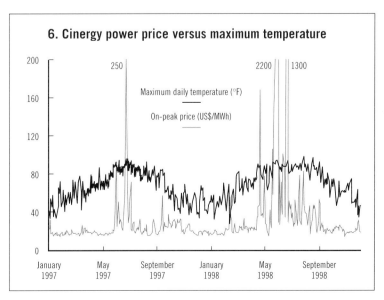

6. Cinergy power price versus maximum temperature

credit derivatives, for instance. This is probably one of the most important problems yet to be solved in the financial theory of derivatives. (Stochastic volatility is a well-known source of incompleteness that holds for all derivative mar-

kets today and is a legitimate subject of concern to practitioners.)

Hedging a short position in weather derivatives

The existence of a perfect hedge for a given derivative – as in the Black–Scholes–Merton (1973) model – has the merit of providing all answers at once: the price of the option, equal to the cost of the hedging portfolio, and obviously the hedging strategy itself. When this exact hedge does not exist, several types of answers can be proposed:

❑ The introduction of a utility function for the representative agent, which leads to the identification of the derivative price as the solution of an optimisation problem. The shortfalls of this approach reside in the questionable identification of this utility function and the assumption of the same utility for all market players

❑ The search for a so-called super-hedging strategy H for the weather derivative, ie a dynamically adjusted portfolio H such that at maturity:

$$-C(T) + H(T) \geq 0 \quad \text{in all states of the world}$$

Unfortunately, the cost of this strategy is in most cases outside the bid–ask prevailing in the option market. Nobody would be willing to buy the option at that price.

❑ Carr–Geman–Madan (1999), observing the limited validity of the previous two approaches to pricing and hedging derivatives in incomplete markets, offer as an alternative the search for a portfolio H such that the position (–C + H) is not necessarily riskless but carries an *acceptable* risk.

When C is a weather derivative, the hedge H will certainly comprise electricity contracts – either spot (such as financial assets) or forwards and options. Since weather is the single most important external factor affecting the demand for power in the US, one can try to represent this demand at date t for a future date t_j (Figures 4 ,5 and 6) as a function:

$$w(t, t_j) = f(I(t_j), a_1, a_2, ..., a_n) \quad (6)$$

where $I(t_j)$ denotes the temperature that will be observed on day t_j at the defined site, and a_1, a_2, ..., a_n are parameters that may vary over time.

For instance, in Figure 7, reconstructed by Dischel (see Chapter 20) using official US data,

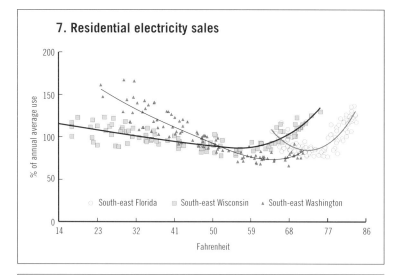
7. Residential electricity sales

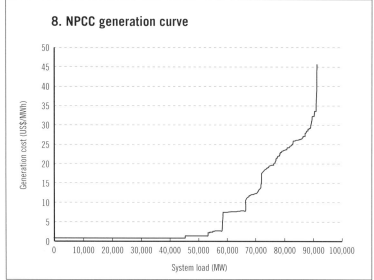
8. NPCC generation curve

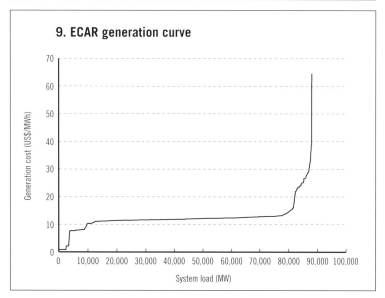
9. ECAR generation curve

the curves associated with regions as different as south-east Wisconsin and south-east Washington have in common the property of showing a high use of residential electricity for low temperatures (below 45°F) and high temperatures (above 68°F). The range of temperatures is obviously much narrower in Florida, where it never gets very cold. Assuming that the quantity $w(t, t_j)$ can be represented as a second-degree polynomial of $I(t_j)$ – not taking into account the other explanatory variables of electricity demand – one or the other root of this polynomial will allow us, depending on the season, to express the temperature as a function of the demand.

Following Eydeland–Geman (1998), one may represent the future price $F(t, t_j)$ as a function of the demand $w(t, t_j)$ and of the power stack function (Figures 8 and 9) prevailing in the area of analysis. Using (5), the futures price becomes in turn a function of $I(t_j)$ and a hedge for the weather derivative can be elaborated using forward contracts. The right parts of the power stack functions in Figures 8 and 9 need to be analysed in detail, since they represent the "extreme events", hence the large payoffs of weather derivatives.

Another way to proceed is to analyse the power demand as a function of temperature through its deviation from the baseload and hedge the weather derivative using volumetric or *swing* electricity options, which become the right protection when temperatures rise sharply. These instruments allow the option holder to call for a bigger volume of power on a number of days, chosen by the holder, during the lifetime of the option (with constraints on the total amount and, possibly, the daily amount as well).

Lastly, to manage their risk exposure, hedgers of weather derivatives may try to benefit from the diversification effect created by several positions within the same region or across different regions, in the same manner as insurance companies hedge part of their underwriting risk through portfolios of insurance contracts. In both cases, the use of insurance derivatives may protect against the catastrophic risk associated with extreme weather events. For instance, when electricity prices in the ECAR (Mid-western) region of the US went from US$25 to US$7,500 in June 1998, with terrible consequences for some market players, the spike was the result of the coincidence of three events: a long heatwave driving prices up because of air conditioning; squeezes in transmission of hydroelectricity coming from Canada; and the destruction by a tornado of a nuclear plant nearby. At least the third event could have been hedged away by a catastrophe option.

Conclusion

Weather specialists are developing a variety of products that enable utilities to manage their weather risk better. Weather risk is the largest source of financial uncertainty for many energy companies and a cause of revenue risk for a large number of economic sectors. Precipitation-related instruments are the next under scrutiny, with particular relevance for hydroelectricity. These products create fresh ways in which banks, insurance and reinsurance companies and energy investors can take advantage of opportunities in this burgeoning market.

BIBLIOGRAPHY

Black, F. and M. Scholes, 1973, "The Pricing of Options and Corporate Liabilities", *Journal of Political Economy*, 81.

Cao, M. and J. Wei, 1999, "Pricing Derivative Weather: an Equilibrium Approach", working paper.

Carr, P., H. Geman and D. Madan, 1999, "Risk Management, Pricing and Hedging in Incomplete Markets", working paper.

Dischel, R., 1998, "The Fledging Weather Market Takes Off", *Applied Derivatives Trading*, November.

Eydeland, A. and H. Geman, 1998, "Pricing Power Derivatives", *Risk*, October.

Geman, H., 1994, "Catastrophe Calls", *Risk*, September.

Geman, H. and A. Eydeland, 1995, "Domino Effect: Inverting the Laplace Transform", *Risk*, March.

Geman, H. and M. Yor, 1993, "Bessel Processes, Asia Options and Perpetuities", *Mathematical Finance*, 3.

Merton, R., 1973, "Theory of Rational Option Pricing", *Bell Journal Of Economics and Management Science*, 4.

GLOSSARY

This glossary provides short definitions of terms and abbreviations that are used, often without further explanation, in insurance and the new and developing area of weather derivatives and the weather risk market. The glossary has been designed for general reference so not all the terms below are used elsewhere in this book. Longer definitions of derivative and risk management terms are available in a glossary called The Chase/Risk Magazine Guide to Risk Management.

act of God A misnomer. A natural disaster such as a flood or tornado

actuary An insurance company mathematician who compiles statistics of losses, develops insurance rates, calculates dividends and evaluates the financial standing of the insurance company

adverse selection Selection against the insurer. The tendency of less desirable exposures to loss, such as people in poor health trying to purchase insurance protection at standard (average) rates

arbitrage An activity which attempts to buy a relatively underpriced security and sell a similar risk-type overpriced security, expecting to profit when the prices resume a more appropriate theoretical relationship

Asian option, or average rate option, is an option whose payoff at maturity depends on the average price of the underlying instrument during all or part of the life of the option, rather than the price of the underlying asset on maturity date. Asian options are among the most popular exotic options in oil and electricity markets. Insurance derivatives and weather derivatives have Asian-type payoffs since these involve cumulative losses or degree-days

basis risk The risk that the value of a futures contract or another hedging instrument will not move exactly in line with that of the underlying position or portfolio that is being risk managed. Basis risk is a form of inefficiency of the hedge, due to the non-existence of the perfect instrument (in terms of period covered and/or compared evolution of the hedge price and the position to be protected). Reserves in cash should be established as provisions against basis risk

call options A European call option written on a stock or another risky security, with maturity T and strike price K, gives to the buyer at date T a cashflow equal to the stock price on that date minus K, or zero if that difference is negative

call spread, or horizontal call spread, is the combination of a long position in a call with strike price K_1 and a short position in a

call with a strike price K_2, both calls being written on the same underlying instrument and having the same maturity

capacity The legal ability to make a binding contract. The amount of insurance an insurance company can write

capped call option Same definition as call option, except that the cashflow received by the buyer of the option (and paid by the seller) cannot be greater than a number specified at inception of the option contract

catastrophe bond A bond coupon (and possibly principal) payment is contingent upon the non-occurrence of a well defined catastrophic event (for example, an earthquake with a magnitude reaching a given number on the Richter scale). Usually, catastrophe bonds are issued with several tranches. The riskier ones have part of the principal at risk but offer a higher coupon rate

credit enhancement insurance A form of coverage in which the insurer guarantees the payment of interest and/or principal of the insured, in connection with debt instruments issued by the insured

credit risk Loss potential caused by a borrower defaulting on a loan or more generally, by a counterparty defaulting on a payment

Currency risk The risk of loss associated with fluctuations in one currency's value against other currencies

degree-day The deviation of a one day average temperature from a benchmark equal to 65°F. A cooling-degree day represents the difference between the average temperature and 65°F, if positive; zero otherwise. A heating degree-day is equal to 65°F minus the average temperature or zero

delta (δ) The sensitivity of the option price to the underlying asset value

dynamic hedging A position risk-management in which an option-like return pattern is created by adjusting over time a position in the underlying (or forwards or futures on the underlying) to simulate the delta change in value of an option price

Earth Satellite Corporation (Earth Sat) The independent service firm designated by the Chicago Mercantile Exchange to define the degree-days indexes to which the weather futures and options contracts are tied

excess of loss reinsurance A form of reinsurance whereby the reinsuring company reimburses the ceding company for the amount of loss the ceding company suffers over and above an agreed aggregate sum in one loss or in a number of losses arising out of any one event

exotic option, or path-dependent, is an option whose payoff at maturity depends on the values taken by the underlying asset over the whole lifetime of the option rather than the single value at maturity

federal crop insurance Comprehensive coverage at rates subsidised by the federal government for unavoidable crop losses, including those that result from hail, wind, excessive rain, drought, freezing plant disease, snow, floods and earthquake

financial risk management A branch of risk management dealing with loss exposures associated with fluctuations in financial markets, in particular losses associated with interest rate changes and currency fluctuations

forward contract A contractual obligation between two parties to exchange a particular commodity or instrument at a set price on a future date. The buyer of the forward agrees to pay (at maturity) the price (defined at inception of the contract) and take delivery of the commodity or instrument; he is said to be long the forward. When the forward contract is related to an insurance or weather index, there is obviously no delivery at maturity but a financial settlement, namely an algebraic cashflow received by the buyer of the forward contract and equal to the nominal amount times the final value of the index minus the price agreed upon at time o. In all cases, there is no cash exchanged before maturity; a possibility of loss for both the buyer and the seller of the forward contract; and credit risk for the two counterparties

future contract An agreement between two parties, a buyer and a seller, to exchange a particular good for a particular price at a particular date in the future, all of which are specified in a contract common to all participants in an organised futures exchange. Futures contracts can be traded freely with various counterparties without credit risk, under the control and guarantee of the

Clearing House of the Exchange. Margin deposits must be posted before entering into transactions and variation margin payments mark futures positions to market at least once a day

gamma (γ) The second derivative of the option price with respect to the price of the underlying

hazard A condition that creates or increases the probability of a loss

hazard rate The probability of occurrence of a catastrophe (or a credit event) in catastrophe bonds (or defaultable bonds) during a unit time period

hedge An action which reduces – possibly eliminates – risk, usually at the expense of a higher return. Hedging is typically accomplished by making approximate transactions that will largely eliminate one or more types of risk. In the narrower sense, the term indicates partially offsetting a long position in one security with a short or short equivalent position in a related security

insurance derivatives A derivative instrument (future, option or swap) whose payout or final settlement is related to a catastrophic event or a loss index; in the case of the instruments traded on the Chicago Board of Trade, the index is a cumulative amount of losses and there are nine distinct regional contracts

Insurance Services Office US national property and liability rate-making organisation. The ISO develops policy forms and computes rates for its member companies

interest rate risk An exposure to losses caused by changes in prevailing interest rates

loss ratio The ratio of incurred losses and loss-adjustment expenses to earned premiums over the same time period, generally a year

moral hazard A dishonest predisposition on the part of an insured that increases the chance of loss

open cargo marine insurance policies These policies provide automatic coverage for importers or exporters for all shipments reported to the insurer. Premiums may be calculated based on monthly reports or may require a year-end adjustment of the initial premium

outage insurance A machinery or equipment coverage for covering loss during the period a piece is inoperable as a result of an accident

plain-vanilla option An option whose payoff at maturity solely depends on the price of the underlying asset on that day. Plain-vanilla options on stocks were the subject of the Nobel-prize winning Black–Scholes–Merton formula in 1973, formula which provides at any date prior to maturity the fair price of the option

pollution The contamination of the environment that includes air pollution, water pollution and disposal of waste materials

premium period The length of time covered by the premium, usually identical with the policy period but frequently not

primary insurer The insurer who first markets the insurance to a consumer/insured. The primary insurer may in turn purchase insurance in an arrangement known as reinsurance and become the ceding company

Property Claim Services (PCS) The independent statistical form defining the cumulative loss indexes to which the nine regional derivative contracts traded on the Chicago Board of Trade are tied

retention Risk management technique whereby the insurance company retains part or all of the losses resulting from a given loss exposure to benefit from the corresponding premium

risk Randomness; and its consequences

risk-free rate The rate of return on the risk-free asset, usually represented by Treasury bills. In the Black–Scholes–Merton model, the risk-free asset and the risky stock are traded in the economy where the price of a call option on the risky stock is analysed

risk premium The difference between the expected total return from a risky investment and the risk-free rate

stochastic process A mathematical representation of the random evolution over time of a security price, interest rate or weather index. Developers of option models attempt to identify the stochastic processes that best match the empirical pattern of the quantity under analysis

theta (θ) The sensitivity of an option price to the time to maturity; a measurement of its rate of time decay

underlying The security, commodity or other instrument or contract (swap, forward, futures contract) to which the option (or another derivative contract) is tied

underwriting The process of selecting and rating (calculating a premium) applicants for insurance

vega Sensitivity of the option price to volatility

volatility risk The risk that the holder or seller of a standard or exotic option incurs if actual or implied volatility varies. Other things equal, an option holder will benefit from an increase in actual or expected volatility and the option seller be hurt by it

weather derivatives See insurance derivatives, with a temperature index replacing the loss index. In the case of the instruments traded on the Chicago Mercantile Exchange, the index is a cumulative number of degree-days and there are eight contracts for eight cities in the US (Atlanta, New York, Chicago, Portland, etc)

yield curve A graph illustrating the level of interest rates as a function of maturity, obtained by plotting the yields of all default-free zero-coupon bonds in a given currency against maturity or, occasionally, duration. Yields on debt instruments of lower quality are expressed in terms of a spread relative to the default-free yield curve

INDEX